Our Glorious Tradition

The religion, history and culture of the Jewish people

Our Glorious Tradition

The religion, history and culture of the Jewish people

Lucien Gubbay and Israel Elia

Chroniclers
26 Linden Lea, London N2 ORG
Publisher

Chroniclers, 26 Linden Lea, London N2 ORG

ISBN 978-0-9527006-3-0

Contents

Jewish History

Preface

It was when undertaking a radical reform of the Talmud Torah at Lauderdale Road Synagogue many years ago that its organisers first became aware of the need for a fully structured programme of learning for its senior pupils. Strange as it may seem, no such programme could be found anywhere. Efforts to commission educational experts to prepare a comprehensive curriculum failed - for no educationalist could be persuaded to undertake so extensive a project. Funding from leading educational charities was not forthcoming as they did not consider the project to be a priority. And so, financed by the far-sighted Elders of the Spanish and Portuguese Jews' Congregation, we undertook the work ourselves on a voluntary basis: it took several years to complete.

Our efforts were at first greeted with scepticism. 'Do you really need to re-invent the wheel?' we were asked repeatedly. And though it is true that the information contained in 'Our Glorious Tradition' exists in other books, nowhere else is it gathered together in such comprehensive form.

Several aspects of the programme are original. The inclusion of Jewish History, from the end of the Biblical period to the present day, may seem surprising - but it is our belief that there are many paths to religious consciousness; and that awareness and pride in their origins may well be the spur needed by some students. The section on Concepts developed from the enthusiasm displayed by young people in our top classes when encouraged to think for themselves and debate vital topics. Workshops on the Jewish origins of Christianity and Islam aroused some initial suspicion but eventually won unanimous approval.

Jewish history, as presented in the lessons, is focussed more on the Sephardi experience than is usual. Though possibly a little unbalanced, this may serve to counter the predominantly Ashkenazi bias of most existing histories of the Jewish people. Those lessons written to illustrate the particular minhag of London's Spanish and Portuguese Jews can easily be adapted for wider use.

Though primarily aimed at young people, the lessons with their notes for teachers and background information, also appealed to many parents. Indeed, taken as a whole, the information and explanations are suitable for adult reading.

This innovative curriculum is now being taught in the Talmud Torah and has proved highly successful. The original lesson packs have not been re-written for publication in book form but were simply edited, collected together and printed.

The publication of this book was funded by generous donations from Gerard Mizrahi, Michael Sultan and Victor Levy; and its production was organized by Michael Ison, Chairman of the Lauderdale Road Education Committee.

Lucien Gubbay

Introduction

This is a comprehensive course of Jewish learning, originally developed for the senior students at the Talmud Torah and for those engaged in supervised private study.

It should also interest adults who wish to learn themselves or supplement their knowledge.

The course is divided into five main sections.

Concepts
a series of discussion papers in which key concepts of Jewish belief and practice are discussed.

The Jewish Year
Shabbat, festivals, fasts and the Jewish calendar.

Prayers and Ritual
the structure of Jewish worship, with its principal prayers and ritual framework.

The Cycle of Life
birth, bar mitzvah, bat mitzvah, marriage and death.

Jewish History and Culture
a selection of salient events from the end of the Biblical period to the present day.

The original lesson packs, now assembled here, contain over one hundred lessons, one or more for each topic. These are supplemented by

Notes for teachers or parents

Material which may be photocopied

Texts or illustrative extracts from other publications by the authors

Charts and maps

Warm thanks are due to Martin Gilbert for kindly allowing the inclusion of so many excellent maps from his Jewish History Atlas, which are an education in themselves.

The audio-tapes, CDs, pictures and books that formed part of the original lesson packs could not be included with this volume. These may be obtained from the Headmaster, Talmud Torah, S & P Synagogue, 2 Ashworth Road, London W9 1JY. The CDs containing the Haggadah in Hebrew and English, with explanations, are particularly recommended.

Hebrew reading, though essential, is not included for practical reasons. Many excellent computer programs and books are available to help teachers.

In the English versions of Hebrew texts quoted throughout, conveying the meaning takes precedence over literal translation of the Hebrew words. The divine name of four letters (which may no longer be pronounced) is always rendered in English as 'the Lord'. Dates are expressed in Jewish terms, with B.C.E. (before the Common Era) for B.C., and C.E. (Common Era) for A.D.

Note

This book is not intended to be read continuously from cover to cover. Its lesson-packs have two main purposes. Firstly, they are presented in such form as to serve as a resource for teachers, providing them with the detailed knowledge and background information necessary to prepare their lessons, and secondly, they are also intended as a text book for senior pupils in the Talmud Torah. Consequently, the text contains two complementary streams of information, one for teachers and the other for children. Much of the teachers' track may well be too detailed and complex for the students.

The difficulty of catering for different age groups as well as conveying background information for teachers has been partly overcome

> by indenting and printing in smaller typeface all such information intended primarily for adults. Longer background notes for teachers have been included as separate notes, apart from the main text

Concepts

God and Creation

What is God?

We accept that the nature of God is so great a mystery that the human mind will never be able to comprehend it. Such knowledge is simply accepted as being so far beyond human intelligence that any discussion is futile and is never attempted.

From the Kippur prayer book:

He, who proclaimed his name to be 'I am, that is what I am' is he who was, who is and who will be eternally … before him no divine power existed and after him none will be

מיוחד באהיה אשר אהיה, הוא היה והוא הוה והוא יהיה , הוא ממית ומחיה, לפניו לא נוצר אל, ואחריו לא יהיה

Can we know anything about God?

Yes. Though we can learn nothing about the unknown (and unknowable) infinite divine essence – pure spirit, whatever that means - we can learn a great deal about those qualities by means of which God makes himself known to man – God's manifestation in the finite world of his creation.

From the Kippur prayer book:

And the Lord passed before him (Moses) and proclaimed 'The Lord, the Lord, a gracious God full of compassion, long-suffering and abundant in mercy and truth, granting mercy to thousands, forgiving iniquity, transgression and sin, and acquitting.

ויעבור ה' על פניו ויקרא: ה', ה', אל רחום וחנון, ארך אפים ורב חסד ואמת: נוצר חסד לאלפים נשא עון ופשע וחטאה ונקה.

For Jews, it is through the Torah that we know how God reveals himself to us in the world. This is described in some detail in the lesson entitled "Revelation and Reason in Judaism" and will not be repeated here.

Creation, from what?

As God is perfect and beyond all limits of space and time, infinite, how then can he have created our finite and imperfect world? If God is all, how can there ever have been a nothing? How can anything possibly exist outside God? That problem has engaged some of the best minds of our sages and philosophers throughout history.

Though a few of them toyed with the idea that God might have created the universe from pre-existing matter, the view was generally accepted that God created the universe from nothing – or "ex nihilo" as it is usually expressed. How that was done is quite another matter.

Several great rabbis – Sa'adia Gaon was the first – attempted to prove the fact of creation ex nihilo; but such proofs are not very convincing to modern minds. It seems that we must just accept that, as interpreted by our Hahamin, the fact of 'creation from nothing' was revealed to us by God in the Torah.

> Jewish mystics propounded their own theories of creation in Kabbalah, the mystical tradition. Though accepting that such matters are beyond human description, they still attempted in some way to describe the creative process by means of an allegory. The actual details of the allegory are not intended to be taken too literally but rather accepted as a way of expressing what is essentially inexpressible.
>
> Their doctrine, called Tzimsum, pictures the unknown, infinite God somehow undergoing a process of contraction, withdrawing himself into himself (so to speak) so as to leave an empty space, a space without God.
>
> Into that void, God then projected his divine power to create the finite universe in which we live. The process of creation was compared by the mystics to breathing - first in and then out; and a similar process of divine contraction and expansion continues as the means by which God sustains the universe.
>
> That idea of God's power continually sustaining the world is not restricted to Kabbalah but has become part of mainstream Jewish thought.

The Scientific view of Creation

Modern science accepts that the universe is constantly expanding in all directions, and at enormous speed. Whether it will go on expanding for ever, or eventually collapse in on itself, remains controversial.

However, the present course of expansion can be tracked backwards by scientists, with the universe becoming smaller and smaller, until its size was once inconceivably tiny – almost infinitely smaller than the head of a pin.

There was then the most awesome explosion, after which the tiny 'particle' started expanding to form the universe we know today – with its countless millions of stars and planets including the earth – and which still continues to expand at an alarming speed. That was the moment when time and space came into being.

Scientists can now detect echoes of that tremendous explosion, the 'big bang', coming back to us from the far reaches of the universe, a huge number of light years distant.

Though scientists are confident of being able to track everything back to a millisecond or so after the "big bang", they can go no further back. All their formulae fail at that point; and they have little confidence of ever getting behind it. Before the "big bang" there was nothing that we can ever visualise – no space and no time. Described in religious terms, the "big bang" may well have been the very moment of "creation".

Can the Religious and the Scientific views be reconciled?

Though some rabbis accept the biblical account of creation in six days in its strict literal sense – how can anything be beyond the power of the Almighty? – many others are prepared to accept the account given in Bereshit as a "poetic" description of what actually occurred; and they interpret the biblical "six days" in a wider sense, not too disturbed by the scientific notion of the vast periods of time involved.

Indeed one's sense of amazement and awe can only be heightened by the revelations of modern science. How much more wonderful does creation now seem than anything our ancestors could possibly have imagined?

Writing in the 9th century, Sa'adia Gaon of Babylon pictured the creation of the world with the sound of great blasts of the shofar – as we still recall in our synagogues each Rosh Hashanah. In the light of our enhanced knowledge today, echoes of the "big bang" may be an even more awe-inspiring reminder of God's absolute power.

The conclusions of science, it seems, may have gone full circle from the once strongly mechanical notions of past years - with no room for creation or a Creator. Science can no longer even attempt to explain what happened at the very beginning of the universe.

Indeed, there may no longer be that much difference between the latest scientific theory of the origin of the universe and that advanced by Judaism, which has always maintained that it was God who created the heavens and the earth, and that he created them from 'nothing'.

Again, from the Kippur prayer book:

Before the heavens and the earth were expanded, the Lord reigned. Before the luminaries shone forth, the Lord reigned. And when the earth shall have waxed old as a garment and the heavens shall have vanished as smoke, the Lord shall reign for ever and ever.

בטרם שחקים וארקים נמתחו

ה' מלך,

ועד לא מאורות זרחו

ה' מלך

והארץ כבגד תבלה ושמים כעשן נמלחו

ה' ימלוך לעולם ועד

Revelation and Reason

Revelation

Judaism, as a faith, is firmly based on revelation. In Jewish history God appeared first to the Patriarchs - Abraham, Isaac and Jacob - and then to Moses.

In an awesome encounter with the entire nation of Israel gathered at the foot of Mount Sinai, God revealed himself to each one of them, collectively and individually. That pivotal event - the giving of the Ten Commandments - so impressed itself on the consciousness of the people, that a *Midrash* (rabbinic parable) has it that all future generations of Jews, yet unborn, were also present at Sinai for that unique revelation.

Through Moses, described in the Bible as the "Man of God," the Divine message was transmitted to the Jews in the form of the *Torah* ('teaching', though often inadequately translated as 'law') in two parallel parts - the written Torah consisting of the first books of the Bible: the Five Books of Moses (Genesis, Exodus, Leviticus, Numbers and Deuteronomy), and the oral Torah which is that body of traditional teaching, faithfully passed on by word of mouth from one generation to another.

Accounts of God's further revelations to man are contained in later books of the Bible. But it is the Torah itself that is the foundation of the Jewish religion; and it is belief in its Divine origin that is one of Judaism's most basic dogmas. In the light of received tradition, successive generations of Rabbis have been able to deepen the understanding of the Torah in their own times by successive reinterpretations of its shades of meaning. However, the actual words of the written Torah and the principles enshrined therein are regarded as God-given, immutable and eternal.

The nature of the Divine

Moses first encountered God on a journey through the desert, when he paused in amazement beside a bush that continued to burn without being consumed. In answer to Moses's question concerning his identity, God replied:

I AM; that is who I am

God's answer defines the traditional attitude towards the nature of the Divine, about which mainstream Judaism hardly ever speculates. God is regarded simply as pure spirit - whatever that may mean - an unknown essence, incapable of comprehension by the human mind. Indeed, in a well known Midrash, God is represented as saying to his people: "Would that you would forget me; but keep my Torah."

In complete contrast, those qualities by means of which God makes himself known to man are revealed in great detail in the Torah. To Moses, God described himself as:

A God compassionate and gracious, long suffering and abundant in mercy and truth...forgiving iniquity, transgression and sin...but one who punishes....

In yet another passage the Israelites are commanded:

You shall be holy, for I the Lord your God am holy.

The ritual, moral and ethical constituents of such 'holiness' are closely defined. Indeed the duties of ritual observance, of doing justice and of practising righteousness are so interwoven in the ideal of 'holiness' as a way of life for the Jewish people that they can hardly be separated one from another:

Each one of you shall revere your father and your mother: and you shall keep my Sabbaths: I am the Lord your God.

In that quotation, the juxtaposition of the commandments of honouring parents and observing the Sabbath with a statement of belief in God show that they are all aspects of the same thing.

Many attempts have been made to summarise the most basic Jewish beliefs concerning God. Joseph Albo, the thinker and philosopher, born in Spain in 1380 C.E., maintained that the essentials of belief can be reduced to the three principles of Divine existence, Divine revelation, reward and punishment; and that once these are accepted there is much scope to interpret God and his laws in ways that appeal to different minds.

However, it may be useful to go a little further in attempting to define the traditional rabbinic view of the Divine. The following characteristics are accepted without reservation:

Unity

Judaism is completely monotheistic. There is one God, and only one God; and to him alone can prayer be addressed.

Incorporiety

God is pure spirit, free from all limitations of created matter.

Omnipotence

God is all-powerful. All forces, natural and supernatural, are subject to his will.

Eternity

God has always existed and will always exist

Transcendence and Omnipresence

Though not part of creation, and far above and beyond it, God is present and indwelling in all creation

Morality

God is 'holy' as described elsewhere in this chapter, and requires man to imitate this quality. He is gracious and merciful, long suffering and constant. He will reward the righteous and will punish the unrepentant wicked. It is often claimed that this concept of a 'moral god' is the principal and most original Jewish contribution to religious thought, for while monotheism, in some form or another may have been known before Abraham, this ethical quality of the Divine was a startling innovation that revolutionised religion - compare it, for example, with the ethical attitudes adopted by the Greek Gods and their flagrantly 'immoral' antics.

Omniscience

God knows the innermost thoughts of man, and it is impossible to hide anything from him.

The above qualities, taken together, give us a view of a God who, though awesome and tremendous beyond human thought and experience is yet a personal God, ever present in everyday life and ever interested and involved in man's least activity. Based on this simple and straightforward concept, many lives of blameless merit and true pity have been built.

> In each generation, though, there are many who have difficulty in reconciling a concerned, personal God with the problem of evil in the world. Where, for example, was God when the Nazis burnt his Torah and compelled those who studied it to dig their own graves? many people ask. For such, the above uncomplicated view will not satisfy, and deeper levels of religious understanding must be sought.

Reason

Jewish philosophy may be regarded by some as a contradiction in terms, for faith is based emphatically on revelation and not on conclusions reached only by the application of logical thought to experience.

However, rational thought processes are not excluded and some can be detected in the Bible itself. Abraham is represented by the Rabbis as a rational thinker. According to a Midrash, Abraham 'discovered' God by using one of the most popular mediaeval philosophical proofs of God's existence. Abraham's life is compared to that of a man who on a long journey comes across a beautiful uninhabited palace: "Is it possible that this building has no master?" asks the traveller, at which point the master makes himself known to the traveller.

Aware that the views on the nature of existence are presented unsystematically in the Bible, without logical supporting argument, later Jewish philosophers discovered a purpose for the human intellect by maintaining that the Bible exists on two levels - the simple literal level, intelligible to all: and a more profound level, discernible only by the application of pure reason in accordance with the methods of philosophy.

Rabbinic thought and writings in general, and the Talmud in particular, are not presented systematically, in logical sequence. Scholars differ as to how familiar with Greek ideas and philosophic methods were the Rabbis who compiled the Talmud, but there seems to be little evidence of direct influence.

Philosophy and philosophers

Jewish philosophy, as such, can be said to have originated in the large and prosperous Greek-speaking community of Alexandria, whose best known exponent was Philo (died in 50 C.E.). According to Philo, God is entirely unknowable and indescribable: between God and the world exists an intermediate being - the Logos - through which God manifests himself to the world and is indwelling in it. Philo's work was of great interest to the early Christian church, but had no lasting influence on Jewish thought.

Sa'adia Gaon, the next prominent name in Jewish philosophy, was born in 882 C.E. and was the principal of the great rabbinic academy in Sura, Mesopotamia. In several works, Sa'adia attempted to convince doubters of his own age that the religious truths transmitted by means of divine revelation can have their validity confirmed by the exercise of pure reason. To Sa'adia, there was no conflict between reason and revelation, as both come from God.

Solomon Ibn Gabirol, born in 1020 C.E., was the first of the Spanish school of philosophers. Between the date of his birth and that of the expulsion of the Jews from Spain in 1492, Jewish philosophy reached its zenith.

Moses Maimonides, one of the greatest scholars of the post-Talmudic era was born in Cordoba, Spain in the 12th century. With the intention of offering the Jewish community a fundamental outline of the true nature of belief, he formulated thirteen principles of faith:

1) The existence of God which is complete and is the cause for the existence of all other beings.

2) God's unity which is unlike all other unity.

3) God must not be conceived in physical terms. All descriptions of God containing human-like qualities should be understood in a metaphorical sense.

4) God is eternal.

5) God alone should be worshipped and obeyed.

6) Prophecy.

7) Moses is unsurpassed by any other prophet

8) The entire Torah was given to Moses.

9) Moses's Torah will not be superseded by any other divine law. Nor will anything be added or distracted from it.

10) God knows the actions of men.

11) God rewards those who fulfill the commandments of the Torah and punishes those who break them.

12) The coming of the Messiah.

13) The resurrection of the dead.

It is outside the scope of this lesson to describe the theories and speculations of other leading figures of that period - Ibn Gabirol, Bahya ibn Paquda, Moses and Abraham Ibn Ezra, Hasdai Crescas and Joseph Albo. Most of those thinkers were well rounded people, who in addition to their preoccupation with Jewish learning and mysticism, were well versed in secular knowledge and pursuits, literature and poetry.

Further developments in Jewish philosophy ceased almost entirely after the Jews left Spain and was revived again only towards the middle of the nineteenth century in Germany.

Though Jewish philosophy itself cannot be said to have had a very significant influence on the development of the religion, there is no doubt that Judaism has been enriched by the work of many of its philosophers - and in particular by their disciplined and systematic approach to Jewish learning as a whole, and the application of that approach to the process of codifying the law and practice.

Some philosophers, Maimonides in particular, are now more highly valued for their work in the field of Halacha (the laws and observances of Judaism) than for their philosophical work. Likewise, Ibn Ezra's Bible commentaries are a subject of study these days much more than his philosophical works and men such as Ibn Gabirol are remembered more for their superb Hebrew poetry than for their edifices of logical thought.

LESSON 3

Human Life and the World to Come

Know then thyself, presume not God to scan: the proper study of mankind is man.

The above quotation from the work of the eighteenth century English poet Alexander Pope touches very neatly on the traditional Jewish attitudes towards man and God. Mainstream Judaism is a practical faith, concerned chiefly with man and this world. It is content, on the whole, to leave vague and unspecified those matters which lie beyond the reach of direct human knowledge.

Two extreme views of life are expressed in the Bible. At his worst man is an animal: in fact he is '*...like the beasts that perish.*' But at his best man is only slightly lower than celestial beings: '*...you have made him little less than the angels, crowning him with glory and honour.*' The choice is open to each individual. He may aspire to reach almost to the level of the angels by observing the teachings of the Torah. Or he may sink towards the level of animals by disregarding God's commandments.

It is stated in the Bible that man was created in the image of God. That, and man's potential for good, renders human life itself sacrosanct. The life of any one man is as important to God as the whole work of creation; and he who kills one man is regarded as if he killed the entire world. The Rabbis teach that Adam was created alone in order to emphasise this very point. The extreme reverence that Judaism attaches to human life is a theme that recurs constantly throughout the whole range of Jewish thought, law and practice.

The Soul

The early books of the bible make little or no distinction between man and his soul and seem to regard both as one and the same. Though the Rabbis hold that belief in the immortality of the soul is implicit in the Torah, comparatively few passages can be quoted to support this view. Perhaps that reticence was caused by the need to wean the Israelites from idolatrous beliefs acquired in Egypt, a country where the cult of the dead often tended to overshadow the needs of the living. Moses, it will be remembered, was originally an Egyptian prince.

Though the later books of the Bible do refer to the afterlife more openly, it is only in the writings of the Rabbis that reference to this belief first became explicit. The world to come was described as the place where all the inconsistencies, anomalies and injustices of this world are put straight; or to quote Maimonidies, it is a place *where God rewards those who keep his commandments and punishes those who break them.*

This concept was developed further with the belief that all souls have already been created by God: they are pure and immortal, and spend only a brief interlude in this world. The first prayer recited by the observant Jew every morning of his life is:

My God, the soul with which you have endowed me is pure: you have created it: you have breathed it into me: you will hereafter reclaim it: and you will restore it to me in the world to come.

The belief in the pre-existence of the soul led the Rabbis to recount that when God gave the Torah to the Jewish people on Mount Sinai, he gave it not only to the generation that had just left Egypt, but also to the souls of future generations yet unborn, who were similarly gathered around the foot of the mountain.

Jewish mystics further extended belief in pre-existence and immortality to belief in Gilgul (transmigration or reincarnation), in which the soul of a dead person may reappear on earth in another human form - though this never became a universally accepted doctrine in Judaism.

The aim of human life

According to Jewish teaching, the duty of man is to cooperate with God in order to achieve his grand design. This is to be done principally by imitating his ways.

As he is merciful, so you shall be merciful:
as he is gracious, so you shall be gracious:
as he is righteous, so you shall be righteous.

The ultimate aim of all human activity is to establish the Kingdom of God here on earth - 'Pie in the sky when you die' - is definitely not a Jewish point of view. The Kingdom of God is visualised as a spiritual and moral Utopia. Belief in the ability of man to perfect himself in stages until the world can finally be redeemed with Divine help is a fundamental principle of faith.

The Messiah

I believe with perfect faith in the coming of the messiah: and though he may tarry, daily will I await his coming.

The Messiah (anointed one) is conceived as a human (and mortal) descendant of the House of David, under whose leadership the exile of the Jewish people from their Holy Land will finally be ended. In the new age that will then start, a great wave of moral and spiritual perfection will influence the whole of mankind into becoming true subjects of the world-wide Kingdom of God then to be established. In the messianic age, to quote the prophet:

the Lord shall be king over all the earth. In that day the Lord shall be one and his name one.

The ambition of a small nation such as the Jewish one, to become the instrument for the redemption of the entire human race, may seem presumptuous, to say the least. This hope can, however, be better understood when it is realised that many concepts of God, of morality and righteousness, now held by large sections of the world's population were originally transmitted to them by means of this same people.

After the messianic age, God's ultimate purpose will be fulfilled, following the Resurrection of the Dead and the Day of Judgment:

I believe with perfect faith that there will be a resurrection of the dead at a time when it shall please the Creator, blessed be his name.

The world to come

The final consummation, leading to the 'world to come', is simply regarded as a principle of faith; and has not been subjected to detailed definition and analysis. On the whole, Judaism is content to concentrate on attempting to establish perfection here on earth and does not try to peer through the veil that cloaks these impenetrable mysteries.

The Rabbis use the words Ha-Olam Habah העולם הבא (the world to come) in two senses: It may either be the place to which the soul goes on the death of the body, or it may be the spiritual existence that will follow the Day of Judgment. Jewish concepts of the hereafter are impossible to summarise, because only belief in reward and punishment is basic.

The Rabbis permitted great scope to their individual imaginations when attempting to picture the after-life. Some believe that the souls of the wicked are punished for up to one year before they are allowed to join the souls of the righteous in Paradise. According to another theory, the souls of the righteous go to Gan Eden גן עדן (the Garden of Eden, or Paradise), while the souls of the wicked go to Gehinam גיהנום (hell). A third theory claims that the souls of the wicked are utterly destroyed.

Likewise, opinions vary on what actually happens in the 'world to come'. One rather pleasing Talmudic passage emphasises tranquillity:

In the world to come there is no eating or drinking, no begetting of children or bargaining, no jealousy, no hatred and no strife. The righteous all sit with crowns on their heads enjoying the light of the Divine Presence.

The preoccupation of some mediaeval Christian theologians with detailed descriptions of Heaven and Hell is not echoed by Jewish sources. A simple Hasidic story on which to leave this subject assumes that as study of the Torah is the ideal occupation of mankind in this world, it will be the only occupation in the world to come. For those who love the Torah, it will be heaven: for those who hate the Torah it will be hell: the choice is with each individual.

The Chosen People and the Gentiles

The Chosen People

The Bible relates how Abraham was chosen by God:

Leave your own country, your kinsmen and your father's house; and go to a country that I will show you. I will make you into a great nation, and will make your name great. You shall be a blessing...

Abraham obeyed the call promptly and started on the long journey. It was a profoundly significant voyage of religious discovery, that led to the acceptance at Mount Sinai of that core of Divine teaching which, during the subsequent course of history, was to develop as the foundation for three of the principal faiths of mankind (Judaism, Christianity and Islam), and through which nearly two thousand million human beings presently derive their notions of God, of morality and of ethical behaviour.

It was also a tremendous physical journey that led Abraham himself from Mesopotamia to Canaan; and took his descendants through the period of enslavement in Egypt to their promised land; and thence after some twelve centuries of turbulent occupation, into almost two thousand years of weary and agonising exile, ending only in the year 1948 when a surviving remnant succeeded in re-establishing the tiny independent State of Israel.

The Bible tells us how the descendants of Abraham, Isaac and Jacob were blessed by God because of the exceptional merit of those three patriarchs; and how, because of this merit, the Israelites were redeemed from their life of slavery in Egypt. From that time on, though, the concept of the 'chosen people' became double-edged. At the foot of mount Sinai, by freely accepting the yoke of the Torah, the Jewish people - so to speak - exchanged their previous bondage to Pharaoh for future bondage to God.

A rabbinic parable describes how God originally offered his Torah to all the peoples of the earth; and how each in turn rejected it because of the heavy burden involved, save for the small and previously insignificant people of Israel.

Jews believe, therefore, that God chose them as the vehicle for his revelation to mankind:

You shall be for me a kingdom of priests, and a holy nation.

They also believe that, by accepting his commandments, the Jews also chose God:

How odd of God to choose the Jews. Oh no it's not, the Jews chose God.

Furthermore, they are taught that those two acts of choice are essentially dependent, one on the other:

If you will listen to my voice and keep my covenant, then you shall be my own treasure from among all the peoples.

Unfortunately, as the prophets of ancient Israel were not slow to point out, God's covenant was not always kept; and the people were often punished for such lapses. The Rabbis teach that the 'chosen people' continue to be punished in every age for failing to live up to the special obligations they have undertaken - though God's unbounded love continues to sustain them, even in the depths of the suffering that he inflicts.

It should be realised, therefore, that there are no arrogant overtones of a 'master race' in the Jewish concept of a chosen people. Any sincere convert, regardless of background, race or colour, is accepted by Judaism and is regarded as a true 'son' or 'daughter' of Abraham. King David himself was a descendant of the convert Ruth.

The term 'chosen' is applied to a people who, because of a highly developed religious and moral sensitivity, freely chose to undertake heavier obligations towards their God than those accepted by much of mankind - and being all too human, they often fail in their endeavours. Nevertheless, Jews do rejoice in what they regard as the special relationship between them and the Divine. They are taught to believe that, despite constant backsliding, the relationship still holds. Pious Jews continue to try to do their best to lead such lives as to fulfil their ultimate ambition of becoming 'a light to the nations.'

The Gentiles

According to Jewish teachings, all men are required to observed the basic laws given by God to Noah, when the earth was renewed after the flood. These fundamental rules of behaviour, deduced by the Rabbis from the biblical text, are known as the Noachide laws (or the laws of Noah); and can be grouped under seven main headings:

 i) Prohibition of idolatry
 ii) Prohibition of blasphemy
 iii) Prohibition of murder
 iv) Prohibition of incest
 v) Prohibition of theft
 vi) Prohibition of eating any part of a living animal
 vii) The obligation to establish courts of justice

Jews are under an obligation to teach pagans and idolaters to conform to these fundamental standards of conduct; but are under no obligation to persuade unbelievers to become Jews - and indeed conversion to Judaism is neither encouraged nor made easy. In no way does Judaism attempt to insist that the rest of mankind must accept its own special and particular 'knowledge' of God: it is sufficient that idolatry, murder, incest etc. are suppressed, and that people live in ordered societies under the rule of laws administered by the courts of justice.

Though Judaism has produced its full share of extreme views in many matters, it has always maintained without dissent that salvation is not reserved exclusively for Jews, and that *'the righteousness of all nations have a share in the world to come.'* The term 'righteous of all nations' is generally understood to include all those who observe the Noachide code.

> Interestingly enough, Maimonides (in the twelfth century) held that to qualify for salvation, the laws of Noah have to be obeyed out of religious conviction, and not merely from natural inclination.

Both Islam and Christianity conform to the Noachide laws. Hence, there is thus no conflict between Judaism and its 'daughter' faiths. Consequently Judaism, though often criticised for being excessively inward-looking, does have the positive virtue of concerning itself mainly with its own progress, and of not trying to coerce its neighbours into following its precise path.

Conversion to Judaism

Judaism has long ceased to be a missionary faith; and those seeking to become Jews are usually rebuffed on first approach with a harshness that can cause distress.

In an increasingly secular world, the Rabbis have much difficulty in maintaining religious standards amongst Jews who do have an obligation to obey the commandments in the Torah. Those who are not Jewish have no such obligation and are free to serve God in their own different ways. As the guardians of Judaism, rabbis will only consider for conversion those who can prove beyond reasonable doubt their belief in the Torah, and their willingness to live their future lives in accordance with its requirements.

> The logic of a faith based on Divine revelation is as simple as it is is unbending. A person wishing to join a particular club must expect to convince the committee that he or she intends to obey its rules, even though many of the existing members may be lax in their

own practices. When it is believed that the rule book was written by the Almighty God, the Creator of heaven and earth, then it is perhaps understandable that there is long and serious hesitation before allowing an outsider to undertake so heavy a set of obligations.

Conversion to traditional Judaism is only possible after years of study, which includes periods of living in a strictly observant, Jewish environment. Once admitted into Judaism, however, the former convert is a full member of the faith, equal in every way to those who were born to it.

Ethics and Law in Judaism

The Structure

The present structure of Jewish morality and law is the result of almost three thousand years of continuous development. The essential principles were handed to Moses on Mount Sinai, and are contained in the first books of the Bible - the five books of Moses - as well as in the parallel oral tradition.

These rules were expanded and amplified in the wealth of ethical injunctions contained in the later books of the Bible.

The Torah was further developed and extended between the years 450 BCE. and 500 C.E., by the many generations of sages whose deliberations and legislation were summarised in the Talmud - the 'classical' statement of religious, civil, criminal, social and moral law.

After the completion of the Talmud, around 500 C.E., the long process of interpretation and refinement of its contents began. This process continues unabated to the present day.

As I am holy, so shall you be holy.

There is no separate word for ethics in the Bible or in the Talmud. In ancient Jewish society, religious practices morality and law were all fused together into that sublime concept of 'holiness' which was stamped with the authority of the Almighty himself.

It has been told to you, 0 man, what is good and what the Lord requires of you. It is to do justice, to love mercy and to walk humbly with your God.

One ingredient is useless without the others. Neglect of the moral code can completely nullify the effect of the most meticulous religious observance intended to fulfill the requirement of walking humbly with God.

Standards

The standard of conduct demanded by Jewish law is exacting. It is not Utopian in the sense of turning the other cheek, but was evolved to accommodate realistic expectations of human conduct. While in some ways human beings may be "only a little lower than angels," they are often overcome by evil impulses. The Rabbis had no illusions about the necessity for firm laws to regulate human behaviour:

pray for the welfare of your government for, but for fear of rulers, every man would devour his neighbour.

Justice and mercy

Justice is based on the often deliberately misunderstood principle of 'an eye for an eye', which was a remarkably enlightened concept for its day. As interpreted in Talmudic times, it meant simply that the punishment must be carefully graded to fit the crime, and certainly must be no greater. The penalty for most crimes, therefore, was related to appropriate monetary penalties or, in other words, to a scale of fines. No one would actually have to lose an eye for blinding another; and no one could possibly be hanged or transported in chains to Australia for the offence of stealing a sheep, which was the practice in England less than two hundred years ago.

Man is commanded to *do* justice and to *love* mercy. The nuances of expression are important, for the opposing concepts of strict justice and mercy run together throughout the entire span of Jewish thought. Justice is stern and unbending; it can be harsh at times; it is impartial and no respecter of persons. One cannot always love justice - even though it is essential for the maintenance of an ordered society. The concept of 'holiness' requires justice to be tempered with the opposing spirit of compassion. Justice and mercy, combined together in the right proportions, sustain a harmonious moral code.

An illustration of the two opposing principles acting together is the biblical ruling that it is permissible to treat 'with rigour' a Canaanite slave - probably captured after a bout of merciless warfare. This was mitigated by the moral code. As expressed by Job:

If I despise the cause of my slave when he argues with me,. . . what shall I do when God rises up . . . did not He that made me in the womb also make him.

This reasoning developed into rules for taking care of sick and infirm slaves and for forbidding slaves to carry out degrading or unnecessary work. Ill treatment of any kind was a sufficient ground to demand the immediate freeing of a slave.

Even the death penalty for murder, though sometimes imposed by the Sanhedrin (Supreme Court), became so hedged with safeguards that its imposition became more and more infrequent.

A Sanhedrin that puts a man to death once in seven years is called a murderous one. Rabbi Eleazar ben Azariah says "or even once in seventy years"; and Rabbis Tarfon and Akiva added "if we had been in the Sanhedrin, no death sentence would ever have been passed".

Though by the time that was written the Roman occupiers of Palestine had already deprived the Sanhedrin of its power to inflict capital punishment, it still serves to illustrate the sentiments of the foremost Jewish sages of almost two thousand years ago and is indicative of the way that the practice of capital punishment had developed since earlier times. The rabbis mentioned by name in the above quotation from the Talmud were not isolated idealists but were prominent amongst those who formulated Jewish law.

Scope

The Jewish legal system embraces all aspects of civil; criminal and religious law; and the moral code is intended to apply to man's every intention and action.

It is hard sometimes to separate one from the other, as the laws themselves are based on the idea of righteousness, with their emphasis on the protection of the poor and underprivileged, and their concern for human rights and dignity.

Any attempt to separate the unenforceable ethical principles from laws administered by courts of justice must commence with the teaching that it may be unfair, in certain circumstances, to insist on full legal rights, without regard for fairness and compassion - the Rabbis condemn the inhabitants of the wicked city of Sodom for doing just that. In any case, they praise the litigant who chooses not to accept the full damages properly awarded to him in a court action against a poor adversary.

When challenged to summarise the whole of the Torah whilst standing on one foot, Hillel (first century B.C.E.) said:

Whatever is hateful to you, do not do to your neighbour. This is the essence of the Torah; the rest is commentary. Now, go and learn.

That, of course, is a paraphrase of a portion of a commandment found in Leviticus, the third book of the Bible

Business practice

The Jewish legal and ethical system deals at length with topics such as business practice and conditions of employment. Hours of work and minimum rates of pay were strictly regulated by ancient law, and any encroachment on the workers' living standards was forbidden. However, slacking at work and taking an unjustified amount of time off, even for prayer, were also regarded as forms of theft.

The moral conduct of business affairs is required to be of a high standard. Unfair competition, cornering the market, all kinds of deceits and tricks of the trade, taking advantage of ignorance or defencelessness: these are only some of the practices which are specifically condemned, even though they may not always be challenged by the law.

Animals

Care for one's fellow creatures also extends to the animal world. It is forbidden to sit down to a meal before having first made sure that one's animals have been fed. The traditional method of ritual slaughter of animals for food was developed from the early biblical laws so as to lessen the suffering of the unfortunate beasts by killing them in the most humane way possible.

Conclusion

The bulk of Jewish civil and criminal law is no longer strictly relevant to most Jews who are obliged to live under the authority of the legal systems of their countries of residence, although the strictly observant will still have internal civil disputes settled by a Beth Din (rabbinic court) rather than submit them to secular jurisdiction.

You shall not take revenge nor bear any grudge; but you shall love your neighbour as yourself; I am the Lord

Rabbi Akiva *(50-135* C.E.) also maintained that this is the essence of the Torah and Ben Azzai observed that the command to love one's fellow was merely a logical extension of the belief that man is made in the image of God.

Jews and non-Jews

There is one and the same law for you and for the resident stranger in your midst, a law binding on your descendents for all time: you and the alien are alike before the Lord

Laws and morality apply equally to Jew and non-Jew alike, and all men must be treated with fairness.

A story is told about the disciples of Rabbi Simon Ben Shetah (90 B.C.E.) who had bought an ass from a pagan Arab as a present for their master. On the beast's neck they found a precious jewel, which they thought of selling to relieve their master's poverty. Rabbi Simon indignantly refused to accept the gem on hearing that the Arab had not known about it when agreeing to the bargain, saying that he would rather hear a heathen praise the God of the Jews than gain all the treasures in this world. The lesson to be learnt by that simple tale is that a fraud against a gentile is considered to be a greater moral offence than one against a Jew, as it involves the desecration of God's name, which is the gravest of sins.

I should have denied the One above if I rejoiced at the destruction of him that hated me, or exulted that evil overtook him

The command to love one's fellow man, whatever the circumstances, is further illustrated by the parable about God's rebuking the angels who were rejoicing at the drowning of the pursuing Egyptian army in the Red sea after the Israelites had passed safely over onto dry land: *'How can you celebrate,'* God is pictured as saying, *'when my creatures are being destroyed?'* This lesson has been carried into the synagogue service; for on the latter days of Passover only half the usual number of psalms of rejoicing, known as the Hallel, are recited for that very reason.

Whoever hates any man hates Him who spoke and the world came into existence

Love of one's fellow man includes a tender care for his self respect. The act of destroying a man's reputation by slander or malicious gossip is compared by the Rabbis to the act of murder; and it is considered a grave offence to put a fellow human being to shame in public 'so that the red leaves his cheeks', that is, as if the blood were draining out of his body after being killed with a knife. One is urged to be specially careful not to risk hurting the feelings of converts by referring to their origins; and one should not embarrass a reformed criminal by alluding to his past misdeeds.

The poor have a right to demand assistance; and charity must be dispensed with tact and sensitivity. It is not considered sufficient merely to give money; and emphasis is put on the duty of constructive aid to enable the recipient to provide for his own needs. Interest on personal loans is forbidden on the grounds that one should not benefit from extending help, and that one person's difficulty should not lead to the enrichment of another.

Commandments and Prohibitions in Judaism

Divine commandments can be divided into two classes:

a) Mitzvot Sihliyot – those commandments which mankind might have derived for itself simply by using the power of reasoning.

b) Mitzvot Shemayot – those which, though they may also have a rational purpose, men could not have discovered by reason alone - but only through the direct command of God.

The differences between these two types of commandment have exercised the minds of our sages throughout the ages. Some of their most interesting views are summarised as follows.

Sa'adia Gaon

Sa'adia, the great Gaon of Babylonian Jewry who lived in the 9th century, was a firm believer in the God-given power of human reason. He maintained that the commandments of the Torah, even though they were revealed to us by the Almighty, are at least partly capable of having been discovered by human reason alone.

Why were they given?
The commandments were given to us as an act of Chesed, of pure kindness.

The first move was that of creation itself, when God brought his creatures into being. Before creation, nothing existed other than God – God created the universe from nothing.

God then gave his creatures the means of attaining happiness and fulfilment by giving them the commandments and prohibitions. He did not make men perfect, as he might have done, because happiness earned by effort is so much greater than unearned happiness that comes automatically and without effort.

In Return
Therefore reason dictates, according to Sa'adia Gaon, that:

i) We must serve God and offer thanks to him for his kindness to us.

ii) We are forbidden to despise or to insult God.

iii) God's creatures must be prevented from harming each other.

This is the basis of the rational commandments (Mitzvot Sihliyot).

Sa'adia claimed that though each one of the revealed commandments (Mitzvot Shemayot) may not be capable of rational explanation, when taken as a whole they do have a rational explanation. Sa'adia's explanation is that God commands his creatures to do certain things merely in order to be able to reward them for their obedience.

However, he also acknowledges that human wisdom cannot grasp the whole of divine purpose but only a small part of it. Divine wisdom is entirely beyond human reach.

Why did the Commandments need to be revealed?

Mitzvot Sihliot

Because, though reason would have provided us with the general principles, it would not have given us the details – so revelation was necessary.

Mitzvot Shemayot

Because we simply could not have discovered them by the use of reason alone.

EXERCISES and QUESTIONS

Give examples of each type of mitzvah.

Give examples of "rational" commandments and their justification.

What was new to Judaism about Sa'adia's formulation?

What do you think of Sa'adia's strictly utilitarian account of the reasons for the commandments in terms of increasing human happiness? Can you think of any inconsistencies or difficulties in this explanation? (There are very many!)

Moses Maimondes

The Rambam, the greatest Jewish thinker and philosopher of the 12th century, adopted a rather more sophisticated approach to the problem. He too believed in the supreme power of reason.

God's Purpose

We all accept that God is all-powerful and all-knowing. It is therefore absurd to think that he can act without reason. It follows that none of his commandments can be arbitrary and without purpose: each of them can only exist because it serves a useful purpose.

Can that argument be accepted without serious doubt?

According to Maimonides, the distinction between mishpatim and hukkim is relative, not absolute.

Mishpatim are self-evidently useful. Hukkim are equally useful but require deep study to understand their purpose. Every one of the 613 commandments is there for a reason that benefits mankind – although there are some (such as the Red Heifer) for which only Moses has so far discovered the purpose.

Though there may be a good reason for some of the commandments as a whole, Maimonides accepts that some of their details may be arbitrary. Sacrifices are one example of this: why was a particular number of sacrifices specified and not another number? Another is shechita (the ritual slaughter of animals for food) - an excellent idea in itself but why must it be done in one particular way and not in another?

The general purpose of the Commandments

The well-being of the soul and, by promoting individual morality and social justice, the well-being of the body. Though the perfection of the soul is a higher aim than that of perfecting the body, it cannot be achieved on its own.

The removal of idolatry and everything that is connected to it or may lead to it. The Rambam believed that a careful examination of the forms of idolatry that existed before the giving of the Torah (or during that period) would reveal explanations for many laws not yet understood.

Examples of these are: prohibition of wearing garments of mixed wool and linen, men wearing women's clothes, eating blood, meat boiled in milk and why salt was placed on every sacrifice.

Recognition of the limits of human nature. It was too much for God simply to forbid all the practices with which the Israelites had been long accustomed. They had to be led gradually to a purer form of divine service; and therefore God allowed pagan practices to continue to some extent, but ordered them to be modified and so transformed to a higher purpose.

In reply to the question as to why God did not alter the nature of man to enable him to dispense with sacrifices without difficulty, Maimonides argued that God changes nature by means of miracles, but never changes the nature of man. If he did so, the concept of freewill would disappear and there would have been no need for the Torah.

Law can never take exceptional cases into account, for if it did so it would vary from circumstance to circumstance and all certainty would disappear. Therefore the failure of a law to produce a beneficial result in one particular case is no argument against the beneficial character of the law as a whole.

Yehudah Halevi

A rather different approach was adopted by Yehudah Halevi, a Spanish poet and philosopher of the 12th century.

He believed that there is an essential difference in the relationship between man and God as perceived by philosophers and that between man and God as perceived by Judaism. Philosophers are interested primarily in knowledge. For the religious Jew, the emphasis is on closeness and attachment to God.

For man to become close to God, specific conditions are needed - a particular people, a particular land and a particular way of life. For the Jew, the way of life is governed by the commandments.

Explanation of the commandments is beyond human reason: they are part of the impenetrable divine mystery. But their result is to bring man closer to God. Human intellect could not have discovered this path alone and only God could have pointed the way.

For Yehudah Halevi also there were two kinds of commandments, which he described as "rational" commandments and "divine" commandments.

He argued that the "rational" commandments came first because they were necessary for the existence of human society. The "divine" commandments came later and are quite different in quality. They are unique to Israel; and only through them can Israel have a special relationship with God.

The Divine Commandments

These are entirely beyond human comprehension. They create order and balance in the world, through which God's influence comes to rest in it.

Each individual receives only as much divine influence as his own actions enable him to receive. Actions that are precisely in accordance with God's commandments establish a special type of harmony in the world – in a manner incomprehensible to us.

Some Examples

1) The sacrificial system was a precise but unfathomable ritual through which the Divine Presence was brought into the midst of the people.

2) Prayer, the Sabbath and the Festivals constitute a regular cycle of establishing closeness to God and purging the soul of the impurities acquired through excessive involvement with worldly concerns.

3) The order of the prayers creates receptiveness to the presence of the Divine.

4) The laws of purity (and leprosy for example) are unique to Israel because of the special sensitivity of the Jewish soul to contacts of this kind.

5) The logic of certain commandments emphasise the priority of the community over the individual.

A QUESTION

Compare Yehudah Halevi's approach to the problem of the commandments with those of the other thinkers described.

Which attitude do you think the most appropriate?

The Problem of Freewill as interpreted by our Sages

The problem of freewill

To put the problem at its very simplest, does God control the universe - the good harvests, the droughts and famines - or can man influence the course of nature? If the past, the present and the future are in God's hands - if all is pre-ordained - what is left for man to decide?

Belief in determinism or fate, thought of in terms of "natural law" or of planetary influence (astrology), was an important element in the thinking of the ancient Greeks. There is an obvious contradiction between the belief that what happens in the world is governed by immutable forces and the belief that the will of man influences the course of events.

Many ancient Greek tragedies, still performed in the theatre, were based on the inexorable working of fate which man is powerless to affect.

That was not, however, the central issue for rabbinic Judaism. Instead the problem lay in Providence - the divine rulership of the universe. And God, unlike 'nature' or the planets, was certainly possessed of freewill. He could be influenced by man, though not as the natural order is influenced, by cause and effect; nor as the supernatural planetary order is influenced, by magic. Rather, he responds to man's actions as the author of justice - watching, judging, rewarding and punishing.

This rabbinic view still poses two problems:

1) If the events in the world are the work of Divine Providence then they cannot be the work of man, and vice versa.

Here we seem torn between two alternatives, both equally unacceptable to rabbinic Judaism:

    i) If Divine Providence is all-powerful and ubiquitous (everywhere at the same time), man cannot have freewill, or
    ii) If man's will is free and can dictate the course of history, God is removed from an active role in the determination of events.

Where is the line to be drawn between what is man's doing and what is God's doing?

2) If God has foreknowledge of all events still to happen, how can man be free? Surely if the way we act is known to God in advance, we cannot do otherwise.

The treatment of the important problem of freewill by the Rabbis was not systematic or philosophical but pragmatic.

The Rabbis were bound to believe in freewill because:

> i) This belief was clearly articulated in the Bible, notably in Devarim; and was also presupposed by the doctrine of divine reward and punishment on which rests the notion of man's responsibility for his acts.
>
> ii) They were committed to a system of law - the halacha - which required a coherent concept of free as opposed to involuntary action on which to base its judicial system.

Equally they were consistent in attributing to Divine Providence its share in the determination of the world. But on exactly where the line was drawn between them, there was a multiplicity of views.

Varying shades of belief in freewill between groups of Jewish thinkers were described by the historian Josephus in the 2nd century C.E. Josephus claimed that the problem of freewill was one of the major sources of difference between Jewish sects at the time of the 2nd Temple.

According to him:

1) the Pharisees combined a belief in Divine Providence with a conviction that man had free choice. They *'attribute everything to fate and to God; they hold that to act rightly or otherwise rests, for the most part with men, but that fate co-operates in each action.'* The Sadducees asserted freewill and denied Providence: *'we are ourselves the cause of what is good, and receive what is evil from our own folly.'*

Freedom of choice

The fundamental Jewish belief is stated in Devarim:

I call heaven and earth to witness against you this day that I have set before you life and death, the blessing and the curse; therefore choose life ...

(Dev. 30:19; see also Dev. 11:26-28).

Here, freedom of human choice is not merely stated as a fact but is the pivot of moral life. Man is not only free but responsible. His acts will be noted and duly rewarded:

...whose eyes are open to all the ways of man, rewarding every man according to his ways and according to the fruit of his doings.

(Jeremiah 32:19)

Despite the fundamental emphasis on man's freedom to be found in rabbinic writings, we must not overlook certain contrary indications. For example:

Resh Lakish said: a person does not commit a transgression unless a spirit of folly enters into him

(Sotah 3a).

This seems to place the cause of sin in something outside of man's volition. R. Jose spoke of the gradual erosion of man's freedom as he becomes habituated to a particular way of life.

Divine Providence

There are at least two facets of the concept of Divine Providence:

1) God's conduct of the universe in general, his authorship of the laws of nature, his provision of food for all the inhabitants of the earth. This Providence extends universally - to non-Jews, to the wicked and even to idolators.

2) God's Providence over the deeds of man, his constant attention to their actions so that he can (in his role as righteous judge of the earth) reward or punish a man according to his deeds:

Your eyes are open to all the ways of the sons of men, to give every one according to his ways, and according to the fruits of his doings.

(Jeremiah 32:19)

This two-edged character of Divine Providence raises an important question: if man is free to choose between good and evil, then he, and not God, determines the allocation of rewards and benefits in the world. If, on the other hand, God determines the conduct of the universe, the good harvests, the famines, and so on, then is the conduct of man also a part of this total scheme, predetermined and leaving no room for choice?

There seems to be an incompatibility between the two aspects of Divine Providence: one assumes, and the other seems to deny, a place for human freedom.

The opposition to determinism

Early statements
1) Psalms of Solomon (9:4):

Our deeds are in the choice and power of the soul, to do righteousness and iniquity in the works of our hands.

2) Ben Sirah (Ecclesiasticus 15: 11-17):

Say not, it was the Lord's fault that I transgressed ... say not, He led me astray ... If you will it, you will keep the commandments; and to deal faithfully is a matter of choice.

R. Akiva

We find strong emphasis on human freedom and responsibility in the saying of R. Akiva.

His famous statement (Avot 3:15): *'Everything is seen (tsafui) and freedom of choice is given'* is not to be understood as a paradoxical statement of belief in both Divine foreknowledge and human freedom. 'Tsafui' has the sense of 'foreseen' only in later, Amoraic writings. Here it simply means, seen, noticed, taken account of.

Man is free to choose his course in life; but all he does is seen by God and will be judged. In his freedom he mirrors his creator: *'Beloved is man for he was created in the image of God'* (Avot 3:14). But he must take the responsibility for all he does:

Everything is given on pledge, and a net is spread for all the living; the shop is open; and the dealer gives credit; and the ledger lies open; and the hand writes. Whoever wishes to borrow may come and borrow, but the collectors make their daily round and exact payment from man, with or without his consent.

(Avot 3:16) (see U. 256-260)

If man is free and is rewarded and punished - does he not then influence Providence? Is there no element of predestination or divine foresight? Akiva's answer seems to be: the rewards and punishments are prepared in advance, but man determines which he will receive:

This attitude is expressed again in a dispute between R. Pappos and R. Akiva on the meaning of the verse, *'Behold man is become like one of us'* (Bereishit 3:22).

R. Pappos interpreted this to mean that man had become *'like one of the ministering angels'*. R. Akiva denied this. Rather, it meant that *'God set before him two ways, one of death and the other of life, and he chose the way of death'*.

In R. Pappos' answer we see the glimmer of an idea that was to be taken up in Christianity, the difference between man before and after the first sin. Before, he was perfect - second only to God, having no possibility of evil. After, he was under the dominion of sin. At neither time was he a freely-choosing being. In R. Akiva we find the rejection of this idea, and the affirmation that after as well as before sin first came into the world, man remains the master of his choices without constraints to his freedom.

The emphasis on freewill made by R. Akiva was also made by Hillel who said that man must fact the consequences of his actions in terms of reward and punishment, and that neither excuses nor an appeal to Zechut Avot, the protective merit of the Fathers, will be of avail:

If I am not for me, who is for me? If I have not made myself worthy in this world, who will make me worthy in the world to come? I have no father, no mother, no brother. Abraham, our father, could not redeem Ishmael; Isaac, our father, could not redeem Esau ...

(Avot deRabbi Nathan ch.27; Sifrei Devarim par. 329).

In other words, certain events are decreed by Providence in advance, yet they are so arranged as to follow as the natural consequences of men's actions. Men act freely, yet God's purposes are still achieved by skilful manipulation without disrupting the natural order. (For another example see U. 297)

Another view: The removal of reward from this world

Another view adopted by Tannaim and Amoraim was to deny any connection between a man's conduct and his this-worldly circumstances. Reward and punishment belong to the world-to-come: only there does man influence his fate. In this world, man is free, but Providence wholly determines the course of events, independently of man's behaviour.

1) Ben Azai (Ethics of the Fathers):

The reward of a precept is a precept and the reward of a transgression is a transgression (Avot 4:2); i.e. in this world, the only reward for virtue is virtue itself.

Limits to Man's freedom

Does Providence ever intrude on man's freedom? Are his acts ever the result of God's will and not his own?

We find, in the school of R. Ishmael, the view that Providence helps a man to make his decisions. Once he has made his own unaided choice of good or evil, he may be strengthened in his chosen path. Only the first decision was his alone:

If a man hearkened to one precept he is enabled to hearken to many precepts ... If a man forgot one precept he is made to forget many precepts.

(Mechilta de-R. Ishmael)

The school of R. Ishmael taught: transgression dulls the heart of man ... if a man defiles himself a little, he is defiled much ... If a man purifies himself a little, he is sanctified much.

(ibid) (see U. 272-3)

Astrology

Amongst the Tannaim and Amoraim there were some who acknowledged astrological, planetary influences, on events and even on human character. But they were often aware of the problem this posed for the belief in freewill.

Various limits on this influence were set. Rav and Shmuel held that fulfilment of the precepts overruled planetary influence. R. Jochanan denied that Israel was subject to this influence at all. He also stressed the power of repentance to *'tear asunder the decree imposed on man'* (Rosh Hashana 17b).

The Illusion of freedom

Some of the late Amoraim even occasionally suggest that God sometimes leads man into actions so that his purposes, which are already decreed, can be achieved. Freedom is, in these cases, partly an illusion. Man is led to think that he brought about what in fact was inevitable.

Thus a Midrash (Tanchuma, Vayeshev, para. 4) tells that death was created before Adam, yet he was blamed for bringing death into the world. Adam says to God:

If you had not prepared death for mankind would you have written thus (i.e. the death penalties prescribed in the Torah, which preceded the world, according to the Midrash, by 2000 years)? Only, you have come to put the blame on me.

A later view - The Rambam

Rambam expressed the dilemma in the following terms.

If God knows in advance that a man will be righteous, then the man must be so. However, if the man also has the freewill to be wicked, then God cannot have real foreknowledge for, if so, we must to conclude that man would not have real freewill.

Rambam's answer is essentially the same as that given to other difficult problems - why the good are made to suffer, for example. It is that God's knowledge is not like man's: God and his knowledge are one, and man cannot hope to be able to understand it.

Everyone has the freewill to govern their own actions - but not the actions of others, who have freewill themselves. God knows the entire pattern, how each one of us is going to act.

According to Rambam, the Bible contains eight examples of cases in which a person's freewill is practically abolished by God's direct intervention. Two such cases are mentioned below.

1) Abimeleh was forbidden by God (in a vision) to regard Sarah as his wife. Though in theory he still had the freedom to proceed, he felt unable to do so against God's direct command and did not touch Sarah.

2) Pharaoh, being a normal human being, would probably have given in and let the Israelites go after the first few plagues. But we read that God "hardened Pharaoh's heart" and so he did nothing.

Many have misinterpreted this last case, thinking it demonstrates that God decrees whether a man should be good or bad.

When man or a society commits a sin deliberately, then it is appropriate to punish them and God acts accordingly. But if the man does teshuvah, Divine Punishment is suspended: just as he is free to sin, he is equally free to do teshuvah.

It is possible that one can commit so great a sin, or so many of them, that God in his justice can deny teshuvah and the possibility of repentance is then removed. (There are 24 things that prevent man from repenting).

The Egyptians had freewill before they first enslaved the Israelites: they were therefore liable to receive punishment - but this was deferred. Thus we read *'I will harden his heart'*; and that means that because the Egyptians had done evil by making slaves of the Israelites, teshuvah was denied to them, and they continued in their course of conduct.

The Jewish Year

Shabbbat שבת

Introduction

Remember the Shabbat day to keep it holy

זָכוֹר אֶת יוֹם הַשַּׁבָּת לְקַדְּשׁוֹ...

... the children of Israel shall keep the Shabbat throughout their generations as an everlasting covenant. It is a sign between me and the children of Israel forever; for in six days the Lord made the heaven and the earth, and on the seventh day he ceased from work and rested.

(Exodus 31:16-17)

ושמרו בני ישראל את השבת לעשות את השבת לדרתם ברית עולם. ביני ובין בני ישראל אות היא לעלם, כי ששת ימים עשה ה' ' את השמים ואת הארץ וביום השביעי שבת וינפש

(שמות ל'א, טז-יז)

Shabbat is the day on which we remember the Creation; and it also symbolises the special covenant between God and the people of Israel. On this day we obey the divine commandment to imitate the ways of our Creator by suspending all work, as "a memorial of the work of creation"; and this has become one of the most important and distinctive marks of our faith.

Remember the Shabbat day to keep it holy. Six days shall you labour and do all your work. But the seventh day is the Shabbat of the Lord your God: in it you shall do no work, you, nor your son, nor your daughter, your manservant, nor your maidservant, your cattle, nor any stranger who is within your gates.

On Shabbat we also commemorate the exodus from Egypt.

On it (the seventh day) ... you shall remember that you were a slave in the land of Egypt, and the Lord your God brought you out of Egypt with a mighty hand and an outstretched arm; therefore the Lord your God commanded you to keep the Shabbat day

(Deuteronomy 5: 15-16)

וזכרת כי עבד היית בארץ מצרים ויצאך ה' אלהיך משם ביד חזקה ובזדע נטויה, על כן צוך ה' אלהיך לעשות את יום שבת.

(דברים ה, יה-טו)

Thus, by remembering the Creation and the exodus from Egypt, we proclaim three main beliefs of the Jewish faith: belief in one God who created the universe, belief in an unique covenant between God and his people, and belief that God directly intervenes in human history as he did in the miracle of the exodus from Egypt

The Shabbat also expresses the idea of equality and the fact that God cares for all his creatures, including animals:

You shall not do any work; you, your son and your daughter, and your man-servant and maid-servant, and your ox and your donkey and all your animals, and the resident in your gates, so that your man-servant and maid-servant shall rest as you.

(Deuteronomy 5:14)

לא תעשה כל מלאכה אתה ובנך ובתך ועבדך ואמתך ושורך וחמרך וכל בהמתך וגרך אשר בשעריך למען ינוח עבדך ואמתך כמוך.

(דברים ה, יד)

Shabbat is a day of family togetherness. It gives the members of families at least one day a week for sitting together and talking to each other instead of watching television or other kinds of activity.

It would be hard to exaggerate the importance of the Shabbat in Judaism. Observance of the Shabbat is listed directly after statements dealing with belief in God in the Ten Commandments. The command to honour the Shabbat day, to keep it holy and to refrain from work on it, is no peripheral injunction to the observant Jew; but is a pivot on which the organisation of his life turns. The Rabbis teach that of all institutions it is the Shabbat that has done most to preserve the Jewish faith and people throughout their long history.

The Jewish idea of dividing time into periods of seven days, with a compulsory rest day in each period, has by now also been adopted by the rest of mankind, to their benefit: however, for reasons of their own, Christianity and Islam observe the day of rest on a day other than the seventh.

Its duration

In Judaism the day begins at sunset, as written in Genesis:

...And it was evening and it was morning, one day

(Genesis 1:5)

Shabbat begins about half an hour before sunset on Friday and ends about half an hour after nightfall on Saturday, lasting 25 hours.

Refraining from work

On Shabbat we are commanded to refrain from all creative activity in order to remind us of our total dependence on our Creator. The tractate Mishnah Shabbat lists 39 activities forbidden on Shabbat; these can be divided into seven categories:

i) Growing and preparing food.
ii) Making clothing
iii) Leatherwork and writing
iv) Providing shelter
v) Creating fire
vi) Completing work
vii) Transporting goods.

Shabbat laws may be neglected only for the purpose of preserving or saving human life, in which case it becomes a positive duty to break them.

Proper observance of Shabbat is often difficult to achieve in a secular society: for example, the early setting of the sun on Friday afternoon in mid-winter will mean that the pious Jew will have to leave work shortly after lunch in order to reach home in time. Though rabbinic interpretation of the prohibition of Shabbat working may seem draconian to some, by forcing the Jew to break his daily routine in this manner the Rabbis have provided a framework by means of which he may add a spiritual dimension to his life. To those who keep it, the Shabbat is a day of tranquillity and joy.

Shabbat as the model for the festivals

In the Kiddush recited on Friday night, we say:

For it is the day which was the beginning of the holy festivals.

Thus Shabbat is perceived as being the first of all festivals. This idea is based on the Torah's list of festivals in Leviticus (Cap. 23) where Shabbat is at the top.

God spoke to Moses, telling him to speak to the Israelites and say to them:
There are special times you must celebrate as sacred holidays to God. The following are my special times:
You may work during the six weekdays, but Saturday is a Sabbath of Sabbaths. It is a sacred holiday to God, when you shall do no work. Wherever you may live, it is God's Sabbath.

These are God's festivals that you must celebrate as sacred holidays at their appropriate times ...

(1-4 Kaplan translation)

The relationship of Shabbat to the Festivals is such that its laws are the basis for the Festival laws.

Bear in mind that when we say "festival" in this section we mean Yom Tov only, i.e. the first two and last two days of Pesach, the two days of Shavuot and of Rosh Hashanah, (Yom Kippur) and the first two and last two days of Sukkot.

In other words, *Melahah* - creative activity - forbidden on Shabbat, is likewise forbidden on Festivals, except that certain *Melahot* (connected with food preparation) are allowed on Yom Tov.

Celebration in the home

Preparation

We are commanded to prepare for Shabbat:

And it shall come to pass on the sixth day that they shall prepare what they bring in ...

(Exodus 16:5)

Erev Shabbat (by which we mean Friday until the start of Shabbat) is a very busy time in a Jewish home for two reasons:

1) We have to make special arrangements in advance to prepare for the negative commandments of Shabbat - for the *Melahot* not allowed on Shabbat itself.

Examples:

i) Cooking is a *Melahah*. However as hot food is desirable, at least for the Friday night meal, it must be cooked before Shabbat and kept warm during Shabbat. As our sages tell us:

He who labours on the eve of Shabbat, shall eat on Shabbat
(Tractate Avodah Zara 3:1)

ii) Lights may not be kindled on Shabbat. So as not to be thrown into darkness, we light candles and switch on electric lights prior to Shabbat. Time-switches may also be used.

2) We are also given the positive commandment to observe Shabbat as a special and joyful day, a day apart from the rest of the week. In order to achieve this, special preparations are

necessary: the home is cleaned, tidied and arranged to look special; the table is laid to look at its most beautiful.

We also prepare our bodies for this holy day by:

    i) bathing,

    ii) washing our hair,

    iii) cutting our nails.

The Table

The Jewish Table (in general)

    i) Eating is not considered a simple necessity, as for animals, but as obeying God's command (a Mitzvah).

    ii) At all times (not just on Shabbat) the Jewish table is likened to the altar in the Temple and must therefore be treated with respect.

    iii) Our meals are always preceded and followed by blessings (berachot).

    iv) One should try to discuss some Torah at the table.

    v) The table is the focal point of the Jewish family where all its members gather.

The Shabbat Table

Each of these points takes on greater importance when it comes to Shabbat:

    i) *Call the Shabbat a delight* (Isaiah 58:13)

    Shabbat meals should be superior to those of weekdays to show that Shabbat is special and to help us to enjoy it.

    ii) The 'altar' takes on a special appearance - not only should the table be beautifully laid and the best dishes put out, but the cloth should remain on the table throughout Shabbat.

    iii) The normal blessings are enhanced by *Kiddush, Zemirot,* etc.

    iv) The leisurely pace allows more time for Torah discussion.

    v) This availability of time also strengthens family bonds. Those who cannot join family meals during the week for whatever reason are re-united every Friday night and at lunch time on Saturday.

On the Shabbat table we usually find:

    i) wine (+ cups - possibly silver - or glasses)

    ii) two Challot (distinctive loaves) (+ Challah board, cloth and knife)

    iii) salt

    iv) (at least) two candles (in ornate candlesticks) (although they do not have to be placed on the table).

Clothes מלבושי השבת

As mentioned, one should change into clean clothes for Shabbat. If possible, one should have separate clothes, only worn on this holy day:

Your dress on Shabbat shall not be as your dress on other days.
(Tractate Shabbat 113:1)

Lighting Candles הדלקת הנרות

1) It is a rabbinic commandment to kindle lights - usually candles these days - in honour of Shabbat (and Yom Tov.). These special lights mark the beginning of Shabbat.

2) The minimum number of candles is two, representing the positive and negative aspects of Shabbat.

According to another custom, one candle is lit for each member of the family.

3) The lady of the house usually performs this mitzvah but a man should carry it out when that is not possible.

In some communities, girls from the age of 12 participate with their mothers in the lighting of the candles.

4) The candles should be lit in the room where the meal will be eaten and placed on or near the Shabbat table.

5) The candles are lit about half an hour before sunset on Friday evening. The times change according to the geographic location and season and a Jewish calendar must be consulted (or the "Jewish Chronicle").

6) The candlesticks are *Muktze*, i.e. objects which cannot be moved on Shabbat.

7) Immediately after lighting the candles, the woman of the house covers her eyes and recites the blessing:

Blessed are you, Lord our God, who has sanctified us with his commandments and commanded us to kindle the light of Shabbat.

ברוך אתה ה', אלהינו מלך העולם, אשר קדשנו במצוותיו וצונו להדליק נר של שבת.

Unlike other blessings, this one is said after performing the mitzvah. The reason for this is that the act of lighting the candles means that the woman of the house accepts the Shabbat and its mitzvot, including the prohibition to light a fire.

8) It is customary in some communities for the woman of the house to put money in a charity box before lighting the candles.

Spiritual preparation (Torah Study למוד תורה)

We prepare ourselves by reading the parasha of the week *'twice in the Bible text and once in translation'* (Berachot 8) before Shabbat begins.

When Aramaic was the everyday language, the parasha had to be read twice in the original Hebrew and once in Onkelos's Aramaic (the *Targum*) which is a translation made to enable the masses to understand the holy text. Nowadays the "translation" read can be Rashi's commentaries or a trusted translation of the text into English.

This reading should be done before Shabbat begins. Where this is not possible it can be done on Shabbat itself or even deferred until the Tuesday of the following week.

Shabbat meals

The more one spends on preparing for Shabbat, and exerting oneself to prepare many good foods, the more one is worthy of praise

(Maimonides 1138-1204)

1) Number of meals

There have to be at least three meals - *Shalosh Seudot* שלש סעודות - on Shabbat. By 'meal' we mean one that usually involves eating bread (or Matzah). They are:

    i) Friday night - immediately after prayers

    ii) Shabbat morning or lunch time

    iii) The 'Third Meal' - *Seudah Shelishit* סעודה שלישית - takes place in the afternoon or early evening (while it is still light).

    This differs from the other two in that if it is not desirable to eat bread (e.g. in the winter when the afternoon is short, the *Seudah Shelishit* may consist of cake or even fruit).

2) Lechem Mishneh

On weekdays, hands are washed if one eats bread and *Hamotsi* and *Birkat Hamazon* are recited. On Shabbat there is an additional requirement: there must be two loaves (again corresponding to the two aspects of the Shabbat) and each must be whole. This is known as *Lechem Mishneh* לחם משנה.

3) As stated, we enjoy more elaborate meals on Shabbat and Festivals. If one comes across a particularly nice item of food during the week, one should try to keep it for Shabbat.

4) However, we are warned not to turn our Shabbat enjoyment into selfish indulgence. It is meritorious to invite guests, especially the poor or lonely.

5) In most communities it is traditional to sing special table songs called *Zemirot* זמירות.

6) Havdalah -

At the sunset on Saturday evening the ceremony of Havdalah (distinction, i.e. between the Shabbat and ordinary days) marks the end of the Shabbat; and the pangs of its departure are lessened by the taste of wine and the scent of fragrant spices.

7) Melave Malkah מלוה מלכה

These words mean "bidding farewell to the Queen", i.e. the Shabbat.

The term refers to the meal eaten on Motse Shabbat. As in the case of Seudah Shelishit, bread is preferable but not essential. It is customary to light candles (without a berahah) for this meal (quite apart from the Havdalah candle).

Friday night services

The basic structure of the services is similar to those for weekdays. However, the services are expanded to honour the Shabbat because there is more time available.

> After the lighting of the candles in the home, worshippers walk to the synagogue. Before reading Mincha, it is customary to read the Songs of Songs, then the Psalm 134 and then Mincha.
>
> The Friday night service is in three parts.
>
> (A) Mincha
>
> (B) Kabbalat Shabbat קבלת שבת:
>
> This is an extra section that precedes Arbit. It includes:
>
> the song, *Lechah Dodi* לכה דודי.
>
> This hymn was composed by Rabbi Alkabetz, one of the kabbalists of Safed in the 16th century. The poem describes greeting the Shabbat as it is a queen or a bride.
>
> This song is chanted by the hazan. The worshippers also recite the last verse as they rise and turn towards the entrance of the synagogue, waiting for the queen or bride - Shabbat - to enter.
>
> (C) Arbit sub-divided into:
>
> i. *Keriat Shema uVir-cho-teha* and
>
> ii. Amidah.

i) Keriat Shema:

The Keriat Shema is the usual version except for the ending of the last blessing Hashkivenu, when we say '*Who spreads the shelter of peace over us and over all your people Israel and over Jerusalem'* (instead of '*who guards your people Israel forever'*.

Sephardim also add two verses, beginning with *Veshamru.*

ii) Amidah:

The Amidah begins after Kaddish is said by the hazan. It is considerably shorter. The first three and last three berachot remain intact; but instead of thirteen middle blessings, we have just one. The middle blessing varies according to the four Amidah prayers (Arbit, Shacharit, Musaph and Mincha) but it ends in all the prayers with the words *'Blessed are You O Lord, who sanctifies the Shabbat.'.*

On Friday night, this middle blessing is "You have sanctified the seventh day, marking the end of the creation of heaven and earth."

The number of blessings in the Amidah was reduced because the Rabbis wanted Shabbat to be a day free from anxiety. So, instead of praying for health, food, forgiveness, etc. (as we do on weekdays) we have one simple berahah which speaks only of spiritual requirements.

The conclusion of Arbit contains more prayers than the parallel weekday service. The hazan and the worshipper rise at the conclusion of the Amidah and repeat aloud the three verses starting with *Va'yechulu* which was also recited with the end of the recitation of the middle Amidah blessings.

Then the hazan recites a blessing for our forefathers and the congregants recite the *Magen avot,* which is repeated aloud by the hazan.

After Kaddish and the recitation of Alenu, Sephardim and Hasidim recite the Psalm 23 ("The Lord is my shepherd").

Some communities include also Kiddush. (see above).

Some communities, including the Spanish and Portuguese, conclude the Arbit with the chanting of *Yigdal.*

Seudah

1) Blessing on children:

It is customary in some communities for the father to bless his children. In other communities the blessing on the children is made only once, on Yom Kippur evening.

The blessing for a son is:

May God make you as Ephraim and as Menasheh.

(Genesis 48:20)

The blessing for a daughter is :

May God make you as Sarah, Rivka, Rachel and Leah.

Both blessings conclude with :

The Lord bless you, and keep you. The Lord make his face to shine on you, and be gracious to you. The Lord lift up his countenance upon you, and grant you peace.

(Numbers 6:24-26)

2) Shalom Alechem שלום עליכם is sung.

3) The head of the family recites: "Sovereign of all worlds, Master of all souls, Lord of peace."

4) The family recites "A woman of valour who can find" אשת חיל מי ימצא from Proverbs 31. This song expresses the unique role of the woman in Judaism.

5) Kiddush קדוש - Sanctification:

We mark the arrival of Shabbat by saying a blessing called Kiddush on the wine or on the grape juice before starting the Shabbat meal.

If one cannot drink alcohol or cannot find kasher wine, the blessing can be said on the two challot alone.

Kiddush is recited by the head of the family who holds a cup of wine on his right hand while standing. All members of the family stand at least for the first part of Kiddush.

The kiddush consists of three parts:

    i) description of the creation of the world

    ii) A blessing on the wine:

...He who created the fruit of the vine..

בורא פרי הגפן

    iii) remembrance of the Exodus from Egypt.

Shabbat morning services

Shacharit

Zemirot and the first part of *Keriat Shema* and its blessings.

Keriat Ha-torah קריאת התורה

1) The actual reading consists of an entire Parashah or, on occasion, two; whereas on all other *Keriat-Ha-torah* days (Mondays and Thursdays) a much smaller section is read usually up to *sheni* (the second portion).

2) Following the Parashah, a *Haftarah* הפטרה is read. This is taken from the Prophets.

3) Various prayers for the community are recited after the *Haftarah* such as memorial prayers, blessings for the Queen, and the State of Israel and the community.

4) These are followed by a *Derashah* דרשה (Exposition or Sermon) or an address to a Barmitsvah.

Musaph

Since an additional sacrifice was offered in the Temple each Shabbat (*Korban Musaph*) we have an "Additional Service" in its place.

Mincha

Keriat Ha-torah - three are called up.
We read the first section of the following week's Parashah;

Arbit of Motse Shabbat

At this service we add a prayer *Ata Honentanu* pointing out the difference between the holiness of Shabbat and the rest of the week and asking the Almighty to bless the coming week.
This is a form of Havdalah.

Music

It is the custom of many Sephardim to sing special poems composed for Motse Shabbat, blessing the coming week and expressing the hope for the coming of the Meshiah.

LESSON 9

Rosh Chodesh ראש חודש

The calendar

There are significant differences between the Jewish calendar employed for all religious purposes and the secular calendar in general use.

The regular waxing and waning of the moon can easily be observed by even the simplest people in the night sky; and so that was used by the Jews and most other ancient peoples as the clearest way of marking the passage of time. They divided time into lunar months, with twelve lunar months in a lunar year.

Ancient peoples, dependent for survival on the growing of food crops also soon realised that the orderly succession of seasons in which seeds are sown, crops grow, ripen and are harvested, correspond exactly to various positions of the sun in the sky. The passage of time very naturally also came to be measured in solar 'years', related to the cycle of the sun's movement through the heavens.

The Jews, like many other early peoples, adopted a luni-solar calendar based partly on the moon (lunar months) and partly on the sun (solar years). They carefully watched the sky for the new moon, and marked the beginning of each lunar month by the reappearance of its crescent. They also attempted to regulate the length of the year by the movements of the sun.

Unfortunately for the makers of calendars, twelve lunar months fall short of a solar year by about eleven days and the two systems cannot easily be reconciled.

> The earth's revolution round the sun takes just over 365 days, while the moon circles the earth in just over 29.5 days.

So, in any calendar based only on the moon, the onset of spring for example would fall 11 days earlier each year until it took place in a month associated with winter - before slowly moving round the calendar again. That did not suit the Jews, an agricultural people, who wished to celebrate their spring festival, for example, in the same month each year.

So a complex system of corrections was devised, to keep bringing the 'year' of lunar months into line with the 'year' measured by the sun and the agricultural seasons. That was done by adding an extra lunar month to the year every few years (called "leap" years, consisting of thirteen lunar months).

In the Jewish calendar, time is divided into cycles of nineteen years, with a leap year in each 3rd, 6th, 8th, 11th, 14th, 17th and 19th year of a cycle. Ordinary years contain twelve lunar months; and leap years contain thirteen lunar months.

A luni-solar calendar of this kind is very complex, as it has to satisfy technical astronomical criteria as well as religious and agricultural needs. The modern Jewish calendar was developed from earlier models, and reached its present form in the tenth century CE.

In contrast, the modern secular calendar is based only on the solar year. Its calendar year contains 365 days, with an extra day added in every fourth year (leap year). The use of the lunar month has been abandoned; and the year is divided artificially into twelve calendar months, seven of 31 days, four of 30 days and one of 28 days (or 29 days in a leap year).

Rosh Chodesh

Rosh Chodesh - the beginning of the month - marks the start of each new month in the Jewish calendar. It was celebrated as a minor festival in former times, when a special sacrifice was offered in the Temple.

Only vestiges of the former significance of the New Moon survive today, when its advent is solemnly announced in the synagogues. If the New Moon falls on the Sabbath, portions are read from two Sepharim (scrolls of Law) instead of from the usual one; and special psalms of rejoicing (the Hallel) are recited.

Before the timing of the New Moon came to be determined by calculation, a special court assembled in Jerusalem on the thirtieth day of each month for that purpose. As soon as two reliable witnesses testified to the appearance of the crescent moon in the sky, the New Moon was proclaimed and a beacon was lit on the Mount of Olives. Signals and messages were then transmitted to all parts of Israel. If the moon's crescent was not seen on the thirtieth of the month, the New Moon was celebrated on the following day.

Jews from beyond the borders of Israel observed the New Moon on the thirtieth day of each month, and again on the thirty-first to make sure that they did not miss the right day. This doubt led to the custom outside Israel of celebrating all the holy days in the calendar (except for Yom Kippur) on two successive days. This, like many other practices in Judaism, continues even though its original purpose has long since disappeared. In Israel only one day is observed (except for Rosh Hashanah).

Rosh Hashanah ראש השנה

Introduction

Yamim Noraim ימים נוראים

Rosh Hashanah is the first of the Yamim Noraim (Days of Awe), or sometimes called the High Holydays to emphasise their solemnity and their importance in the Jewish calendar.

The idea of "awe" is clearly stated in the Amidah for Rosh Hashanah, when we pray to God to:

... impose your awe on all your works and your dread upon all you have created, that all your works may revere you and all your creatures prostrate themselves before you, and all together do your will with a perfect heart.

It is a time to remind oneself of the majesty of creation - perhaps by looking up at the myriads of stars in the night sky or by contemplating the scale and wonders of the universe revealed by the discoveries of modern science - a time for realising the insignificance of man before his Creator and of accepting that the fear as well as the love of God must have an important place in our lives.

The Yamim Noraim are more personal and less national in their character than other festivals. For not only is God awesome and tremendous beyond description, but he is also a personal God who cares for each one of us. At the same time, we pray for all the Jewish people because of our special feelings of responsibility for each one of them: therefore most of our prayers start with "We" rather than "I".

It is a time therefore of introspection - of looking carefully into our actions and thoughts during the past year - of making amends for wrongdoing and for resolving the behave better in future.

The Ten Days of Penitence עֲשֶׂרֶת יָמֵי תְּשׁוּבָה

The ten days which start with Rosh Hashanah and end with Yom Kippur ten days later are called the Ten Days of Penitence, during which we recite special prayers (Selichot) imploring God's forgiveness for our sins.

The minor fast of Gedaliah immediately follows Rosh Hashanah on 3rd Tishri; and following Shabbat, also falling within the Ten Days of Penitence, is known as Shabbat

Shuva (The Shabbat of Repentance) after the opening line of its haphtarah from Hosea - Shuva Yisrael (Return, O Israel).

Gedaliah was a descendant of King David who was appointed Governor of Judah by the Babylonians. (Some Jews were allowed to stay in the country by the Babylonians after most had been deported to Babylon). He was assassinated by Jews led by Yishmael ben Netanya at the suggestion of the king of nearby Ammon; and Jewish hopes of rapid return to independence vanished. Reacting to the murder of Gedaliah, the Babylonians ensured that all Jews were exiled from Judah.

The fast, which lasts from morning to evening, also helps one to prepare for the full-day fast on Yom Kippur.

The Month of Elul אֱלוּל

Elul is a month of preparation for Rosh Hashanah.

Selichot are recited from the second day of Elul early in the morning.

Every morning, in most Sephardi synagogues, the shofar is blown after Shacharit. Spanish & Portuguese synagogues blow the Shofar only from Rosh Hashanah to Kippur.

The sound of the shofar awakens us to repent - to say sorry for bad deeds and ask for forgiveness.

In the month of Elul we should put time and effort into:

    i) Repentence תְּשׁוּבָה

    ii) Prayer תְּפִלָּה

    iii) Charity צְדָקָה

Doing acts of charity, to help others in difficulty, is a very great mitzvah. It reminds us that whatever we have is sent from God and is meant to be shared.

On 1st of Elul, tradition has it that Moses went up Mount Sinai to collect the second set of tablets of the Ten Commandments. He came down on Yom Kippur forty days later. The gift of the second set showed that the Almighty had forgiven the Israelites for the golden calf.

Selichot סְלִיחוֹת

Selichot are special prayers which are said from the day after Rosh Chodesh Ellul (for Sephardim) or from the Sunday before Rosh Hashanah (for Askenazim) until and including Erev Kippur. The service is held in the synagogue early in the morning before dawn.

The shofar is blown at the end of Shacharit (This is custom not law and therefore no beracha is said). The exception is the day before Rosh Hashanah when the shofar is not heard so as to distinguish the customary "build-up" from the blowing of the shofar on Rosh Hashanah.

Haphtarot הפטרות

During Elul, the special haphtarot of comfort following Tisha Be'Av assure us of God's mercy while increasing our fear of him at the same time.

Rosh Hashanah רֹאשׁ הַשָּׁנָה

Rosh Hashanah is the beginning of the New Year.
The festival is celebrated on 1st and 2nd of the month of Tishri.

וּבַחֹדֶשׁ הַשְּׁבִיעִי בְּאֶחָד לַחֹדֶשׁ מִקְרָא קֹדֶשׁ יִהְיֶה לָכֶם כָּל מְלֶאכֶת עֲבוֹדָה לֹא תַעֲשׂוּ.

In the seventh month on the first day you shall have a holy festival, you shall do not work.

On the first day of the seventh month there will be a day of rest, a holy gathering - together of the community, an occasion for remembering and hearing the shofar. You shall do no work and shall bring a fire offering to God.

(Vayikra 23.23-25)

It is the New Year of Years - that is the date on which the number of the year (e.g. 5750) changes. There are other "New Years" such as New Year for Festivals on 1st Nisan, the first month of the year - but these are of far lesser importance.

Rosh Hashanah is the start of the agricultural year. The harvest has been gathered in and the period of planting and regeneration starts.

Rosh Hashanah is a solemn time - a time when we turn our thoughts to God. In our prayers we say sorry for wrong deeds over the past year; we ask God to forgive us and we pray for a Good Year לְשָׁנָה טוֹבָה to come.

Tradition holds that three books are opened on Rosh Hashanah. One for the completely evil, one for the totally good and the third for everyone else. Judgment is suspended for the last group until Kippur. Hence the greeting, *leshana tova tikatevu* and *hatima tova* and particularly for Sephardim *Tizku le shanim rabot* (may you be worthy of many years).

The Names of the Festival

There are 4 names:

Rosh Hashanah רֹאשׁ הַשָּׁנָה

As written in the Mishnah:

(Tractate Rosh Hashanah)

בְּאֶחָד בְּתִשְׁרֵי רֹאשׁ הַשָּׁנָה לַשָּׁנִים.

On the first of Tishri is the New Year of Years.

Yom Hazikaron יוֹם הַזִּכָּרוֹן

In the Amidah of Rosh Hashanah we say:

וַתִּתֶּן לָנוּ ה' אֱלֹקֵינוּ בְּאַהֲבָה יוֹם הַזִּכָּרוֹן הַזֶּה.

...You have given us with love this day of remembrance.

One of the recurrent themes of Rosh Hashanah is the plea that God will remember in our favour the good deeds of the Patriarchs and his promises to them.

Yom Teruah יוֹם תְּרוּעָה

Day of blowing (the Shofar). This name is used in the Torah where it is written:

וּבַחֹדֶשׁ הַשְּׁבִיעִי בְּאֶחָד לַחֹדֶשׁ יוֹם תְּרוּעָה יִהְיֶה לָכֶם.

In the seventh month on the first of the month it shall be a day of blowing (the shofar) for you.

Yom Ha-din יוֹם הַדִּין

In Mishnah Rosh Hashanah:

On Rosh Hashanah all the inhabitants of the world pass before God in judgment like a flock of sheep.

Rosh Hashanah is a day when the Almighty reviews each person's merit to decide their fate. Nachmanides suggests that Rosh Hashanah is a day of judgment with mercy and that Yom Kippur is a day of mercy with judgment. Either, judgment is cast on Rosh Hashanah subject to mercy given on Yom Kippur; or for most people, judgment is left over until Kippur.

Its purpose

On Rosh Hashanah we focus our minds on the idea of God sitting in judgment in the new year just beginning. In our prayers we state, again and again, that God is our king.

Although the King or Judge is reviewing our past year's conduct, we have ten days left (until Kippur) to prove ourselves, to repent and show that we mean to make the new year better than the past one.

Any wrong a person has done to his fellow man or woman has to be settled personally. We ourselves must right wrongs done to those around us. Asking forgiveness for such sins must not be left until Yom Kippur; and we should seek out those we have wronged to ask their forgiveness.

We ask forgiveness in our prayers for sins committed against God and his Torah.

Teshuvah:

Teshuvah means "return". The analogy is drawn in the Tanach (Bible) between God and Israel as partners in a difficult marriage:

Turn back to me and I will turn back to you.

Sins fall into three categories:

i) avon (an act of unaware wrong-doing)

ii) het (an accidental act) and

iii) pesha (an act of rebellion).

These words are used throughout the Rosh Hashanah and Kippur prayers and each can be forgiven by atonement.

Philo argued that the act of teshuvah removes the stain of sin from the person concerned. Indeed Teshuvah may make a person who did wrong in the past do better in the future than someone who never did the bad act. Voluntary repentance brings the individual closer to God and to improved behaviour. For this reason, it is forbidden to remind a sinner of his past acts. If an individual fails to pardon someone after repeated requests for forgiveness, the sin is transferred onto the person whose forgiveness was sought.

While Succot is a festival of relatively uninhibited joy, the Yamim Noraim are concerned with self-criticism and doubt. Although Rosh Hashanah celebrates the birthday of the world, it is more in the nature of a stock-take than a birthday party.

Tefillah:

Being a day of judgment, we do not say Hallel on either Rosh Hashanah or Yom Kippur as we do on other festivals and on Rosh Chodesh. As part of the heightened atmosphere of prayer, we say *Melech Hakadosh* instead of *El Hakadosh* during the amidah. We also add a number of requests that we may be written down for good fortune in the future.

Sedaca

The true meaning of Sedaca is "righteousness", not "charity" - not something we choose to bestow on another, but something we must do to be righteous. By doing good deeds, we set the pattern for the year ahead. Our sages teach that the best acts of charity are those done anonymously i.e. with no thought of thanks, in this world at least.

The Shofar   תְּקִיעַת שׁוֹפָר

The commandment unique to Rosh Hashanah is Tekiat Shofar תקיעת שופר (Blowing the shofar).

It is written in the Torah:

וּבַחֹדֶשׁ הַשְּׁבִיעִי בְּאֶחָד לַחֹדֶשׁ מִקְרָא קֹדֶשׁ יִהְיֶה לָכֶם... יוֹם תְּרוּעָה...

In the seventh month on the first day, you shall have a holy day of assembly... a day of blowing it shall be for you.

The shofar is built into the Torah's description of the festival. The shofar was blown at Mount Sinai when the Torah was given. It is also connected to the ram who was sacrificed instead of Isaac.

In biblical times, the shofar also proclaimed the succession of a new King and announced the Jubilee every fiftieth year.

The shofar is not blown on Shabbat to prevent people from accidentally carrying it to synagogue.

The purpose of the blowing of the shofar was summarised by Sa'adya (the great Gaon of Baghdad in the 10th century) as follows:

1) As a memorial of the day of creation, when God assumed kingship over the world - the triumphant sound of coronation.

2) As a warning to repent from evil ways, on this first of the Ten Penitential Days.

3) As a reminder of the giving of the Torah on Mount Sinai, when *'the sound of the SHOFAR waxed exceeding loud.'*

4) As a reminder of the warnings of the Prophets - compared to blasts on the trumpet.

5) As a reminder of the destruction of the Temple - a sound of warfare.

6) As a reminder of the willingness of Isaac to be bound as a sacrifice to God, and of God's mercy - a ram was sacrificed instead.

7) To make its hearers *'tremble and quake with fear'*, so that they may humble themselves before God.

8) As a reminder of the great Day of Judgment to come, which will be proclaimed by the sound of the shofar.

9) As a reminder of the messianic age to come, when the outcasts of Israel will return to worship in Jerusalem to the sound of the shofar.

10) As a reminder of the resurrection of the dead, when the shofar will be sounded.

Hearing the shofar is thus a very important mitzvah.

The basic sounds of the shofar are:

i) Tekiah   תְּקִיעָה   a long sound

ii) Shevarim   שְׁבָרִים   3 short sounds

iii) Teruah   עָה תְּרוּ · 9 short blasts

(Each of the three basic sounds lasts for a equal time)

The above sounds are made separately or in different combinations:

i) Tekiah the plain sound

ii) Shevarim the tone broken into three

iii) Teruah at least nine staccato notes

iv) Shevarim-Teruah a combination of (ii) and (iii).

(ii), (iii) and (iv) are always preceded and followed by (i) but an entire sequence ends with:

v) Tekiah Gedolah a very long Tekiah

The first thirty Shofar blasts are sounded before the Sifre Torah are returned to the Ark Thirty are sounded during the Repetition of the Musaph and the remaining forty towards the end of the service. [The shofar is not blown on Shabbat].

One of the reasons why the sounds are made in so many different combinations is because we are no longer quite sure of their sequence when the shofar was blown in the Temple; and by doing this we hope to hit on the right sequence.

Bamidbar 29.1 and 10.5 use the first two notes as alternate names for the blowing of the shofar. So, the Rabbis concluded that there were two sounds. In the Talmud, the story is told of the debate about the correct sounding of Teruah. What is now Shevarim was the minority view that was rejected. Isaac Arama thinks that Tekiyah is the sound of joy and optimism and Teruah is the sound of awe and fear of the judgment to be made on Rosh Hashanah.

Maimonides said the following about the Shofar:

Although the Torah gives no explicit reason for blowing the Shofar the implicit message is:
Wake up, you slumberers, from your sleep:
Look closely at your past deeds.
Turn back in repentance
And remember your Creator.

These words, continues Maimonides, *are directed to people who are so concerned about being 'with it' that they lose sight of any sense of true values.*

The mitzvah is to hear the shofar, not to blow it. This is reflected in the first beracha said before the blowing of the shofar on Rosh Hashanah. No beracha is said when blowing the shofar during Elul, as we are not fulfilling a mitzvah then.

A shofar can be made of the horn of any clean animal except a cow or an ox, preferably a ram to commemorate the Akedah. (The cow is excluded because of the golden calf). The horn is boiled in water until it gets soft. The inside is then hollowed out and the horn flattened a little: the mouthpiece is shaped and the shofar put aside to harden. A shofar must not have a hole in its side and it cannot be painted.

Prayers and readings

As noted above, the blowing of the Shofar occupies a prominent place in the synagogue service.

The synagogue services are also considerably extended by special poems (piyyutim).

Like on Shabbat, there is a special additional service - מוּסָף - which corresponds to the additional sacrifice offered in the Temple at Rosh Hashanah.

There are 3 very important groups of prayers during שַׁחֲרִית : מוּסָף

i) Malchuyot:מַלְכוּיוֹת

About God's kingship over us and the whole world.

ii) Shofarot שׁוֹפָרוֹת:

A section about the call of the shofar to all of us.

iii) Zichronot זִכְרוֹנוֹת:

Remembrances - telling about good deeds of our ancestors, and asking God to remember their merits and allows us to share in them.

Keriat Ha-Torah:

On both days of רֹאשׁ הַשָּׁנָה two scrolls are taken out.

The reading for the second is the same for both days.

1st DAY

i) The birth of Isaac בראשית כ"א Chapter 21

ii) Offering at the Temple on יום תרועה.

במדבר Chapter 29, 1-7

הַפְטָר - The birth of Samuel and dedication to Temple service.

2nd DAY

i) The binding of Isaac עקדת יצחק

בראשית Chapter 22, 1-20.

ii) Offerings on הַפְטָרָה, Jeremiah's vision and hope of return after exile. Jeremiah 31, 1-21.

On the two days of Rosh Hashanah, we read the two halves of *Parashat Vayera* about Abraham and Isaac. On the second day, we read the story of how Isaac was almost sacrificed.

In the first day's reading, we learn about Hagar and Ishmael being sent away from Abraham and finding themselves totally at the mercy of God when they ran out of water. We also learn of the birth of Isaac, the product of prayer. This matches the haphtarah on the first day which tells of the birth of Samuel. Both stories tell of God's total power. In the latter two case, it was the Almighty's ability to transform someone unable to have children into the mother of the key prophet of the period.

Other customs and traditions

According to our liturgy, '*On this day the world was created*' (*hayom harat haolam*).

The Midrash pictures Rosh Hashanah as the anniversary of the sixth day of creation; and that on that day, Adam and Eve broke the instruction about the apple, were punished and then re-established a relationship with their creator.

There are a number of Minchagim associated with the Yamim Noraim and, as for Pesach, these vary from community to community. In many synagogues there is a special Ark Curtain coloured white; and among Ashkenazim, the hazan and Baal Tekiah wear a kittel (white robe), which is the shroud in which he will be buried eventually.

Greetings

On the first evening of Rosh Hashanah, after the עַרְבִית of לֵיל ר אֹש הַשָּׁנָה people greet one another with the special greetings:

To a man:

לְשָׁנָה טוֹבָה תִּכָּתֵב וְתֵחָתֵם

May you be written and sealed for a good year.

To a woman:

לְשָׁנָה טוֹבָה תִּכָּתֵבִי וְתֵחָתֵמִי

Some times also:

כְּתִיבָה וַחֲתִימָה טוֹבָה

The most usual greeting amongst Sephardim is:

May you merit many years

תִּזְכּוּ לְשָׁנִים רַבּוֹת

or simply *Many Years*.

God considers each person individually and judges him or her according to good or bad deeds performed during the past year. It is because of this that we pray to be inscribed (written) by God in the Book of Life for the year to come.

Symbolic Foods

On the evening meal of Rosh Hashanah we eat various foods to symbolise a good year.

Sephardi and Ashkenazi communities have some different customs. In all communities, however, apples soaked in honey are eaten to symbolise the intended sweet new year. This is accompanied by the prayer *Yehi ratzon*. On the second night, one eats a fruit not previously eaten during the season to symbolise the renewal involved in the new year. The *beracha sheheheyanu* is recited as being the blessing on new things.

The festival challot are rounded in shape to show the continuity of the years, which go round and round, with each starting at the end of the preceding one. These are also dipped in honey before being eaten.

The following symbolic foods are usually to be found on the tables of Sephardi families; with a special blessing accompanying each one. The ceremonies around the table are full of joy and pleasant thoughts.

1) Pomegranates: May we be full of mitzvot as the pomegranate is with seeds.

2) Dates: May our enemies cease.

3) Black-eyed beans: May our merits be very many.

4) Pumpkin: May we be judged by our good deeds, not our bad ones.

5) Spinach: May our enemies disappear.

6) Fish: May we be fruitful like the fish.

7) The Head of a sheep: May we be like the head, not the tail; and may you remember the ram of Isaac.

QUESTIONS

1) What exactly is a shofar?

2) What kind of festival is ראש השנה:

     i) a time of fasting.

     ii) a time of rejoicing.

     iii) a time of serious prayer.

     iv) a time of mourning.

3) Put into your own words why we blow the shofar.

4) Explain three customs connected with food.

5) Why is a set of scales an important symbol of ראש השנה

6) Find out two customs connected with the synagogue.

7) What does 'repentance' mean?

8) לְשָׁנָה טוֹבָה תִּכָּתֵבוּ וְתֵחָתֵמוּ What is the idea behind the words of this greeting?

9) Why do you think the portions about the birth of Isaac and the Akedah are read on ראש השנה?

10) After Rosh Hashanah, write 6 sentences about what you remember most about it.

Activities:

Pupils should write out and discuss their goals and wishes for the coming year. These should be personal goals and community goals.

What does the shofar make the pupils think of? Ask them to write down their own list. Then discuss, using Sa'adya Gaon's list as a way of comparison.

Discuss what is achieved by confessing one's sins on Rosh Hashanah and Yom Kippur.

Build a simple scale (a kitchen set of scales would do). Encourage class members to tell you of mitzvot and sins that they have committed. Write them each on a sheet of paper and put them on a plastic bag which should be placed on the appropriate arm of the scales.

Pupils should compose a Rosh Hashanah message to modern Jews on the line of the prophet's advice to repent.

More Activities for Older Children:

Draw up a calendar with the months on the left. In the second column, write what you did during the year. In the third column, put in all the bad things you did at those times. Finally, in the fourth column, write how next year you could do better and avoid the sins you committed. Pupils must not worry about being precise about the dates.

Pupils can then write their column 3 answers on a sheet divided in three. Against that, they can write sins committed by society during the same period. In the third column, they should note what society and the pupil can do next year to try to reduce the number of sins in either column.

Discuss why this should be a day of rejoicing.

Discuss why pray in the first person plural and confess sins which we as individual have not committed.

When discussing Tefillah draw up a table in advance for each pupil of biblical examples of prayer on the following lines:

Source	Who is praying?	Who is the prayer for?	What is the prayer?	Outcome of the prayer
Bereshit 20. 17-8				
Bereshit 24. 12-20				
Bereshit 25. 21				
Bereshit 32. 9-12 & 33. 4				
Shemot 32. 11-14				
Bamidbar 14. 13-20				
Devarim 3. 23-27				

Ask students to complete:

When I touch the shofar I fell ...
When I try to blow the shofar, I am ....
When I hear the shofar sounded, I think ...

Give the students a pre-printed list of Sa'adya Gaon's reasons for blowing the shofar. Ask students to rank them order of importance. Discuss the ranking and seek to establish a consensus. Then ask which reasons are most important for the survival of Judaism and compare the two sets of rankings.

Ask pupils to do a report on the world's progress since creation.

LESSON 11

Yom Kippur יום כיפור

Its Names

1) Yom Kippur יוֹם כִּפּוּר

2) Yom Hakippurim יוֹם הַכִּפּוּרִים

3) Kippur כִּפּוּר -perhaps the most popular name amongst Sephardim.

Its date

On the tenth day of the seventh month there shall be a Day of Atonement; it shall be a holy convocation for you, and you shall afflict your souls...

(Leviticus 23:27)

According to one translation, וְעִנִּיתֶם אֶת נַפְשֹׁתֵיכֶם means *'you must fast'* instead of *'you shall afflict your souls.'*

Kippur is observed on the tenth day of Tishri.

Its meaning and purpose

Yom Kippur is the last of the Ten Days of Penitence. It is the most solemn day of the year when we fast (no food or drink) from sunset on one day until one hour after sunset on the next. It is a day of complete abstention from normal activities, a Sabbath of Sabbaths, devoted entirely to introspection (examining our lives) and prayer.

In the day-long succession of synagogue services, worshippers are made conscious of human inadequacy and sinfulness. Humbled in spirit and afflicted by self-imposed deprivation, they confess their shortcomings to God, and seek forgiveness.

A central part of the services is the detailed description of former proceedings in the Temple, when the High Priest sacrificed to make atonement for the people, and the scapegoat carrying their sins was driven out of the city and killed: all bow low when the Divine Name is referred to in the recital, for God's presence is felt to be close.

In the last service of the day - the *Ne'ilah*, the symbolic closing of the gates of heaven - members of the congregation throw themselves more confidently on God's mercy: *'The Lord is near those ... who call upon him in truth ... He will hear their cry, and will save them'*; and pray that they may *'enter your gates'*.

The service concludes with a triumphant blast on the shofar, proclaiming the new freedom gained by self-imposed afflictions, prayer and Divine grace; and the day which began with bodily mortification ends with spiritual exaltation: *'Go, eat your bread with joy, and drink your wine with a glad heart; for the Lord has already accepted your works.'*

Yom Kippur is the day on which God pardons man for sins committed against him. On this day Moses came down from Mount Sinai with the second set of tablets; and on this day God forgave Israel for the sin of the Golden Calf. Therefore, the day is a day of mercy, forgiveness and the acceptance of our prayers.

Forgiveness of sins is a matter of Divine Grace. It is not automatic and can occur only if there is genuine repentance expressed by remorse for the sinful act, a determination not to repeat it and positive effort to make amends and do good. The Talmud states that the Day of Atonement will not bring pardon if a man says: *'I will sin and Yom Kippur will bring me pardon.'*

As written in the Ashkenazi Prayer Book:

On the first day of the year (Rosh Hashanah) it is inscribed, and on the Day of Atonement (Kippur) it is sealed and determined how many shall pass away, and how many be born; who shall live and who shall die; whose appointed time is finished, and whose is not; who is to perish by fire, who by water, who by the sword and who by wild beasts ... who shall reap enjoyment and who shall be painfully afflicted; who shall get rich and who shall become poor; who shall be cast down and who exalted. But penitence, prayer and charity will avert the evil decree.

Kippur is the day on which the decree of life or death, drafted for us by God on Rosh Hashanah, is sealed.

Its laws

On Kippur, all the laws of Shabbat apply (but not those of Yom Tov).

In addition, it is forbidden:

1) To eat and drink for 25 hours
2) To wash, except when essential
3) To use perfumes or ointments
4) To use leather shoes, which are a symbol of comfort

5) To have sexual relations

By abstaining from daily pleasures such as eating and drinking, one is better able to concentrate on prayer, clear the soul from sin and prepare it for repentance.
The aim is to obtain forgiveness for our wrongdoings.

Its services

There are 5 services held on Kippur. Each contains a confession (Vidduy).
There are two forms of the Vidduy:

i) Ashamnu אשמנו   which is a shorter version and
ii) Al Chet על חטא   which is a longer one.

The Services are:

i) Arbit (Kal Nidre)
ii) Shacharit
iii) Musaph
iv) Mincha
v) Ne'ilah

Arbit עַרְבִת

The evening service is opened with the chanting of *Shema koli* (Hear our voices).

The hazan continues with *Kohaneha*, and then the members of the congregation who have been assigned the special honour of carrying the Torah Scrolls from the ark to the tebah, remove the Scrolls from the echal and begin their procession to the tebah.

Kal Nidrei is recited three times before the beginning of the holiday. This prayer is in Aramaic, once the everyday language of the people. In this prayer we absolve ourselves, of any oath to God we may have taken during the previous year.

By reciting *Kal Nidrei* (All vows), all promises and vows made by man to his Creator are cancelled. This does not apply to obligations and promises made between one person and another person.

Kal Nidrei is recited in unique fashion by the Spanish and Portuguese congregation. The first half until *Sheba aleinu leshalom* is recited by the hazan, and the congregation continues with *Nidreina la nidrei* until the end of *Ki lekhol haam bishegaga*. At the conclusion of the third recitation, the hazan recites the *Sheheheyanu*.

Special prayers are offered for the Queen, the congregation, the Hatan Torah, the Hatan Bereshit, for the holy city of Jerusalem, for those who are held in captivity, for those who are journeying and for the sick. These two last prayers are unique to the Spanish and Portuguese congregation.

The services concludes with the chanting of *Yigdal* based on the 13 principles of the Jewish faith formulated by Maimonides.

The greeting on leaving the synagogue is:

Tizke (Tizku) leshanim rabot

(May you merit many years)

In some congregations (but not the Spanish and Portuguese) it is the custom for men to remain in the synagogue after Arbit to read *Tehillim*, *Masekhet Yoma* (selections of the *Zohar* which relate to Yom Kippur) and the *Keter Malkhut* of Rabbi Shelomo ibn Garbirol.

Shacharit שַׁחֲרִית

The service is longer than usual. In the *zemirot* of the morning service, Psalms 17, 25, 32, 51, 65, 85, 86, 102, 103, 98, 121, 122, 123 and 124 are all added. *Piyutim* are also recited. The *Hashem negdeha and Elohim Keli ata*, are recited before Nishmat.

The *Birkat Kohanim* is recited (though this is not recited by the Spanish and Portuguese Jews on an "ordinary" Shabbat).

Musaph מוּסָף:

In the Musaph, additional prayers of supplication are recited.

An important part of the Musaph is called *"Seder Ha'avodah"*. This describes the procedures carried out by the High Priest in the Temple on Yom Kippur, when he offered sacrifices to make atonement for the people; and the scapegoat carrying their sins was driven out of the city and killed.

Birkat Kohanim is recited.

Mincha מִנְחָה

The Sepher is read during Mincha, as on Shabbat. The very long Haphtarah comes from the Book of Jonah.

Here we mention a very special prayer repeated again and again in the Kippur liturgy, when we ask the all-powerful King sitting on the Throne of Mercy to pardon and be gracious to all sinners. We ask God to remember his revelation to Moses when, hidden in the cleft of a rock, God's glory passed before him:

And the Lord passed before him (Moses) and proclaimed: the Lord, the Lord, a God full of compassion and gracious, long-suffering and full of mercy and truth; keeping mercy unto thousands, forgiving iniquity, transgression and sin, and acquitting.

In this prayer, we implore God to pardon our wrongdoing and sin. It ends by recalling the actions of the High Priest in the Temple on the day of Kippur:

כִּי בַיּוֹם הַזֶּה יְכַפֵּר עֲלֵיכֶם לְטַהֵר אֶתְכֶם מִכֹּל חַטֹּאתֵיכֶם לִפְנֵי ה' תִּטְהָרוּ

For on this day shall he make atonement for you, to cleanse you. From all your sins shall you be clean before the Lord.

The words of God's proclamation to Moses are, of course important for another reason. From those very words our Sages have deduced the thirteen qualities through which God reveals himself to man. These are known as the Thirteen Attributes of God.

The Ne'ilah (Concluding Service) נְעִילָה

This is the high point of the day. As the gates of heaven close in judgment, we realise that it is our very last chance to repent. We feel that God is close and that he will hear our prayers if they have been said with sincerity.

Ne'ilah is recited before the open *echal* (ark) before sundown.

The introductory prayer, *El nora alila*, is sung to one of the best known tunes in Sephardi liturgy and its chanting is very similar in all Sephardi congregations.

The timing of the service is critical; for the *Birkat Kohanim* must be reached before the sun sets and the hazan must stretch out the remainder of the service until the first stars appear in the sky. At these very last moments before the future is decreed, the word *"kotvei'nu"* (may we be inscribed) is substituted by the word *"chotmei'nu"* (may we be sealed) in the book of life.

'*Shema Yisrael*' and '*Baruch Shem Kevod...*' are recited at the end of the *Ne'ilah*, which ends with the solemn proclamation, seven times over, '*The Lord, he is God.*'
This is the climax of the service, its most tense and concentrated few moments.

After that the *Teki'at Gedola* is sounded on the shofar to remind us of the Redemption. We are told to go away, eat, drink and be merry for God has accepted our repentance.

The custom in some congregations is to make at least a token start of building the succah immediately after we have broken the fast. Thus one mitzvah immediately follows on the last one.

Other customs

Many synagogue customs are similar to those of Rosh Hashanah.

On the day before Kippur, people carry out a practice, again symbolic, of getting rid of sins called Kapparot כפרות ("Atonement"). This consists of taking a hold of fowl (or money), holding it over the head and reciting a special formula. The fowl (or money) is subsequently given to the poor.

Other customs for the day before Kippur are:

1) Mikveh:

It is customary to immerse oneself in the Mikveh (ritual bath) for purification.

2) Many people refrain from work.

3) They give charity.

4) Among Spanish and Portuguese Jews, the father of the household blesses his children with the traditional blessing for boys and girls followed by the Priestly Benediction.

5) Seuda Mafseket סְעוּדָה הַמַּפְסָקֶת Concluding Meal:

Early in the afternoon, we eat the final meal before the fast. The meal must end about a half hour before sundown.

Following the seudah, lights are kindled in the home, as on the Sabbath with the appropriate blessing for Yom Kippur.

6) White Garments:

White clothes are worn by both Ashkenazim and some Sephardim on Kippur for, as the prophet Isaiah said:

Though your sins be like scarlet, they will become as white as snow

(Isaiah 1:18).

Among Ashkenazim only, some men (the hazan in particular) wear a long white robe called a "*kittel*", which is in fact the shroud in which they will eventually be buried. This symbolises our humbleness and abasement before God on this day of judgment.

Succot   סוכות

Introduction

You shall live in huts (tabernacles) for seven days ... So that your descendants may be reminded how I made the Israelites live in booths when I brought them out of Egypt: I am the Lord your God.

(Leviticus 23:42-3)

לְמַעַן יֵדְעוּ דֹרֹתֵיכֶם כִּי בַסֻּכּוֹת הוֹשַׁבְתִּי אֶת בְּנֵי יִשְׂרָאֵל בְּהוֹצִיאִי אוֹתָם מֵאֶרֶץ מִצְרַיִם, אֲנִי ה' אֱלֹקֵיכֶם.

This has become the prime significance of the festival of Succot, when we erect temporary huts (succot) and "live" in them for the seven days of the holiday.

On the fifteenth day of the seventh month, when the harvest has been gathered, you shall keep the Lord's pilgrim feast for seven days ... you shall take the fruit of the citrus tree, palm fronds and willows from the riverside, and you shall rejoice before the Lord your God ...

(Leviticus 23:39-40)

Succot is also a harvest festival, celebrating the *'ingathering from the threshing floor and from the winepress'*, and the succah is lavishly decorated with hangings of fruit and vegetables - the produce of the harvest just gathered in.

> The Bible promised the Israelites land to farm: thus, agricultural festivals and religious events were tied together. A farmer works much harder in summer than in the rest of the year. By the time autumn comes, most of the harvest has been gathered in. The farmer knows the result of his work and can then celebrate - particularly if things have gone well. This is the agricultural background to Succot.
>
> In order to give thanks for the produce of the land, each man was sent on pilgrimage to Jerusalem with some produce to offer in the Temple.
>
> It is Jewish tradition, to celebrate the finishing of things generally. So, when finishing the study of a Mishnah, one holds a siyum or party. Similarly, Simchat Torah celebrates the end of the reading of the Torah for the year.

Succot is one of the three Pilgrim Festivals (or Foot Festivals, as at least the last part of the pilgrimage was performed on foot), when all Jewish males were commanded to present themselves with offering in the Temple.

Three times a year, all your men shall appear before the Lord your God at a place he will choose at the festivals of Pesach, Shavuot and Succot. And they shall not appear before God empty-handed. Each man is to give in accordance with what he can, in line with the blessing he has received from the Lord your God.

(Devarim 16: 13-17)

Its date and duration

Succot is celebrated on 15th Tishri, three days after Kippur. It marks the beginning of the rainy season in the Land of Israel.

As at Pesach, the first two and last two days are holy, the middle four days are called hol hamo'ed, the ordinary days of the festival - when we are permitted to do some work.

	Tishri		
Yom Tov	15		
	16		Succot
Hol Hamo'ed	17		
	18		Succot
	19		
	20		
	21	Hosha'ana Rabbah	
Yom Tov	22		Shemini Atseret
	23	Simchat Torah	

Its several names

1) Succot סוכות
'Tabernacles' (temporary huts)

2) Chag Ha'asif חג האסיף
'The Festival of the Gathering'
This refers to Succot as the time when the harvest is finally gathered in.

3) Zeman Simchatenu זמן שמחתנו

'The Season of our Rejoicing'

As we have just read, the Torah commands us to rejoice in the festival and to be joyful.

4) Chag חג

'The Festival'

This term is used in the Torah and more particularly in the Mishnah.

Its significance

This commemoration of life in the desert continues the theme of remembering the going out of Egypt described in the Bible. It reinforces the sense of the Jews belonging to a historical people.

Succot commemorates the fact that the Israelites lived in temporary huts in the wilderness. It is also an opportunity to give thanks at the end of the fruit harvest.

> The two are connected; for this is the occasion on which we thank God for the food gathered in at harvest time, and also on which we remember how the Almighty sheltered our ancestors in the wilderness and protected them from the oppressive heat of the sun and the coldness of the desert nights.

During Succot we are close to nature and to the basic things of life - food and shelter. By dwelling in the succah, as did our ancestors, we too express our trust in God to protect us when all else fails.

The laws of Succot

The succah

The Torah commands us:

בְּסֻכֹּת תֵּשְׁבוּ שִׁבְעַת יָמִים כָּל הָאֶזְרָח בְּיִשְׂרָאֵל יֵשְׁבוּ בַּסֻּכֹּת

You shall dwell in succot for seven days; all who are Israelite-born, shall dwell in sukkot.

(Leviticus 23:42)

Most Sephardi congregations begin the construction of the succah immediately before breaking the fast of Yom Kippur.

All meals are eaten in the succah and some people sleep there. The commandment is to "leshev basuccah". Thus, when we enter a succah, we say a blessing. This commandment actually requires us to live (and therefore presumably sleep each night) in the succah. However, rainfall exempts one from this. Women are exempt from these rules as they are time-based commandments. Another view is that leshev basuccah requires us to treat the succah like our home, when we move from our home and dwell in the succah.

> The succah is also a symbol of peace, Succat Shalom. In Temple times, it was the custom to sacrifice seven oxen (offered by other nations) at Succot as a symbol of peace between Israel and the "seventy nations" of the world.

The succah must be a temporary structure - usually built in a garden, yard or on the balcony or roof. It may also be built in your parking space if you live in a block of flats. A succah must have at least three walls and be able to withstand the ordinary strength of the wind. So, temporary or permanent walls can be used. You can build a succah on the balcony of a flat or up against the walls of a house. You must be able to see the stars through the roof but the covering must provide more shade than sunlight. The roof consists of leaves (usually laurel or another evergreen and capable of lasting for the full week) or any other non-edible vegetation that has been cut from the ground or from a tree (s'chah סכך).

The succah is decorated with fruit and vegetables, the produce of the harvest just concluded. According to our Sages, we should perform every mitzvah in the most beautiful manner possible for, as written in Exodus 15:2,

This is my God and I will glorify Him.

There are many different customs relating to the decoration of the succah. Some Sephardim decorate the succah so that it is completely covered in green - like a real hut. Others hang the chair of Elijah the prophet (Kise shel Eliyahu hanavi כיסא של אליהו הנביא) on the wall of the succah to symbolise the time when Elijah will return to earth to prepare the way for the Messiah and all Israel will dwell in the Succah shel Leviatan (the Hut of Leviathan).

Arba'a Minim ארבעה מינים The Four Species

And you shall take for yourself on the first day the fruit of the beautiful tree, branches of the palm tree, boughs of thick trees and willows of the brook; and you shall rejoice before the Lord your God seven days.

(Vayikra/Leviticus 23:40).

וּלְקַחְתֶּם לָכֶם בְּיוֹם הָרִאשׁוֹן פְּרִי עֵץ הָדָר כַּפֹּת תְּמָרִים וַעֲנַף עֵץ־עָבֹת וְעַרְבֵי־נַחַל וּשְׂמַחְתֶּם לִפְנֵי ה' אֱ־לֹקֵיכֶם שִׁבְעַת יָמִים

ויקרא 23, 40

According to the above verse, the Four Species are:

i) *Fruit of the beautiful tree.* the Etrog אתרוג - "fruit of a citrus tree" or Citron.

The citron must be elongated and not round, with its two ends (oketz עקת and pitam פטם) undamaged. It must be at least the size of an egg.

ii) *Branches of palm trees* - the Lulav לולב.
This is a palm branch that has not yet opened.

It must be no less than 40 centimetres long and the spine must not be split at the ends.

iii) *Boughs of thick trees* - Hadassim הדסים
"branch of a myrtle tree"

Three twigs of myrtle must be kept together. They must be about 30 centimetres long. The ideal hadas should be "triple", i.e. with three leaves growing out at each level of the branch.

iv) *Willows of the brook* - Aravot ערבות "brook willows".
For the mitzvah, two willow branches are required.

The ideal should have reddish stems with long narrow leaves whose tips are unbroken.

The Arba'a Minim are taken from plants or trees which require much water to grow well.

The branches of palm, myrtle and willow are bound together with the palm branch "lulav" in the middle. Taken together, they are generally called by the term Lulav (even though "lulav" specifically means the palm). The term Lulav is also sometimes used to describe all four i.e. the branches bound together and the Etrog.

To fulfil the mitzvah, hold the lulav in the right hand and the etrog in the left hand with its stem (pitom) pointing downwards. Then say the following blessing:

Blessed are you, Lord our God, King of the universe, who has sanctified us with his commandments, and commanded us to take (raise) the Lulav.

Each Succot, when saying the beracha for the first time, add the beracha "Sheheheyanu". When you have finished the blessing, turn the etrog upside down and holding them together, shake the lulav in all four directions and up down.

There are different ways of approaching the symbolism of the lulav.

One way of looking at it is that it represents the different parts of the body. The etrog is the heart: the lulav is the backbone: the myrtle, because of its oval leaves, is the eyes; and willow is the mouth. The Rabbis said that, together, they show that the whole body and mind must work together to perform a person's religious duties.

With different smells, shapes and ways of growing, one can also see the lulav as the representing the different types of people that make up the world. The etrog has both taste and smell. The fruit of the date palm (the date) from which the lulav is a branch has taste but no smell. The myrtle has smell but no taste and the willow has neither taste nor smell. The Rabbis argued that some people have both knowledge of Torah and do good deeds, some have one and not the other, some have neither. The idea is that a community is always stronger than the individuals who make it up. Together, the types of people represented by the lulav and etrog can pool their strengths.

The commandment in the Torah about the arba'a minim uses uses the word lachem. Thus, the lulav and etrog have to belong to you. In practice, people can obtain a lulav and etrog from their synagogue. They also temporarily give theirs to those who do not own them in order to enable them to perform the mitzvah.

In synagogue, the Arba'a Minim is held in the hands before Hallel in Shacharit when the blessing is recited. It is also held during Hallel (when it is shaken in all directions) to acknowledge God's total power everywhere), in the Amidah for Musaph, and also during the circuits (Hakafot הקפות)

Services - special features

After Arbit on the first night, congregants greet each other by saying "Moadim leSimha" (Festival for joy) מועדים לשמחה to which the proper response is "Hagim u'z'manim le-sasson" ("Holidays and Festivals for gladness") חגים וזמנים לששון.

The whole of Hallel (Psalms 113-118) is said on each day of Succot when the Arba'a Minim are waved. The Hallel is recited standing.

Hosha'ana

Hosha'ana is a special series of prayers recited after Musaph on Succot. It consists of supplications to God, arranged as hymns in alphabetical order. Its name means "Save us" and this forms the first word of each verse.

The order of reciting the Hosha'anot is as follows:

i) The Sefer Torah is brought by the person honoured to the tebah.

ii) The first four verses are recited by the hazan.

'Save us, For Your Sake, our God, save us.'

'Save us, For Your sake, our Creator, save us.'

'Save us, For Your sake, our Redeemer, save us.'

'Save us, For Your sake, our Benefactor, save us.'

iii) Members of the congregation, holding the Arba'a Minim in hands, join the hazan in the recitation of a short verse (the hazan remaining on the tebah).

iv) The Hakafah (procession around the tebah), is undertaken by members of the congregation led by the Hazan. This reminds us of similar circuits around the altar in the Temple.

v) The hazan returns to his place on the tebah and the concluding verses are said.

vi) The Torah scroll is returned to the echal (ark).

Rejoicing on Succot

The element of rejoicing is strong at Succot. Indeed, it is called *'The Season of our Rejoicing'* because of the commandment to rejoice at Sukkot:

and you shall rejoice before the Lord your God seven days

(Leviticus 23:40)

In Temple times, there was a festival called Simchat Bet Hasho'eva during Sukkot. It consisted of a procession to and from the spring that supplied the water for the Temple, the Pool of Siloam. The procession was accompanied by dancers and the playing of flutes, harps, and cymbals. In the Mishnah we read:

He who has not witnessed the joy of the water-drawing has never in his life experienced real joy.

Today, parties called Simchat Bet Hasho'eva שמחת בית השואבה are sometimes held in the succah during hol hamo'ed.

Some Sephardi congregations have the custom of commemorating Simchat Bet Hasho'eva by staying in the synagogue each night of hol hamo'ed and reciting special prayers after Alenu.

Hol Hamo'ed:

The middle days of Succot, though still a part of the festival, are of minor importance. We still wear festive clothes, eat in the succah (saying the blessing) and rejoice with our families. Sephardim do not wear Tefillin (but Ashkenazim do) during hol hamo'ed.

The morning service includes the full Hallel, Hosha'ana (but no procession with the lulav on Shabbat) and Musaph.

Ushpizin אשפיזין

According to tradition, each succah is visited every year by seven Ushpizin אשפיזין, "guests". They are Abraham, Isaac, Jacob, Joseph, Moses, Aaron and David. All the Ushpizin have one thing in common: they were all wanderers who moved from one place to another, both within the boundaries of Israel and beyond them.

Each guest is welcomed with a short prayer on each of the seven days of Succot and a chair is left vacant for them.

In some congregations, the visit of the Ushpizin is highlighted by the hanging of a chart or painting with their names on it as part of the decoration of the succah

The welcoming of the Ushpizin also reflects the opening of our homes to guests and the giving charity to the poor - which is a mitzvah:

Rejoice (to include) the outsider, the orphan and the widow within your gates

(Devarim 16:14)

Hosha'ana Rabbah - הושענא רבה

The seventh day of Succot is known as Hosha'ana Rabbah. It means The Great Hosha'ana or the Great Prayer For Help.

Since it is the seventh day of Succot, one makes seven circuits around the synagogue instead of the usual one.

The day marks the very final sealing of God's judgment, started on Rosh Hashanah and completed on Kippur. It is thus a solemn day as well as one of rejoicing, as is reflected by some of the Kippur tunes used in the synagogue services.

The lulav has performed its function; and the palm branches, willow and myrtle may be thrown away. A bunch of willows is carried on the last hosha'ana and beaten against the benches at the end of the circuit until most of the leaves fall off. This represents the successful atonement for all our sins.

Shemini Atseret and Simchat Torah
שמחת תורה   שמיני עצרת

The eighth day is actually a separate festival. שמיני עצרת is sometimes translated as "Eighth Day of Solemn Assembly" but Atseret also means "conclusion".

Outside Israel there are two days, the second being known as Simchat Torah שמחת תורה - "The Rejoicing of the Law".

In Israel Simchat Torah is combined with Shemini Atseret in one single day.

On Shemini Atseret, we pray for rain during Musaph: this looks forward to the winter season in the Land of Israel when abundant rain is a blessing for farmers.

It marks the end of Succot, a gradual "letting go" of the festival, the atmosphere is more solemn: we do not wave the lulav and are not required to sit in the succah.

Simchat Torah is a festival of rejoicing to mark the end of the cycle of readings of the Torah and the start of a new cycle. It is post-talmudic in origin.

On the evening of Simchat Torah, all the sefarim but one (which remains in the ark) are carried around the synagogue (hakafot הקפות) seven times in procession. The hakafot are accompanied by singing and dancing in celebration. (Similar hakafot were once made around the altar in the Temple).

Four Sifrei Torah are used in the Spanish and Portuguese Congregations for services on the morning of Simchat Torah:

i) For completing the annual cycle of readings

ii) For the Hatan Torah - Bridegroom of the Law (who completes the annual reading of the Torah)

iii) One for starting the new cycle of readings

(by the Hatan Bereshit - Bridegroom of the Beginning)

iv) One for a subject specially related to the festival - Pinchas.

The last verses of the Torah are read out on the morning of Simchat Torah: we also read the beginning of Bereshit from a second Sepher Torah immediately after to ensure that our study of Torah remains continuous. We then repeat the reading from Bereshit the following Shabbat. The Hatan Torah traditionally reads the last parashah *Vezot Haberacha* and the Hatan Bereshit starts off *Bereshit*.

Vezot Haberacha is both sad and happy, an end and a beginning. It represents the end of Moses's life and the beginning of the Israelites' entry into the Land of Israel. *Bereshit* is of course all about the wonders of creation.

EXERCISES

You are inviting some friends (who know nothing about Succot) around to help you build a succah. Write down and draw what you will be doing to build it and what a succah is.

Take pupils to the window and ask them to say what changes are occurring in the trees and the grass.

Bring in a lulav and etrog and have the students say the beracha. Preferably do this in the synagogue's succah.

Prepare sheets of paper with the different elements of the arba'a minim on them with their smell and taste characteristics, and another four sets with the characteristics of the different kinds of people as described above. Ask pupils to match them up. Then discuss whether an ignorant but good Jew is better than a knowledgeable but wicked one.

Discuss - How does the requirement of praying for rain apply if one is in Australia or in England?

Why do we keep harking back to the going out of Egypt. Discuss why this was such a pivotal event for the Jews.

Take the biblical texts and then ask the students to work out how the rules on the succah are derived from them.

Why do we not have a procession with the lulav on shabbat. After all, one can always bring the lulav to synagogue on Friday afternoon.

Ask students to prepare a manual on how to build and decorate the succah. Tell them to take it home with them. This could be done in groups.

Discuss: What do the arba'a minim stand for and why do we bring them together?

Consider what causes most famines.

Is it lack of water or food or/and problems distributing it?

Why is it necessary to pray for rain in the autumn? (when it is needed to help newly planted and existing vegetation to grow.)

Discuss: What is the significance of a pilgrim festival for a nation that does not have a Temple?

Discuss the effect of reading the last and then the first part of the Torah immediately after each other. (Brings back memories of everything in between.)

LESSON 13

Chanukah   חנוכה

Historical background

In the year 333 B.C.E., Judah - a small self-governing province of the once mighty Persian Empire - fell to Alexander the Great.

> Alexander, whose conquests stretched from his native Greece as far as India, wished to spread Greek culture throughout his empire. However, he respected the particular beliefs of the Jews and confirmed all their former privileges. Tradition has it that he personally offered a sacrifice in the Temple; and though this is unlikely, the existence of such a story does illustrate Alexander's benevolent attitude to his Jewish subjects.

After Alexander's death, his empire was split between his generals. The province of Judah was fought over repeatedly but somehow managed to survive, despite many hardships, until Antiochus IV assumed the throne of what had by then become the Seleucid (Greek) Empire.

Antiochus was a megalomaniac, who gave himself the title of the The Manifest God. He was determined to unite his kingdom as never before by stamping religious and cultural uniformity on it. Judaism was banned; and all religious obligations such as keeping the Sabbath and Festivals, and the practice of circumcision, were prohibited on pain of death. Copies of the Torah were destroyed and its possession declared a capital offence. Even worse, the Temple was converted to the worship of the Greek god Zeus and pigs' flesh offered on its altar. Worship was made compulsory at the many pagan altars set up in the towns and villages.

Matityahu (Mattathias), an aged priest with five sons, was the first to raise the standard of revolt, which soon spread throughout the country. After his death, Judah (Judas Maccabeus) assumed the lead and eventually managed to defeat Antiochus's troops and their allies.

On 25th Kislev of the year 165 B.C.E., Judah entered the Temple, cleansed it of all traces of idol-worship and re-consecrated it to the one true God of Israel. A special festival to mark the kindling of lights in the restored Temple was celebrated for eight days and this has continued on each anniversary ever since - now called Chanukah.

A much later tradition tells that there was only one jar of unpolluted oil left in the Temple when the time came for kindling the lamp; and that, by a miracle, that one jar of oil lasted for the full eight days of the festival even though it only contained enough oil for one day.

Antiochus IV died soon after the dedication of the Temple and, some two years later, the Greeks finally made peace with the Jews and granted them full freedom to live in accordance with the customs of their ancestors.

Our present joyful celebration of Chanukah masks the fact that the Maccabean revolt sparked off the most painful and ferocious civil war in Jewish history.

Greek culture, in its debased Hellenistic form, had become very popular with the Jewish upper classes, from the High Priest downwards, most of whom greatly appreciated the many material advantages of mingling on easy terms with the Greek rulers of the country. We read that Shabbat was publicly desecrated and the rite of circumcision neglected. Jewish athletes competed naked in the Greek arenas of Jerusalem. People increasingly worshipped Greek idols: they were ashamed of the Torah, which they considered backward, and opted for what they considered to be the civilised, international way of life.

The Hellenised Jews of the Holy Land reacted badly to what they saw as a "fundamentalist" revolt which threatened their prosperity and comfortable life-styles. They repeatedly joined their Greek friends and allies in battle against the Maccabees; and they continued to wage implacable civil war against their Jewish brethren until the final triumph of Judah the Maccabee and his party of Torah-loving Jews. After that event, the Hellenised Jews rapidly lost their grip on the country and dwindled away.

The rebellion against Antiochus IV was called the revolt of the 'Hasmoneans' or 'Maccabees'. There are many explanations of the origin of these two names. One is that the name Maccabee can be traced to the nickname used by Antiochus's troops for Judah, i.e. "hammer" = Maccabi.

According to another explanation, the origin of the word can be traced to the Hebrew phrase: מי כמוך באלים ה' , i.e., "Who is like you among the gods, O Lord?".

The term Hasmonean has its origin in the word "hashman", which refers to a person with rare qualities of leadership.

Its date

As written in the Book of Maccabees:

And Judah and his brothers commanded them (the Jewish people) to celebrate the dedication of the altar on the twenty-fifth day of the month of Kislev, eight days each year, to praise and thank the Lord.

(1 Maccabees 4:59)

Therefore, as our Sages stipulated, we celebrate Chanukah for eight days, from the 25th of Kislev to the 2nd or 3rd of Tevet (in some years Kislev has twenty-nine days and in others it has thirty days).

Its name

Chanukah is:

i) The "Feast of Lights", as mentioned in the Talmud.

ii) The Festival of Dedication. In Hebrew, Chanukah is the word for "dedication" in the sense of setting apart for sacred purposes.

We read in the Book of Maccabees:

And they celebrated the dedication of (Chanukkaht in Hebrew) the altar for eight days ...

iii) We should also remember that the name Chanukah refers to the fact that the first stage of the war ended on the 25th of Kislev when the soldiers then rested. Therefore the name has its origin in the Hebrew phrase חנו-כ"ה, which means "They rested on the 25th כ"ה".

Its purpose and significance

On Chanukah we remember the heroism of those who fought to defend their right to perform the God's commandments.

We also celebrate re-dedication of the Temple.

On this festival, we remember that God did not abandon his people in their time of need.

Its laws

The laws of Chanukah are:

> Light the candles
>
> Read the full Hallel after morning Amidah
>
> Recite the For the miracle על הנסים during the Amidah and in the Grace after Meals.

Laws and customs concerning "lighting the candles"

1) Number of lights per house:

According to the Babylonian Talmud, we should have a single light per household or a single light for each individual.

2) *Shamash* שמש:

It is forbidden to use the Chanukah candles for any secular purpose (such as lighting the room) and so we use an extra candle called *shamash* for lighting the others. After lighting the candles we put the *shamash* in the central stem of the Hanukkiah.

3) When are the candles lit?

The candles are lit after Arbit (i.e. after nightfall).

The lights must burn for at least half an hour after nightfall. So, on Friday evening, since the Chanukah lights are lit before the Shabbat candles, longer-burning candles are used instead of the regular Chanukah ones. (They should last for at least one and a half hours).

4) How do we light the candles?

According to Shammai's school, we should light eight candles on the first day and after that we should reduce the number by one each night.

According to Hillel's school, we should light one candle on the first day and thereafter we should increase the number of lights each day by one.

We now follow the custom of Hillel's school; and the procedure for lighting the candles is as follows:

> i) On the first day of Chanukah, we light the candle on the extreme right of the hanukkiah and say three blessings:
>
> ...*Who has sanctified us with his commandments and commanded us to kindle the light of Chanukah;*
>
> .. אשר קדשנו במצותיו וצונו להדליק נר של חנוכה
>
> ...*Who performed miracles for our fathers in those days at this season;*
>
> ...שעשה נסים לאבותינו בימים ההם בזמן הזה
>
> ...*Who has kept us alive and preserved us and enabled us to reach this time.*

On the following seven days, only the first two blessings are recited.

Each night, the new light (or candle) is put on the left of the earlier ones and is lit first.

ii) *Ha nerot alalu:*

When the candles are being lit we say הנרות הללו. *ha nerot alalu:*

We kindle these lights on account of the miracles, the deliverances and the wonders, which you performed for our ancestors.

iii) The *Mizmor shir Chanukaht habayit leDavid* is recited.

iv) Some Sephardim sing the "modern" poem of *Ma'oz Tzur*.

This consists of five-verses by the 13rd century poet Mordehai. Each verse starts with a letter of the author's name, i.e. Mordehai מרדכי, and mentions an event in which those who tried to destroy us were themselves destroyed.

5) Where do we put the Chanukah candles?

The lights must be put in a place where they can be seen, not only inside the house but also from the outside, because we should "publicise the miracle".

Chanukah prayers and readings:

i) The full Hallel is read after the Amidah of Shacharit.

ii) The *Al Hanisim* על הנסים, is recited during the Amidah and in the Grace after Meals.

iii) The Sefer (Numbers, chapter 7) is read on each day of Chanukah in the synagogue when three people are called up.

Customs

1) Eat fried food:

We eat food fried in oil, such as doughnuts and latkes (shredded potato-cake fried in oil), to commemorate the miracle of the oil.

Some Sephardim eat deep-fried puffy fritters called buermuelos. The buermuelos are served warm and are dipped in honey and/or sprinkled with sugar or cinnamon.

2) Dreidle:

It is a special children's game for Chanukah. The dreidle is a spinning four-sided top with Hebrew letters, נס גדול היה שם. The children spin the dreidle and make up words with the letter that falls uppermost when it stops spinning.

3) Children are given presents.

---

4) The women of the house refrain from work while the Chanukah lights are lit.

This is a way of honouring the women who kept the mitzvah of circumcising their sons, despite of the tortures and humiliation they suffered by the Antiochus's troops when they were caught.

5) Charity in the form of food or money to buy food is given to the poor.

LESSON 14

Tu Bi-Shevat   ט״ו בשבט

Introduction

The Mishnah establishes four different dates for the New Year, and one of these is Tu Bi-Shevat ראש השנה לאילנות. It marks the end of the rainy season in Israel when the sap rises again in the trees - bringing new life to them and, eventually, a new crop of fruit.

As its name indicates, Tu Bi-Shevat is celebrated on the fifteenth day of Shevat שבט, the eighth month in the Hebrew Calendar. It was not originally celebrated as a festival and only became one long after the Talmudic period.

The New Year for Trees is observed as a joyous occasion since Jews regard the changing cycle of nature as evidence of God's constant care for his world.

Tu Bi-Shevat cannot fall on a Friday or on a Sunday.

The Jewish people and the trees

כי תצור אל עיר ימים רבות להלחם עליה לתפשה, לא תשחית את עצה לנדח עליו גרזן, כי ממנו תאכל ואתו לא תכרת, כי האדם עץ השדה לבא מפניך במצור. רק עץ אשר תדע כי לא עץ מאכל הוא, אתו תשחית וכרת, ובנית מצור על העיר אשר היא עשה עמך מלחמה עד רדתה.

(דברים כ, יט-כ)

When in your war against a city you have to besiege it a long time in order to capture it, you must not destroy its trees and wield the ax against them. You may eat of them but must not cut them down. Are the trees of the field human to retreat before you into the besieged city? Only trees that you know do not yield food may be destroyed; you may cut them down for constructing siegeworks against the city that is waging war on you, until it has been reduced.

(Deut. 20, 19-20)

This passage illustrates the special care the Jewish people have for trees, and specially for fruit trees. The pasuk: *Ki haadam etz asade* כי האדם עץ השדה is interpreted by the Hahamim to teach us that human life depends on and is connected with the trees.

Many legends and customs also reflect the special relationship between the Jewish people and the trees. In some, trees are given human characteristics: for example, they speak to each other. Our hahamim have often compared human beings to trees (Masechet avot 3, mishnah 17)

Its significance

Tu Bi-Shevat is the agricultural New Year on which farmers in ancient Israel had to set aside a proportion of their crops for the priests and the poor (tithes).

Tu Bi-Shevat is the festival which expresses the close relationship between the Jews and their land. In modern Israel, the festival acquired new significance when the tradition was added of planting a tree on this day.

This is the festival of the flowering of nature פריחת הטבע and the trees in the Land of Israel.

Its date

The minor festival of Tu Bi-Shevat is not biblical and is not mentioned in the Torah.

Nevertheless, the Torah commands farmers to tithe their crops (i.e., to set aside a certain percentage as gifts for the priests and the poor) of the same year. It was forbidden to tithe crops of the former year. Therefore, it was necessary to fix the day for the New Year of Trees.

The date for the New Year of Trees was fixed during the period of Bet Shamai בית שמאי and Bet Hillel בית הלל in the first century B.C.E. The date for the New Year of Trees was fixed on the fifteenth of Shevat in favour of Hillel's opinion.

When the Hahamim fixed the date for the New Year of Trees, they had to face the fact that in Israel spring begins on different dates in different areas. As most of the population lived in the mountains, the date was fixed according to the beginning of spring in the mountains.

Therefore, the fifteenth of Shevat became the cut-off date for all tithes of fruits: fruit harvested before 15 Shevat belong to the previous year's crop and must be tithed separately from fruit harvested after that date.

Laws and customs

Tu Bi-Shevat is observed according to the customs enumerated in Sefer Peri Ez Hadar. This sefer contains all the procedures for reciting blessings over the many fruits for Tu Bi-Shevat, as well as the appropriate readings (tikkun) from the Zohar and the Bible.

Minor Festival

The customs of Tu Bi-Shevat are those of the Yom Tov, e.g., it is forbidden to mourn or deliver a eulogy over a dead person.

The תפילת התחנון (confession of our sins) is not said.

In Israel

In Israel, the New Year of Trees is marked by tree-planting.

Jews living in other parts of the world often contribute money to plant trees in Israel.

The tree-planting is, of course, not carried out in the שנת השמטה (Fallow Year).

Eating of fruits

On Tu Bi-Shevat, we eat the fruits of Eretz Israel to remind us of our land.

Berachot on the fruits

It is the custom to eat a new fruit, one that has not yet been eaten this year. Then, the beracha *sheheheyanu* is said.

In addition to its beracha, special prayers are recited similar to the *Yehi razon* prayers on Rosh Hashana night.

> Some have the custom of starting with the שבעת המינים shivat haminim (the seven types or kinds) and recite the regular beracha over the fruit according to the order in which they appear in the Pasuk.

It is customary to eat 15 kinds of fruit, because of the date of the festival. We try to eat as many of the seven species שבעת המינים as possible.

The seven types

כי ה' אלהיך מביאך אל ארץ טובה, ארץ נחלי מים ... ארץ חטה ושערה וגפן ותאנה ורמון, ארץ זית שמן ודבש (דברים ח, ז-ח)

For the Lord your God is bringing you into a good land ... a land of wheat and barley, of vines, figs and pomegranates, a land of olive trees and honey ... When you have eaten your fill, give thanks to the Lord your God for the good land which he has given you.

(Deut. 8, 7-8)

The seven types became the symbol of the Land of Israel.

1) Wheat חטה

- is the first in importance, the most basic of foods.

Bread is made out of wheat.

2) Barley שעורה

- is an important cereal.

3) Grapes גפן

In the Torah, the first vine was planted by Noah after the Flood. The importance of grapes in the Biblical period is reflected by many proverbs and metaphors.

4) Figs תאנה

In the Tanach, the fig is considered to be the fruit that represents the fertility of the land.

The fig was one of the fruits brought back to Moshe by the spies as a proof of the fertility of the Land of Israel.

The fig became a symbol of peace and calm. As the prophet Micah said when he described the calm of the days to come, the Messianic age.

וישבו איש תחת גפנו ותחת תאנתו ואין מחריד ...

(מיכה ד, ד)

Every man shall sit under his vine or fig tree with no one to disturb him.
(Micah 4,4)

5) Pomegranates רמון

The pomegranate is a juicy fruit whose shape is much used for decoration, such as the silver pomegranates that often adorn a Sepher Torah.

6) Olives זית

The olive tree and its fruit were considered holy in Biblical times. Olive oil was used for anointment by the priests in the Bet Hamikdash. The מנורת שבעת הקנים in the Temple was lit with pure olive oil.

The branch of the olive tree is a symbol of peace. It is also a symbol of Israel because it is the most common tree in the Holy Land and because of its deep roots like the roots of the Jewish people in Eretz Israel.

7) Dates תמר (דבש)

The date palm is the only one of the Seven Types that is also one of the Arba'a Minim that make up the Lulav.

Hahamim compared Israel with the palm tree because all its parts are useful.

Purim   חג פורים

Historical background

Following the destruction of the first Temple in 586 BCE, the Jews were deported from the Holy Land to Babylon, currently Iraq. About 50 years later, King Cyrus of Persia conquered Babylonia and gave permission to the Jews to return to the Holy Land and rebuild the Temple. However, many Jews decided to remain in Babylon, by then one of the most splendid cities in the world; and they were to become the ancestors of the Sephardim.

The historical events we commemorate at Purim occurred during the period of the Persian King Ahashverosh (identified with Xerxes, 486 BCE - 465 BCE), and are related in the Book of Esther.

We read in the Book of Esther that King Ahashverosh banished his queen, Vashti, after a domestic quarrel. He then decided to choose a new wife from amongst the most beautiful women in his kingdom. Eventually he chose Esther, a Jewish orphan girl who had been brought up by her uncle Mordecai. Following her uncle's instructions, Esther did not reveal her Jewish origin to the king.

Mordecai felt very lonely without his niece and began taking daily walks through the grounds of the palace in the hope of catching sight of her. It was during one of those walks that Mordecai discovered the existence of a plot by two slaves to assassinate the king. He promptly told Esther about the plot and asked her to pass on the message to the king. After investigation, the two slaves were found guilty and hanged. The whole affair was recorded in the Book of Chronicles.

Following that incident, King Ahashverosh appointed a nobleman called Haman as prime minister. Haman was a descendant of Agag, king of the Amalekites and an ancient enemy of the Jews: Haman too was counted amongst the enemies of the Jews at the Persian court for having opposed their return to the Holy Land and their rebuilding of the Temple. After his appointment as prime minister, Haman issued an order requiring all to bow down to the ground before him. Mordecai, however, who would not prostrate himself to any earthly minister, refused to bow down to Haman.

Haman seized upon Mordecai's disobedience as a pretext to do away with the Jews of the kingdom. He persuaded King Ahashverosh to sign a decree ordering the massacre of all the Jews in Persia and the confiscation of their possessions: this was to come in effect on the thirteenth day of the month. Copies of the decree were sent to the governors in charge of all the different provinces of the empire and, according to its terms, the Jews were to be given no opportunity to defend themselves.

Mordecai put on sackcloth and covered himself with ashes, as a sign of mourning, when he heard of the decree and positioned himself outside the palace gates, where he was soon noticed by Esther. She sent her personal servant to Mordecai to find out what had happened; and the servant returned to the queen with a copy of the decree and a message from Mordecai begging her to plead with the king for its cancellation.

Esther agreed to approach the king but there were grave risks involved: anyone approaching the king's presence without an invitation could be instantly put to death. She therefore asked Mordecai to have all the Jews of Shushan fast and pray to God on her behalf for three days before her planned visit to the king.

Esther managed to reach the king without mishap and invited him and his prime minister Haman to a banquet. She also asked them to favour her by coming to a second banquet on the following day. After the first feast, all bowed down to Haman as he left the palace - except Mordecai. Haman was so furious that he decided to hang Mordecai and built a special gallows for that purpose.

That night the king had a dream in which he was reminded that he had not yet rewarded Mordecai for his good deed in uncovering the murder plot. He then decided to heap honour on Mordecai and chose Haman for the task.

On the day after Haman had attended the second of the queen's banquets, Esther finally told the king about her Jewish identity and Haman's plan to annihilate the entire Jewish nation, herself included. Then King Ahashverosh, in fury, had Haman and his ten sons executed. Mordecai was appointed prime minister in his place.

However, according Persian law, any decree already issued could not be withdrawn; so instead, the king issued a new decree permitting the Jews to defend themselves and strike back against their enemies. On 13th day of Adar the Jews of Persia fought fiercely against those who wished to destroy them and succeeded in killing several thousand: on 14th Adar, they rested. The Jews of Shushan, the capital city of empire, were allowed an additional day in which to destroy their enemies; and so they fought on the 14th Adar as well and rested on the 15th.

A year later, Mordecai and Esther sent letters throughout the empire instructing the Jews to celebrate Purim on 14th Adar generally, but on 15th Adar in walled cities.

Throughout the ages, Jews have used the example of Purim to celebrate deliverance from particular perils that came close to overwhelming them. Thus many local communities either have a "second" Purim, or else also use Purim itself, to commemorate their being saved from imminent destruction on other occasions.

Name

These days are called Purim, after the pur (lottery).

(Esther Chap.9)

על-כן קראו לימים האלה פורים על שם הפור...

Haman was a superstitious person who drew lots to fix the day for the extermination of the Jews. The name of the holiday relates to that 'pur' or lottery cast by Haman.

Date

We commemorate Purim on the 14th of Adar when the Jews were finally able to rest after overcoming their enemies.

Purpose and significance

On Purim we celebrate the deliverance of the Jews from the decrees of Haman; and we remember not only Haman but also his heirs throughout history who have also sought to destroy the Jewish people.

We also remember the struggle of the Jewish people for physical survival and celebrate its success with joy.

The name of God is not mentioned once in the entire Book of Esther. Therefore Purim reminds us that God is always present, guiding and assisting his people, even when he seems to be absent.

This festival is one of hope to all Jews, and in particular to those living in difficult conditions.

Shabbat "Zachor" ("Remember")

The Shabbat before Purim is called Shabbat Zachor "remember". On this Shabbat we read an additional Torah portion from Deuteronomy 25:17-19, which begins with the word "remember":

Remember what Amalek did to you on your journey out of Egypt...

- and so we remember Amalek's deeds by reading this portion of the Torah.

In some Sephardi congregations, it is customary for men to stamp their feet and clap their hands softly when the name Amalek is mentioned.

Sephardi congregations recite special piyutim, such as *Mi kamoha* by Rabbi Yehuda Halevi. Sephardim call this Sabbat *Shabbat Mi Hamoha*.

Fast of Esther

On the 13th of Adar we fast in order to commemorate the three days' fast observed by Esther and the Jews of Shushan before she approached the king.

The fast lasts from daybreak to nightfall.

At Mincha in the synagogue, a special tray is used for the donation of the symbolic half-shekel, symbolising the half-shekel given during the Temple period. In some communities the donation consists of three special coins that are later exchanged for donations to charity.

It is customary for some Sephardi communities to send the money to Israeli institutions of Torah learning. Other Sephardim simply put the money into Sedaca (charity) boxes located behind the teba.

Laws

...they made it a day of feasting and rejoicing.

(Esther 9: 17)

ועשה אתו יום משתה ושמחה

(מגילת אסתר ט, יז)

The Jews were to observe these days as seasons of feasting, rejoicing, sending delicacies to one another, and alms to the needy.

(Esther 9, 22)

לעשות אותם ימי משתה, ושמחה ומשלח מנות איש לרעהו ומתנות לאביונים

(מגילת אסתר ט, כב)

According to the Megillah, the four basic mitzvot of Purim are:

1) Reading the Megillah קריאת המגילה

2) Having a festive meal סעודת פורים

3) Sending gifts of food to friends - mishloach manot משלוח מנות

4) Giving alms to the poor - matanot la'evionim מתנות לאביונים

Three additional mitzvot were decreed by our Sages:

5) Reciting Al Hanisim על הנסים

6) Reading the Torah קריאה בתורה

7) Prohibition of fasting or delivering eulogies to the dead.

Reading the Megillah

קריאת המגילה

When is the Megillah read?

The Megillah is read twice during Purim, after Arbit and again on the following morning during Shacharit.

One is obliged to read the Megillah at night, and to repeat the reading during the day.

(Talmud Bavli, Tractate Megillah 4a)

Minyan is not necessary.

Characteristics of the Megillah

The Megillah must be written by the scribe in the same fashion as a Sefer Torah, i.e., on a parchment scroll. Some Sephardi communities place the Megillah in a specially decorated case.

Blessings before the reading

Before the Megillah is read, the scroll is unrolled so as to resemble an *iggeret* and three blessing are said by the Reader.

The blessings are:

i) *Blessed are you, Lord our God, King of the universe, who has sanctified us with his commandments and commanded us concerning the reading of the Megillah;*

ברוך אתה ה' אלקינו מלך העולם, אשר קדשנו במצותיו וצונו על מקרא מגלה.

ii) *Blessed are you, Lord our God, King of the universe, who performed miracles for our fathers in those days at this season;*

ברוך אתה ה' אלקינו מלך העולם שעשה נסים לאבותינו בימים ההם בזמן הזה.

iii) *Blessed are you, Lord our God, King of the universe, who has kept us alive and preserved us and enabled us to reach this time;*

ברוך אתה ה' אלקינו מלך העולם שהחינו וקימנו והגיענו לזמן הזה.

The blessings are said by the Reader (ba'al koreh בעל הקורא) and the congregants answer "Amen". Everyone should recite the three blessings, but if one hears another reciting them and then responds "Amen", it is as if one had recited them for oneself.

Concluding blessing

After the reading, the concluding blessing is said by the Reader with the congregants responding "Amen":

Blessed are you, Lord our God, King of the universe, who fights our battles, performs judgments for us, avenges wrongdoings for us and punishes all the enemies of our soul, causing those who trouble us to pay the price. Blessed are you, God, who acts on behalf of his people Israel in the face of all who trouble them, the God of salvation. 'Amen'

ברוך אתה ה' אלקינו מלך העולם, הרב את ריבנו, והדן את דיננו, והנוקם את נקמתנו, והמשלם גמול לכל אויבי נפשנו, והנפרע לנו מצרינו, ברוך אתה ה', הנפרע לעמו ישראל מכל צריהם, האל המושיע.

By answering Amen it is as if we had read the Megillah ourselves (שומע כקורא).

Every word must be heard

For the fulfilment of the mitzvah one must hear every single word of the Megillah. Therefore:

    i) one must concentrate,

    ii) one should not make noises

    iii) children must be kept as quiet as possible.

Verses recited by the congregants

Four verses of the Megillah are recited aloud by the congregants before the Reader says them:

    i) *There was a Jew, a resident of Shushan, and his name was Mordecai, the son of Yair, the son of Shim'i, the son of Kish, of the tribe of Benjamin*

(Esther 2:5)

איש יהודי היה בשושן הבירה, ושמו מרדכי בן יאיר בן שמעי קיש איש ימיני

(מגילת אסתר ב, ה)

    ii) *And Mordecai went out before the king, donning royal garments of fine blue and white linen, and a large golden crown, and a fine linen cloak of purple, and the city of Shushan was jubilant and exultant.*

(Esther 8:15)

ומרדכי יצא מלפני המלך בלבוש מלכות, תכלת וחור, ועטרת זהב גדולה ותכריך בוץ וארגמן, והעיר שושן צהלה ושמחה

(מגילת אסתר ח, טו)

    iii) *The Jews had light and joy and delight and honour*

(Esther 8:16)

(מגילת אסתר ח, טז)

iv) *For Mordecai the Jew, the viceroy of King Ahashverosh, was renowned among the Jews and greatly favoured by his brethren; and he sought good fortune for his nation and harmony for all his issue.*

(Esther 10:3)

כי מרדכי היהודי משנה למלך אחשורוש וגדול ליהודים ורצוי לרב אחיו, דרש טוב לעמו ודבר שלום לכל זרעו

(מגילת אסתר י, ג)

A commandment for woman

Women are commanded to hear the reading of the Megillah despite the fact that this is a "time-bound" mitzvah.

Some Sephardi congregations have a special reading for the women on the afternoon of Purim.

Erase Haman's name

In some Sephardi communities it is customary to write the name of Haman on the floor or on a stone and then rub it out.

It is also customary, to make noises each time the name Haman is mentioned. This symbolises the eradication of the names of our enemies. However, some Sephardi congregations are discouraged from making to much noise.

To be sure that each word of the Megillah is heard clearly, the ba'al koreh waits for the hubbub to stop before he continues reading; or else he repeats words that may not have been heard clearly.

Festive Meal סעודת פורים

The Seudah must be held on the day of Purim itself.

The festive meal resembles the wine banquet prepared by Esther for King Ahashverosh and Haman.

Some Sephardi communities call this feast Seudat Esther.

At this meal, we should drink enough wine until we can no longer distinguish between *"Blessed be Mordecai"* and *"Cursed be Haman"* - but this is not compulsory!

Mishloah Manot משלוח מנות

This commandment consists of sending portions of food to our friends on Purim.

The word 'mishloah' means "sending" and the word 'manot' means "portions" (in the plural). Therefore, in order to fulfil the mitzvah, one must send at least one gift of more than one item of food. The gifts usually include a drink and some food - often a tray of cakes or other sweets.

Traditionally, children are sent with the gifts so that they may learn the mitzvah of generosity.

It is customary for some Sephardi communities to set the manot on a special silver dish (platos de Purim) which is taken by children from house to house.

Gift to the poor.

Matanot la'evionim מתנות לאביונים

'Matanot' means "gifts" in plural and 'evionim' means "poor" also in the plural. Therefore, the minimum requirement for the fulfilment of this commandment is to send two gifts to at least two less fortunate persons.

On Purim, one should give charity to anyone asking for it, as we read in Tractate Megillah 2, 16:

One does not count coins when giving charity on Purim; one must give to anyone who extends his hand to receive.

The money can be given directly or by means of a Sedaca box.

It is customary in some Sephardi congregation to give money both to poor Jews and to poor non-Jews as well.

Al Hanisim על הנסים

Al Hanisim is recited in the beracha of Modim in the Amidah and in the second paragraph of the Grace after Meals (birkat hamazon).

We thank God for delivering us from our enemies:

For the miracles, and the salvation, and the mighty deeds, and the victories, and the wonders, and the consolation, and the battles which you performed for our ancestors in those days, at this time.

על הנסים, ועל הפרקן, על הגבורות, ועל התשועות, ועל הנפלאות, ועל הנחמות, ועל המלחמות, שעשית לאבותינו בימים ההם בזמן הזה.

Reading the Torah קריאה בתורה

The Torah is read at Shacharit before the reading of the Megillah.

The Torah reading is Exodus 17. The parasha is Beshallah which describes the war of the Israelites against the Amalekites (ancestors of Haman) who attacked them when they had just left Egypt.

The minimum permitted length of a reading from the Torah is ten verses: so, in order to fulfil this requirement, Sephardi congregations repeat the last verse of *Vayabo Amalek*.

Hallel is not recited

Hallel is not recited for two main reasons:

a)The Book of Esther is considered a substitute for Hallel

because it is in itself a book of praise and thanksgiving to God for the miracle.

b)The Hallel is only recited in gratitude for a miracle that

occurred in the Land of Israel (Babylonian Talmud, Tractate Megillah 14a).

The one exception to this rule is the recitation of Hallel at Pesach, when we celebrate our Exodus from Egypt at a time before the Land of Israel became our homeland.

Customs

1) Many humorous and satiric plays have been written for performance at Purim.

2) Children dress-up
On Purim we celebrate the transformation of Jews from victims to victors; for that reason we demonstrate that transformation by dressing up to change our appearance.

3) Eating delicacies:
It is customary to bake special delicacies for Purim, which are also used for the mishloah manot. Some typical Purim delicacies are:
Oznei Haman (Haman's ears) which are biscuits in the shape of a triangle.
Purim Hallah is a sweet hallah with raisins.
Baklava, ghraybe, pita de susam, halva, etc.

4) Seudah shel Haman or Hebura di Haman:
It was customary in some Sephardi communities to ridicule Haman at a special breakfast on Purim morning.

5) Images of Haman:
Some Sephardim make images of Haman and his ten sons, mock them and hang them from a gallows and burn them (like Guy Fawkes in England).

6) Adloyada עדלידע:
In Israel a carnival parade called *Adloyada* is held on Purim day.

7) Pizmonim:
Some Sephardi communities have special pizmonim for Purim. These songs are to be found in the prayer books or in *Shir Ushebaha Hallel Vezimra*

Shushan Purim or Purim of Kerachin (walled cities)

On Shushan Purim, we commemorate the struggle of the Jews of Shushan who fought their enemies both on the 13th and on the 14th of Adar and rested only on the 15th of Adar.

As Shushan was then a walled city, it was decreed that in the cities of the Holy Land that had been enclosed with walls since the time of Yehoshua bin Nun, Purim would fall on the 15th of Adar. The time of Yehoshua was chosen as a reference point because he was the first to fight Amalek

In some places, such as Acre, Gaza, Lod, Tiberias, Jaffa, Nablus, Hebron, S'fat and Haifa, it is uncertain whether or not the cities were fortified at the time of Yehoshua. There, Purim is celebrated on 14th of Adar, but the Megillah is read both on the 14th and on the 15th of Adar.

Pesach   פסח

Introduction

You shall keep this day as a remembrance ... for all time

(Exodus 12:14)

Pesach is an eight-day long celebration of the deliverance of the tribes descended from the patriarchs - Abraham, Isaac and Jacob - from slavery in Egypt.

The Lord brought us out of Egypt with a mighty hand and with an outstretched arm, with great terribleness and with signs and wonders.

And the Lord bought us out of Egypt, not by means of an angel or a seraph, or a messenger - but by the Holy One, blessed be he, himself in his glory ...

(Haggadah)

Even though this is where the towering figure of Moshe first appears in Jewish history, great stress is laid throughout the festival on God's own personal role in the redemption.

For seven days you shall eat unleavened bread ... anyone who eats leavened bread shall be outlawed from Israel

(Exodus 12:15)

... and the people picked up their dough before it had risen

(Exodus 12:34)

The dough they had brought from Egypt was baked into unleavened cakes, because there was no leaven; for they had been driven out of Egypt and allowed no time even to get food ready for themselves before departing

(Exodus 12:39)

The festival starts in the home with a special ceremonial meal called the Haggadah (by some Sephardim) or the Seder (order, or arrangement) by others. The youngest person at table asks "Why is this night different from all other nights?" and the answer to that question forms the basis of the narrative that follows, when we - the actual or the spiritual descendants of the slaves - remember the time of oppression and lovingly recount the traditional story of the events that led to our freedom, whilst leaning back in our chairs, drinking wine and feasting.

Unfortunately, human oppression did not end with the exodus from Egypt and grievous circumstances now and in the past serve constantly to keep fresh the message of Pesach, the festival of freedom.

Date of the festival

Pesach is observed at a full moon in early spring and marks the transition from winter to summer. Prayers for dew *"to slake the scorching earth"* are included in the synagogue service for the first day of the festival.

Pesach is the first of the Shalosh Regalim (Pilgrim Festivals) when the Torah commands all males to come up to Jerusalem and offer sacrifices in the Temple. It occurs on 15th Nisan, the first month in the Hebrew calendar - the 1st Nisan being the New Year for Festivals. There is more than one other "New Year" in the Hebrew calendar - what are they and when do they occur?

ערב פסח   Nisan

	14	night*	Bedikat Hamets (Search for leaven)
		day	Biur Hamets (Disposal of leaven) Taanit Bechorim (Fast of the Firstborn) The Korban Pesach was offered that afternoon in the Temple.

Yom Tov	15	night	1st Seder
	16		2nd Seder. Start of Sefirat HaOmer
Hol Hamo'ed	17		
	18		
	19		
	20		
Yom Tov	21		
	22		

*Note: The Jewish "day" commences at sundown on the previous evening.

Its different names

1) Hag Hamatsot חג המצות

The Festival of Unleavened Bread is the name used in the Torah.

2) Pesach פסח

In the Torah the word Pesach actually refers to the Korban Pesach (sacrificial lamb) offered on the day before the festival (14 Nisan) and eaten during the first evening (at which time we now celebrate our Seder).

3) Hag Ha'aviv חג האביב

This means 'Spring Festival' and the Torah uses the word Aviv to describe the month of Nisan. Its agricultural significance is that on the second day of Pesach an Omer (a measure of barley) was brought to the Temple in gratitude for the new crop.

4) Zeman Herutenu זמן חרותנו -

"The Season of our Freedom". This is the phrase most often used in our prayers.

Its purpose

Though all three Pilgrim Festivals (Pesach, Shavuot and Succot) are strongly linked to the story of the Exodus from Egypt, the event actually took place at Pesach. Thus we constantly refer to the Exodus from Egypt (Yetsiat Mizrayim יציאת מצרים) in our prayers for the entire eight days; and that event remains uppermost in our minds. One of the main reasons for eating Matzah is to remind ourselves of the food eaten by the Children of Israel during their hurried departure from Egypt.

Its laws מצות

1) Hamets חמץ (Leavened)

Food prepared from any one of the Five Species of Grain (שבעת המינים) which has fermented is termed Hamets. It is forbidden to eat it, to have benefit from it or to own it from the day before Pesach until the end of the last day of Pesach.

> The ban on eating applies from half-way through the morning and the ban on benefit and ownership comes into force a little later that morning.

2) Matzah מצה (Unleavened Bread)

Matzah is eaten through Pesach. It is a special mitsvah to eat Matzah at the Seder. For this reason the beracha על אכילת מצה. is only said at the Seder.

3) Seder סדר (Order)

On the first night in Israel and on the first two nights elsewhere, a special home service takes place. The purpose of this service is to relate the history of the Exodus and to celebrate our freedom from slavery in Egypt. See Appendix B for a full explanation of the Seder and its significance.

Very briefly, the most important elements of the Seder are:

Haggadah הגדה (Telling)

A large part of the evening is devoted to explaining the departure from Egypt. This is particularly directed towards children as we read in Exodus:

And you shall tell your son on that day...

(13: 8)

The book used on this evening is the Haggadah (Narrative) and it contains appropriate Biblical, Talmudic and Midrashic selections. In addition it includes all the relevant blessing and prayers (e.g. Birkat Hamazon and Hallel). It gives full instructions as to what to do at each stage.

The Four Cups ארבע כוסות

A cup of wine is drunk at four specific points in the evening, making four cups in all, to celebrate our freedom.

Three Matzot

The three matzot are placed on the seder table - two as is normal on Shabbat and Yom Tov, and a third which is to be broken into two pieces: the smaller part symbolises *'poor man's bread'* לחם עני (he cannot afford complete pieces) while the larger section becomes the Afikoman.

Elijah's Cup כוסו של אליהו

This is a fifth cup of wine, reserved for the prophet Elijah, and which is not drunk.

Karpas כרפס

This is the vegetable eaten at the start of the Seder.

Maror מרור (Bitter Herbs) .

A vegetable such as lettuce is eaten near the start of the meal to recall the bitterness of slavery.

Haroset חרוסת

This is a paste (made, for example, from apples, nuts, dates, cinnamon and wine) which represents the mortar used by the slaves in Egypt for building work. The Maror is dipped in Haroset.

Shankbone זרוע

A roasted bone from a sheep is placed on the table in memory of the Passover Lamb קרבן פסח which, in the Temple times, was eaten on this night. However, it is not eaten at the Seder; and the Afikoman is substituted for it at the end of the meal in memory of the eating of the sacrificial lamb.

Egg ביצה

A roasted egg appears on the Seder plate to remind us of the Korban Hagigah קרבן חגיגה, the "Festival Sacrifice" (offered on each of the Shalosh Regalim).

4) Sefirat Ha'Omer ספירת העמר
(Counting the Omer)

The Torah says:

You shall count from the day after the rest-day, from the day you bring the Omer as a wave-offering, there shall be seven complete weeks, until the day after the seventh week...

(Leviticus 23: 15-16)

Although we are now unable to bring the wave-offering (since we have no Temple) we still maintain the counting. Each night - from the second night of Pesach until the night before Shavuot - we count the day of the Omer.

Its customs מנהגים

As is the case with all the festivals, there are many different customs associated with Pesach, particularly at the Seder. These vary considerably and there are too many to list here.
Here is just one of them:
Among some eastern communities the children dress up as the Benei Yisrael just leaving Egypt. They stand outside the room where the Seder is taking place. Then, they knock on the door and a dialogue is acted out between them and the Seder leader - who are you? where have you come from (Egypt)? and where are you going (the Land of Israel)? what was it like in Egypt?, etc.

Think of the customs you have seen at the Seder, whether it be the use of a special Seder Plate, the eating of certain foods (in addition to those listed above) or the singing of particular tunes.

Its prayers תפילות

In addition to the special prayers of the Haggadah, Ya'aleh Veyavo is included in the Amidot (apart from Musaph) throughout the eight days.

Hallel and Musaph are recited throughout the eight days.

In the synagogue, in Israel and among some Sephardim and Hasidim outside Israel, Hallel is said just before the Seder (as well as at home during the Seder).

Two Sifrei Torah are used on each of the eight days. The service on the days of Yom Tov is similar to that of Shabbat.

The special Prayer for Dew is added in the Musaph of the first day. This is known as *Tefillat Tal* תפילת טל (In Sephardi prayer books it appears as *Tikkun Ha'tal* תקון הטל).

The Torah reading for the seventh day contains the Song of the Sea שירת הים (אז ישיר, etc.).

On the Shabbat of Pesach, the *Megillah of Shir Hashirim* שיר השירים (Song of Songs) is read in many Ashkenazi congregations. On the eighth day a short memorial service is held in Ashkenazi synagogues. This is called *Yizkor* יזכור or *Hazkarat Neshamot* הזכרת נשמות. It offers the individual an opportunity to remember departed relatives. It also includes public memorial prayers for martyrs including those who perished in the Holocaust. Sephardim do not have these customs.

Shir Hashirim is read in Sephardi synagogues on the last day of Pesach.

APPENDIX A

Timetable in connection with Hamets and the Korban Pesach

14 Nisan	Night	Search for Hamets
	Day	By 1/4 day (= approx. 10.30am): Latest time for eating Hamets By 5/12 day (=approx. 11.45am): Latest time for owning Hamets. Afternoon: Korban Pesach offered in Temple times.
15 Nisan	Night	Korban Pesach eaten in Temple times. Nowadays, no Korban but the Seder instead.

APPENDIX B

The Passover Seder סדר ליל פסח

1) Recite the Kiddush. קדש ורחץ.

2) Wash the hands.

3) Eat the greens dipped in salt water. כרפס יחץ.

4) Break the middle matzah and keep half for the afikoman.

5) Recite the Haggadah.

6) Wash the hands for the meal. מגיד רחצה.

7-8) Say Hamotzi and a special blessing over the matzah מוציא מצה.

9) Eat the bitter herb dipped in Haroset.

10) Eat the maror and matzah sandwich. מרור כורך.

11) Serve the Pesach meal. שלחן עורך.

12) Distribute parts of the afikoman to all present. צפון ברך.

13) Say grace after the meal.

14) Chant the Hallel הלל נרצה.

15) Recite the closing prayer.

16) Sing the special Seder songs - optional for Sephardim.

Lag Ba'Omer   ל״ג בעומר

The Omer

The Omer was the offering brought to the Temple after Passover on 16th Nisan. Only after it had been offered in the Temple was it permissible for people to eat the produce of the new harvest. (Leviticus 23:9)

The name "Omer" was then used to designate the period between Pesach and Shavuot; for Torah commands us to count the 49 days between Pesach and Shavuot. Each day is counted after saying a special beracha.

The Omer is regarded as a period of semi-mourning for the disciples of the great sage, Rabbi Akiba, who died of a plague caused *"because they did not treat each other with respect."*

Lag Ba'Omer

Lag Ba'Omer is the thirty-third day of the Omer. It is the anniversary of the death of another great sage, Shimon bar Yohai. In some congregations it is also used as an occasion for honouring their own Zaddikim by visiting their graves.

In the Midrash, Rabbi Shimon bar Yohai is compared to Moshe Rabbenu. He was assured acceptance into the celestial abode because of his exemplary way of life; and he wanted us all to share in his happiness. Therefore, on Lag Ba'Omer we observe a *hilula* ("wedding" or "celebration") to rejoice on the night of his *Nahala* (anniversary).

Lag Ba'Omer also indicates the end of the period of sadness commemorating the death of Rabbi Akiba's disciples, during which it is forbidden to celebrate weddings or any kind of *sema-hot.*

In some congregations, *semachot* can take place on Lag Ba'Omer but most Sephardim allow *semachot* to be celebrated from ל"ד 34th day of the Omer.

Customs

The celebration of Lag Ba'Omer is called *hadlakah or hilula*. Its main features are:

1) The lighting of candles in memory of Rabbi Shimon bar Yohai.

2) Pizmonim.

During the hadlakah, *pizmonim* are sung.

The main pizmon is the *Bar Yohai* (about Rabbi Shimon bar Yohai).

3) The Zohar (*Idra Zuta*), which is attributed to Rabbi Shimon bar Yohai, is studied.

4) Morrocan Jews visit local cemeteries and pray at the

graves of their *zaddikim.*

5) Many congregations have the custom of burying all items that have to be put in the *geniza* (in the cemetery) on that day. While they are in the cemetery, they also visit the graves of their special *zaddikim*.

6) In Israel, it is the custom to visit the grave of Rabbi Shimon bar Yohai in Meron.

7) Our own Spanish and Portuguese Congregation does not usually mark Lag Ba'Omer with any special celebration.

Shavuot שבעות

Introduction

...I have carried you on eagles' wings and brought you here to me. If only you will now listen to me and keep my covenant, then ... you shall be my kingdom of priests, my holy nation

(Exodus 19: 4-5)

The act of gaining freedom from slavery in Egypt was not enough to forge a nation; and seven weeks after Pesach, we celebrate one of the supreme moments in our history when, in the desert of Sinai, we received the Torah from God.

There were peals of thunder and flashes of lightning, dense cloud on the mountain and a loud trumpet blast: the people in the camp were all terrified

(Exodus 19:16)

By accepting God's Torah at Sinai, the Children of Israel acquired the reason for their freedom, a stamp of nationhood to which Jews have clung with remarkable tenacity ever since.

The receiving of the Torah on Mount Sinai has now become the primary reason for celebrating Shavuot; but in Temple times it also marked the end of the barley harvest and the beginning of the wheat harvest, when the first ripe fruits of the season were brought to the Temple.

The day of the first-fruits is when you bring a new grain offering to God as part of your Shavuot festival.

(Leviticus 28:26)

The names of the festivals

1. Shavuot שבעות which means "Weeks."
This name refers to the fact that this festival begins seven weeks after Pesach.

2. Chag Hakatsir חג הקציר which means "The Festival of Reaping."

On the second day of Pesach an Omer (a measure of grain) was brought as a "wave" offering to the Temple. Fifty days later, on Shavuot, the new harvest was gratefully celebrated by the offering of two loaves made from the new crop.

3. Yom Habikkurim יום הבכורים "The Day of the First Fruits."

In Temple times farmers would also bring certain first-fruits to the Temple in thanksgiving.

4. Zeman Mattan Toratenu זמן מתן תורתנו "The Season of the Giving of our Torah."

The sixth of Sivan was the day of Revelation, when God "revealed" himself to our ancestors through the giving of the Ten Commandments and indeed of the entire Torah.

5. Atseret עצרת "Conclusion"

This is the Mishnaic term for the festival. Connected by Sefirat Ha'omer, Shavuot forms the conclusion to Pesach.

Its date

On 6th and 7th Sivan in the diaspora (i.e. outside Israel) and on 6th Sivan only in Israel.

> The three days before Shavuot are known as the *Sheloshet Yemei Hagbalah* שלשת ימי הגבלה "The Three Days of Bordering". This name is derived from the fact that the Children of Israel were told to prepare for Mattan Torah three days prior to the event and to keep away from Mt. Sinai's border.
>
> The day after Shavuot is known as *Isru Chag* אסרו חג. This also describes the day after the end of Pesach and the day after Simchat Torah.

Its laws

Shavuot is one of the three Pilgrim Festivals (also called Foot Festivals, because at least the last stage of the pilgrimage was always made on foot), when the Torah commands every male to go up to Jerusalem and offer a sacrifice in the Temple.

Shavuot has no distinctive laws, other than the general rules for Yom Tob.

Its prayers

The services are much the same as those for Pesach except that the references are, of course, to Shavuot. The Torah portion for the first day contains the Ten Commandments when all present in the synagogue stand for its reading.

The Book of Ruth is also read during the festival.

Its customs

1) The synagogue is decorated with flowers and plants for the festival.

2) Dairy food (food containing milk) is served for at least one meal at home on Shavuot. The reason for this is that the Torah is compared to milk and honey:

Your lips drop sweetness like the honeycomb, my bride. Syrup and milk are under your tongue.

(Songs of Songs 4:11)

3) A charming old practice, still observed in Gibraltar and elsewhere, is the reading of a *ketubah* (marriage contract) in the synagogue to symbolise the symbolic wedding between Israel and the Torah.

4) In memory of the night spent by the Benei Yisrael in anticipation of Mattan Torah, many stay up to study Torah for the whole of the first night of Shavuot. Some use a special book called *Tikkun leil Shavuot.*

> The order of the study of the *Tikkun leil Shavuot* varies from congregation to congregation, but in general it consists of:
>
> *Tanach* (Bible Prophets and Hagiographa):
>
> Reading of several verses from the beginning and end of each *parashah*
>
> *Taryag Mitzvot* (613 commandments)
>
> Selections from the Midrash
>
> *Idra Rabba*
>
> *Idra Zuta*

Moses

They never arose in Israel a prophet who, like Moses, did behold the likeness of God.

(Deut. 34:10)

Moses, venerated above all other men in Jewish tradition, played a key role in the events commemorated at Shavuot. However this is the festival which celebrates the giving of the Torah at Sinai. It is concerned primarily with the central relationship of the Jewish nation to its God, compared to which the significance of individual people and places is unimportant. For example, Moses - who negotiated with Pharaoh for the freedom of his people, who led them through the desert to the boundary of the Promised Land, and who received the Ten Commandments and the Torah on their behalf - has no shrine: his place of burial remains unknown: and no festival, not even Shavuot, is consecrated to his memory. Also, Mount Sinai, the dramatic setting for the act of revelation, is no longer regarded by Jews as a holy place; and the late (Egyptian) President Sadat's suggestion of building a synagogue, together with a mosque and a church, on its supposed summit was received with indifference in Israel.

Fast of Gedaliah   צום גדליהו

Its date

We observe this fast day on the 3rd of Tishri ג' בתשרי (the seventh month of the year). It falls on the day after Rosh Hashanah and lasts from dawn to nightfall.

As a fast day can never fall on Shabbat (the only exception being Kippur) the Fast of Gedaliah is postponed to Sunday if Rosh Hashanah falls on Thursday and Friday.

Historical background

Following the destruction of the first Temple, thousands of Jews were expelled from the Holy Land and deported to Babylon. The Babylonian King Nebuchadnezzar allowed some Jews to remain in Eretz Israel and appointed Gedaliah as their governor. Gedaliah was a peaceful man who tried to convince the Jews to give up all idea of further rebellion. Under Gedaliah's rule, the situation of the Jews in the Land improved.

Five years after the destruction of the Temple, Gedaliah and some Babylonian soldiers in his palace were assassinated by a group of Jews. After that event, the Babylonian army moved in to quell the uprising. Some Jews escaped to Egypt and most of the others were deported to Babylonia (modern Iraq). That was the real beginning of the exile that lasted for 70 years.

Its purpose and significance

On this day we commemorate the assassination of Gedaliah ben Ahikam.

We mourn Gedaliah's murder because it marked the loss of the last chance for some time to rebuild the Temple and the ending of Jewish self-rule in the Land.

Features

1) At Shacharit:

i) Special *Selichot* are added.

ii) *Avinu Malkenu* is said after the hazan repeats the Amidah.

iii) The hazan says an additional blessing in the *Amidah* :

עננו:

"*Answer us, O Lord*" עננו ה' ביום צום תעניתנו

iv) "The Thirteen Attributes of Mercy" are recited.

v) The Torah portion for a fast-day is read.

2) At Mincha:

i) The Torah portion for a fast-day is read again.

ii) In the *Amidah*, everyone who is fasting adds עננו *"Answer us, O Lord"* in the שמע קולנו prayer.

Fast of Tevet   צום עשירי בטבת

Its date

As its name indicates, this fast day falls on the 10th of Tevet, which is the tenth month (the months are counted from Nisan). We fast from dawn to nightfall.

The fast is not postponed if it falls on Friday, as are other fasts, because of Ezekiel's verse:

on the self-same day (Ezekiel 40:1)

Its purpose and significance

Commemoration of the destruction of the Temple

The Fast of Tevet is one of the four fast-days set aside in the Jewish calendar to mourn the destruction of the Temple.

This day marks the beginning of the siege of Jerusalem by the Babylonians in 587 BCE. The siege ended over 18 months later on the 17th of Tamuz, when the walls of the city were finally breached and the Babylonian army completed their conquest.

And in the ninth year of his reign, in the tenth month, on the tenth day, Nebuchadnezzar, king of Babylon, and all his army came to Jerusalem, and he camped there and built a fort about it. And the city remained under siege until the eleventh year of King Zedekiah.

(II Kings 25: 1-2)

Although it is a day of mourning, we hope that it will eventually become a day of celebration in accordance with Zechariah's prophesy:

Thus said the Lord: the fast of the fourth month, the fast of the sixth month, the fast of the seventh month, and the fast of the tenth month shall be transformed for the House of Judah to joy and gladness and good times.

(Zechariah 8:19)

"General Day of Kaddish"

The Chief Rabbinate of Israel established this day as a *"General Day of Kaddish"* for the remembrance of the six million Jews who were exterminated in the Holocaust. As the date of their individual deaths is unknown, this date has become the day for saying Kaddish for all of them.

Do not confuse this day with *"The Day of the Holocaust and of Valour"* which commemorates the valour of the Jews in Warsaw's Ghetto who fought the Nazis during the Second World War.

Its laws and customs

Mourning

On this day we mourn as our Sages did:

By the rivers of Babylon, there we sat down and wept when we remembered Jerusalem.

(Psalms 137:1)

על נהרות בבל, שם ישבנו גם בכינו בזכרנו את ציון

A *Hashkabah* (memorial prayer) is recited, memorial candles are lit and *Mishnayot* are studied in memory of the Jews killed by the Nazis.

Features

1) Shacharit:

During the repetition of the Amidah, the hazan says a special prayer:

Answer us...   .עננו ה' ביום צום תעניתנו

This prayer finishes with:

Blessed are you O Lord who answers His people Israel at times of distress"

ברוך אתה ה' העונה לעמו ישראל בעת צרה

This benediction is also said by the worshippers during Mincha.

2) Torah reading:

i) The Torah is read both at Shacharit and Mincha.

ii) Three persons are called up to the Torah.

iii) The portion read describes how Moses beseeched God to forgive the Jewish people for the sin of the Golden Calf and how God finally forgave them.

iv) Tallit and tefillin are worn by some Sephardim during the afternoon service.

The Seventeenth of Tamuz   שבעה עשר בתמוז

The Fast of Tammuz

The Fast of Tamuz commemorates the breaching of the walls of Jerusalem after the siege of the city by the Babylonians in the 6th century BCE, leading to the destruction of the First Temple; and also the breaching of the walls of Jerusalem by the Romans in the 1st century CE, resulting in the fall of the Second Temple.

Through the earlier event took place on the 9th of Tamuz and the later one on the 17th of Tamuz, both are commemorated on the 17th of Tamuz because the scale of the second destruction was far greater.

Events that occurred on the Seventeenth of Tamuz

According to the Mishna (Tractate Ta'anit 4:6):

i) Moses broke the Tables of the Law when he descended from Mount Sinai and saw the nation worshipping the golden calf.

ii) The Korban Tamid (the weekly sacrifice), which took place every Monday while the Temple stood, ceased on that day during the siege of Jerusalem, when it became impossible to bring in lambs for the sacrifice.

iii) An idol was set up in the Temple during the time of King Menashe of Judah (First Temple).

The Three Weeks of Calamity ימי בין המצרים

The three weeks שלשת השבועות

The three weeks between the 17th of Tamuz and the 9th of Av are called Bein HaMetzarim (in the midst of the straits) - weeks of past calamity and potential calamity in the future.

Roman armies broke through the walls of Jerusalem on the 17th of Tamuz of the year 70 CE. During the three weeks that followed, fierce hand-to-hand fighting took place between Jews and Romans as the Jews were gradually driven back towards the Temple itself, which fell on the 9th of Av.

Because of this, we observe a period of partial mourning from 17th Tammuz onwards. During this time the following are forbidden:

i) cutting one's hair

ii) shaving

iii) listening to music, singing, dancing, playing music

iv) wearing new garments

v) getting married

Some communities delay implementing these restrictions until the 1st of Av.

"The Nine Days" תשעת הימים

The period called 'the nine days' spans between 1st and the 9th of Av.

On these days additional mourning customs are observed:

i) one stops eating meat and drinking wine,

ii) it is forbidden to swim for pleasure or

iii) to visit places of entertainment.

Some Sephardim do eat meat on the day of Rosh Chodesh Av itself. Other congregations begin not eating meat and not drinking wine only in *shabua shehal bo* (the week in which Tisha Be'Av falls): then, meat is not eaten until the afternoon of the 10th of Av.

"The Three Shabbatot of Troubles" שלוש שבתות הפרענות

The three Shabbatot that occur during the "Three Weeks" of troubles are called the "Shabbatot of Troubles".

Their name refers to the the fact that, on each of them, we read a Haphtarah in which the prophet warns the people of Israel of the impending destruction.

The three Haphtarot, sometimes called *'Shelosha depuranuta'*, are sung by Spanish and Portuguese Congregations in a specially sad melody and not in the usual chant. These Haphtarot also contain some sentences of "comfort" which are always chanted in the normal melody.

In some Sephardi communities, these Haphtarot may only be recited by an adult.

"The Shabbat of the Prophecy" שבת חזון

The third of these three Shabbatot is called the Shabbat of the Prophecy, *Shabbat Hazon*. It is also called Shabbat Eiha by some Sephardi Jews.

On this Shabbat, we read from *Isaiah 1* the portion which warns of imminent destruction. This Haphtarah begins with the words:

The prophecy of Isaiah son of Amoz, which he prophesied on Judah and Jerusalem.

Some read it in the chant used for the Book of Lamentations.

Its customs

It is the custom for a small child to drink the wine at the Havdalah ceremony after Shabbat Hazon (instead of an adult), as drinking wine is a symbol of joy.

In some Sephardi communities the hazan chants the Shabbat melodies in a special *makam* (musical mode) to reflect the sadness of the 9th of Av when the Temple was destroyed.

Tisha Be-Av   תשעה באב

Its significance

Tisha be-Av is the date on which both Temples were destroyed and when many other tragedies occurred in Jewish history.

The Temple had stood in Jerusalem with only one interruption of about seventy years (after the First Temple was destroyed) since the days of King Solomon, a thousand years before. For Jews it had become the centre of their national identity, the focus of their faith. God's presence had hovered in the Sanctuary - a bare room considered so sacred that entry was restricted to the High Priest, and then only once a year at the climax of the service on Kippur.

The Mishnah tells of ten miracles that took place in the Temple every day:

...the rain did not put out the fire on the altar, the wind did not move the vertical column of smoke ... when the people stood they were crowded together but when they bowed they had ample room ...

The destruction of the Temple was a catastrophe - a disaster so keenly felt that, almost two thousand years later, we still observe a fast on each anniversary.

The words of Psalm 137 movingly describe the Jewish feeling of loss for Jerusalem and its Temple:

If I forget you, O Jerusalem, let my right hand wither!
Let my tongue cleave to the roof of my mouth,
if I do not remember you,
if I do not set Jerusalem
above my highest joy!

אם אשכחך ירושלים תשכח ימיני תדבק לשוני,

לחכי אם לא אזכרכי

אם לא אעלה את ירושלים על ראש שמחתי

Several other tragic events also took place on Tisha be-Av:

1) The twelve spies sent by Moses to spy out the Land of Israel returned with the report that the Land was exceedingly fruitful, but that its inhabitants were giants who could not be defeated. Upon hearing this, the nation wept. Our sages tells us that God proclaimed that on that day, when the nation wept for nothing, they would be given reason to weep in the years

to come. On that day, too, God decreed that the generation which had left Egypt would die in the desert, after 40 years of wandering, and that only the next generation would enter the Land of Israel.

2) Jerusalem was ploughed under by the Roman conquerors in 132 CE.

3) The fortress of Betar, the last stronghold of the Bar-Kokhba revolt, fell on this day in 135 CE, 65 years after the destruction of the Second Temple. There Bar-Kokhba breathed his last, and the revolt was finally suppressed.

4) In 1290 CE, the expulsion of the Jews from England took place.

5) In 1492 CE, the expulsion of the Jews from Spain took place.

Tisha be-Av is one of the four days on which we mourn and fast in memory of the tragedies suffered by us in the past. The other three are the Fast of Tebet (10th Tebet), the Fast of Tammuz (17th Tamuz) and the Fast of Gedaliah (3rd Tishri). Tisha be-Av is the most important of these fast, ranking only after Kippur in its significance.

Though Tisha be-Av is a sad day, its prayers also express a strong element of hope. Jews look forward to a glorious Messianic Age when, according to the tradition, the Temple will be rebuilt and the 9th of Av will become a day of rejoicing.

Its date

As its name indicates, Tisha be-Av is commemorated on the 9th of Av.

The burning of the Second Temple began on the Ninth of Av and continued until the Tenth of Av. Therefore, some communities also continue mourning (but not fasting) on 10th of Av as well.

The destruction of the First Temple

And it came to pass in the ninth year of his reign, on the tenth day of the tenth month, Nebuchadnezzar King of Babylon and his army camped around Jerusalem, building a wall to surround the city. Jerusalem remained under siege until the twelfth year of the reign of Zedakiah. In the month of Tammuz, famine gripped the city, and the city's walls were breached ...

(Kings II 25: 1-4)

The First Temple was built on Mount Moriah by King Solomon, in the glorious period of the Kingdom of Israel in the latter half of the tenth century BCE. It became the religious and national centre of the Kingdom of Israel.

During the first Temple period, the kingdom split into two: the Kingdom of Judah and the Kingdom of Israel. The two kingdoms steadily declined, both morally and religiously. Then, according to the prophets, Nebuchadnezzar was sent as the messenger of God to punish the Jewish people for their lapses.

The siege of Jerusalem began on the 10th of Tebet in 589 BCE. It lasted two and a half years until the 9th of Tamuz, when the walls of the city were breached. On the 9th of Av, in the afternoon, Babylonian soldiers burned the Holy Temple.

The second destruction

In 537 BCE, the Babylonian empire fell to the Persians. Then, the Persian king Cyrus allowed the return of the exiles from Judah to their Land and the rebuilding of their Holy Temple. The first Return to Zion began under Ezra and Nechemiah. Only some members of the tribes of Judah and Benjamin went back to the Land: other members remained behind in Babylon. The other ten tribes disappeared from history, some probably merging with those who chose to stay behind in the Persian empire.

The building of the Second Temple was finished in 525 BCE; but it was considerably extended and embellished during the next 500 years, especially by King Herod The Great. Jerusalem and its Temple enjoyed periods of success and misery, independence and foreign rule, until the Temple was destroyed in the year 70 CE.

The Temple was destroyed after the Jews revolted against the Romans and refused to offer sacrifices in honour of the Caesar. In 69 CE the Roman commander Titus placed Jerusalem under siege. On the 17th of Tammuz, the walls were breached, and the Roman soldiers poured in. The Jewish defenders barricaded themselves in the Temple and held out for three weeks. On the 9th of Av, the Romans broke through to the Temple and burned it to the ground. This was the beginning of the long and bitter exile that lasted for almost two thousand years.

Its laws and customs

Fasting
On the Ninth of Av, as on all the four days of mourning in our calendar, we abstain from food and drink. The fast lasts for 25 hours, from the sunset of the day before until dark on the 9th of Av).

The other three fasts (Tebet, Tamuz and Gedaliah) last only from dawn to sunset on the actual day of the fast.

Other prohibitions

i) One does not bathe

ii) One does not use perfumes.

iii) Sexual relations are forbidden

Concluding meal

Though customs vary from place to place, the Seudah hamafseket basically consists of a cooked meal, followed by a hard boiled egg (one dish only).

In some Sephardi communities, a cooked dish of lentils and hard-boiled eggs is eaten.

It is traditional to eat the meal alone, in a low chair or on the ground. If three men are present, they sit separately and each one recites the *Birkat Hamazon* for himself (not with *Zimun)*. Some eat at the table.

Reading of the Book of Lamentations מגלת איכה

After evening prayers, the *Book of Lamentations* (one of the five "scrolls" in the Bible), is read in the synagogues by candlelight. The worshippers sit on the ground.

The book begins with the words:

How does the city that was full of people (Jerusalem) sit solitary; how has she become desolate, like a widow?

The book ends with words of hope:

Return us to you, O Lord, and we shall return. Renew our days as of old.

According to tradition, the author of the *Book of Lamentations* was Jeremiah, the prophet, who had warned the nation of the coming destruction.

Reading of Kinot קינות

On the 9th of Av we recite *"Kinot"*, which are poems describing the calamities and tragedies that have befallen the Jewish people throughout its history. Some of them were written in remembrance of entire communities massacred in the Middle Ages, others refer to the more recent Holocaust.

Some Sephardi congregations have the Kinot (*Kol Tehina* by R. Abraham Ancoua) printed in their special prayer book for the fast-days. The last poems read are those of Rabbi Yehuda Halevi (one of the greatest Hebrew poets of Spain, 1080-1140), which include words of comfort and hope for the coming redemption.

Most Sephardi communities chant a special *kina* called *Aleikhem eida kedosha eshal mikem she'eilot* which is similar to the Four Questions of the Haggadah. According to the tradition, when Tisha be-Av and Pesach fall on the same day of the week, this special *kina* shows the connection between the two. A similar *kina* is also recited in the morning service of Tisha be-Av, entitled *Madua beyom zeh*. Some Sephardim recite a special Mah Nishtanah that also shows the connection between the two commemorations.

The Book of Job is read.

In the Synagogue

Custom differ between community and community. Here, we describe the customs of the Sephardi and Portuguese synagogues of London.

On 9th Av, the lighting is kept low and a black curtain covers the *echal* (ark).

The Torah, covered in a black cloak, is read from a table, also covered in black, and not from the teba.

In order to show the confusion and sadness we feel on this day, Sephardi congregations do things in a way opposite to the normal. For example:

i) the Torah, is read using a black wooden *yad* (pointer) in place of the usual silver one, or sometimes without using the *yad* at all,

ii) there is no *levantar* (raising of the Torah before it is read),

iii) individuals are not called to the Torah by name

iv) the normal salutations of *Hashem imahem* and *Yebarekhekha Hashem* are not said, when approaching the Torah.

v) people do not sit in their usual seats; they sit on the floor when reciting the *Kinot*.

Number of years since the destruction

In synagogue, the hazan announces the number of years since the destruction of the Temple. The number is calculated by subtracting 68 (in gematria 68 = hayyim, which means life) from the current year in the secular calendar.

Tallit and Tefillin

Tallit and tefillin are not worn on Tisha be-Av.

However, in some Sephardi communities men do put on the tallit and tefillin at home in private (with the beracha) on the morning of Tisha be-Av.

People do not greet one another.

The Western Wall

In Israel, on the eve of the 9th of Av and during the day, thousands of Jews congregate at the Western Wall, the only surviving remnant of the Temple. At the Wall, they sit on the ground, read the Book of Lamentations and mourn the destruction.

Customs

1) Abstain from work

In some Sephardi communities people abstain from working on Tisha be-Av because it is felt that little will be gained from the day's toil. There is a popular saying: *Kaspei heikha vekhaspei mi kamokha ein bahem siman berakha.*

2) Honouring the dead:

It was traditional in some Sephardi congregations to designate the day of Tisha be-Av as a day for honouring dead relatives. Many therefore visit the cemeteries and make hashkaba (the memorial prayer for the dead).

3) Sleep on mattress:

On the night of Tisha be-Av, it is the custom in some Sephardi communities, to sleep on a mattress spread out on the floor and to put a small stone under the pillow as a sing of mourning.

4) Breaking the fast:

> The fast finishes one hour after sunset but the mourning period continues until midday on 10th Av because the ruins of the Temple continued to smoulder until them.

Prayer and Ritual

Tefillah   תפילה

Introduction to Tefillah (Prayer)

Prayer is the most important method of communicating with God. It therefore plays a significant role in the spiritual life of the Jew.

There are two types of prayer.

Spontaneous Prayer

The spontaneous cry to God is often a plea for help or an expression of gratitude or wonder. The words are formed by the person praying; and they can, of course, be in any language. Spontaneous prayers may be said at any time and as often as we wish.

Formulated Prayer

This type of prayer has a fixed form of words, which are usually taken from the Bible (e.g. the Shema, שמע) or composed by the Rabbis (e.g. the Amidah, עמידה). Although prayer must be a personal expression uttered *"with all our heart"* (the Shema), our Sages did nevertheless institute forms of prayer to be followed by Jews.

These are generally to be said at fixed times (e.g. Shacharit must be said in the morning), or on specific occasions (e.g. the blessing bore peri ha'etz בורא פרי העץ, is pronounced before eating fruit grown on trees). Most of these prayers, too, may be said in any language.

Nusach - Prayer Rite - נוסח

A Nusach is the particular order of prayers adopted by a Jewish community and incorporated in their Siddur (prayer book). One Nusach will differ from another in the order of the prayers, in the particular prayers included and in the actual wording of those prayers that do not come directly from the Bible.

Thus Sephardim say *"Baruch Sheamar"* ברוך שאמר later in the service than do Ashkenazim. The weekday Amidah, varies considerably between Ashkenazim and Sephardim. However, any direct quotation from the Tanach, such as the Shema, is obviously the same in all Nushaot.

The most ancient Siddur we know was prepared specially by Amram Gaon (the head of the yeshiva of Sura in Babylon in the 9th century), for the Jews of Spain. About 100 years later, Sa'adia Gaon (head of the same yeshiva) prepared a Siddur for the Jews of Arab countries. Later, other prayer books were compiled by many rabbis, including Maimonides and Simcha Vitri.

The principal rites in use today are:

The Sephardi Siddur (used by the Spanish and Portuguese Synagogue).

The Nusach Sepharad (used by Hasidim).

The Nusach Ashkenaz: (used by all other Ashkenazim).

Reform and Liberal Jews have their own prayer books, which include new prayers and omit those they consider irrelevant today.

For convenience, the prayer book of our own Spanish and Portuguese Congregation is divided into the following six volumes:

Daily and Occasional – including Shabbat and prayers for various special occasions.

Pesach פסח

Sukkot and Shavuot סוכות ושבועות

Rosh Hashanah ראש השנה

Kippur כיפור

Ta'aniot – fasts other than Kippur תעניות.

The three daily services

We read in Psalms: (IV, 17)

Evening, morning and noon will I pray

We are taught (Berachot 27b) that:

The (three daily) prayers were instituted by the Patriarchs

and that Abraham instituted the Shacharit, Isaac the Mincha and Jacob the Arbit.

Jewish worship had once been focused on the Temple in Jerusalem, where sacrifices were offered to God in a fixed order.

After the destruction of the Temple, when it was no longer possible to offer sacrifices, our Sages established daily services for the recitation of prayers. The prayer services correspond to the original sacrificial services of the Temple and were intended as substitutes for them.

The three daily services are as follows:

    i) Shacharit שחרית - the morning service, corresponding to the dawn sacrifice.

    ii) Mincha מנחה – the afternoon service.

    iii) Arbit ערבית – the evening service.

On Shabbat, Festivals and High Holy Days there is an additional service Musaph מוסף, which corresponds to *the Additional Sacrifice, Korban Musaph* קורבן מוסף, offered in the Temple on these special days.

On Yom Kippur, a Concluding Service, the Ne'ilah נעילה, is said just before the end of the fast.

The Synagogue

The Minyan מנין

In the multitude of people is the king's glory

(Prov. xix, 28)

Whenever we can, we must try to pray בציבור, with a congregation.

Minyan, in this context, is best translated as "quorum" and refers to the minimum number of people required to form a congregation for the recital of public prayers.

According to the Talmud, a minyan consists of ten Jewish males of bar mitzvah age or over. It is based on the verse: *"How long this evil congregation"* (Numbers 16:21), referring to the ten spies sent by Moses to the Promised Land who came back and reported that it was inhabited by giants who could not be defeated.

A full congregational prayer service cannot take place in the absence of a minyan. That means that certain prayers have to be omitted and there can be no public reading of the Torah.

Separation of Men and Women

Men and women must pray separately in the synagogue. This is to remind us that we are not at a social event but in a house of prayer, where we must concentrate and pray with kavanah כוונה (maximum devotion).

This separation is achieved by building a ladies gallery in the synagogue or, when everyone is seated on the same level, by installing a Mechitzah מחיצה (dividing screen) between the men and the women.

Direction of Prayer הכתל המערבי

When a Jew says the Amidah, whether in synagogue or not, he faces towards Jerusalem: in this country, that means facing east מזרח. That is why the ark is housed on the corresponding wall, so that we may also face the scrolls of the Torah contained within it when we turn towards Jerusalem in prayer.

There are further opportunities for facing Jerusalem in prayer, such as when reciting the Kedushah קדושה and the Barechu ברכו.

The Rabbi הרב

The Rabbi's function should be primarily educational, teaching and guiding his congregation in matters of Halacha (Jewish Law). In some English speaking countries this position is held by someone without a rabbinic diploma, called a Minister: many of his duties are similar to those of a rabbi.

Haham חכם, is an alternative name for the rabbi.

The Hazan (Reader or Cantor) החזן

The primary function of the Hazan is to read the services. He also may be given other titles such as Sheliah Tsibbur שליח ציבור, Representative of the Congregation, or Baal Tefillah בעל תפילה, Master of Prayer. These titles may also be used to describe a lay leader of the services.

The Shamash (Beadle) השמש

The Shamash assists in all the duties required to run the synagogue and its services - including the provision of tallit, tefillin and prayer books, collecting charity and all other tasks connected with looking after the synagogue and the worshippers.

The Parnas (Warden) גבאי

It is the duty of the Parnas (the Gabbai in Ashkenazi synagogues) to direct the conduct of the services, and he is said to "preside" over them. In the Spanish and Portuguese Synagogue, the Parnas is usually a member of the Mahamad, which is the elected executive committee of the Board of Elders, responsible to the members for the running of the affairs of the Congregation.

The Siddur in more detail

The main division of the siddur for weekdays, Shabbat and festivals is as follows:

a) weekdays

Each of the services on weekdays can be subdivided further:

Shacharit

Section	Translation	From
Birhot Ha'shahar ברכות השחר	Morning Blessings	Start of Shacharit
Zemirot זמירות	Verses of Song	"Baruch She- amar" "Hodu"
Keriat Shema Uvirhoteha קריאת שמע וברכותיה	The Reading of the Shema and its Blessings	"Baruch"
Amidah עמידה		

The Following sections are included on some days but not on others:

Section	Translation	From
Selichot סליחות (fasts except 9 Av)		(Selichot prior ro Rosh Hashanah are said before Shacharit).
Tahanun תחנון (omitted mainly on festive occasions)	Supplications	Mon.&Thu. אל מלך יושב Sun, Tue, Wed, & Fri. ויברך דוד
Hallel (certain festivals)	Praise	
Keriat Hatorah קריאת התורה (Mon, Thur, fasts, Chanukah & Purim - 3; Rosh Chodesh and Hol Ha'Moed - 4)	Torah Reading	"Vayhi" + "H immash"
Conclusion		"Ashre"

Mincha

Keriat Ha'Torah (only on fasts)

Amidah

Tahanun

Psalm

Alenu

Arbit

Keriat Shema Ubirhoteha

Amidah

Yehi Shem

Shir Lama'alot

Alenu

b) Sabbath and festivals

This splits up into the following parts:

Kabbalat Shabbat

Arbit

Shacharit

Keri'at Ha'torah

Musaph

Mincha

Rules for Keri'at Ha'torah

On Shabbat, 7 men and the Maftir are called to the reading of the Torah. First comes a Cohen and then a Levi, acknowledging the historical role of the priests and Levites in Judaism. Some men, usually a rabbi or a bar mitzvah, will read their own portions for themselves: others will have the portion read out for them.

The portion Maftir is usually a repetition of the last few verses of the Parasha; but on special Shabbatot and on Yom Tov, the Maftir is a separate reading from the second Sepher Torah.

The person called for Maftir will himself read the Haftarah after

the conclusion of the readings from the Sepher

The Haftarah for the day is taken from one of the books of the Prophets (second part of Tanach). On most Shabbatot it is connected to the subject matter of the Parasha but on a special occasion it will reflect an aspect of that occasion

At Mincha on Shabbat and on the following Monday and Thursday mornings, the first part of the following week's Parasha is read to 3 men.

At Mincha on Fasts, 3 men are called to the Sepher and the 3rd reads the Haftarah.

On Yom Tov (except for Kippur), 5 + the Maftir are called to the Sepher.

On Yom Kippur, 6 men + the Maftir are called.

A Haftarah is read on the mornings of Shabbat, Yom Tov, Rosh Hashanah, Kippur and Tisha beAv.

A Haftarah is read on the afternoons of all fasts.

Rules for Musaph

Musaph is recited on Shabbat, Rosh Chodesh, Kippur, Rosh Hashanah, Yom Tov and Hol Hamoed.

Rules for Hallel

Hallel is chanted on:

Rosh Chodesh,

Pesach, Shavuot and Sukkot, including Hol Hamoed,

Chanukah,

Yom Ha'atsmaut,

Yom Yerushalayim.

The Shema שמע

Introduction

The Shema is not really a prayer at all, in the sense of asking God to satisfy our needs, but is rather a declaration of the fundamental principles of Jewish belief.

By reciting the Shema, we affirm our belief in God as the supreme ruler of the universe, our awareness of our duties towards him and the principle of reward and punishment.

The recitation of the Shema formed a part of the daily service in the Temple and it was taken over by the synagogue when the Temple ceased to exist.

The Shema consists of three separate paragraphs from the Torah:

i) Paragraph 1 Deut. 6: 4-9
ii) Paragraph 2 Deut. 2: 13-21
iii) Paragraph 3 Numbers 15: 37-41

The very words of the Shema instruct us when it should be recited:

And you shall speak of them ... when you lie down and when you rise up

ודברת בם ... ובשכבך ובקומך

This is interpreted by the Oral Law to mean in the morning and again in the evening.

The three letters that form the word Shema can also be taken as confirming that view:

Shin .. שחרית....Shacharit

Mem מ יטה Mita (before going to bed)

Ayin ערבית Arbit

The word Shema is given another profound and mystical meaning. The letters that make up the word - Shin, Mem and Ayin - are an acronym for the expression "Lift up your eyes on high" שאו מרום עינים and they also stand for "To the Almighty, Supreme King" שדי

מלך עליון. This helps show us that we should look to God for guidance and protection throughout our lives. He is supreme, and only he has the power to help us.

The first paragraph

The first verse of the Shema

Hear (this) Israel, the Lord is our God, the Lord is one

שמע ישראל ה' אלקינו ה' אחד

is the supreme statement of our belief in monotheism. There is only one God, the creator of heaven and earth. These are the first Hebrew words taught to young children, even before they are able to read; and they are very often the last words uttered by a person just before the moment of death. It is customary to close one's eyes, or to cover them with the tallit, in order to achieve the utmost concentration when saying this verse during prayers.

The next line, *Baruch Shem* ברוך שם, expressing our adoration of the wonder and power of God, is the only one not taken directly from the *Tanach* (Bible). It is said quietly, in an undertone.

There is a story that when Moses went up to receive the Torah from God on Mount Sinai, he heard an angel singing this prayer to God. He thought it so beautiful that he wanted to take it back to earth for the Jewish people to enjoy. The angels objected saying that the Jewish people were not angels, so how could they say this prayer? Therefore Moses made a promise to the angels, that when we say Baruch Shem, we will say it quietly.

There is only one time we say Baruch Shem aloud and that is on Yom Kippur, when we do not eat. For one day we concentrate on our spirit rather than our body; so perhaps then we are almost like the angels who always recite Baruch Shem in a loud voice.

The first paragraph contains seven Mitzvot:

1) To know and affirm the unity of God.
How did Abraham discover God when his father and all the people around him worshipped idols? Do idols have any power? Can worshipping stone statues offer us protection and guidance?

2) To love God.
We must do more than simply to believe in God; we must also love him for his gifts to us. Even if things do not always turn out in the way we want, we must realise that God's purpose is ultimately for the good.

Has anything ever happened to you that at first appeared to be bad but eventually turned out to be a good thing?

3) To learn God's commandments and to teach them to our children.

By learning the Torah we constantly see the greatness of God and reaffirm our belief in him. By teaching Torah, we pass this knowledge on to others, and so pass on the gift of our heritage.

What happens if we do not learn and teach Torah? Our heritage become forgotten, leading to assimilation.

4) To recite the Shema twice every day.

Twice a day we re-affirm our belief in God. No matter what is happening to us - whether we are happy, sad or frightened - we still believe in him. We still love God and know that all good things come from him. Only he can help us through bad times.

5) To put Tefillin on one's arm, opposite the heart.

Both boxes of the Tefillin contain written words of the Shema. In ancient days, people believed that we love with our heart; so putting Tefillin on the arm is a powerful symbol of our love for God.

6) To put Tefillin on one's head.

Through logical thought we conclude that God is the one true God. Wearing Tefillin on the head shows that we believe in God with our intellect.

7) To fix a Mezuzah מזוזה (containing the words of the Shema) on one's doorposts.

The origin of a Mezuzah comes from the time when the Jewish people in Egypt put the blood of the Korban Pesach on their doors. By smearing the blood on the doorpost, Bnei Yisrael demonstrated their faith that God would offer them complete protection. Even today, putting a Mezuzah on our door is an outward and open sign that we are Jewish and have faith in God.

EXERCISES

Discussion topic

The concept of *Emunah* אמונה (belief in God)

Suggested drama sketches for some of the seven mitzvot

Abraham in his father's idol shop. How he proved to his father that they were worthless and that only God has power.

Something that at first appears to be bad turns out to be good. Your friends refuse to go out with you on Sunday - it turns out they planned a surprise party to you. You are the only one of all your friends who is not going on holiday; you think you will have to spend a boring, lonely summer at home when you suddenly received a letter from an aunt in Florida inviting you to Disneyland.

You meet a new child at school who turns out to be Jewish but does not know anything about what that means and you are able to teach him all about it.

You wake up in the morning worried about a big test at school. You have not prepared properly and you are going to fail. You say the Shema, believing that God will help you. In school you discover the test has been postponed until the following week. However, a good friend was run over by a car that morning and is in hospital. That night, saying Shema, you are grateful for the test but sad and worried about your friend; but you have faith that God will help. The following morning you are awakened by the phone. It is your friend calling to say that she is getting better and will be out of hospital in a week. You say Shema feeling relieved and happy.

Conversation in Egypt between father and son. The son is concerned about what will happen when the Egyptians see lamb's blood on the doorpost. The father explains that nothing will happen to them for God had commanded them to do it.

The second paragraph

The second paragraph of the Shema teaches us to submit to the Divine; and also teaches us the concept of reward and punishment in an agricultural and national context.

If you observe my commandments with diligence ... I will send the rain for your land in due season ... and you shall eat and be satisfied.

Neglect of God's commandments, on the other hand, will lead to disaster.

He will shut up the heavens, that there will be no rain ... and you shall perish quickly off the good land which the Lord has given you.

The paragraph continues by repeating the obligations to love God, to teach children and to make physical display of "these words" so that

Your days and the days of your children may be as long as the days of the heavens above the earth, in the land which the Lord promised to your ancestors.

EXERCISES

Introduce the concept of *Bechira* בחירה - choice

The Torah tells us what we should and should not do; but we have the choice to do good or bad. People cannot be rewarded for doing something good when they have no choice. The challenge is to know what is good and what is bad and to decide which one to choose. It may be harder to choose good but the reward will be much greater.

Give the class situations to think about and discuss. For example: You have a test for which neither you or anyone in the class has prepared. Everyone else has decided to cheat in order to get a good mark.

Do you cheat like the rest of the class; after all everyone is doing it, you will not be the only one.

Do you take the test honestly knowing that you are the only one in the class who is going to fail and will get into trouble with the teacher.

Tell the teacher that the whole class has cheated, knowing you will get them into trouble and that they will probably be very angry with you?

Announce to the class that you are going to take the test honestly and are brave enough to fail and take the consequences. Are they such cowards that they have to cheat.

Tell the teacher in advance that you did not learn and warn her in advance that you probably won't do well.

Any other suggestions?

A great aunt of yours is ill in hospital and your mother wants you to go and visit her in hospital on Sunday afternoon. However, she is old and you do not find her that interesting to talk to. Furthermore, your friends have invited you to go to the cinema with them in the afternoon.

Do you listen to your mother and go to visit your great aunt?

Do you go with your friends to the cinema?

Any other suggestions.

Introduce the concept of community

The second paragraph of the Shema is mostly written in the plural to indicate that it is preferable to perform Mitzvot communally rather that privately. Why? As a community we show God our unity. We have more strength when we are all together - if there are some great people in the community, their merits benefit everyone. In general, you do things better if you have good examples to copy. For example if you play football with much better players, you try hard since you don't want to be seen as a bad player.

The third paragraph

The third and last paragraph of the Shema contains the commandment to wear fringes on the corners of our garments as a constant reminder of God's words

...that you may look upon them and remember all the commandments of the Lord, AND DO THEM

The Tzitzit ציצית symbolise the number 613; and so wearing them reminds us of the 613 Mitzvot we are commanded to keep.

> One of the threads of the Tzitzit (*Petil Tehelet*) used to be blue, as commanded in the Torah. These days we substitute a white thread, as we no longer know how to make the dye that gives the correct shade of blue. (The colour blue is to remind us of heaven).

The Shema ends with a final reminder of the covenant made with the Jewish people when God redeemed them from a life of slavery in Egypt.

I am the Lord your God who brought

You out of the land of Egypt to be

Your God: I am the Lord your God

EXERCISE

Craft activity

Teach children how to knot the Tzitzit. This can be done using string tied round a square piece of cardboard.

The Amidah   עמידה

Introduction

The Amidah is the core of each of the three daily services in the synagogue (or home) and was adopted to replace the sacrifices once offered in the Temple.

> Thus the synagogue services - Shacharit, (Musaph on Shabbat and Holydays), Mincha and Arbit - are each timed to take place when sacrifices were offered in the Temple.

> The prayer is of great antiquity. Parts are said to have been compiled by Ezra and the Men of the Great Assembly about 400 B.C.E.; and the prayer reached its final form in about 100 C.E.

The prayer is known as the Amidah (standing) עמידה because it is always said standing. It is so important that, for centuries, it was simply known as Ha-Tefillah (The Prayer) התפילה.

It is also called the Shemoneh-Eshreh (Eighteen) שמונה עשרה because it once consisted of 18 blessings, even though it now contains nineteen. (On Shabbat it is reduced to 7 blessings).

Approaching the Amidah

Ask the children to imagine that you are granted an audience with the Queen and can ask for anything you want. A lady-in-waiting opens huge double doors and shows you into the throne room. This has a marble floor with expensive rugs, huge chandeliers, and the walls are adorned with paintings. At the far end of the room sits the Queen on her throne wearing the crown and regal dress, just waiting to listen to you.

Would you grab the nearest chair, lounge across it and say: "Hi! I'd like a new computer, a new bike and a trip to New York" and then get up and wander around the throne room ignoring the Queen?

> Ask for a reaction from the children. Then ask "How would you approach her? How would you act? What would you say? What would you ask for?"

You would probably walk in slowly, with great respect. Then you would bow, stand to attention and speak very politely, asking only really important requests.

Do you realise we get such an opportunity every day, not just once but three times and that our audience is with someone even higher than the Queen - it is with God himself? Three times every day we approach God who is waiting to listen and answer our requests. To make it even easier for us, what we really need is already written out in a special prayer so that we know exactly what to ask for. This prayer is called the Amidah from the Hebrew word *Amed* meaning to stand. We stand in front of God, the King of Kings, and present him with our requests set out in 19 separate benedictions.

Ask the children to imagine the scene in the throne room once again. How should you present this special prayer to God? How would you approach him? How would you begin your prayer?

Ask for suggestions.

The Amidah is recited with the utmost concentration and devotion: no interruption is permitted until the prayer has been completed. We stand, with feet together, facing the site of the Temple in Jerusalem.

We begin by taking three steps backwards and then three steps forwards, to show that, as we approach God, we remain in awe of him. We bless God, our King, bow and then stand up straight with our feet together.

Before the last verse of the prayer, we take three steps backwards - withdrawing, as it were, from the Divine presence.

The Amidah is not a random collection of verses but is carefully organised.

i) The first 3 verses are blessings of praise to God. No requests are included.

ii) The following 13 verses consist of petitions of various kinds.

On Shabbat, these are reduced to a single verse expressing appreciation of the joys of Shabbat.

iii) The final 3 verses are considered as expressions of thanks to God.

The first three blessings

אבות (Avot - Patriarchs)

This refers to our forefathers, and of God's promise of blessings to their descendants (i.e. to us).

God is adored as the God of the Patriarchs Abraham, Isaac and Jacob. Even if we are unworthy, we express the hope that God will bring redemption to us because of the merits of our forefathers (זכות אבות).

גבורות (Gevurot - Mighty Deeds)
This refers to the power of God.

God is adored as the Supreme Power of the universe, the God of Nature, who *'sustains the living with loving-kindness, resurrects the dead, supports the fallen, heals the sick, frees the captives and keeps faith with those who sleep in the dust'*.

Who are those who 'sleep in the dust'?

קדושה (Kedusha - Holiness)
This, proclaiming the holiness of God, is said only during the repetition of the עמידה in synagogue. The קדושה is said aloud by the congregation and the שליח ציבור (the Reader) to show its importance.

The Kedusha starts with the words said to be uttered daily by the angels who minister to the Divine Presence.

Holy, holy, holy is the Lords of Hosts

Why do you think we need to tell God how powerful and holy he is? Doesn't he know? Does he need us to tell him?

Imagine your audience with the Queen. Would you start immediately by asking for what you want? You would start off by addressing her as "Your Majesty" and talk of her greatness. Traditionally, such language is used to kings and queens to show respect; we show equal respect to God.

The middle verses
(replaced by a single verse on Shabbat)

The next 13 benedictions form the second section of the Amidah, in which we ask for what we need most - things which affect every aspect of our lives. Jews are commanded to pray in groups rather than alone. These prayers address God in the plural; "Please give us" not "Please give me".

Why do you think we speak in the plural when we are saying the prayer quietly, by ourselves?

To show that we consider all Jewish people to be one community, in which people help to look after each other.

בינה (Binah - Insight)

We pray for wisdom and understanding to enable us to choose between good and evil.

> Ask for examples from everyday life when we require "Binah"? If the children need help, suggest situations such as cheating in a test, or joining a friend in making fun of someone.

> Then ask for similar examples.

תשובה (Teshuvah - Repentance)

In this and in the next ברכה, we refer to God as "our father".
God is asked to cause us to repent and to draw near to his teaching.
We are confident that God will show the love and compassion of a father to his child when there is sincere תשובה.

סליחה (Selichah - Forgiveness)

We pray that God will forgive us and not punish us for past sins and transgressions.

גאולה (Ge'ulah - Redemption)

We pray that God will free us from all our afflictions (spiritual and physical) and redeem us from our sufferings; also that he will protect us from our enemies.

רפואה (Refu'ah - Healing)

We pray that God will send us a complete and speedy recovery from our illnesses. Here we may add the name of a person who is seriously ill.

> Do you know anyone at the moment who is not well? If so, you can pray for them in "Refuah".

ברכת השנים (Birkat ha-Shanim - Blessing of the Season)

We pray that God will bless the year's crops so that we will all have enough to eat.

Can you imagine how terrible it would be if there was not enough rain and the crops died; or so much rain that the fields flooded; or if insects ate all our crops? Famine is one of the most ancient scourges of mankind.

קיבוץ גלויות (Kibbuts Galuyot - Ingathering of the Exiles)

We pray that all בני ישראל will once again be brought together from all over the world to ארץ ישראל- the Land of Israel

Does anyone have family or friends in another country? Where do they live? Would you like us all to live together so we meet more often. More important, would it be good for all Jews to live together in their own country without enemies trying to harm them ?.

דין (Din - Justice)

We pray for honest and wise judges, as in former times (i.e. in our own country), who will rule with justice and wisdom to ensure that innocent people do not suffer and the guilty are punished.

ברכת המינים (Birkat ha-Minim - Against heretics)

According to one view, this ברכה was added later to the original eighteen prayers (שמונה עשרה). In this ברכה, we pray to God to teach ignorant Jews the right way to understand religion. We also ask God to save us from wicked Jews who try to harm the people of Israel.

צדיקים (Tsaddikim - The Righteous)

We pray that God will reward righteous people - those who are good to others and do not only think of themselves.

בנין ירושלים (Binyan Yerushalayim - Rebuilding Jerusalem)

We pray for the rebuilding of the holy city of Jerusalem.

Earlier, we prayed that all Jews will return to the land of Israel. We now pray that our holy city Jerusalem, which has been destroyed so many times, will be rebuilt and will stand for ever.

Have any of you been to Jerusalem? Where did you stay? Did you see houses and streets? Jerusalem is no longer a pile of rubble, but a modern city with buildings and paved roads. Why then do we still ask for it to be rebuilt? What do you think Binyan Yerushalayim is really asking God? We are asking for Jerusalem to be rebuilt completely - complete with the Bet Hamikdash, the Temple. When will that happen?

מלכות בית דוד (Malchut Bet David - The Kingdom of David)

We pray that God will restore the Royal House of David and hasten the coming of the Messiah משיח. In that ideal age all Jews will again live at peace in the Land of Israel, with the Temple rebuilt in Jerusalem. Then the whole world will be ruled in the spirit of righteousness, according to the will of God.

קבלת תפילה (Kabbalat Tefillah - Acceptance of Prayers)

We have now completed our list of petitions to God. Therefore, in this last ברכה of the second section of the עמידה we pray that God will listen to our תפילה and accept them favourably.

Personal petitions may be added by the worshipper at this point.

> Why don't we ask God for toys or luxuries like CD's? Why do we ask only for the basic things of life food and safety?

The last verses

These blessings are regarded, to some extent, as thanks for what we now have and for what we once had but lost because of our sins.

עבודה (Avodah - Service in the Temple)

Here, we remember with gratitude the service which took place in the Temple. Without the Temple we cannot perform the Avodah; instead we pray that God will restore the Temple and its worship.

הודאה (Hoda'ah - Thanksgivings)

We began the Amidah by praising God's greatness: then we asked him for what we need. In this beracha we thank God for all he has already given us, for his unfailing mercies and for the good he bestows on us each day.

> Can you give any examples of what we have to thank God for?

> What good things has God done for you? For your family? For the Jewish people as a whole?

שלום

We conclude the עמידה as we do the קדיש and ברכת המזון by praying that God will grant us peace and blessing. Only in times of peace can we serve God completely and live full and happy lives. In the repetition of the Amidah in synagogue, God is asked to bless us with the blessing with which the priests were commanded to bless the people:

May the Lord bless you and keep you.
May the Lord cause his face to shine upon you and be gracious to you.
May the Lord look kindly on you and give you peace.

After the last blessing of the Amidah we say the prayer, *Elohai Netsor* א' נצור, asking God to guard us from speaking evil and saying deceitful things. We pray that we shall behave humbly to everyone, including those who abuse us and that God will protect us against all evil people who rise up against us to plot our downfall.

After *Elohai Netsor* the '*Yehi Ratson*' יהי רצון is recited, consisting of another short prayer for the restoration of the Temple.

EXERCISES

Craft activity

Make a collage based on our requests to God in the Amidah and our gratitude to God for all the goodness he has given us.

Ask the class to bring in magazines and travel brochures, and find pictures to link the requests we make of God in the Amidah e.g. crops in a field, pictures of Jerusalem, Jewish people around the world, a judge in court, pictures of doctors or nurses, etc.

Kaddish קדיש

Introduction

The Kaddish is of ancient origin, and dates from before the destruction of the Temple.

The word 'Kaddish' is Aramaic (the everyday language spoken by most Jews of that time) for 'holy'; and the prayer is written in a mixture of Aramaic and Hebrew. It is both an expression of praise and glorification of God, and a messianic prayer calling for the speedy establishment of his kingdom on earth.

The Kaddish is a 'public' prayer and may only be recited in the presence of *minyan* מנין (ten males).

When Kaddish is recited

1) It was originally employed to conclude the regular public exposition of the Torah, which had become an established feature of Jewish life by the end of the first century B.C.E. This was done to demonstrate the belief that study of the Torah is not only an intellectual pursuit, but is also the beginning of knowledge that leads to the love and to the fear of God.

The Kaddish is still used, roughly in this manner, to mark the conclusion of certain sections of the synagogue service.

2) The Kaddish was first adopted by mourners as a prayer specially suited to their needs during the period of severe persecution of Jews in the thirteenth century (the Crusades). It is now the only public prayer recited by mourners.

It may, at first sight appear strange that these particular verses were chosen above all others as the mourner's prayer; for they contain no reference to death, or to the soul of the departed.

Its meaning

Man is obliged to praise his Creator at all times; but when he has just lost a loved one, and has the greatest temptation to doubt God, that act of praise has heightened significance. It then expresses resignation to the will of God and submission to his judgment, rather in the spirit of Job's declaration on the loss of his children: *'The Lord has given: the Lord has taken away: blessed be the name of the Lord'*. Man's longing for the coming of the messianic age, when God's Kingdom will be established on earth, is at its most intense at times of suffering; and the messianic aspect of the Kaddish therefore becomes specially appropriate at moments of acute personal distress.

Viewed in this light the Kaddish is an eloquent declaration of submission to God's decree, coupled with a plea for the early advent of the final redemption, when pain and suffering in the world will cease for ever.

The core of the Kaddish is considered to be the congregation's response to the mourner, יהא שמיה רבא מבדך *'Yehe sheme rabba mebarach* (May his great Name be blessed and glorified for ever and ever); and this is the key to a range of further meanings assigned to this ancient prayer. Jewish tradition holds that God rewards us for the good deeds of our parents, and indeed for those of our forefathers. In like manner therefore it is argued that parents can benefit after death from the merit of their children. Consequently the recital of the Kaddish by a mourner becomes particularly significant; for it is hoped that the deceased parent may thus be rewarded for the mourner's pious act of leading the congregation in prayer, and causing those present to bless and glorify God's great Name in their responses.

Mystical interpretations

Amongst the many mystical interpretations of this prayer, the one that has most captured the public's imagination, is again based on the great value attached to the congregation's response '*Yehe Sheme Rabba...*'. Kabbalists have gone so far as to maintain that the 'evil decree' is cancelled for those who make this response in a spirit of true devotion; and also that 'evil decrees' against the House of Israel as a whole are continually deferred from day to day because of the responses of its people.

According to Kabbalah, the souls of the departed are punished for their sins on earth for a period of up to twelve months after death; and the congregation's response in the Kaddish has the power of instantly lessening this suffering. Thus the recital of Kaddish by a son of the deceased is a form of direct intercession for the soul of his parent - in other words, a prayer of special efficacy for the dead, as it is in fact generally regarded.

Widespread though this idea became, it was also opposed by some rabbis, who warned that the dead would be judged for their actions on earth, and not on account of the prayers offered by their sons; and who preferred to view the Kaddish more as a method of honouring the memory of a parent, by causing a congregation to assemble and join the mourner in giving public praise to God.

Customs

Sephardim sit (and Ashkenazim stand) when Kaddish is recited by the hazan in synagogue.

Mourners stand, facing Jerusalem, when they recite Kaddish at home or in synagogue.

On the whole, women do not say Kaddish (though some rabbis permit them to do so); but simply respond with the rest of the congregation.

Sephardi and Ashkenazi versions of the Kaddish vary, with Sephardim saying a longer and more florid form of the prayer.

A translation

Though difficult to capture the full flavour of the Kaddish in translation, the following free version of the form most frequently used will give a fair impression:

Hazan or mourner

Glorified and sanctified be God's great name throughout the world, which he has created according to his will. May he establish his Kingdom (cause salvation to spring forth and hasten the coming of his Messiah - Sephardim only) in your lifetime and within that of the whole House of Israel, speedily and soon.

And let us say Amen.

Congregation

May his great Name be blessed for ever and ever.

Hazan or mourner

May his great Name be blessed for ever and ever. Blessed and praised, glorified and exalted, adored and honoured, be the Name of the Holy One, blessed be he, far more than any blessings and praises that can ever be uttered in this world.

And let us say Amen.

May abundant peace descend from heaven, with life (and plenty, healing and liberation, atonement and forgiveness, redemption and salvation - Sephardim only) for us and for all Israel.

And let us say Amen.

May he who creates perfect harmony in his heavens (through his infinite mercy - Sephardim only) grant peace to us and to all Israel.

And let us say Amen

When the Kaddish is recited immediately after the reading of a rabbinic passage in the service, the following additional verse is inserted:

For Israel, for our Rabbis, for their disciples and pupils, and for all who study the Torah, here and everywhere - for them and for us, may grace, loving kindness and mercy come from the Lord of heaven and earth.

And let us say Amen.

Alenu   עלינו

Introduction

This is one of the most ancient prayers in the liturgy. According to an old tradition, it was composed by Joshua when he entered the Promised Land. It was Rav, the great Babylonian sage of the 3rd century C.E., who is said to have introduced Alenu into the Musaph for Rosh Hashanah. About a thousand years later, Alenu came into use also as the concluding prayer for each of the three daily services.

The story is told that the great Ottoman Sultan, Suleiman the Magnificent, once asked his Jewish physician and confidant to translate one of the Hebrew prayers for him. On hearing the words of Alenu, Suleiman is said to have been so impressed that he declared that, with a prayer like Alenu, the Jews have no need for the rest of prayer book.

Its message

The prayer is an eloquent testimony to God's rule over his people, Israel and over the entire world. It ends with the messianic hope that eventually God will be acknowledged as King over all the earth.

Alenu starts by declaring that it is our duty to praise God, the creator of all.

שלא עשנו כגויי הארצות

... for he has not made us like the nations of the lands...

According to this, God chose the Jews for particular responsibility. No superiority is implied by this: only the very special task of observing the commandments and setting an example to the nations of the world.

שהוא נוטה שמים ויוסד ארץ

He stretches out heaven and establishes earth's foundation...

The use of the present tense, נוטה "stretches" and יוסד "establishes", (not "stretched" or "established"), emphasises the Jewish belief that the Almighty did not just create the world and then leave it alone but that he is continually involved with the world he made.

The prayer continues with the optimistic belief that, one day, all the nations of the world will acknowledge God and worship him alone.

The missing sentence

One sentence is missing from most of Ashkenazi versions of Alenu.

שהם משתחוים להבל וריק ומתפללים אל אל לֹא יושיע

For they bow to vanity and emptiness and pray to a god which helps not.

(It should appear between ככל המונם and ואנחנו.)

In 1400 a baptised Jew spread the slander that this verse ("*For they bow...*") refers to the founder of Christianity.

> His proof was based on the numerical value of one of the words in Alenu, even though the 'objectional' words come from Isaiah, a prophet venerated by Christians.

Despite stout Jewish defence of Alenu, on the grounds that the sentence referred to pagans and not to Christians or Muslims, the Church, backed by Christian governments, continued to persecute the Jews on account of this prayer. As a result, the Ashkenazim removed the sentence from their version of the prayer.

Sephardi Jews who mostly lived in Muslim countries were unaffected by this particular brand of anti-semitism. Therefore, the Sephardi version of Alenu retains the verse intact.

Askenazim and most Sephardim add a second paragraph to Alenu, which is omitted from the prayer recited by some Sephardim.

The Reading of the Torah   קריאת התורה

The reading of the Torah - קריאת התורה

Our Sages established that we have to read a portion from the Chumash, the Five Books of Moshe חמשה חומשי תורה on Mondays, Thursdays and on certain Hagim; and also twice on Shabbat.

Why do we read the Torah on Mondays and Thursdays?

Ezra the Scribe, who was a *kohen* and the leader of the Jews of Eretz Israel who had returned from the Babylonian exile in the fifth century B.C.E, established that Mondays and Thursdays would be days of Torah Reading. On those days, the Torah is read after *Tahanun.*

The main reasons for why the Torah is read then are as follows:

i) Those were market days and the days on which the Law Court functioned in ancient Palestine. Therefore, reading the Torah on these days would allow farmers who came to town to attend the Law Court or to visit the market, to hear it.

ii) In the Torah we read:

They went three days in the desert and did not find water.

(Exodus 15.22)

The Torah is compared by our Sages to water. Therefore, our Sages concluded that three consecutive days should not pass without our reading the Torah.

Reading the Torah on Mondays and Thursdays allows us to hear the Torah being read without an interruption of three consecutive days.

Procedure for reading the Torah

On Weekdays

1) The Ark is opened. This Mitzvah is called 'Portas' (gates) in the Spanish and Portuguese Synagogue.

2) The one who is honoured takes the Torah scroll out of the Ark and carries it to the Teba. It is customary to kiss the Torah when it passes on its way to the Teba.

3) Sephardim raise the Torah (Levantar) at this point, unlike Ashkenazim (*Hagbaha*) who do it after the reading of the Torah has been completed.

4) The Aliyah עליה ('calling up' to the Torah reading) takes place. Three adults are called to the Torah on a weekday: first a Cohen, second a Levi and finally an Israelite. More are called on Shabbat and festivals.

5) The person called to the Torah recites: ברכו את ה' המבורך

Bless the Lord, who is to be blessed.

6) The congregants respond: ברוך ה' המבורך לעולם ועד

Blessed is the Lord, who is blessed for all eternity.

7) The person called up recites the rest of the blessing beginning with ברוך אתה ה'...

... who has chosen us from among all the other nations ....

8) The worshippers respond "Amen".

9) The portion from the Torah is read.

10) The Torah is kissed by the person called up when he has finished reading it.

11) The person called up recites:

... who has given us the Torah of truth and implanted eternal life within us; Blessed are you, O Lord, who gave us the Torah.

12) Kaddish is recited when the third portion has been read.

13) Sephardim, after the Torah reading, continue with the service and return the Torah to the Ark later. Ashkenazim return the Torah to the Ark immediately after the Torah reading has been completed and then continue with the service.

14) The Torah is returned to the Ark.

Then the Shacharit services continues.

On Shabbat

1) The actual reading consists of an entire Parashah or, on occasion, two; whereas on all other *Keriat-Ha-torah* days (Mondays and Thursdays) a much smaller section is read usually up to *sheni* (the second portion).

2) Following the Parashah, a *Haftarah* הפטרה is read. This is taken from the Prophets.

3) Various prayers for the community are recited after the *Haftarah* such as memorial prayers, blessings for the community, the Queen and the State of Israel.

4) These are followed by a *Derashah* דרשה (Exposition or Sermon) or an address to a Barmitsvah.

Some laws concerning the reading of the Torah

1) The Torah is always carried on the right arm.

2) The person called up should wear a Tallit.

3) The Scroll must always be touched with the Tallit and held by its rollers, never with bare hands.

4) It is forbidden to speak while the Torah is being read.

Torah reading on diverse occasions:

		Torah Reading	Number of Aliyot
Shabbat		Weekly Sidrah	Arvit: 3 Shacharit: 7 + Maftir
Mon. & Thurs.		First Parasha of the weekly Sidrah	3
Rosh Chodesh		Numb. 28: 1-15	4
Hanukka		Numb. 7	3
	8th day	Numb. 7 + part of 8	3
	On Shabbat	weekly Sidrah + Numb. 7	
Purim		Ex. 17	3
Pesach	each day	Numb. 28:19 +	5 + maftir
	1st day	Ex. 12	
	2nd day	Leviticus 23	(4 in Israel)
	3rd day	Ex. 13	
	4th day	Ex. 22	
	5th day	Ex. 34 (if it falls on Shabbat, the	(if it falls on Shabbat: 7 + Maftir)

		reading begins from 33:12	
	6th day	Numb. 9	
	7th day	Ex. 13-15	
	8th day (outside Israel)	Deut. 15-16	
Shavuot	1st day	Ex. 19 - 20	5+ Maftir
	2nd day	Deut. 15 - 16	
Sukkot	1st day	Levit. 22:26 + 23:44 Numb. 29:12-16	5 + Maftir
	Hol Hamoed	Numb. 29	
Rosh Hashanah	1st day	Genesis 21	5 + Maftir
	2nd day	Genesis 22	
Kippur		Levit. 16:29	6 + Maftir
Simchat Torah		last passage of Deut. + first passage of Genesis	as many as possible

Mezuzah   מזוזה

It is the duty of every man to perform the commandment of fixing the Mezuzah. Whenever we enter or leave the house, we are confronted with the name of the Holy One, blessed be he; and recalling his loving kindness, we are reminded that in this world nothing endures but God, that all is vanity but the love of God and his commandments.

(Maimonides, Hilkot Mezuzah VI, 13)

What is a Mezuzah?

The Mezuzah consists of a scroll of parchment containing the two paragraphs of the Shema written by a Sofer סופר.

The first paragraph is from Deuteronomy 6: 4-9:

Hear (this) Israel: The Lord is our God, The Lord is One. You shall love The Lord your God, with all your heart, with all your soul, and with all your might .... and you shall write them (these words) on the doorposts of your house and upon your gates.

and the second paragraph is from Deuteronomy 11: 13-21:

If you obey the commandments that I command you today, to love the Lord, your God, and to serve him with all your heart and with all your soul ... and to write them on the doorposts of your house and upon your gates...

On the back of the scroll the name Shaddai, which means Almighty, is written so that only this name is visible when the scroll is rolled up.

Where are the Mezuzot placed

The Mezuzot are placed into a tube of metal or wood and fixed on the upper third of the right-hand of every doorpost (right, as you enter) of Jewish residences except on the doors of the bathrooms or toilets. The Mezuzah is placed vertically, in the Sephardi tradition, unlike the Ashkenazim who fix it with the top sloping toward the house (or room).

Before a Mezuzah is fixed into position a beracha is said:

... who has sanctified us with his commandments and commanded us to fix a Mezuza.

Spanish and Portuguese Jews recite the beracha *Likboa Mezuzah* לקבוע מזוזה when they fix it for themselves; but if they fix the Mezuzah for someone else, the beracha *Al kebiat mezuzah* is recited instead.

It is customary to touch the Mezuza and then kiss our hand each time we enter or leave the house.

Its purpose

The Mezuzot, like the Tefillin and Tsitsit, act as reminders, or "visual aids". Each time we enter or leave a room we are reminded of God and his special covenant with his people. We are also reminded (see the second paragraph of Shema) of the duty to obey God's commandments.

Tsitsit and Tallit   ציצית וטלית

ויאמר יהוה אל-משה לאמר: דבר אל-בני ישראל ואמרת אלהם ועשו להם ציצת על-כנפי בגדיהם לדורותם ונתנו
על-ציצת הכנף פתיל תכלת ...

במדבר טו, לז-לֹח

*The Lord said to Moses as follows:"Speak to the Children of Israel and instruct them to make fringes
on the corners of their garments, throughout the generations. And they shall attatch a cord of blue to
the fringe at each corner.*

(Num. 15: 37-38)

This passage (Num. 15: 37-41) also forms the third paragraph of the Shema.

גדלים תעשה-לך על-ארבע כנפות כסותך אשר תכסה בה

(דברים כב, יב)

You shall make fringes on the four corners of the garment with which you cover yourself.

(Deut. 22:12)

The Tsitsit are fringes attached to four-cornered garments. One of the fringes is longer than
the others: it is the thread known as the Shamash which is used for winding round the other
threads.

    The garment (prayer shawl) to which they are attached is called a Tallit. The Tallit
should be square or rectangular.

There are two kinds of Tallit:

    i) The Tallit Katan טלית קטן - often referred to as the *Arba Kanfot* ('Four Corners'). It is a
vest-like garment worn under the shirt throughout the day.

    ii) The Tallit Gadol טלית גדול - often referred to simply as a Tallit - is like a robe.

    As its beracha ("...*enwrap ourselves...*") suggests, the Tallit Gadol has to be large
enough to cover a sizable part of the body.

Its purpose

... that you may see it (tzitzit) and remember all the commandments of the Lord and practice them...

(Numbers 15: 39)

... וראיתם אותו וזכרתם את כל-מצות יהוה ועשיתם אתם ...

(במדבר טו, לט)

The Tsitsit are an ancient 'visual aid' which serve as a reminder, like the knots we make in our handkerchiefs, to remind us of something we must not forget to do.

Being weak and easily distracted, we all need constant reminders of our higher purpose on earth.

As the Talmud says:

...seeing leads us to remembering, and remembering leads to acting.

(Menachot 34b)

Our Sages taught us:

Whoever has a Mezuzah on his doorpost, Tzitzit on his garment, and Tefillin on his arm and head, will assuredly not sin.

When are they worn and who wears them?

and it shall be unto you for a fringe, that ye may look upon it

(Num. 15:39)

והיה לכם לציצת וראיתם אתו

(במדבר טו, לט)

Therefore, Tzitzit may be worn only when they can be seen. The Tallit Katan is worn daily during daylight hours whereas the Tallit Gadol is worn daily for morning prayers only.

There are also other occasions (such as Mincha on Shabbat) when the hazzan and those specially honoured (e.g. by being called to the Reading of the Torah) wear a Tallit - but this is not the case in all synagogues.

In the Spanish and Portuguese Synagogue, the Cohanim wear the Tallit over their heads when blessing the congregation. The person blowing the Shofar also covers his head with the Tallit as do the hazan and the seganim (those supporting him on either side) for certain parts of the high holiday services. Otherwise, the Tallit is not generally worn on the head.

On Tisha Be'Av, Tallit and Tefillin are worn only for Mincha. Some would put them on at home before they come to the synagogue.

Sepharadim wear Tallit in synagogue, even from the age of five or six. Ashkenazim do not wear a Tallit regularly until they get married.

Although the mitzvah is that "*you may look upon it*", blind people are not excepted from wearing a Tallit since the reason for the mitzvah is also that "*you may remember*".

Women are exempt from wearing Tallit and Tzitzit since this is a time-bound mitzvah.

What are Tallitot and Tzitzit made of?

The Tallit Gadol should preferably be made of wool but many are made of silk or cotton.

The Tallit Katan is also often made of wool but other materials, such as cotton may be used.

The Tzitzit are usually of wool but may also be made of silk.

Colour of the Tzitzit

And they shall place upon the fringe of each corner a thread of blue

(Num. 15: 38)

ונתנו על-ציצת הכנף פתיל תכלת

(במדבר טו" לח)

Then, why are all our Tzitzit white?

The dye originally used to produce the "blue" colour was obtained from a shell fish called the Hilazon which is now thought to be extinct. Therefore, as we can no longer hope to match the particular shade of blue with confidence, a white thread is used instead.

Blessing said when wrapping oneself with the Tallit

The beracha on putting on the Tallit Gedolah is להתעטף בציצית *Lehitatef betzitzit* (" ... *to wrap ourselves in the Tallit*") and על מצות ציצית *Al mizvat Tzitzit* ("... *concerning the commandment of Tzizit*") for the Tallit Katan.

> However, some Sephardim do not recite *Al Mizvat Tzitzit* since the *Lehitatef betzitzit* applies to the Tallit Katan as wel.

After the recitation of the blessing we wrap our head with the Tallit and gather the Tallit over one shoulder, and then over the other shoulder. After this, we wear it in the usual manner for the rest of the prayers.

Some customs

1) Kiss the Tzitzit:

It is the custom to kiss two Tzitziot at the end of *Baruch She'amar*.

It is also customary to hold the Tzitzit in front of the eyes and kiss them while the word Tzitzit is mentioned in:

     i) the recitation of the third paragraph of Shema,

     ii) the recitation the last word of the Shema and

     iii) the recitation the prayer that follows.

     2) Most Sepharadi Jews use 26 windings for making

     Tzitzit. They tie knots in the sequence of 10, 5, 6, 5, so as to spell the equivalent of the four Hebrew letters comprising the name of God (YKVK).

3) Sephardim cover the eyes with the Tallit during the recitation of the first line of the Shema.

4) Some Jews wear the fringes over their clothes so that they can be seen but this is not the Sepharadi custom.

Tefillin   תפילין

Introduction

Bind them as a sign upon your arm and let them be a symbol between your eyes

(Deut. 6, 8)

וקשרתם לאות על-ידך והיו לטטפת בין עיניך

(דברים ו, ח)

This command appears (with slight variation) four times in the Torah.

The Tefillin consist of two small black leather boxes containing the four portions of the Bible in which we are commanded to wear them. They are strapped to the left arm (except for a left-handed person who puts them on the right hand) and to the forehead .

Tefillin are sometimes wrongly translated as Phylacteries, after the Greek word which means "charm". No such idea is suggested by this commandment and no magical properties are associated with Tefillin.

Biblical sources for Tefillin and Mezuzah

	Name of Parashah	Full Name		Source			Main Message
			Book	Sidrah	Cap.	vv.	
1	Kaddesh	Kaddesh Li קדש לי	Exod	Bo	13	1-10	Remember the Exodus
2	V'hayah	V'hayah Ki Y'viaha והיה כי יביאך	Exod	Bo	13	11-16	
3	Shema שמע		Deut.	Vaet.	6	4-9	Unity of God; Love of God

4	V'hayah	V'hayah Im Shamoa והיה אם שמע	Deut.	Ekev	11	13-21	Reward and punishment

Passage numbered 3 and 4 are contained in the Mezuzah; and all the four passages are included in the Tefillin.

What is in the Tefillin?

The Tefillin consist of the Tefilla of the hand Shel-Yad של - יד, and Tefilla of the head Shel-Rosh של - ראש.

Each has three parts:

1) Bayit בית which is the box, joined to the Mabarta מעברתא which is the base. They are made of leather from a kasher animal (even when it was not prepared for a kasher market) and should be cubic and black.

The Bayit of a Tefilla Shel-Rosh contains the Hebrew letter Shin on the sides but not on the front or on the back.

2) Parchment scrolls containing the four Parashot (פרשות or פרשיות). There are four separate scrolls in the Tefillin Shel-Rosh and only one long one in the Tefillin Shel-Yad.

> As our Sages explain, when thinking about taking action, there can be many possibilities before us. For this reason the Tefilla Shel-Rosh contains various scrolls. However, when we do act there is only one action undertaken by our hand, for this reason the scroll of the Shel-Yad contains a single scroll.

The parchment scrolls are written by a Sofer סופר and must be checked by him approximately every three years to find out if they have faded or cracked. Some Sephardim inspect them every Elul.

> According to Rashi's tradition, the parchment scrolls should be placed in the boxes from right to left according to the order in which the texts appear in the Bible. However, according to Rabbenu Tam, the order in which we place the portions must be inverted, i.e. the portions from Deuteronomy must be placed first since they are more important than the portions from Exodus as they are a dialog with God rather than a historical message. Some people wear Tefillin arranged according to Rashi and later on they replace it for Tefillin arranged according Rabbenu Tam's interpretation.

3) Retsuot רצועות. They are leather straps, enabling the Batim to be worn.

The Sephardi Tefillin are smaller than the Ashkenazim ones. This enables them, if they wish, to wear two pairs of Tefillin at the same time, one arranged according to Rashi's tradition and the other according to Rabbenu Tam's. Very few observe this custom.

Its purpose

Great is the sanctity of the tefillin, for while the tefillin are on a man's head and about his arm, he is humble and God-fearing; he is not drawn away by levity and idle conversation, nor does his heart entertain evil thoughts; but he fills his heart with thoughts of truth and righteousness.

(Maimonides, Hilkot Tefillin iv, 25)

The Tefillin act as a reminder of the bond of love between us and God.

One of the four Parashot says:

And they shall be ... for reminder between your eyes.

Therefore, the Tefillin also remind us of the ideas contained within them, particularly the Exodus, God's unity and the love of God.

Who wears Tefillin and when?

Tefillin are worn by males of Barmitsvah age, during morning prayers.

In some Sephardi congregations, it is customary for children to begin wearing the Tefillin before the age of 13 as a way of preparing them for the Bar-Mitzvah.

However, the Spanish & Portuguese Jews put them on for the first time usually on the Thursday before the ceremony. Of course, a boy must put on Tefillin the moment he reaches the age of 13.

Women are exempted from wearing Tefillin since this is a time-bound mitzvah.

Tefillin are worn daily except on Shabbat and Hagim חגים. We do not wear Tefillin on these days because we read in the Torah:

And it shall be for a sign unto thee

(Ex. 13, 9)

and the three mitsvot described by the Torah as 'a sign' ('ot') are: Milah (Circumcision), Shabbat and Tefillin. On Shabbat (and on Yom Tov) the role of the Tefillin 'sign' is taken over by the sanctity of the day ('*It is a sign between Me and the children of Israel for ever*', Ex. 31, 17) and therefore there is no reason for wearing Tefillin on these days.

The customs as regard to Hol Hamoed vary but most Sephardim do not wear Tefillin during these days.

How to put on Tefillin

Tefillin are put on in following sequence immediately after putting on the Tallit:

1) The Shel-Yad is placed on the upper part of the biceps of the left arm with the knot of the strap in the form of the Hebrew letter yod. Sephardim put on the Shel-Yad while seated.

The Bayit should be placed in such a way that, when the arm is at rest, it faces our heart. This is a reminder that we should serve God with all our heart.

2) A beracha is recited before tightening the strap

...Who commanded us to put on Tefillin

Sephardim stand while reciting the beracha.

3) The Retsua (leather strap) is tightened and wound round the arm seven times (seven symbolises perfection in Judaism).

4) The Shel-Rosh is placed roughly in the centre of the head, '*between the eyes*'; the forward edge must be not lower than the line on which hair begins to grow. The strap is then knotted with the knot placed on the nape of the neck. The knot is in the form of the Hebrew letter daled.

Sephardim put on the Shel-Rosh while standing.

5) A second beracha Al Mitzva Tefillin על מצוה תפילין is said by Ashkenazim only:

...Who commanded us about the law of the Tefillin.

This beracha is not recited by Sephardim unless there is an interruption חציצה between putting on the Shel-Yad and the Shel-Rosh.

6) The Bayit and Retsuot are secured correctly.

7) Baruch Shem is said by Ashkenazim, but not by Sephardim.

Blessed (is his) name whose glorious kingdom is forever and ever.

8) The strap of the Shel-Yad is wound (making three coils) around the hand and around the middle finger. Sephardim make the three coils around the finger bringing the strap back twice so that they can form the Sephardi Shin.

This Shin, together with the daled formed by the hand and the yod formed by the part that hangs down from the retsua, constitute the word Shaddai, meaning Almighty.

Most Sephardim make the windings outwards.

There should be nothing between the Tefillin and the body - only the hair.

9) Tefillin are removed in exactly the opposite sequence in which they were put on. The Sephardim remove them seated, unlike the Ashkenazim who do it standing.

In Sephardi communities, it is customary for anyone who drops the Tefillin to give money to Tzedaca to show respect, or even to fast.

Kashrut כשרות

Dietary laws (Kashrut)

These fall into three main parts:

    i) Permitted and forbidden foods

    ii) Preparation of meat for consumption

    iii) Separation of milk and meat

The laws are complicated; and a short summary of aspects that most affect observant Jews in English-speaking countries is given here.

1. Permitted and Forbidden Foods

Fruit and Vegetables

I give you all plants that bear seed everywhere on earth, and every tree bearing fruit which yields seed

In compliance with that biblical statement, all fruit and vegetables may be eaten.

Animals

Animals which both chew the cud and have cloven hooves are permitted for food. All all others are prohibited, including pig, rabbit and horse.

    Animals which have died of natural causes may not be eaten, nor may those suffering from disease.

Fish

Only fish that have both scales and fins (at least one of each) may be eaten. All others are forbidden, including sturgeon (caviar), eel, shark, and shellfish.

Reptiles and Insects

Reptiles, insects and 'creeping things' are not allowed, including frogs.

Birds and Fowl

A list of permitted birds and fowl is included in the Bible. Amongst others, all birds of prey are forbidden

2. Preparation of Meat for Food

You shall eat none of the blood, whether of bird or beast, wherever you may live. Any person who eats any of the blood shall be cut off from his father's kin.

All animals intended for food must be killed in the specified manner, the process being known as Shechitah (ritual slaughter): this can only be done by a qualified man, the Shochet, who has been highly trained in the minutiae of this facet of religious law.

The instrument used is the knife, which must satisfy exacting standards of sharpness, in order to minimise pain and cause almost instantaneous unconsciousness.

The throat of the animal is cut; and as much blood as possible drained from the carcass, which is then examined carefully for any defects or injuries that would render the meat unfit for use.

Abdominal fat is removed, as this was once sacrificed on the altar.

In memory of Jacob's struggle with the angel, the sciatic nerve is also removed:

Israelites to this day do not eat the sinew of the nerve that runs in the hollow of the thigh.

For her home, the observant Jewish housewife will obtain all her meat and poultry from a Kasher butcher, who will only sell meat that has been slaughtered under strict rabbinic supervision.

Most butchers will also 'kasher' the meat – that is removing all traces of blood from it by soaking it in cold water for half an hour, then sprinkling it with salt and allowing it to drain for a further hour before washing it again two or three times in cold water. If the butcher does not 'kasher' the meat, this must be done at home.

Shechitah is without doubt one of the most humane methods of slaughter available. However, since the development of modern methods of stunning beasts prior to killing, Shechitah sometimes comes under attack. A powerful lobby periodically attempts to have Shechitah banned on the grounds of cruelty; but Jews and their supporters continue to maintain stoutly that their method is still as humane as any other, and that it minimises suffering.

3. Milk and Meat

You shall not boil a kid in its mother's milk.

This biblical command has been expanded by the Rabbis until it now involves the complete separation of all foods containing traces of any milk product (such as butter or cheese) from those containing meat.

Food containing meat and food containing milk may not be eaten together at the same meal.

Meat can be consumed soon after milk if the mouth is first rinsed, or bread is eaten.

Milk may not be eaten after meat before an interval of several hours, the precise period depending on the degree of strictness demanded by local custom.

Complete separation of milk and meat in the kitchen must be ensured. Separate storage, washing facilities (two sinks), sets of cooking utensils, sets of crockery and cutlery must be provided for each type of food: the pans and dishes must be washed and dried apart from each other.

In essence the Jewish housewife runs two parallel kitchens in the space of one room; and though this may sound awkward, it is not nearly so difficult in practice when it simply becomes routine.

As milk and meat foods are kept completely apart throughout all stages of storage, preparation, cooking and eating, most orthodox Jewish institutions and hotels maintain two separate kitchens, one for milk and the other for meat. Restaurants will usually be equipped to serve only one or the other.

Neutral food (Parve), such as bread, eggs, vegetables and fruit, may be consumed either with milk or with meat.

Reason for Kashrut

And why, a disinterested observer might ask, have Jews developed such awkward and elaborate laws to regulate their eating habits? Why must they afflict themselves with standards of observance so much higher even than those set out in the Bible, and from which many of them sometimes fall short?

The Torah itself is clear about the reason for its lists of permitted and forbidden foods, and its strictures on the drinking of the blood of animals:

You shall be holy unto me, therefore you shall not eat...

and

I have set you apart from the peoples that you shall be mine.

In other words certain rules of 'holiness' or 'apartness' are imposed on the Jewish people to enable it to become 'a light to the nations' and transmit the Divine message to all mankind.

The Rabbis, in their own words, made 'a fence round the Torah', and developed the original basic laws to the extent that the simple prohibition of boiling a kid in its mother's milk expanded into the elaborate rules described above, involving the complete separation of food containing any trace of milk from that containing meat.

The Rabbis of the Talmudic era had no doubts concerning the primary purpose of Kashrut - it was to refine man by disciplining his basic appetites:

. . . what does the Holy One, blessed be he, care whether a man kills an animal by its throat or by the nape of its neck. Hence its purpose is to refine man himself.

In later ages all kinds of practical and pseudo-rational reasons for Kashrut were advanced. The most popular is that founded on the need to preserve man's health. For example, pigs scavenged in filth, as they still do in India today, and carry disease. Shellfish breed best in polluted water and so are prone to contamination.

That kind of argument can easily be refuted. The horse, to quote only one instance, has always been a 'clean' animal, but is forbidden nevertheless.

When all has been said, it is the early reasons that still seem the most valid today.

Dietary laws were introduced to set the people apart in order to enable them better to fulfil their role as interpreters and teachers of God's law. The rules were then developed to give man an opportunity of disciplining his appetites above the level of the animal world, and to remind him constantly of the higher plane of existence to which he must aspire.

At the Table   השלחן היהודי

This table is before the Lord

Man does not live by bread alone

(Dt. 8, 3)

לא על הלחם לבדו יחיה האדם

(דברים ח, ג)

The importance of the Jewish table is reflected in the fact that 50 of the 613 Commandments are connected with it.

Judaism stresses the importance of proper nutrition and disapproves of unnecessary fasting. For example: during the Temple period some men and women (Nazirites = those who deprive themselves) denied themselves legitimate food, such as wine or meat. Although they are referred in the Torah as "holy", they still had to bring a sin offering to the Temple at the end of their period as Nazirites.

What was the sin committed by the Nazirites?

Their sin was to refuse to take wine. Our sages regarded the refusal to drink wine as a sin because the vine was created by God for man's enjoyment.

In Judaism we are commanded to keep our bodies functioning and to enjoy the benefits of the world. For this reason, eating, drinking and other activities related to our bodies are regulated by Halacha (Jewish law).

The Jewish table is an altar and the act of eating is a symbol of the sacrificial offering. As eating may be considered a way of serving the Almighty, there are many restrictions involved - such as when and what we may eat and what blessings we must recite.

These restrictions are not intended to stifle our legitimate needs and enjoyment, but rather to enable us to lead holy lives by regulating and controlling our natural desires.

that the soul (the seat of man's inclinations) might perform its appointed functions without being restricted by the ill disposition of the body or the dullness of the ear

(Sefer HaHinuch, Mitzvah 154)

Laws regarding the act of eating

1. Washing the Hands - על נטלת ידים

You shall sanctify yourselves

(by washing the hands before eating)

Like the Kohanim, who had to wash their hands before performing the service, our sages decreed that we must wash our hands before fulfilling the sacred obligation of eating.

How do we wash our hands?

i) Nothing must separate the hands from the water. For this reason we clean our nails, remove any sticky dirt and take off our rings before washing the hands.

ii) The hands should be washed once.

iii) We should use clean water.

iv) We should use a vessel.

v) We begin with the right hand and then turn to the left hand.

vi) The water must flow to cover the entire hand from the wrist downwards.

vii) The blessing should be recited after washing, but before drying:

Blessed are you, O Lord our God, King of the universe who has sanctified us with his commandments and commanded us concerning the washing of the hands.

אשר קדשנו במצותיו וצונו על נטילת ידים

We recite the blessing after performing the mitzvah (and not before as is usually done) because God's name cannot be mentioned with unwashed hands.

viii) After saying the blessing, we are forbidden to speak until we say *Hamotzi* המוציא and swallow the first bite of bread. However, if necessary, we can ask for things connected to eating the bread, such as "knife", as that is not considered a pause הפסק.

2. Hamotzi המוציא - The Blessing on the Bread

אלקינו מלך העולם, המוציא לחם מן הארץ

Blessed are you, O Lord our God, King of the universe, who brings forth bread from the earth.

Its laws

1) There should be no interruption between washing the hands and the recitation of *Hamotzi*

2) One should eat immediately after saying *Hamotzi*.

3) After the *Hamotzi*, the bread is cut up and distributed to all those present.

Its customs

1) It is customary to place the hands on the loaf of bread while saying *Hamotzi*.

2) We also dip the bread on which we recited *Hamotzi* into salt. The Torah says:

With all your offerings you shall offer salt.

(Lev. ii, 13)

3. Blessing Before Enjoying the Gifts of The World
Why must we bless God before we eat?

The earth is Lord's, and the fullness thereof.

Everything belongs to God, but after being consecrated by a benediction, it becomes man's privilege to enjoy it.

(Rabbi Levi)

whoever enjoys this world without first reciting a blessing is as if he has stolen from the Holy One, blessed be he, and from the Jewish people.

(גמרת ברכות 35)

Though everything belongs to God, we are free to enjoy it after saying the appropriate blessing.

Its laws

1) One must say a blessing before eating or drinking anything.

2) One should say the blessing appropriate to each kind of food:

> i) On bread and all baked products whose main ingredients are flour and water, we say *Hamotzi*:

המוציא לחם מן הארץ...

... Who brings forth bread from the earth

ii) On wine, we say *Ha'Gefen*:

... בורא פרי הגפן

... Who creates the fruit of the vine.

iii) On baked products whose principal ingredients are not flour and water, or on those whose principal ingredients are flour and water but were cooked before being baked, we say *Mezonot*:

... בורא מיני מזונות

...Who creates various types of baked goods

iv) On eating vegetables or fruit which grow on annual trees we say *Ha'adama*:

... בורא פרי האדמה

... Who creates the fruit of the earth.

v) On fruit which grows on perennial trees, we say *Ha'etz*

... בורא פרי העץ.

... Who creates the fruit of the tree.

vi) On all other food or drink not included in the above categories, we say *Shehakol*:

... שהכל נהיה בדברו

... Whose word make everything exist.

3) There should be no interruptions between the blessing and the consumption of the food or drink. In case of interruption, the blessing should be repeated.

4) We should say the blessing on the whole article of food, i.e. before cutting it. However, if we suspect the food may be bad, we may cut it to check before saying the blessing

4. Grace after Meals - Birkat Hamazon ברכת המזון

ואכלת ושבעת וברכת

(דברים 8:10)

You shall eat and be satisfied and bless the Lord for the good land which He gave you.

(Deuteronomy 8:10)

We are commanded to thank God for having provided us with food and are not allowed to leave our seats, except temporarily, without reciting Birkat Hamazon.

According to the Torah, one is commanded to say it when one is "satisfied" ושבעת. However, the Talmud establishes that the Jews have voluntarily accepted the obligation of reciting Grace even when they are not satisfied.

Birkat Hamazon consists of four blessings:

i) The first is a long blessing which expresses gratitude to God for the food.
It begins with 'ברוך אתה ה 'Blessed are you, O Lord..' and ends with אתה ה' הזן את הכל *'Who sustains all'*.

ii) Blessing of the land ברכת הארץ
It expresses a general thanksgiving to God.

iii) *Boneh Yerushalayim* Who builds Jerusalem בונה ירושלים
Please, O Lord our God, have mercy upon Israel your nation, and Jerusalem your city...
This is actually a prayer rather than a blessing of thanksgiving.

iv) He who is good and who does good הטוב והמטיב

This blessing was added after the destruction of the Second Temple. It expresses gratitude for the miracle performed when the bodies of Jews killed in a revolt against the Romans in Betar (in 70 C.E) did not decompose until the Romans granted permission to bury them.

Following these blessings, we recite a series of prayers which are petitions for individuals, for groups or for the Jewish nation as a whole. Each of these prayers begins with the phrase *'Merciful One'* הרחמן.

At the conclusion of *Birkat Hamazon* we say:

May he who makes peace in his heavens, make peace for us and for all Israel ... May the Lord give his nation strength; may the Lord bless his nation with peace!

Its laws

a) *Mayim aharonim* מים אחרונים

and you shall be holy

(by washing the hands after the meal)

We must wash our hands before saying the Grace.

b) The tablecloth and the bread must be still on the table when we recite *Birkat Ha-mazon*.

c) The Grace after Meals must be recited while seated.

d) *Zimun:*

If three (or more) men have eaten bread together, they are commanded to unite in saying the Grace after Meals. In this case, one of the participants has to lead the blessing, inviting the others to join by saying: "Gentlemen, let us say Grace!"

Women cannot join the men in the *zimun*. However, women eating together are permitted to say the communal Grace.

Customs

a) It is customary to recite a Psalm before saying Grace.

i) During the week, we read Psalm 137:

על נהרות בבל

By the rivers of Babylon

ii) On Shabbat and Holidays as well as after meals following weddings, circumcisions or other religious ceremonies, we read Psalms 126:

שיר המעלות

A song of ascents.

b) It is also customary to remove or cover any knives left on the table before reciting Grace after Meals since the table is considered an altar and in the Torah is written:

You shall not lift up any iron upon them

(Deuteronomy xxvii, 5)

5. The Latter Blessing - Beracha Aharona - ברכה אחרונה

This blessing is recited after eating meals that do not require the recitation of *Hamozi*, i.e. cake or biscuit, or one of the Seven Species שבעת המינים, as well as after drinking wine.

   The *Beracha Aharona* consists of a long blessing which condenses the three first blessings of the Grace after Meals.

6. The Borei Nefashot - בורא נפשות

Blessed are you the Lord our God who creates many living things with their needs, for all the means you have created to sustain the life of each of them. Blessed is he who is the life of all worlds.

The *Borei Nefashot* is said after eating:

   i) vegetables,

   ii) a fruit other than one of the Seven Species or

   iii) those products for which the initial blessing is *shehakol*.

Kiddush   קדוש

Its purposes

To observe Shabbat is both a positive commandment (מצות עשה) and a negative one (מצות לא תעשה). The negative aspect is to refrain from certain creative acts (מלאכה) and the positive aspect is to celebrate the day by performing certain acts.

The positive observance is expressed by the Kiddush of the day (Kiddusha Rabba - קדושא רבא), the Havdalah - הבדלה, by wearing special clothes, eating special meals and reciting special prayers.

The meaning of the word Kiddush is "sanctification". We make holy or sanctify Shabbat and other festivals by reciting Kiddush.

Kiddush in Synagogue

The Talmud (Pesachim) relates that Kiddush was said by the hazan in the synagogue on Friday and Festival nights for the benefit of guests lodging on synagogue premises. Although the synagogue no longer functions as a boarding house, some communities (Hasidic Ashkenazim outside Israel) still retain Kiddush as part of the service in the synagogue.

> The exception is on the first two nights of Pesach when everyone would be attending the Seder and there was no need for the synagogue Kiddush

It is normal for children to drink the wine over which the hazan has recited Kiddush.

How the Kiddush is recited

Kiddush is recited over wine which symbolises the sweetness and joy of the day.

It must be recited in the home where the meal is eaten; and supper is commenced immediately after it. The head of the family recites Kiddush standing up while holding a cup of wine in his right hand. All those present stand up for at least the first part of Kiddush.

The Kiddush consists of three parts:

i) Reading of Biblical verses taken from the very end of Genesis Cap.1 and the beginning of Cap.2 (ויכולו...ויהי ערב until לעשות). These verses describe the creation of the world and how God rested on the seventh day. They are, however, omitted from the version recited in the synagogue.

On this day God rested from all His work which God (in creating) had made

(Genesis 2:3)

כי בו שבת מכל מלאכתו אשר ברא אלהים לעשות

ii)The blessing on the wine is recited:

...He who created the fruit of the vine...

בורא פרי הגפן

iii)A reference to the Exodus from Egypt is made.

When the leader of the family finishes the reciting the Kiddush, everybody responds "Amen" and tastes the wine.

In some families it is customary for the children to recite Kiddush.

TheChallot

The recital of Kiddush is followed by the washing of the hands and the saying of *Hamotsee* המוציא, the blessing over bread.

Two loaves of bread often specially baked and braided as a bride's hair (Hallah = bride) are required for this to commemorate the double portion of Manna which the Israelites in the wilderness collected on Fridays - for that day and also for Shabbat.

The bread is kept covered with a cloth during Kiddush to symbolise the dew which formed on the Manna every morning in the wilderness.

As always, the bread is sprinkled with salt after the blessing and before being eaten. This is to remind us that salt was offered with every sacrifice in the Temple.

Absence of wine

When a person is not allowed to drink alcohol or cannot find kasher wine, Kiddush may be said over the twochallot alone.

At home, in the absence of wine (or grape juice), Kiddush on Friday night must be said over bread alone.

However, during the day, Kiddush may only be said over an alternative drink (such as whisky, etc.).

Night and day

The Kiddush recited at night on Sabbath and Yom Tov differs from that said in the day.

Special combinations

1) At the Seder: The first of the 'four cups' (Arba Kosot - ארבע כוסות) 'double' as Kiddush.

2) When a Festival occurs on Shabbat, the texts of the Shabbat Kiddush and that for Yom Tov are combined.

3) When a Festival occurs on Saturday Night (Motse Shabbat - מוצאי שבת): The Kiddush for Yom Tov and Havdalah for Shabbat are combined.

4) Shehecheyanu: The seasonal blessing, Shehecheyanu - שהחיינו, is added to all Festival night Kiddushim except for those on the last two nights of Pesach.

Customs

It is customary, in some Sephardi communities for parents to bless their children after Kiddush. The children then kiss the hands of their parents and grandparents.

> Some Sepharadim mix water with the wine before Kiddush. The practice of watering down wine (*meziga*) has its origin in the Kabbalah, where wine symbolises *midat hadin* (harsh justice) and water symbolises *midat harahamim* (mercy). Thus, by mixing them, we hope to temper judgment with mercy. Another reason is simply that pure wine is too strong for some.

Havdalah   הבדלה

Introduction

Havdalah means "division" and it marks the difference between Shabbat (or Festivals) and weekdays - between "Kodesh - קדש" "holy" (special) and "Hol - חול" "ordinary" (weekdays).

Remember the Shabbat day, to sanctify it

זכור את יום השבת לקדשו

We welcome the Sabbath as we would a bride and recite Kiddush to sanctify it. We perform the ceremony of Havdalah on its departure, consoling ourselves with the taste of wine and the scent of the fragrant spices.

Havdalah is recited after nightfall in the home and also (for some communities) in the synagogue.

It is forbidden to eat after sunset on Saturday before Havdalah has been recited.

For Havdalah we need:

    i) wine in a cup overflowing as a symbol of abundance.

    ii) a candle

    iii) a box of spices or herbs.

Havdalah ceremony

The ceremony consists of:

1) The reading of verses from the Bible.

2) The recital of four blessings:

    a) *bore peri hagefen* בורא פרי הגפן on the wine.

    In the absence of wine we can say the blessing on another kind of beverage but then we have to recite *sheakol* שהכל instead.

    b) *bore miney besamim* or *atzey besamim* is said on the spices.

...בורא מיני בשמים   (עצי בשמים)

... Who creates diverse spices

בשמים spices symbolise the N'shamah Yeterah - נשמה יתרה (the "Extra Soul") which gives us higher sensitivity on Shabbath and which leaves us when the Shabbat ends.

c) *Boreh me'orey ha'esh* is said on the flame of the candle:

He who created the lights of fire

בורא מאורי האש

The use of light in Havdalah is to recall that the first thing God created was light. (On Motse Shabbat we enter the beginning of six days of work, parallel to the six days of creation).

d) *Hamavdil* המבדיל is recited:

... Who makes a distinction between the sacred and the secular ...

המבדיל בין קודש לחול

This is the most important blessing, and constitutes the actual Havdalah.

Note that after Shabbat the blessing ends with ...המבדיל בין קודש לחול ("...Who divides between holy and profane"); after Yom Tov it concludes with ...המבדיל בין קודש לקודש ("...Who divides between holy and holy.")

3) Drinking the wine:

The person who recites Havdalah drinks most of the wine in the cup and the rest is used to extinguish the candle.

4) Singing songs: e.g. *Eliyahu Hanavi* אליהו הנביא (Elijah the prophet).

What we do during the ceremony:

1	Hold wine in right hand, spices in left. (Standing)"*Hinneh*".	"Bore peri hagefen"
2	Hold wine in left hand, spices in right.	"Bore miney besamim
3	Smell spices.	
4	Continue holding wine in left hand, bend	"Bore me'orey ha'esh

	fingers towards light.	
5	Hold wine in right hand, spices in left.	"Hamavdil"
6	Sit. Drink. Extinguish the candle.	

Types of Havdalah

There are three types of Havdalah הבדלה:

    i) Saturday Night (Motse Shabbat)

    ii) After Three Pilgrim Festivals (Shalosh Regalim) and Rosh Hashanah (Motse Yom Tov)

    iii) After Yom Kippur (Motse Kippur)

Structure	Biblical verses	Blessing wine	for spice	candle	Concluding blessing
Sat. Night (Motse Shabbat) (synagogue)		+	+	+	+
Sat. Night (home)	+	+	+	+	+
*Night following Shalosh Regalim and Rosh Hashanah (Motse Yom Tov)		+			+
* Night following Kippur		+		+	+

* There is no difference between the ceremony performed in the synagogue and that in the home.

Havdalah in the Amidah

Although Shabbat ends at dusk, it is not permissible to do Melahah until one has recited the Havdalah of the Amidah. It is the paragraph "*Attah Honantanu* - אתה חוננתנו which is inserted into the fourth beracha of the Amidah of Motse Shabbat.

"Baruch Hamavdil"

If one wants to perform a weekday activity before Arbit, one recites the short formula ברוך המבדיל בין קודש לחול. When Yom Tov occurs on Motse Shabbat the formula is: ברוך המבדיל בין קודש לקודש.

Customs

1) Some Sephardim look into the wine on which *bore peri hagefen* is recited, to see their faces reflected in it. This practice is intended to fulfil the *Hatabat panim* (beautifying the face).

After the recital of bore peri hagefen, it is customary to laugh aloud and so enter the new week with joy.

2) The spices used for the blessing vary in each community. Some Sephardim use rose water (mayet zaher); others use lemons, hadassim (myrtle twigs) or mint.

It is customary for children to pass the spice-box around.

3) It is customary to put our fingertips close to the flame during the recital of the blessing in order to enjoy the heat and the light and so pronounce the blessing with conviction.

After drinking the wine, some Sepharadim put a drop of it behind the ears, on the back of the neck, over the eyes and into the pockets to symbolise health and good fortune in the week to come.

4) In some Sephardi communities, fathers bless their children during Havdalah. The children kiss their father's hand and the father then blesses them with the blessing וברכך וישמרך (the Priestly Benediction).

The Cycle of Life

Circumcision ברית מילה
and
Naming a Girl זבד הבת

Berit Milah (covenant of circumcision) and naming a girl

Berit Milah ברית מילה

... you, and your offspring to come throughout the ages, shall keep my covenant. This is the covenant between me and you and your descendants after you...
Every male among you shall be circumcised. You shall circumcise the flesh of your foreskin; and that shall be the sign of the covenant between me and you.

(Genesis: 17: 9-11)

ויאמר אלהים אל-אברהם ואתה את-בריתי תשמר אתה וזרעך אחריך לדרתם: זאת בריתי אשר תשמרו ביני וביניכם ובין זרעך אחריך המול לכם כל-זכר: ונמלתם את בשר ערלתכם והיה לאות ברית ביני וביניכם ...

(בראשית יז, ט-יב)

What is circumcision?

The Berit Milah (sometimes also called *Birkat Milah*) is a minor surgical operation in which the foreskin of the penis is removed. The operation is performed by a qualified person called a *Mohel*. The Mohel need not necessarily be a doctor but he must be highly trained and religiously observant. The Berit Milah may be performed at home, in the hospital or in the synagogue.

Its history

Circumcision was not invented by the Jews, and dates back to prehistoric times. Abraham circumcised himself in his old age, in obedience to God's command, as a sign of the Covenant; and since then the rite has assumed great significance for the Jews.

The Children of Israel were circumcised by Joshua before entering the Promised Land, for the practice had been discontinued during the rigours of the long march through the wilderness.

When the institution lapsed again during the reign of King Ahab and Queen Jezebel (874 BCE), it was triumphantly revived by the prophet Elijah who thus earned himself a place in all future circumcision ceremonies.

The banning of *Berit Milah* by Emperor Hadrian was one of the causes of Bar Kochba's revolt against Roman rule in 132-135 CE; and many Jews through out the ages have faced martyrdom rather than forgo this sacred obligation.

The philosopher Spinoza once declared:

Such great importance do I attach to this sign of the Covenant, that I am persuaded it is sufficient in itself to maintain the separate existence of the Jewish people for ever.

When a Roman official, questioning the attachment to circumcision, asked Rabbi Oshaya why God had not made man as he wanted him (i.e. without a foreskin), the reply given was that in order that man should have the opportunity of perfecting himself.

Circumcision is a visual sign of the covenant; and any child born of a Jewish mother is Jewish whether circumcised or not.

It is sometimes claimed that circumcision may have certain health and other benefits. However, this is not the reason for this ritual. The Torah firmly states that circumcision is the visible sign of that special relationship between the Jewish people and their God by means of which the Divine message was transmitted for the benefit of mankind.

Who is circumcised?

At the age of eight days every male among you shall be circumcised ...

(Genesis 17, 12)

ובן-שמונת ימים ימול לכם כל-זכר לדרתיכם

(בראשית יז, יב)

Thus, in obedience to the Torah, every newborn male should be circumcised. Adult Jews who have not been circumcised before, and non-Jews wishing to convert to Judaism must also be circumcised.

When does and where does circumcision take place?

On the eighth day after the birth, even if it falls on Shabbat or Yom Kippur. An exception is made only if the infant has health problems, when the circumcision must be delayed until the baby is fit.

It preferably takes place in the morning as *"Those who are zealous try to perform the commandments as early as possible"* זריזים מקדימים למצוות (Arukh Hashulhan 262:8-9).

Mitzvot described as signs 'ot' אות in the Torah

There are three: Shabbat, Tefillin and Circumcision.

Circumcision is the most important because it remains with us regardless of the time or the day or where we are.

As stated in the Talmud:

The mitzvah of Berit Milah is equal in importance to all the 613 precepts of the Torah together.

Shabbat Abraham Zaken (Shalom Zachar)

It is customary to hold a festive gathering on the Friday before the circumcision, which is called *Shabbat Abraham Zaken* because Abraham was the first to be circumcised. The Ashkenazim call it Shabbat *Shalom Zachar* i.e., peace to the male.

The ceremony of Berit Milah

On the Shabbat previous to the Berit Milah, the father of the child is called up to the Torah as *Baal haberit* בעל הברית.

Sephardim often read sections of the Zohar on the night before the Berit Milah, which is called *The Night of the Zohar.*

Then, on the 8th day after the birth, the Berit Milah is performed, preferably but not necessarily in the presence of a *minyan* (a quorum of ten adult male Jews). Some participants have special honours, such as the *Mohel*, the *shushbinim* ('escorts') who take the child from his mother and give him back to her after the circumcision, the *Sandak* and the person who pronounces the blessing over the wine. It is customary for the father, the Mohel and the Sandak to wear a Tallit.

Specially honoured guests

The Sandak (father's companion) has the honour of holding the baby on his lap during the ceremony. "Sandak" is sometimes translated as "Godfather". This is incorrect as there are no godfathers in Judaism - only in Christian tradition.

Also specially honoured is the woman who takes the infant from his mother and carries him into the room in which the ceremony takes place. Honoured too is the man who received the baby from the woman and hands him to the Mohel.

Elijah's chair

The prophet Elijah is the unseen witness at all Berit Milah ceremonies.

Ever since the prophet Elijah revived the practice of circumcision, he has had a chair reserved for him at each circumcision. God said to him:

Since you were so zealous for the precept of circumcision, you will forever be present at every circumcision.

In some Sephardi communities, Elijah's chair is occupied by the *Sandak* who holds the baby on his lap. Other Sephardi communities put a Bible on the chair.

Some Sephardim decorate Elijah's chair to resemble a throne; but this is not the custom among Spanish and Portuguese Jews, who do not decorate the chair

The procedure for the circumcision is as follows:

1) When the *Mohel* is ready, the woman who acts as escort takes the child from his mother to the room in which the circumcision will take place.

2) Those presents recite: *baruch haba* ברוך הבא *'Blessed be he who comes!'*

3) The woman hands the infant to her husband who takes him to the *Mohel.*

4) The child is placed on the lap of the *Sandak.*

5) The father of the child should perform the circumcision if he is qualified to do so. Otherwise the *Mohel* asks his permission to perform the operation on his behalf.

6) The circumcision takes place.

7) The father says the blessing:

...Who has sanctified us with his commandments and commanded us to enter him (the child) into the covenant of our father Abraham

... וצונו להכניסו בבריתו של אברהם אבינו

8) The father recites *shehecheyanu*.

9) Those present respond:

Just as he entered the covenant, may he also enter to Torah, the wedding canopy, and good deeds.

אמן. כשם שנכנס לברית, כן ייכנס לתורה ולחופה ולמעשים טובים.

10) The child is held by an honoured guest. Another guest, usually the *Mohel*, says a blessing over a cup of wine (*birkat hagefen*). Then, he drinks the wine and blesses and names the child with his Hebrew name.
According to some Sepharadi traditions, the child is named after a close living relative. Ashkenazim only give children the names of deceased relatives.
Some Sephardim then recite the blessing over spices.

11) The child is taken by the same person who brought him to the *Mohel* before the circumcision. He passes the baby to his wife who, in turn, passes him back to his mother.

12) A celebration called *Seudat Mitzvah* סעודת מצוה takes place then.

Naming a girl (zebed habat)

The naming ceremony for girls varies from one community to another.

In some communities the custom is to name the baby girl when the father visits the synagogue for the first time after her birth and has the honour of being called to the Torah. The girl is then named (in her absence) from the Tebah.

Some Sephardim name their daughters in a ceremony when the mother visits the synagogue for the first time after giving birth in order to recite *Birkat hagomel*, a thanksgiving for successful childbirth.

Other Sephardim conduct this ceremony at home when the mother has recovered.

The procedure for naming a daughter consists of reciting a prayer for the daughter after which she is named as follows:

May he who blessed Sarah, Rebecca, Rachel and Leah, ... bless this beloved child, and may her name be.

Pidyon Haben   פדיון הבן

Pidyon Haben פדיון הבן

For every firstborn of the Children of Israel became mine ...

(Numbers 8, 17)

כי לי כל-בכור בבני ישראל ...

(במדבר ח, יז)

Firstborn males enjoyed many privileges in the ancient world. In Jewish tradition the firstborn belong to God's service and were originally intended to serve in the sanctuary.

However, they lost that honour to the Levites, who remained loyal to God when the Israelites turned aside from God in the desert of Sinai to worship the golden calf.

... And you shall redeem every human firstborn among your sons.

(Exodus, 13: 13)

וכל בכור אדם בבניך תפדה

(שמות יג, יג)

Apart from the children of the hereditary priestly families (Cohen) and the hereditary Levitical families (Levy), every such boy must therefore be redeemed by his father from the priests.

The child of a woman whose father is a priest or Levite is also exempt from the obligation.

No redemption is required for a child born of a Caesarean operation, or after his mother had a previous miscarriage. He must be 'firstborn of the womb' to need redeeming.

The ceremony

The ceremony, which is a short one, takes place on the thirty-first day after birth, unless this a Sabbath or festival.

Those that are to be redeemed - from one month shall you redeem according to the valuation, five shekels by the sacred shekel.

(Numbers 18: 15-16)

The redemption of the firstborn must be performed by the father as follows:

1) The infant is brought in on a cushion by the father to the Cohen.

2) The father declares:

This is my first-born son, who opened the womb of his Jewish mother. ...

In Sephardi ceremonies the mother intervenes by saying:

This is my son, my firstborn, I have not (previously) miscarried.

זה בני בכורי, לא הפלתי

3) The Cohen asks the father whether he wants to redeem his son or leave him with the priests.

What do you want more - this first-born son of yours, or the five shekalim that you are required by the Torah to pay to redeem him?

4) The father answers that he wants to redeem his son.

5) The father recites the blessing על פדיון הבן:

... Who has sanctified us with his commandments and commanded us concerning the redemption of the son.

6) The father recites *shehecheyanu.*

7) The father gives the value of five silver coins to the Cohen who takes it placing his hands over the infant's head.

These five coins are given at this time because on the thirtieth day it becomes more certain that the child will continue to live.

> The coin used for the exchange must contain at least 4.2 oz of silver. The old American coins (before 1964) and the coins issued by Israel Coins and Medal Authority are suitable for this symbolic exchange.

8) The Cohen blesses the child.

May the Lord bless you and keep you.
May the Lord cause His face to shine upon
you and be gracious unto you.
May the Lord look kindly on you and give
you peace.

9) The Cohen says a blessing on a cup of wine (*hagefen*) and drinks the wine. In some Sephardi ceremonies, the blessing on spices (*Bore minei besamim*) or over hadasim (*Bore azei besamim*) are also recited.

10) A festive meal סעודת מצוה takes place.

Bar Mitzvah and Bat Mitzvah
בר מצווה ובת מצווה

Age of obligation

The ages of thirteen for a boy and twelve for a girl are those at which, in Jewish law, a child assumes the full moral and legal responsibilities of an adult.

These ages, representing the onset of physical maturity, relate originally to the distant past. The Rabbis teach that both Abraham and Jacob made crucial decisions governing the future conduct of their lives at the age of thirteen - Abraham abandoned the idol worship of his father, and Jacob parted from Esau.

The age of maturity for boys was deduced by our sages.

At thirteen years the age is reached for the fulfilment of the commandments.

(Avot 5, 21)

In Isaiah 43:21 we read: '*This nation which I created shall tell my praise.*' and this, zu זו in Hebrew, has the gematric value of 13. Thus, our Sages deduced that at the age of 13 is when a boy is required to praise God, i.e. to fulfil his commandments.

Girls reach the state of adulthood earlier than boys, at the age of twelve. According to our Sages it is because:

The Almighty has endowed woman with greater natural wisdom than man.

(Nida 46a)

To view the traditional age of majority in perspective, it should be remembered that the first modern attempt to control the abuse of child labour in mines and factories was passed by the English parliament only in 1802, and then proved ineffective; and also that children, often as young as seven, still constitute up to a tenth of the total labour force of many countries of Asia, Latin America and the Middle East.

From the age of thirteen years and one day, a father is no longer responsible for the actions of his son. The boy is then considered an adult in Jewish law: he is eligible to form part of a Minyan (quorum of ten adult males required for the holding of a public religious service): with very few exceptions, he is able to engage in legally valid transactions for which he is held to be fully accountable.

A girl is, in theory, able to marry at the age of twelve years and one day. This now has a significance that is more historic than real; for even in Israel, where religious law governs the personal status of Jews, a girl is not normally permitted to marry under the age of seventeen.

Terms

The terms Bar Mitzvah (son of the commandment) and Bat Mitzvah (daughter of the commandment) are used in two ways.

The first is to describe the state of adulthood entered into at the age of thirteen for a boy and twelve for a girl. The second is the name of the ceremony and celebration accompanying the attaining of those ages.

Contrary to popular belief, no ceremony of any kind is necessary. All Jewish children automatically become Bar Mitzvah or Bat Mitzvah at the appropriate age, even if they are entirely unaware of that fact. The lack of a ceremony to mark the event may possibly leave a person with a feeling of deprivation; but it has no more significance than that.

Attempts of middle-aged men (mostly in America) to arrange a 'Bar Mitzvah' ceremony for themselves, to make up for one missed in youth, are based on total misunderstanding of Jewish teaching.

Ceremony

There are records indicating that Bar Mitzvah was occasionally celebrated as a public ceremony from the 10th century; but it was not until the 15th century that the custom first became more common.

The custom of celebrating a boy's attaining the age of Bar Mitzvah has now assumed great importance in Jewish family life. The boy will study hard for his performance in synagogue on the great day; and the subsequent festivities can sometimes equal those for a wedding in their scale, and in the feelings of joy and pride that are aroused.

The custom of celebrating a girl's becoming Bat Mitzvah is of even more recent origin, and dates back only to the nineteenth century. Some parents will merely treat the event as a rather special birthday; but others will use it to demonstrate their love for their daughter. As women are not permitted to take any part in the ceremonial of the statutory synagogue services, the ceremony is of a different type to that of the Bar Mitzvah.

Bar Mitzvah

The first three commandments that the Bar Mitzvah has to fulfil are:

    i) to say the Shema שמע

    ii) to wear Tefillin תפילין

    iii) to be given an Aliya עליה

The Bar Mitzvah must first be prepared for accepting and fulfilling the commandments. Then he spends the weeks before the ceremony learning the part of the Torah which he will recite at his Bar Mitzvah ceremony (sometimes boys even learn the entire *Parasha*) and learn how to put on Tefillin.

In the Sephardi community and some others, the Bar Mitzvah attends the Shacharit service on the Monday or Thursday after his 13th birthday (according to the Jewish calendar). Mondays and Thursdays are the days of the week in which the Torah is read and Tefillin are worn (on Shabbat, the Torah is read but Tefillin is not put on).

On that Monday or Thursday, the boy will wear Tefillin and will be called up to read the Torah for the first time in his life. This practice is often carried out in Israel by the Western Wall (Kotel) where many Bar Mitzvah ceremonies are performed simultaneously.

This, in some Jewish communities, is the Bar Mitzvah. In many others, it is either omitted altogether or else is followed by a more public ceremony on the following Sabbath (which is the custom in the Spanish and Portuguese Synagogue).

In what is now commonly understood as the Bar Mitzvah service, family and friends are invited to the Sabbath morning service in the synagogue.

The father and other male members of the family will be allotted Mitzvot מצוות, which are honoured roles in the ceremonial.

The father recites *baruch she patrani*.

Blessed be he who has relieved me from being punished for this one

ברוך שפטרני מעונשו של זה

The father is responsible for his son's actions until he reaches the boy's religious majority after which the son will be responsible for his own actions. With the recitation of *baruch she patrani* the father expresses his satisfaction that the boy has reached adulthood and has become responsible for his own actions.

The Bar Mitzvah will be called to the reading of the Torah; and will often sing his own portion with some display of virtuosity. A boy with a good voice may also read the other portions, the Haftarah (portion from the Prophets) or other parts of the service, depending on local custom.

The Rabbi will address the boy in a sermon, stressing his new responsibilities as a full member of the Jewish community. In some synagogues the boy also recites a special prayer affirming his devotion to the faith of his ancestors.

After the service there is a celebration in synagogue, often a special Kiddush.

It is customary also to have a celebration dinner סעודה מצוה at home or in a hall with friends and relatives. At this celebration the Bar Mitzvah delivers a *derasha* or a speech of thanksgiving to his family and teachers.

Bat Mitzvah

The Bat Mitzvah ceremony varies from community to community. Some communities do not even mark the occasion with a special ceremony.

In the Spanish and Portuguese Synagogue, the Bat Mitzvah ceremony is held on the Shabbat or on the Sunday after the girl reaches womanhood.

If held on Shabbat, the father is called up to the reading of the Torah. In some synagogues he will recite *baruch she patrani* on that occasion.

At the conclusion of the Shabbat morning service, before Alenu, the girl is addressed by the Rabbi. She then recites extracts from Tehilim, Pirkei Avot and the Torah. She may also give a short *d'var Torah*.

Being of comparatively recent origin, the Bat Mitzvah service has not yet become standardised. In the Spanish and Portuguese Synagogue, its framework is still evolving in the attempt to achieve the most satisfactory form.

Marriage and Divorce   נישואין

Importance of marriage

It is not good for man to be alone. I will provide a partner for him ... a man leaves his father and mother and is united to his wife, and the two become one flesh.

The institution of marriage is one of the pillars of Judaism, considered essential for the preservation of society.

The Rabbis view the married state so highly that they use that analogy to illustrate the significance of many of the most important combinations in Jewish life. God is said to be 'married' symbolically to the Jewish people: the Jews are said to have contracted a 'marriage' with their Torah; and the Sabbath is regarded as the 'bride' of the Jewish people, as expressed by the hymn sung on Friday evenings to greet its onset:

Come my beloved to meet the bride; let us welcome the presence of the Sabbath.

Marriage was established by Divine law. Conduct within a marriage, and rules for its dissolution are regulated by Divine law. A person is not fulfilled until married; and celibacy of any kind is strongly discouraged by traditional Judaism.

Concept of marriage

The Jewish attitude to marriage differs subtly but decisively from that of the Catholic Church, and from that of modern secular society.

Jews have never regarded marriage as a concession to man in order to cope with his sinful sexual instincts (as does the Catholic Church) - on the contrary, within limits, sex is regarded as an essential ingredient of a complete life.

Jews have never regarded marriage as an experimental association between two people, free to make up rules to suit themselves as they go along. Divine law regulates conduct within marriage. Consequently a Jewish marriage is different in concept, and perhaps even in quality, from one entered into under other laws and in other societies.

Jews have never regarded marriage as indissoluble except through the death of one of the partners - a Jewish divorce, if by mutual consent, is always available.

From a technical point of view a Jewish marriage is a simple contract between two people, imposing obligations on both and specifying conditions to be met in the event of breakdown. If both parties agree, a divorce can be effected by a simple legal ceremony, after which they are each free to remarry at will.

However since earliest times the plain legal aspect of the marriage union has acquired overtones of holiness. Many rabbinic legends refer to God's interest and approval in the making of marriages; and we read that the Divine altar in heaven 'sheds tears' at the news of a divorce. Marriage therefore is not merely a cold legal arrangement; but is also a holy institution, blessed by God.

Equality of men and women

The commonly held fallacy that a Jewish husband 'acquires' a wife, as he might acquire a chattel, is based on total misunderstanding of Jewish law and practice.

Though the man is the actual instigator of the making and of the breaking of a marriage contract, the full force of Jewish law is directed towards the protection of the woman's rights, both in marriage and subsequently.

It must be remembered that Jewish marriage laws were framed and developed at a time when wives in general had few rights. For example, though a married woman has always been allowed to own property in her own right in Jewish law, this was not possible in England until the passing of the Married Women's Property Act about one hundred years ago.

The marriage contract (Ketubah) signed by the bridegroom just before the actual wedding had two main purposes:

> i) to guarantee the material, social and sexual rights of the woman during the marriage.
> ii) to protect the woman's financial position in the event of a divorce or the death of her husband.

The marriage settlement included in the Ketubah is a specific sum of money that the husband is legally obliged to hand over to his wife in case of divorce. It is the first charge on the husband's estate on his death.

The status of the Jewish woman in marriage and in the home is long established and unassailable:

Who can find a capable wife for her worth is far above rubies. Her husband's whole trust is in her....
She is clothed in dignity and power.

The parody of the Jewish mother, repeatedly portrayed with such humour in modern American fiction, is nevertheless firmly based on the age-old concept of the vital importance of the woman's role as a full partner in the marriage.

Polygamy

Polygamy was not forbidden by the Torah, and the Bible includes many instances of men who had more than one wife.

In practice however Jewish society had become almost completely monogamous by Talmudic times. In the tenth century, polygamous unions were absolutely forbidden to all Ashkenazim by Rabbi Gershon; and this prohibition gained widespread acceptance by Sephardim too, even though the practice of polygamy was normal in the Moslem lands in which most were living.

It is interesting that even amongst those Sephardim who did allow polygamy (living in Muslim lands), their marriage contracts stipulated that a husband could only undertake a second marriage with the express permission of his first wife. This was only permitted when the first wife had failed to produce children over a ten-year period.

In modern Israel, where Jewish law governs family and personal matters, polygamy is forbidden.

Divorce

Divorce is easy, if by mutual consent.

In Jewish law, the husband prepares the GET (bill of divorce), and the wife accepts it in a simple ceremony.

Should the woman refuse to accept the Get, the man can appeal to the court (BETH DIN) for assistance. Should a husband refuse to grant a divorce, then no divorce is possible - and it is this aspect that is often criticised today.

In Jewish society great moral and social pressure is exerted by rabbis on an unreasonable husband who refuses to grant a divorce: in Israel, where religious law is paramount in such matters, rabbinical courts have been known to impose sanctions on a recalcitrant husband until he agrees to deliver the required bill of divorce to his wife.

These days, when we live under the civil law of the land, no Beth Din will agree to sanction a Jewish divorce until a civil divorce has first been obtained.

Preparation for marriage

The date for the wedding must be fixed for a time when the bride is not menstruating. The reason for this is that the marriage must be consummated after the wedding and sexual relations are forbidden during menstruation. Weddings may not take place on Shabbat or festivals.

It is customary for the future bridegroom to be called to the reading of the Torah on the Shabbat before the wedding. The engaged man is called He'Arus in the Spanish and Portuguese Synagogue. Families and friends attend synagogue on that day Shabbat He'Arus, and celebrate afterwards.

Some Sephardim also call the bridegroom, the Hatan, to the reading of the Torah on the Shabbat after the wedding.

Marriage ceremony

This consists of two distinct and separate parts. The first ceremony, that of Erusin (betrothal) - or Kiddushin (sanctification) - establishes the legal bond between husband and wife.

Betrothal is roughly equivalent to a modern engagement, with the important difference that a divorce is necessary to break the bond. After the betrothal the couple are legally married, though they are not permitted to live together.

The second ceremony is that of Nissuin (nuptials), and is celebrated under the Chuppah (wedding canopy). After the nuptials, the marriage is complete and may be consummated.

In Talmudic times there was an interval of at least a year between the two ceremonies, during which the bride remained in her father's house and could not live with the bridegroom. Since the twelfth century the general practice has been to combine the bethrothal and the nuptials as two parts of the same wedding ceremony.

The order of the modern wedding ceremony varies slightly between Ashkenazim and Sephardim, and in different communities. However the differences are unimportant.

The service in the synagogue commences with the reading of the normal statutory afternoon service, if the timing is suitable: otherwise a selection of psalms may be recited.

The bridegroom and the bride's father, together with two witnesses (often the officiating ministers) will go to the reading desk. The Ketubah (marriage contract), or an extract from it, is read to the bridegroom, who will sign the document and give the traditional pledge to the witnesses as a sign of having taken an oath. The witnesses will then sign the Ketubah.

The bridegroom next proceeds to the Chuppah (marriage canopy) to await the bride. The bride's father escorts the bride into the synagogue and to the canopy, whilst the choir sings Psalm 118: 'Blessed be you who comes in the name of the Lord.'

In some communities the bridegroom is escorted by his father and future father-in-law and the bride by her mother and future mother-in-law.

With the bride and groom standing under the canopy together with the officiating minister and both sets of parents, the first part of the ceremony, Erusin (betrothal), begins.

The blessings of betrothal are then pronounced over a cup of wine, and God is praised for having instituted the laws of morality and marriage. The couple then drink the wine, and the bridegroom places the wedding ring on the right index finger of the bride, stating:

Behold, you are wedded to me by this ring according to the law of Moses and Israel.

The recital of this formula by the bridegroom, and the willing acceptance of the ring by the bride in the presence of the witnesses effects the marriage. With this act, the ceremony of Erusin is completed.

The Rabbi or minister will deliver an address.

The minister then proceeds to recite the seven blessings of Nissuin (nuptials) over another cup of wine:

> Blessed are You, O Lord our God, King of the universe, who has created the fruit of the vine.
>
> Blessed are You, O Lord our God, King of the universe, the Creator of man.
>
> Blessed are You, O Lord our God, King of the universe, who has created man in your image . . .
>
> May Zion, who was barren, rejoice at the speedy regathering of her children within her .
>
> ....
>
> May this loving couple delight in the same joy that you created at the Garden of Eden.
> Blessed are you, 0 Lord, who brings joy to the Bridegroom and to the Bride.
>
> Blessed are you, O Lord our God, King of the universe, who has created joy and gladness, Bridegroom and Bride, love and harmony, delight and pleasure, peace and companionship. O Lord our God, may there soon be heard in the cities of Judah and in the streets of Jerusalem the voice of joy and the voice of gladness, the voice of the Bridegroom and the voice of the Bride, the sound of wedding celebrations and the festive songs of youths.

Blessed are you, 0 Lord, who causes the Bridegroom to rejoice with the Bride, and who blesses their welfare. 'Give thanks to the Lord for he is good; for his mercy endures for ever.'

May all sorrows depart from Israel, and may joy increase amongst us.

The bride and groom then drink the wine; and the nuptials are concluded by the bridegroom's breaking a glass (by stamping his foot upon it) as a reminder of the destruction of the Temple - for our Rabbis teach us that there must be an element of sorrow, even at moments of the greatest joy.

The religious marriage is now concluded; and the couple proceed to the reading desk where they both sign the civil marriage register, thus completing the marriage in accordance with English law.

After the wedding the couple will retire to a room adjoining the synagogue for a few moments of privacy, symbolising their new status of man and wife, and where they may also break their fast.

The seven nuptial blessings will be recited again after the meal given at the wedding reception; and also (in the presence of the bride and groom) after all meals taken during the first week of marriage, providing that at least ten men are present.

Sex in Marriage

Sex drive

Mankind has developed widely differing attitudes towards basic human instincts such as sex, eating, drinking, and the acquisition of wealth and power.

On the one hand the old pagan world often gloried in satisfying some appetites: Romans would gorge themselves with food and then induce vomiting so that they could gorge themselves all over again. The early Church, on the other hand, together with Jewish sects such as the Essenes, regarded sex as sinful and urged celibacy instead: food and drink were consumed only in sufficient quantities to ensure physical survival: power and wealth were scorned in favour of what was thought to be the ideal life of poverty, chastity and obedience.

Both of these extremes are unacceptable to Judaism, which teaches lofty ideal of

Make yourself holy with that which is permitted to you.

התקדשתם... במה שמותר לכם.

In other words, most human instincts are neither to be suppressed, nor glorified. Instead they are to be indulged in moderation, with self-discipline, so that they may be consecrated to God. This is the reasoning behind the elaborate Jewish laws concerning the preparation and consumption of food (Kashrut), and those concerning the channelling of the sex drive (Marriage).

Were it not for the sexual instinct, no man would build a house, marry a wife or beget children.

The above quotation from the Talmud is a good example of the Rabbis' thinking on the subject.

> Sexual relations are an essential part of marriage; and their denial is a prime ground for divorce. The marriage contract itself specifically refers to the obligation to maintain a full and regular sex life.

Sex and marriage דיני אישות

Judaism regards sex as a normal and essential ingredient of life. It has nevertheless developed detailed laws to channel sexual act. Put at their very simplest the laws contain two main requirements:

i) Sex is not permitted outside marriage.

ii) In marriage, sexual relations may not take place within a woman's menstrual period, or during the week after its end - meaning that sex is barred for at least twelve days in each month.

The Mikveh

The Mikveh (ritual bath) is a large bath of specified dimensions. It contains natural spring or rain water; or else may be filled with ordinary tap water and then connected to a source of natural water, such as a rainwater cistern on the roof.

A woman is rendered 'ritually impure' by her menstrual flow; and immersion in a Mikveh is required to purify her after menstruation, before she is free to resume sexual relations with her husband. The observant Jewish woman will therefore visit the ritual bath before her marriage, and thereafter every month, one week after the ending of her period.

Laws of purity טהרת משפחה

It must be said at once that the laws of ritual purity and sexual abstinence may seem strange and even archaic to some modern minds. The Rabbis have advanced many different reasons for them, including the idea that they are intended to teach man self-discipline so that he may raise his behaviour above that of the animal world.

It is hard to find rational reasons for many of the laws themselves. The ritual bath is not connected with personal hygiene - in fact women have an ordinary bath before entering the Mikveh.

For the traditional Jew all explanations are unnecessary, interesting though they may be. The laws were given by God to the Jewish people to live by:

You shall be holy, for I the Lord your God am holy.

והיתם קדושים כי קדוש אני.

We are encouraged to discuss the laws and to study them: ultimately, though, the laws exist to be accepted and obeyed. Man will never understand God's purposes and ways. Attempts to find satisfying rational explanations for his commandments are secondary and, in most cases, futile.

It should be noted that these laws, like many others in the Torah, are intended to apply to Jews only, and to no one else.

You shall be unto me a kingdom of priests, and a holy nation.

Death and Mourning

To everything there is a season,
and a time to every purpose under the heaven.
A time to be born and a time to die,
A time to weep and a time to laugh;
A time to mourn, and a time to dance.

The system

The practices and customs of traditional Jews relating to death differ from those of their gentile neighbours. A comprehensive pattern of ritual and behaviour has been developed by the Rabbis throughout the ages in an attempt to cope with almost every possible situation.

The Jewish way represents the distillation of many centuries of concern for the bereaved. It recognises the place for natural feelings of sorrow and anguish, and for their expression; but also, teaches submission to the will of God and discourages wild and extravagant displays of emotion. The Rabbis have recognised that close relatives of a recently deceased person are at their most vulnerable, and can easily be upset by a thoughtless word or deed.

> Suffering and its disciplines are, in retrospect, often found to be curiously enriching experiences, helping to deepen sensitivity to the feelings and needs of others.

Care of the dying

The Jewish faith is far from fatalistic. A sick person must be nursed with care, and every effort made to preserve the precious gift of life.

Indeed, so important is this task that the Rabbis have ruled that even the Sabbath may be broken for that purpose - as the preservation of life takes precedence over almost every other consideration.

All the skills of medical aid are to be employed; and God's help should also be invoked in private prayer. If requested a special prayer can be recited before the open Ark in a synagogue.

Care of the body

The human body, dwelling place of the soul and part of the highest form of creation must always be treated with reverence:

God created man in His own image . . . male and female

The Rabbis regard the reduction of a corpse to ashes by fire as an indignity and an outrage. Consequently no traditional Jewish organisation will sanction cremation.

Rending of garments

Keriah (rending) is the traditional Jewish sign of grief, first mentioned early in the Book of Genesis, when Jacob was brought the mangled and blood-stained coat of Joseph:

Jacob rent his clothes, put on sackcloth, and mourned his son ....

The rite is performed at home, on hearing of the death of one's parent, spouse, child, brother or sister. It may also be carried out at the cemetery.

The mourner stands; and a vertical tear (started by a cut) is made down the jacket, shirt or under-garment. This is done on the left hand side for the death of a parent, and on the right hand side in other cases.

The following blessing is recited:

Blessed are you 0 Lord our God, King of the universe, the true judge.

For a parent, the rent must never be fully mended, though it may be stitched together roughly after thirty days. For other relatives it may be repaired loosely after seven days, and the repair completed after thirty days.

The burial

In many communities women did not attend funerals until comparatively recently, but simply remained at home or in the house of mourning. These days women often do go to the cemetery, but they may sometimes be asked to stay in the prayer hall during the actual interment.

The burial service is simple and short. Psalms and appropriate verses from the Bible are read and a memorial address is given by the rabbi or minister. In the Sephardi ritual, some of those present may make seven circuits round the bier (of a male), whilst chanting prayers for the soul of the deceased:

Have mercy upon him, we beseech you ...

Remember the good that he did in life.

May the Gracious One, in the abundance of his

mercy, forgive his transgressions... May he find the

gates of Heaven open ... and may the angels

receive him there....

After the actual burial, the memorial prayer *(hashkabah)* is read and mourners recite the Kaddish. In the Sephardi tradition, the mourners sit in line along one side of the hall while everyone else files past, shaking hands with each mourner, and murmuring words of sympathy and wishes for a long life. The traditional phrase is:

המקום ינחם אתכם

Mourning

My son shed bitter tears for the dead; raise a lament for your grievous loss ... with bitter tears and passionate lament, make your mourning worthy. . . .

The concept of the 'stiff upper lip' is not accepted in Judaism, which has always regarded displays of emotion as natural, healthy and entirely appropriate to times of great sorrow or great joy.

We Jews are however warned by our sages that mourning must be restrained both in manner and in duration:

Mourn for a while ... and then take comfort....
Do not abandon yourself to grief....You cannot help him,
and can only injure yourself.

Tradition recognises three main periods of formal mourning:

> i) the first week
> ii) the first month
> iii) the first year

These are decreed to honour the memory of the dead and to impose some limits on the suffering of the mourners. They are intended as a discipline, by means of which the mourners may be led back in stages from the initial numbness of grief to normal life.

Shivah

Joseph observed seven days mourning for his father.

Shiva, or seven (days of mourning), is observed for a parent, spouse, child, brother or sister.

The period commences with the day of the burial (day one); and continues for seven days, unless prematurely terminated by the advent of one of the festivals, the New Year, or the Day of Atonement.

No mourning is permitted on the Sabbath, a day of joy except for restrictions observed in private. So formal mourning is suspended for that day, even though it is included as one of the seven.

The first three days, described as the time of weeping, is the strictest period; and mourning may be slightly less intense during the last four days, known as the time of lamentation.

On returning home from the funeral, mourners eat the Meal of Consolation. This is served to them the by their friends, who must provide the food themselves and bring it to the house. It consists usually of bread and hard boiled eggs, which symbolise the continuity of life. This must not be bought by the mourners.

A memorial candle is lit and the light maintained for the full seven days or a full year.

Except for possible visits to the synagogue, mourners are obliged to remain in the house of mourning, for the entire week. They no longer sit on the ground, wear sackcloth and sprinkle ashes over their heads as in former days; but now sit on low chairs or stools, refrain from wearing leather shoes or slippers indoors, and dress sombrely and with discretion.

The wearing of black is no longer as widespread as it was and is now discouraged in some communities, unless the mourner feels very strongly about this custom.

Other than in exceptional circumstances, mourners may not work or pursue any occupation during the Shivah. Mourners are not allowed to shave, to cut their hair and nails, or to wear cosmetics. All forms of entertainment and pleasurable activity (including sexual relations) are forbidden; and this ban extends even to the reading and study of the Torah, other than for certain mournful parts such as Lamentations and the Book of Job.

Statutory daily services are held in the house of mourning every day, except on the Sabbath; though where this is not practicable, they may be held in the synagogue. The order of service is varied slightly from the usual, with the addition of the Memorial Prayer and the omission of various passages considered inappropriate. Mourners recite the Kaddish.

> The rules of mourning fulfil two main functions, the first of which is to show respect for the memory of the dead. So far as the mourners are concerned, Shivah serves to shield them from the distractions of everyday life at the time of their greatest vulnerability; and to allow a pause within which they can attempt to adjust gradually to their loss.
>
> Well-wishers often bring food to the mourners. This is a very old custom that has as its object the wish to spare the mourners the effort and distraction of having to provide food for themselves. The bringing of a meal, or part of a meal, by neighbours and friends is an act of kindness that is usually very much appreciated.
>
> Unfortunately the practice, when not properly understood, can go badly wrong. Gifts as such (including chocolates!) must never be brought; and it is both wrong and tactless to do so. Cakes and biscuits are sometimes given; and they may be useful and acceptable when intended for serving to other visitors.
>
> In some communities the rabbi or minister will call at the house of mourning at the conclusion of the Shivah in order to 'raise' the mourners from their state. After reciting a short prayer he will physically help the mourners up from their low stools to mark the ending of the Shivah.

Sheloshim

.. and the children of Israel mourned thirty days for Aaron ....

Sheloshim (thirty) is the name given to the prescribed month of mourning, starting on the day of the burial (day one), and continuing for thirty days. This mourning period is observed for a parent, spouse, child, brother or sister.

After the end of the Shivah (first seven days), the requirements of mourning become very much less onerous, with the mourners returning to work and to most of their usual everyday activities.

Mourners are still forbidden to shave or to cut their hair. They may not marry or visit places of entertainment. Attending festivities, listening to music and similar pleasurable activity is not allowed. Mourners are required to attend daily services at the synagogue, and to recite Kaddish.

Year of mourning

For a parent only, mourning continues for a full year from the day of burial, though in a much modified form.

The only practical restriction that remains after the ending of Sheloshim is the ban on attending places of entertaimnent, or festivity, particularly where music is played, or wearing new clothes.

Though not allowed to shave during the year, the Rabbis permit this rule to be relaxed as soon as the mourner is 'reproached' by friends or acquaintances for looking unkempt.

The conscientious male mourner will continue to attend the daily services in the synagogue so that he may recite Kaddish during the first eleven months

All periods of mourning are measured in accordance with the Jewish calendar.

Memorial stone

At some time during the first year, and usually towards the end of the period, it is customary to place a tombstone over the grave of the deceased. Ashkenazim generally wait for the full year before erecting the memorial.

Rules concerning the inscription vary from community to community; but the text is usually fairly simple, and is inscribed in both Hebrew and English. Ashkenazi tombstones are fixed in a vertical position; and those for Sephardim are laid flat over the grave.

Anniversary

The anniversary of the death of a parent is known as Yahrzeit to Ashkenazim, and as Nahalah (or Annos) to Sephardim. It is marked in a special manner.

The Nahalah, is observed on each anniversary of death according to the Jewish calendar except on the first year of the day of the burial.

On the Sabbath prior to the anniversary, the son of the deceased should ask to be called to the reading of the Torah in the synagogue; and a memorial prayer will be read (Sephardim only). Kaddish will be recited.

Most will observe the actual day of the anniversary quietly, refraining from obvious amusements. It is an opportunity to give charity and to study at least a little Torah. The Nahalah of the parents is observed by a fast when we are able (i.e. not on Shabbat and festivals).

Jewish History

In the Beginning

This is the first lesson in a history course specially prepared for this Talmud Torah. It tells the story of the Jewish people from its earliest beginning down to the present day.

MESOPOTAMIA

Mesopotamia the once fertile strip of land between the rivers Tigris and Euphrates, now known as Iraq, was one of the cradles of human civilisation, possibly even pre-dating that of Egypt. As long as five thousand years ago, its people had already mastered the art of writing and were living in walled cities. Quite the most splendid was Ur of the Chaldees, capital of the Sumerian kingdom, situated on the river Euphrates within easy reach of the Persian Gulf. Its people had attained a high level of artistic achievement, as shown by the beautiful musical instruments, furniture and statues discovered in its ruins and now to be found in the museums of the world.

Visit the British Museum and see some of the wonderful objects, over 4000 years old, dug up from the site of Ur of the Chaldees.

We know from the archaeologists that Ur was conquered and sacked by wild invaders from neighbouring Persia in about 1960 B.C.E. And that date has key significance in the history of the Jewish tradition for, according to the Torah, Mesopotamia was also the origin of the Jewish people.

The story is told in Genesis of how, some time before the destruction of Ur, Abraham's father and his family quit that city and moved to Haran in the north of the country. It was in Haran that Abraham had his vision of the one true God, the creator of heaven and earth. Abraham came from a society of idol-worshippers: his 'discovery' of God was one of the great achievements in human history.

Do you think God can be 'discovered' and his existence proved by the exercise of pure reason?

It was from Haran that Abraham started on his epoch-making journey – in physical terms to establish his family, his followers and their descendants as a distinct people in the land of Canaan, later to be called Israel – and in religious terms, the journey that was to end in the adoption of at least a part of his remarkable insight by over two thousand million human beings.

Why did so many people follow at least part of Abraham's beliefs and who are they?
(Jews, Christians and Muslims)

The next great milestone in the history of the Jewish tradition occurred about eight hundred years later in Egypt, the other leading centre of ancient civilisation. Famine in Canaan had previously driven Abraham's descendants to leave that country and settle in the eastern part of the Nile delta, called the Land of Goshen in the Bible. And it was from Egypt that Moses led his people out into the desert for a renewal of that revelation of the Divine previously granted to their ancestors Abraham, Isaac, and Jacob.

Mesopotamia and Egypt, at each end of the Fertile Crescent where civilisation began, represented the two peaks attained by human society at the dawn of Jewish history. Abraham left the luxury and comfort of his homeland because of its spiritual decay. He and his followers emigrated to an unsophisticated new land – one in which they could live their lives and worship the one true God undisturbed by the corruption that had surrounded them. In similar manner, Moses later led his followers into the uncertain perils of the desert, departing from the splendour and moral laxity of Egypt without a backward glance.

Those migrations, at the very start of the Jewish tradition, were both prompted by the idealism which chose absolute, divinely-inspired values in preference to those compromised by luxury, conformity and security. And that, in essence, is the Jewish story.

Are all the Jewish people today descended from Abraham?
No, there have been many converts throughout history. Even Abraham himself made converts from his servants and those living around him

Can you name any famous converts in Jewish history?
Ruth, from whom King David was descended, was a convert to Judaism

Are converts regarded as full members of the Jewish people?
Yes, all sincere converts to Judaism are regarded as if they were personally descended from Abraham and are equal in every way to his physical descendants.

MATERIAL FOR LESSON 1

MAP

Map of the Fertile Crescent.

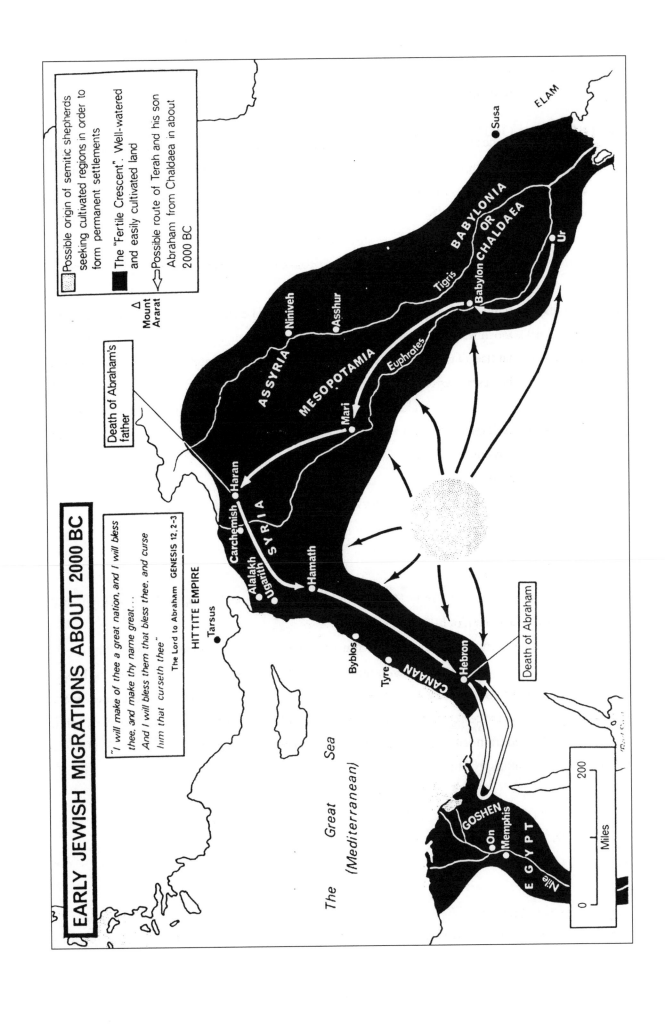

EARLY JEWISH MIGRATIONS ABOUT 2000 BC

"I will make of thee a great nation, and I will bless thee, and make thy name great...
And I will bless them that bless thee, and curse him that curseth thee"

The Lord to Abraham GENESIS 12, 2-3

Death of Abraham's father

Death of Abraham

Possible origin of semitic shepherds seeking cultivated regions in order to form permanent settlements

The "Fertile Crescent". Well-watered and easily cultivated land

Possible route of Terah and his son Abraham from Chaldaea in about 2000 BC

Mount Ararat

HITTITE EMPIRE

Tarsus

Alalakh
Ugarith
Carchemish
SYRIA
Haran
Hamath

ASSYRIA
Niniveh
Asshur
MESOPOTAMIA
Mari
Euphrates
Tigris

BABYLONIA OR CHALDAEA
Babylon
Ur

Susa

ELAM

Byblos
Tyre
CANAAN
Hebron

GOSHEN
EGYPT
On
Memphis
Nile

The Great Sea
(Mediterranean)

Miles
0   200

Abraham, Founder of Monotheism

At Pesah, we read in the Haggadah:

> *Originally our ancestors worshipped idols, but God brought us to worship him.*

Abraham's discovery that there is only one God – the creator of heaven and earth – and that belief in other gods (idols) is worthless, was a truly epoch-making event.

Though some societies of that time believed in a 'high god' or a 'chief god', above all the other gods, the idea of only one God – known as monotheism – was then unknown.

In Haran, God commanded Abraham to leave his father's house and the luxurious idol-worshipping society of Mesopotamia and travel to the far more primitive land of Canaan where he could worship God without distraction.

> *Go out from your land, from your relatives, and from your father's house to the land which I*
> *will show you.*
> *(Genesis 12.1)*

There Abraham started his own family. His first son Ishmael (traditionally regarded as the 'father' of all Arabs) was born to a woman of his household.

God commanded Abraham to circumcise himself and his followers as a special mark of the special relationship – known as a covenant, or solemn agreement – between God and Abraham. Then God blessed Abraham and Sarah with a son Isaac, and promised that Abraham's descendants would become as numerous as the stars in the sky and that they would inherit the land of Canaan – the Promised Land.

Circumcision was not new to the ancient world: it was routine in Egypt. For Abraham's people, it became the necessary sign of their covenant with God.

> *What is circumcision called in Hebrew?*
> Brit Milah – Covenant of Circumcision

> *When is it performed?*

One of the highlights of Abraham's experiences in the Promised Land was God's testing his faith by commanding him to take his beloved son, Isaac up to Mount Moriah and offer him as a sacrifice. Can you image how Abraham would have felt when given such a command. He and Sarah had longed for such a son, and their wish was finally fulfilled in their old age. And now God commanded Abraham to take this child and offer him as a sacrifice!

Was it fair for God to have asked Abraham to make such a sacrifice?

What would you (or your father) have done in Abraham's place?

How would you have felt if you were Isaac?

Without questions, Abraham got up early in the morning, saddled his own donkey, took his son Isaac, and wood, and headed for Mount Moriah [which would later be the site of the Temple in Jerusalem]. When God saw that Abraham was prepared to sacrifice Isaac, he sent an angel to command Abraham not to kill his son, Abraham saw a ram entangled in the bushes, and offered the ram in Isaac's place.

An account of this episode, known as the 'Akedah' is read on the second day of Rosh Hashanah - because that is when it took place. A beautiful poem by Judah Samuel Abbas, describing what happened, is sung before the blowing of the shofar on both days of Rosh Hashanah. This is called 'Et Sha'are Ratson' (which means 'When the gates of mercy are opened').

When Isaac, Abraham's beloved son, wanted to marry, his father sent a trusted servant back to Mesopotamia to choose a wife for him from his own people.

Why do you think he did that?

Isaac inherited God's covenant from his father Abraham. So too did Isaac's son Jacob.

Jacob had twelve sons and one daughter, Dinah. The future Twelve Tribes of Israel are descended from his sons.

Famine in the land of Canaan caused Jacob and his sons to take refuge in Egypt, where they settled in Goshen, the eastern part of the Nile delta.

There, we read in the Torah that they were enslaved by the Egyptians and ill-treated.

MATERIAL FOR LESSON 2

MAP

Abraham's journey from Haran to the Promised Land.

PHOTOCOPY

from Rosh Hashana Prayer Book 'Et Sha'are Ratson'

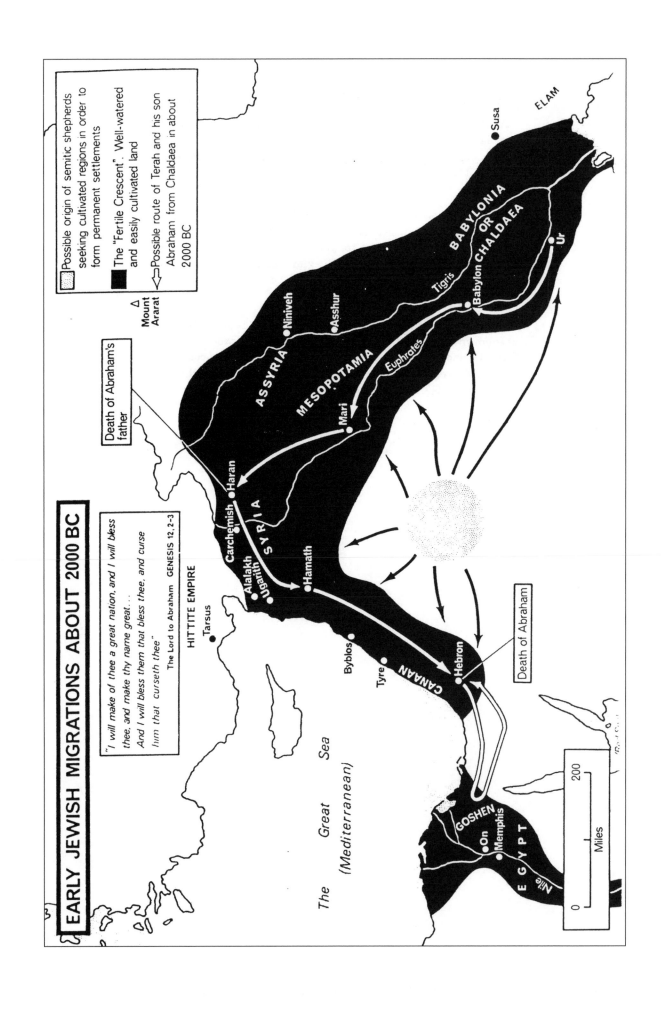

EARLY JEWISH MIGRATIONS ABOUT 2000 BC

"I will make of thee a great nation, and I will bless thee, and make thy name great...
And I will bless them that bless thee, and curse him that curseth thee"

The Lord to Abraham GENESIS 12, 2-3

HITTITE EMPIRE

Possible origin of semitic shepherds seeking cultivated regions in order to form permanent settlements

The "Fertile Crescent". Well-watered and easily cultivated land

Possible route of Terah and his son Abraham from Chaldaea in about 2000 BC

△
Mount
Ararat

Death of Abraham's father

Death of Abraham

Tarsus

Carchemish Haran

Alalakh
Ugarit

S Y R I A

Hamath

Byblos

Tyre

Hebron

C A N A A N

GOSHEN

On
Memphis

E G Y P T

Nile

The Great Sea
(Mediterranean)

Niniveh

Asshur

ASSYRIA

MESOPOTAMIA

Mari

Euphrates

Tigris

Babylon

BABYLONIA
OR
CHALDAEA

Ur

Susa

ELAM

0 200 Miles

Et Sha'are Ratson

Chanted by the Congregation.

Composed by Judah Samuel Abbas, whose name forms the acrostic.

At the time that the gates of favour are about to be opened; on this day on which to thee, O God! I spread forth my hands. On this day of judgment, O remember in my favour, Abraham who bound, Isaac who was bound, and the altar.

At the last of Abraham's trials, the last of the ten[1]: (God said to him) "The son which Sarah hath borne unto thee—that son to whom thy soul is bound—go, and offer him up as a pure burnt-offering, on the mount where my glory shall appear unto thee with shining splendour." "O remember," &c.

The Patriarch then said unto Sarah, "Thy beloved Isaac has now grown up, but he has not yet been taught the worship of God: I will therefore go and instruct him according to God's command." "Go, my lord, (she answered) but not too far." "Let thy heart confide in God," he replied. "O remember," &c.

At the dawn of day he arose to proceed early on his journey, and with him two of his heathen servants. On the third day he

עֵת שַׁעֲרֵי רָצוֹן לְהִפָּתֵחַ

יוֹם אֶהְיֶה כַפַּי לְאֵל שׁוֹטֵחַ

אָנָּא זְכוֹר נָא לִי בְּיוֹם הוֹכֵחַ

עוֹקֵד וְהַנֶּעֱקַד וְהַמִּזְבֵּחַ:

בְּאַחֲרִית נִסָּה בְּסוֹף הָעֲשָׂרָה

הַבֵּן אֲשֶׁר נוֹלַד לְךָ מִשָּׂרָה

אִם נַפְשְׁךָ בּוֹ עַד מְאֹד נִקְשָׁרָה

קוּם הַעֲלֵהוּ לִי לְעוֹלָה בָרָה

עַל הַר אֲשֶׁר כָּבוֹד לְךָ זוֹרֵחַ:   עוקד

אָמַר לְשָׂרָה כִּי חֲמוּדֵךְ יִצְחָק

גָּדֵל וְלֹא לָמַד עֲבוֹדַת שַׁחַק

אֵלֵךְ וְאוֹרֵהוּ אֲשֶׁר לוֹ אֵל חָק

אָמְרָה לְכָה אֲדוֹן אֲבָל אַל תִּרְחָק

עֲנֵה יְהִי לִבֵּךְ בָּאֵל בּוֹטֵחַ:   עוקד

שָׁחַר וְהִשְׁכִּים לַהֲלוֹךְ בַּבֹּקֶר

וּשְׁנֵי נְעָרָיו מִמָּתֵי הַשֶּׁקֶר

approached the sought-for place, where he beheld the appearance
of the divine resplendent glory: there he paused to consider how
to perform worthily the divine behest.   "O remember Abraham
who bound, Isaac who was bound, and the altar."

The young men understood that he asked them when he said,
"Have ye seen a splendid light shining on the summit of mount
Moriah?"   They answered, "We see nought but caverns."   "Stay
here with the ass, (he replied) ye stolid and dull people; whilst I
and the lad go yonder to prostrate ourselves."   "O remember," &c.

They both proceeded to perform the sacred work, when Isaac
addressed his father thus, "Father, I see the fire and the wood
prepared, but where, my lord, is the lamb, according to the established
rule; hast thou then this day forgotten thy law?" "O remember," &c.

His father answered, "Trust in the living God, for he will provide
the lamb for the burnt-offering; for know, that whatsoever pleaseth
God, that he will do; let us this day, my son, erect a throne[1] before
him; and then, the sacrifice and sacrificer shall both be exalted."
"O remember," &c.

Then the son willing to be made a sacrifice, and the father ready
to sacrifice him, knocked at the gates of mercy, that they might
be opened, both confident in God, and firmly trusting to his mercy;
for "They who trust in the Lord shall obtain renewed strength."
Thus they sought to join the inheritance of God.   "O remember," &c.

With strength and might did Abraham prepare the wood for the
burnt-offering, and bound Isaac as if binding a lamb: then it was

[1] An altar.

Rosh Hashana Prayer Book 'Et Sha'are Ratson'

יוֹם הַ־שְּׁלִישִׁי נָ־גְעוּ אֶל חֵקֶר

וַיַּרְא דְּמוּת כָּבוֹד וְהוֹד וַיֶּקֶר

עָמַד וְהִתְבּוֹנֵן לְהַמְשֵׁחַ

עוֹקֵד וְהַנֶּעֱקָד וְהַמִּזְבֵּחַ :

יָדְעוּ נְעָרָיו כִּי קְרָאָם לֵאמֹר

אוֹר הֲרְאִיתֶם צִץ בְּרֹאשׁ הַר הַמּוֹר

וַיֹּא־מְרוּ לֹא נֶחֱזֶה רַק מַחֲמוֹר

עָנָה שְׁבוּ פֹּה עַם מְשׁוּלִים לַחֲמוֹר

וַאֲנִי וְהַנַּעַר לְהִשְׁתַּטֵּחַ : עוקד

הָלְכוּ שְׁנֵיהֶם לַעֲשׂוֹת בִּמְלָאכָה

וַיַּ־עֲנֶה יִצְחָק לְאָבִיו כָּכָה

אָבִי רָאֹה אֵשׁ וַעֲצֵי מַעֲרָכָה

אַיֵּה אֲדֹנִי שֶׂה אֲשֶׁר כַּהֲלָכָה

הֲאַתְּ בְּיוֹם זֶה דַּרְ־תְּךָ שׁוֹכֵחַ : עוקד

וַיַּ־עֲנֶה אָבִיו בְּאֵל חַי מַחְסֶה

כִּי הוּא אֲשֶׁר יִרְאֶה לְעוֹלָה הַשֶּׂה

דַּע כֹּל־אֲשֶׁר יַחְפּוֹץ אֱלֹהִים יַעֲשֶׂה

נִבְנֶה בְּנֵי הַיּוֹם לְפָנָיו כִּסֵּא

אוֹ יַ־אֲמִיר זֶבַח וְהַזּוֹבֵחַ : עוקד

דָּפְקוּ בְּשַׁעֲרֵי רַ־חֲמִים לִפְתּוֹחַ

הַבֵּן לְהִזָּבֵחַ וְאָב לִזְבּוֹחַ

קֹוִים לָאֵל וּבְרַ־חֲמָיו לִבְטוֹחַ

קֹוֵי יְיָ יַחֲלִיפוּ כֹחַ

דָּרְשׁוּ בְּנַחֲלַת אֵל לְהִסְתַּפֵּחַ : עוקד

הֵכִין עֲצֵי עוֹלָה בְּאוֹן וְחַיִל

וַיַּ־עֲקוֹד יִצְחָק כְּעָקְרוּ אַיִל

that the bright light of day appeared to them as dismal night; tears rushed down their cheeks, the eye in truth weeping bitterly, but the heart rejoicing. "O remember Abraham who bound, Isaac who was bound, and the altar."

"O tell my mother (said Isaac), that her joy has now departed, for the son she bore at ninety years of age has become a prey to the knife and to the fire: where, oh where shall I seek for one to comfort her? Oh how I grieve for my mother! in her weeping and distress." "O remember," &c.

"Through the knife my speech faltereth; yet sharpen it, father, I beseech thee. Have courage and bind me strongly! and when the fire shall have consumed my flesh, take with thee the remains of my ashes, and say to Sarah, Behold, this is the savour of Isaac." "O remember," &c.

Then all the angels of the throne were deeply moved; Ophanim and Seraphim interceded and implored for mercy for this chief of the host and said, "O grant a redemption and appoint a ransom for him. Deprive not the world of so great a luminary." "O remember," &c.

The Lord of heaven then said to Abraham, "Lay not thy hand on him, who is one of the three illustrious lights; and ye angelic hosts return in peace, for this will be a meritorious day for the children of Jerusalem, and thereon will I pardon the sin of Jacob's posterity." "O remember," &c.

וַיְהִי מְאוֹר יוֹמָם בְּעֵינָם לַיְל

וַהֲמוֹן דְּמָעָיו נוֹזְלִים בַּחֵיל

עַיִן בְּמַר בּוֹכָה וְלֵב שָׂמֵחַ

עוֹקֵד וְהַנֶּעֱקָד וְהַמִּזְבֵּחַ :

שִׂיחוּ לְאִמִּי כִּי שְׂשׂוֹנָהּ פָּנָה

הַבֵּן אֲשֶׁר יָלְדָה לְתִשְׁעִים שָׁנָה

הָיָה לְאֵשׁ וּלְמַאֲכֶלֶת מָנָה

אָנָה אֲבַקֵּשׁ לָהּ מְנַחֵם אָנָה

צַר לִי לְאֵם תִּבְכֶּה וְתִתְיַפֵּחַ : עוקד

מִמַּאֲכֶלֶת יֶהֱמֶה מִדְבָּרִי

נָא חַדְּדָהּ אָבִי בְּעֵת מַאְסָרִי

חֹזֶק וְאֵת יְקַךְ יְקוֹד בִּבְשָׂרִי

קַח עִמְּךָ הַנִּשְׁאָר מֵאֶפְרִי

וֶאֱמוֹר לְשָׂרָה זֶה לְיִצְחָק רֵיחַ : עוקד

וַיֶּהֱמוּ כָּל־מַלְאֲכֵי מֶרְכָּבָה

אוֹפָן וְשָׂרָף שׁוֹ־אֲלִים בִּנְדָבָה

מִתְחַ־נְּנִים לָאֵל בְּעַד שַׂר צָבָא

אָנָּא תְּנָה פִּדְיוֹם וְכוֹפֶר הָבָה

אַל נָא יְהִי עוֹלָם בְּלִי יָרֵחַ : עוקד

אָמַר לְאַבְרָהָם ׀ אֲדוֹן שָׁמַיִם

אַל תִּשְׁ־לָחָה יַד אֶל שְׁלִישׁ אוֹרַיִם

שׁוּבוּ לְשָׁלוֹם מַלְאֲכֵי מַחֲנַיִם

יוֹם זֶה זְכוּת לִבְנֵי יְרוּשָׁלֵם

בּוֹ חֵטְא בְּנֵי יַעֲקֹב אֲנִי סוֹלֵחַ : עוקד

O thou who dwellest in the highest heavens, remember thy covenant and oath to this tempest-tossed and suffering nation! [On Week-days say, Hearken to the modulated sounding of the Shofár [1]] [On the Sabbath say instead of the preceding line, Hearken to the prayer which reminds us of the sounds of the Shofár]; and say unto Zion the time of her salvation has come, "Behold, I send Yinnon [2] and Elijah unto you [3]."

On Sabbath begin "Let thy mercy," p. 111.

לִבְרֵי־תֶךָ שׁוֹכֵן זְבוּל וּשְׁבוּעָה

זָכְרָה לְעֵדָה סוֹ־עֲרָה וּנְגוּעָה

בחול

וּשְׁמַע תְּקִיעָה תְּרוּ־קְעָה וּתְרוּעָה

(בשבת אומרים

וּשְׁמַע תְּפִלָּה זָכְרָה וּתְרוּעָה)

וֶאֱמוֹר לְצִיּוֹן בָּא זְמַן הַיְשׁוּעָה

יָנוֹן וְאֵלִיָּה אֲנִי שׁוֹלֵחַ: ינון

בשבת מתחילים: יהי חסדך דף קי״א׳

_____

כתב רבינו סעדיה מה שצונו הבורא יתברך לתקוע בשופר בר״ה יש

בזה עשרה ענינים:

The Birth of a Nation

God had promised Abraham that:

> *Your offspring shall be strangers in a land not belonging to them, and they will be enslaved*
> *and oppressed for four hundred years.*
> *(Genesis 15: 13)*

and also

> *I shall also judge the nation that they (the Israelites) shall serve, and afterwards they shall*
> *leave with great wealth.*
> *(Genesis 15: 14)*

We all know the story of how God delivered the children of Israel from slavery in Egypt and how Moses – who had been brought up as a prince in Pharaoh's household – led the people out of Egypt, from slavery to freedom.

We read in the Torah (Exodus 12: 38) that 'a mixed multitude went up with them'.

> *What does the Torah mean by a 'mixed multitude'?*

> *Were people other than the children of Israel allowed to share in God's message?*

> *What lesson does that teach us?*

The Israelites did not rejoice at their freedom until they had crossed the Red Sea and seen Egyptian army drowning in the waters;

Then Moses and the Children of Israel sang this song to the Lord saying:

> *I will sing to the Lord, for He has triumphed gloriously: the horse and his rider He has*
> *hurled into the sea...Exodus 15: 1)*

The Song of Moses is called 'Az Yashir Moshe' or the 'Shirah' (song) in Hebrew. Listen to it being sung – can you sing it as well?

Do you know which other parts of the service use this tune?

It is written in the Book of Job:

I should have denied the One above if I rejoiced at the destruction of him that hated me or exulted that evil overtook him.

Do you think that God fully approved of the rejoicing at the drowning of the Egyptian army in the Red Sea?

A midrash (rabbinic parable) describes how God rebuked the angels rejoicing at the drowning of the Egyptians in the Red Sea. '*How can you celebrate*', God is pictured as saying, '*when my creatures are being destroyed?*'

How is that lesson carried into the synagogue service?
Only half the Hallel, psalms of rejoicing are recited on the latter days of Pesah for that very reason.

The act of gaining freedom from slavery was not enough to forge a new nation. Seven weeks after Passover we celebrate the supreme event in our history when, in the desert of Sinai, we received the Torah from God.

What is that celebration called?
Shavuot

In an awesome encounter with the entire nation of Israel gathered together at the foot of Mount Sinai, God revealed himself to them, both collectively and individually.

There were peals of thunder and flashes of lightening, dense cloud on the mountain and a loud trumpet blast: the people in the camp were all terrified.

and that pivotal event in Jewish history – the giving of the Ten Commandments – so impressed itself on the consciousness of the people that a midrash (rabbinic parable) has it that all future generations of Jews yet unborn were also present at Sinai for that unique revelation.

Do you regard the events at Sinai as the key event in the history of the Jews?

At Sinai, by freely accepting the yoke of the Torah from God the Jewish people, so to speak, exchanged their previous bondage to Pharaoh for future bondage to God.

A rabbinic parable describes how God originally offered his Torah to all the peoples of the earth and how each in turn rejected it because of the heavy burden involved, save for the tiny and previously insignificant people of Israel.

By their act of accepting God's Torah at Sinai, the Hebrew tribes acquired a reason for their freedom, a stamp of nationhood to which they have clung with remarkable tenacity ever since.

When did it all happen?
In about 1200 BCE, that is over 3,000 years ago.

What else was going on in the world at that time?
The Greeks were fighting the Trojan war, as described by the poet Homer.

Although one should not measure one Mitzvah against another, The Ten Commandments have become known as the most important Mitzvot in the Torah. Not only do the Ten Commandments portray God's revelation to us on Mount Sinai, they also represent all the 613 Mitzvot contained in the Torah.

The Ten Commandments are divided equally into two parts, representing those Commandments between God and man, and those between man and his fellow man.

Some commandments are positive – 'You shall ...' and others are negative – 'You shall not ...' Of the 613 Mitzvot there are 365 positive commands and 248 negative commandments.

THE TEN COMMANDMENTS

1. I am the Lord your God who has brought you out of the land of Egypt out of the house of bondage.

2. You shall have no other gods before me, and you shall not make for yourselves any graven images...

3. You shall not take the name of the Lord your God in vain...

4. Remember the Sabbath day to keep it holy...

5. Honour your father and your mother...

6. You shall not murder

7. You shall not commit adultery.

8. You shall not steal.

9. You shall not bear false witness against your neighbour (do not lie).

10 You shall not covet your neighbour's house, you shall not covet your neighbour's wife, nor anything belonging to your neighbour.

As the receiving of the Torah at Mount Sinai was one of the most important events in our history, we relate it in a very dramatic way. When this part is read in Synagogue on Shabbat Yitro and on the Festival of Shavuot, it is sung using special notes (called Ta'amim). It is usual for the Rabbi of the Synagogue to be given the honour of being called for the reading of the Ten Commandments, and the whole congregation stands.

MATERIAL FOR LESSONS 3

BOOKS

a) Haggadah

b) Daily and Occasional Prayer Book

MAP

Egypt and the Land of Goshen. From Slavery to the Promised Land.

PHOTOCOPIES

a) 'The Song of Moses'

b) 'The Ten Commandments'

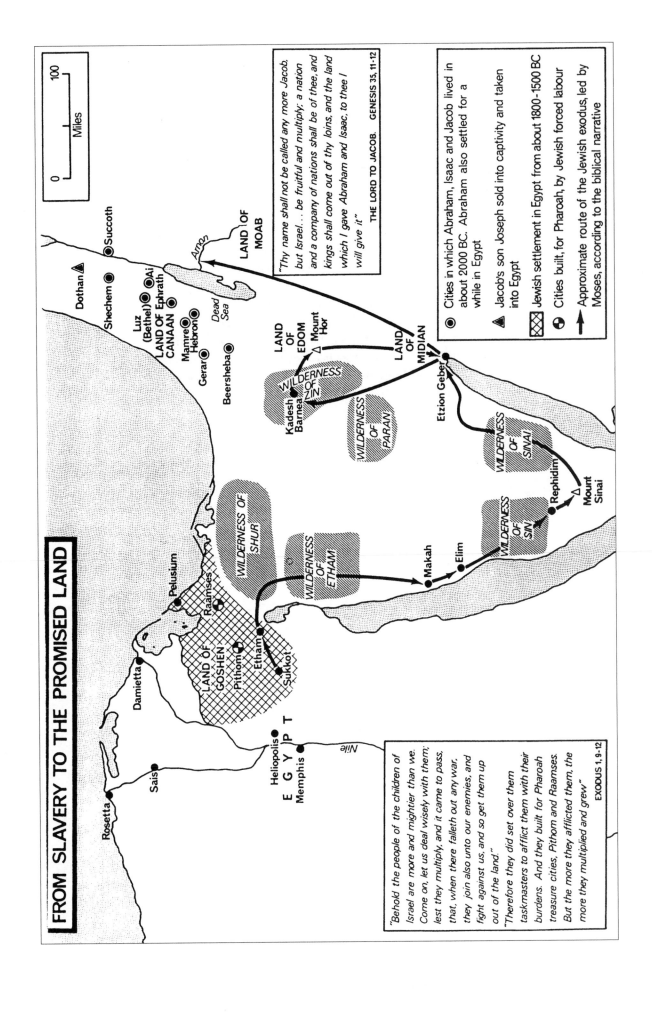

FROM SLAVERY TO THE PROMISED LAND

Rosetta
Sais
Damietta
Heliopolis
Memphis
E G Y P T
Nile

Pelusium
LAND OF GOSHEN
Raamses
Pithom
Etham
Sukkot

WILDERNESS OF SHUR
WILDERNESS OF ETHAM
WILDERNESS OF SIN
WILDERNESS OF SINAI

Makah
Elim
Rephidim
△ **Mount Sinai**

Etzion Geber
LAND OF MIDIAN

WILDERNESS OF PARAN
WILDERNESS OF ZIN
Kadesh Barnea
LAND OF EDOM
△ **Mount Hor**

Beersheba
Gerar
Mamre **Hebron**
LAND OF CANAAN
Luz (Bethel) **Ai**
Ephrath
Shechem
Dothan ▲
Succoth
Dead Sea
Arnon
LAND OF MOAB

Miles
0 ___ 100

"Thy name shall not be called any more Jacob, but Israel . . . be fruitful and multiply: a nation and a company of nations shall be of thee, and kings shall come out of thy loins, and the land which I gave Abraham and Isaac, to thee I will give it"
THE LORD TO JACOB.   GENESIS 35, 11-12

◉ Cities in which Abraham, Isaac and Jacob lived in about 2000 BC. Abraham also settled for a while in Egypt

▲ Jacob's son Joseph sold into captivity and taken into Egypt

▨ Jewish settlement in Egypt from about 1800-1500 BC

◓ Cities built, for Pharoah, by Jewish forced labour

→ Approximate route of the Jewish exodus, led by Moses, according to the biblical narrative

"Behold the people of the children of Israel are more and mightier than we. Come on, let us deal wisely with them: lest they multiply, and it came to pass, that, when there falleth out any war, they join also unto our enemies, and fight against us, and so get them up out of the land."

"Therefore they did set over them taskmasters to afflict them with their burdens. And they built for Pharoah treasure cities, Pithom and Raamses. But the more they afflicted them, the more they multiplied and grew"
EXODUS 1, 9-12

"Then sang Moses and the children of Israel this song unto the Lord, and thus did they say :—I will sing unto the Lord, for he hath triumphed gloriously : the horse and his rider hath he thrown into the sea. The Lord is my strength and song, and he is become my salvation : he is my God, and I will glorify him ; my fathers' God, and I will exalt him. The Lord is the Lord of war : the Lord is his name. The chariots and host of Pharaoh hath he cast into the sea : his chosen captains are sunk in the Red Sea. The deeps have covered them : they went down unto the depths like a stone. Thy right hand, O Lord, glorious in power, thy right hand, O Lord, hath crushed the enemy. And in the greatness of thy excellency thou overthrowest them that rise up against thee : thou sendest forth thy wrath, it consumeth them as stubble. And with the blast of thy nostrils the waters were piled up : the fluids stood upright as a wall, and the deeps became congealed in the heart of the sea. The enemy said, 'I will

אָז יָשִׁיר מֹשֶׁה וּבְנֵי יִשְׂרָאֵל אֶת־הַשִּׁירָה הַזֹּאת לַיְיָ וַיֹּאמְרוּ

לֵאמֹר   אָשִׁירָה לַיְיָ כִּי גָאֹה גָּאָה   סוּס

וְרֹכְבוֹ רָמָה בַיָּם: עָזִּי וְזִמְרָת יָהּ וַיְהִי־לִי

לִישׁוּעָה   זֶה אֵלִי וְאַנְוֵהוּ   אֱלֹהֵי

אָבִי וַאֲרֹמְמֶנְהוּ:   יְיָ אִישׁ מִלְחָמָה יְיָ

שְׁמוֹ:   מַרְכְּבֹת פַּרְעֹה וְחֵילוֹ יָרָה בַיָּם   וּמִבְחַר

שָׁלִשָׁיו טֻבְּעוּ בְיַם סוּף: תְּהֹמֹת יְכַסְיֻמוּ יָרְדוּ בִמְצוֹלֹת כְּמוֹ־

אָבֶן: יְמִינְךָ יְיָ נֶאְדָּרִי בַּכֹּחַ   יְמִינְךָ

יְיָ תִּרְעַץ אוֹיֵב: וּבְרֹב גְּאוֹנְךָ תַּהֲרֹס

קָמֶיךָ   תְּשַׁלַּח חֲרֹנְךָ יֹאכְלֵמוֹ כַּקַּשׁ:   וּבְרוּחַ

אַפֶּיךָ נֶעֶרְמוּ מַיִם   נִצְּבוּ כְמוֹ נֵד

נֹזְלִים   קָפְאוּ תְהֹמֹת בְּלֶב־יָם: אָמַר

אוֹיֵב אֶרְדֹּף אַשִּׂיג   אֲחַלֵּק שָׁלָל תִּמְלָאֵמוֹ

pursue—overtake—divide the spoil : my soul shall be satisfied upon them : I will unsheath my sword, my hand shall destroy them.' Thou didst but blow with thy wind—the sea covered them : they sank as lead in the mighty waters. Who is like unto thee, O Lord, amongst the mighty? Who is like unto thee, glorious in holiness, tremendous in praises, working miracles? Thou stretchedst out thy right hand, the earth swallowed them. Thus dost thou guide with thy kindness the people which thou hast redeemed, and leadest them in thy strength to thy holy habitation. The people have heard it, and tremble ; pangs have seized the inhabitants of Philistia. Then were the chieftains of Edom troubled ; trembling took hold of the mighty men of Moab : all the inhabitants of Canaan are melted away. Fear and dread falleth upon them ; by the greatness of thine arm they are as still as a stone ; till thy people pass over, O Lord, till the people pass over which thou hast acquired. Thou wilt bring them and plant them in the mount of thine inheritance, the place, O Lord, which thou hast made for thy residence ; in the sanctuary, O Lord, which thy hands have established. The Lord shall reign for ever and ever."

"For unto the Lord is the sovereignty[1]; and he governs the nations. And deliverers[2] shall go up to mount Zion, to judge the mount of Esau : and the kingdom shall be the Lord's. And the Lord shall be king over all the earth : in that day shall the Lord be One, and his name One[3]."

נַפְשִׁי   אָרִיק חַרְבִּי תּוֹרִישֵׁמוֹ יָדִי׃   נָשַׁפְתָּ

בְּרוּחֲךָ כִּסָּמוֹ יָם   צָלְלוּ כַּעוֹפֶרֶת בְּמַיִם

אַדִּירִים׃   מִי־כָמֹכָה בָּאֵלִם יְיָ   מִי

כָּמֹכָה נֶאְדָּר בַּקֹּדֶשׁ   נוֹרָא תְהִלֹּת עֹשֵׂה־

פֶלֶא׃   נָטִיתָ יְמִינְךָ תִּבְלָעֵמוֹ אָרֶץ׃   נָחִיתָ

בְחַסְדְּךָ עַם זוּ גָּאָלְתָּ   נֵהַלְתָּ בְעָזְּךָ אֶל נְוֵה

קָדְשֶׁךָ׃   שָׁמְעוּ עַמִּים יִרְגָּזוּן   חִיל

אָחַז יֹשְׁבֵי פְּלָשֶׁת׃   אָז נִבְהֲלוּ אַלּוּפֵי

אֱדוֹם   אֵילֵי מוֹאָב יֹאחֲזֵמוֹ רָעַד   נָמֹגוּ

כֹּל יֹשְׁבֵי כְנָעַן׃   תִּפֹּל עֲלֵיהֶם אֵימָתָה

וָפַחַד   בִּגְדֹל זְרוֹעֲךָ יִדְּמוּ כָּאָבֶן   עַד

יַעֲבֹר עַמְּךָ יְיָ   עַד יַעֲבֹר עַם זוּ

קָנִיתָ׃   תְּבִאֵמוֹ וְתִטָּעֵמוֹ בְּהַר נַחֲלָתְךָ   מָכוֹן

לְשִׁבְתְּךָ פָּעַלְתָּ יְיָ   מִקְּדָשׁ אֲדֹנָי כּוֹנְנוּ

יָדֶיךָ׃   יְיָ יִמְלֹךְ   לְעֹלָם וָעֶד׃

כִּי לַיְיָ הַמְּלוּכָה וּמוֹשֵׁל בַּגּוֹיִם׃ וְעָלוּ מוֹשִׁיעִים בְּהַר צִיּוֹן לִשְׁפֹּט

אֶת־הַר עֵשָׂו׃ וְהָיְתָה לַיְיָ הַמְּלוּכָה׃ וְהָיָה יְיָ לְמֶלֶךְ עַל כָּל־

הָאָרֶץ׃ בַּיּוֹם הַהוּא יִהְיֶה יְיָ אֶחָד וּשְׁמוֹ אֶחָד׃

THE TEN COMMANDMENTS.

Exodus xx. 1–17.

And God spake all these words, saying:

1. I am the Lord thy God, who brought thee out of the land of Egypt, out of the house of bondage.

2. Thou shalt have no other gods before me. Thou shalt not make unto thee a graven image; nor the form of anything that is in heaven above, or that is in the earth beneath, or that is in the water under the earth; thou shalt not bow down thyself unto them, nor serve them: for I the Lord thy God am a jealous God, visiting the iniquity of the fathers upon the children, upon the third and upon the fourth generation, unto them that hate me: and shewing lovingkindness to the thousandth generation, unto them that love me and keep my commandments.

3. Thou shalt not take the name of the Lord thy God in vain; for the Lord will not hold him guiltless that taketh his name in vain.

4. Remember the sabbath day to keep it holy. Six days shalt thou labour, and do all thy work: but the seventh day is a sabbath unto the Lord thy God: in it thou shalt not do any work, thou, nor thy son, nor thy daughter, thy manservant, nor thy maidservant, nor thy cattle, nor thy stranger that is within thy gates: for in six days the Lord made heaven and earth, the sea and all that is therein, and rested on the seventh day: wherefore the Lord blessed the sabbath day and hallowed it.

עשרת הדברות:
שמות כ׳ א׳–י״ז

וַיְדַבֵּר אֱלֹהִים אֵת כָּל־הַדְּבָרִים הָאֵלֶּה לֵאמֹר:

א אָנֹכִי יְהוָה אֱלֹהֶיךָ אֲשֶׁר הוֹצֵאתִיךָ מֵאֶרֶץ מִצְרַיִם מִבֵּית עֲבָדִים:

ב לֹא־יִהְיֶה לְךָ אֱלֹהִים אֲחֵרִים עַל־פָּנָי: לֹא־תַעֲשֶׂה לְךָ פֶסֶל וְכָל־תְּמוּנָה אֲשֶׁר בַּשָּׁמַיִם מִמַּעַל וַאֲשֶׁר בָּאָרֶץ מִתָּחַת וַאֲשֶׁר בַּמַּיִם מִתַּחַת לָאָרֶץ: לֹא־תִשְׁתַּחֲוֶה לָהֶם וְלֹא תָעָבְדֵם כִּי אָנֹכִי יְהוָה אֱלֹהֶיךָ אֵל קַנָּא פֹּקֵד עֲוֹן אָבֹת עַל־בָּנִים עַל־שִׁלֵּשִׁים וְעַל־רִבֵּעִים לְשֹׂנְאָי: וְעֹשֶׂה חֶסֶד לַאֲלָפִים לְאֹהֲבַי וּלְשֹׁמְרֵי מִצְוֹתָי:

ג לֹא תִשָּׂא אֶת־שֵׁם־יְהוָה אֱלֹהֶיךָ לַשָּׁוְא כִּי לֹא יְנַקֶּה יְהוָה אֵת אֲשֶׁר־יִשָּׂא אֶת־שְׁמוֹ לַשָּׁוְא:

ד זָכוֹר אֶת־יוֹם הַשַּׁבָּת לְקַדְּשׁוֹ: שֵׁשֶׁת יָמִים תַּעֲבֹד וְעָשִׂיתָ כָּל־מְלַאכְתֶּךָ: וְיוֹם הַשְּׁבִיעִי שַׁבָּת לַיהוָה אֱלֹהֶיךָ לֹא־תַעֲשֶׂה כָל־מְלָאכָה אַתָּה וּבִנְךָ וּבִתֶּךָ עַבְדְּךָ וַאֲמָתְךָ וּבְהֶמְתֶּךָ וְגֵרְךָ אֲשֶׁר בִּשְׁעָרֶיךָ: כִּי שֵׁשֶׁת־יָמִים עָשָׂה יְהוָה אֶת־הַשָּׁמַיִם וְאֶת־הָאָרֶץ אֶת־הַיָּם וְאֶת־כָּל־אֲשֶׁר־בָּם וַיָּנַח בַּיּוֹם הַשְּׁבִיעִי עַל־כֵּן בֵּרַךְ יְהוָה אֶת־יוֹם הַשַּׁבָּת וַיְקַדְּשֵׁהוּ:

5. Honour thy father and thy mother: that thy days may be long upon the land which the Lord thy God giveth thee.

6. Thou shalt not murder.

7. Thou shalt not commit adultery.

8. Thou shalt not steal.

9. Thou shalt not bear false witness against thy neighbour.

10. Thou shalt not covet thy neighbour's house, thou shalt not covet thy neighbour's wife, nor his manservant nor his maidservant, nor his ox, nor his ass, nor any thing that is thy neighbour's.

ה כַּבֵּד אֶת־אָבִיךָ וְאֶת־אִמֶּךָ לְמַעַן יַאֲרִכוּן יָמֶיךָ עַל הָאֲדָמָה אֲשֶׁר־יְהוָה אֱלֹהֶיךָ נֹתֵן לָךְ:

ו לֹא תִרְצָח׃

ז לֹא תִנְאָף׃

ח לֹא תִגְנֹב׃

ט לֹא־תַעֲנֶה בְרֵעֲךָ עֵד שָׁקֶר:

י לֹא תַחְמֹד בֵּית רֵעֶךָ לֹא־תַחְמֹד אֵשֶׁת רֵעֶךָ וְעַבְדּוֹ וַאֲמָתוֹ וְשׁוֹרוֹ וַחֲמֹרוֹ וְכֹל אֲשֶׁר־לְרֵעֶךָ:

The Promised Land

The Children of Israel travelled for 40 years in the wilderness of Sinai until they reached eastern side of the River Jordan, from where they would enter the Land of Canaan, the Promised Land.

Ten spies sent on ahead to report on the land, its inhabitants and the state of its defences, brought back a very negative report, thus revealing lack of trust in God's promise. As a result God decreed that none of those who had been slaves in Egypt, except for Joshua and Caleb, would be permitted to enter the Promised Land. They would all die in the wilderness. Their children, who had grown up in the wilderness would instead be given the task of entering the Land, conquering it and becoming a new nation there.

Moses was not allowed by God to lead the Children of Israel into the Promised Land. He was to die on Mount Nebo, after appointing Joshua as his successor. Joshua was well qualified to become the new leader of the Israelites. He had already proved a capable military general when he had defeated the Amalekites at Rephidim. Joshua had also been a faithful assistant to Moses during 40 years in the wilderness and had learnt the art of leadership from him. Nevertheless, Moses knew how hard the task of leading the Israelites would be. So when he summoned Joshua, he told him:

> *Be strong and brave, since you will be the one to bring this nation to the land which God*
> *swore to their fathers, that He would give it to them. You will be the one to inherit it for*
> *them. But God will go before you, and will be with you. He will never forsake you or*
> *abandon you, so do not be afraid and do not let your spirit be broken.*
> *(Deuteronomy Chapter 31, verses 7 and 8)*

Although Moses was not to cross the River Jordan, God allowed him to view the Promised Land from Mount Nebo. From this vantage point, Moses could see the mountains of Judah and, in the north, the majestic Mount Hermon with its crown of snow. Moses could also see as far as the Mediterranean Sea.

Can you spot Mount Nebo on the map?

Moses then blessed the people and urged them to be faithful to the Torah. Then he died on Mount Nebo. To this day we do not know exactly where he was buried. Moses had been teacher, father and prophet to his people; and despite his 120 years of age, he had not lost his faculties.

The Torah (The Five Books of Moses) ends with the account of Moses' death, and this is read every year on Simhat Torah. The Haftarah which is taken from the beginning of the Book of Joshua tells of God's charge to lead the Israelites:

Moses my servant is dead; now therefore arise, go over this Jordan, you and all this people,
to the land which I am giving to them, even to the Children of Israel ... Be strong and of
good courage, for you will cause this people to inherit the land which I swore to their fathers
to give them.
(Joshua – Chapter 1, verses 2 to 6)

Because this Haftarah is one of the shortest, in many communities it is the tradition for a young boy to read this Haftarah on Simhat Torah. Listen to the tape of this being sung. Why not try and learn it yourself!

On assuming the leadership of the Jewish people, Joshua's first task was to prepare for the invasion of the Land of Canaan. He sent his officers though the great throng of Israelites encamped near the River Jordan, and instructed them to prepare for the crossing. Firstly the Ark of the Covenant was carried across by the Cohanim. When all the tribes who were to settle in the Promised Land followed, they took 12 boulders from the River Jordan and built an altar on the west bank of the Jordan.

Who were the Cohanim?
The descendants of Aaron, the High Priest

Not all the 12 tribes were to settle in the Promised Land, as Moses had already agreed that the tribes of Manasseh, Reuben and half of the tribe of Gad, would settle in the territory of Gilead, east of the Jordan, which had already been conquered by the Israelites. This was good grazing land, ideal for the herds these tribes possessed. Nevertheless, the men from these tribes did help the others to conquer the land.

MATERIAL FOR LESSON 4

BOOK
Chumash

MAPS
Journey through the wilderness.
Territories of the 12 tribes

PHOTOCOPY Haftarah for Simhat Torah

FROM SLAVERY TO THE PROMISED LAND

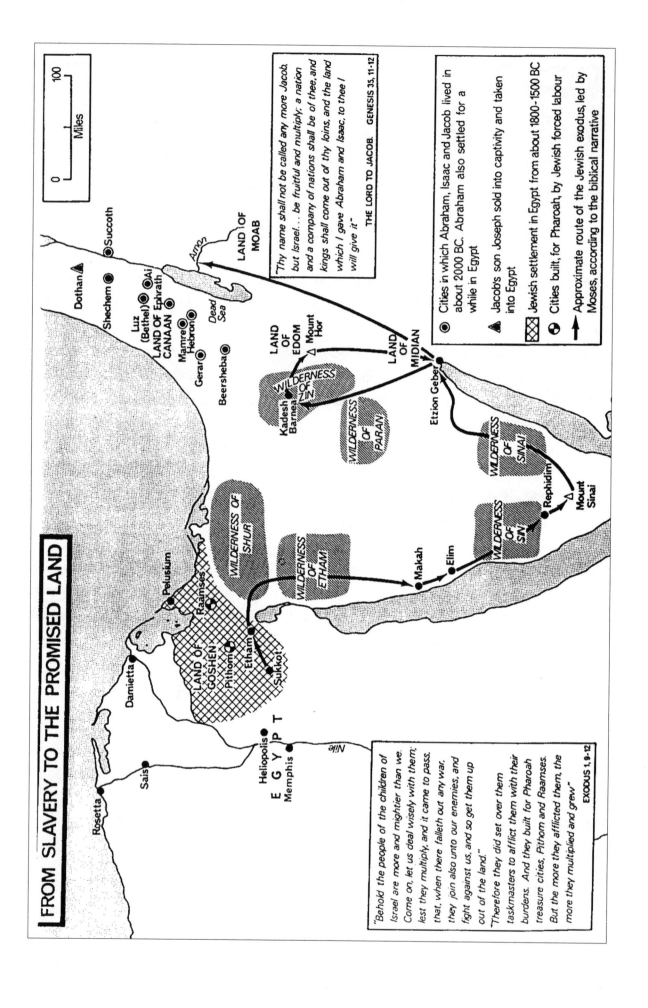

0 ————— 100
Miles

"Thy name shall not be called any more Jacob, but Israel... be fruitful and multiply; a nation and a company of nations shall be of thee, and kings shall come out of thy loins, and the land which I gave Abraham and Isaac, to thee I will give it."

THE LORD TO JACOB.   GENESIS 35, 11-12

⊙ Cities in which Abraham, Isaac and Jacob lived in about 2000 BC. Abraham also settled for a while in Egypt

▲ Jacob's son Joseph sold into captivity and taken into Egypt

⊠ Jewish settlement in Egypt from about 1800-1500 BC

⊕ Cities built, for Pharoah, by Jewish forced labour

→ Approximate route of the Jewish exodus, led by Moses, according to the biblical narrative

Succoth

Dothan ▲

Shechem ⊙

Luz (Bethel) ⊙ ⊙ Ai
LAND OF ⊙ Ephrath
CANAAN
Mamre ⊙
Hebron ⊙   Dead
Gerar ⊙   Sea

Beersheba ⊙

LAND OF MOAB

Arnon

LAND OF EDOM

Mount Hor △

Kadesh Barnea ⊙   WILDERNESS OF ZIN

WILDERNESS OF PARAN

LAND OF MIDIAN

Etzion Geber

WILDERNESS OF SINAI

Rephidim

Mount Sinai △

WILDERNESS OF SHUR

WILDERNESS OF ETHAM

WILDERNESS OF SIN

Makah

Elim

Pelusium

Raamses

LAND OF GOSHEN
Pithom
Etham
Sukkot

Damietta

Nile

Heliopolis
E G Y P T
Memphis

Sais

Rosetta

"Behold the people of the children of Israel are more and mightier than we. Come on, let us deal wisely with them; lest they multiply, and it come to pass, that, when there falleth out any war, they join also unto our enemies, and fight against us, and so get them up out of the land."

"Therefore they did set over them taskmasters to afflict them with their burdens. And they built for Pharoah treasure cities, Pithom and Raamses. But the more they afflicted them, the more they multiplied and grew"

EXODUS 1, 9-12

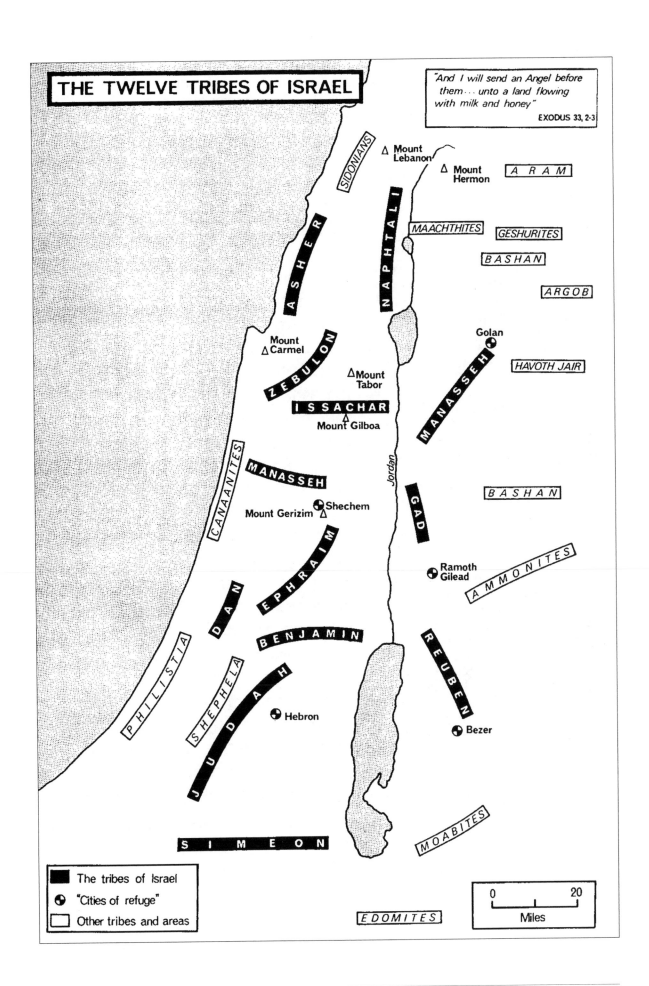

THE TWELVE TRIBES OF ISRAEL

"And I will send an Angel before them... unto a land flowing with milk and honey"

EXODUS 33, 2-3

SIDONIANS

△ Mount Lebanon

△ Mount Hermon

A R A M

MAACHTHITES

GESHURITES

BASHAN

ARGOB

ASHER

NAPHTALI

Mount △ Carmel

ZEBULON

△ Mount Tabor

Golan

HAVOTH JAIR

MANASSEH

ISSACHAR

Mount Gilboa

CANAANITES

MANASSEH

Jordan

BASHAN

Mount Gerizim △ Shechem

GAD

EPHRAIM

Ramoth Gilead

AMMONITES

DAN

BENJAMIN

REUBEN

PHILISTIA

SHEPHELA

JUDAH

Hebron

Bezer

S I M E O N

MOABITES

The tribes of Israel

"Cities of refuge"

Other tribes and areas

0   20

Miles

EDOMITES

LESSON 4   THE PROMISED LAND

269

This selection takes up the Scriptural narrative from the death of Moses.

1:1. And it was after the death of Moses, the servant of the Lord, that the Lord said to Joshua the son of Nun, Moses' minister, saying. 2. "Moses my servant has died; and now arise cross this Jordan, you and all this nation, to the land which I give the children of Israel. 3. Every place on which the soles of your feet will tread I have given to you, as I have spoken to Moses. 4. From this desert and Lebanon to the great river, the Euphrates, all the land of the Hittites to the great sea westward shall be your boundary. 5. No man shall stand up before you all the days of your life; as I was with Moses, so shall I be with you. I will not weaken My grasp on you nor will I abandon you. 6. Be strong and have courage; for you will cause this nation to inherit the land that I have sworn to their ancestors to give to them. 7. Just be strong and very courageous to observe and do in accordance with all of the Torah that Moses My servant has commanded you. Do not stray therefrom right or left, in order that you succeed wherever you go. 8. This book of the Torah shall not leave your mouth; you shall meditate therein day and night in order that you observe to do all that is written in it, for then will you succeed in all your ways, and then will you prosper. 9. Did I not command you, be strong and have courage, do not fear and do not be dismayed, for the Lord your God is with you wherever you go." (*Sephardim conclude here.*) 10. And Joshua commanded the officers of the nation, saying: 11. "Go through the midst of the camp and command the nation, saying: 'Prepare provision for yourselves, for in another three days you will cross this Jordan to come and inherit the land that the Lord your God is giving you to inherit.'" 12. And to the Reubenites and the Gadites and the half tribe of Manasseh, Joshua said, saying: 13. "Remember the word that Moses, the servant of the Lord, commanded you,

א וַיְהִ֗י אַחֲרֵ֛י מ֥וֹת מֹשֶׁ֖ה עֶ֣בֶד יְהוָ֑ה וַיֹּ֤אמֶר יְהוָה֙ אֶל־יְהוֹשֻׁ֣עַ בִּן־נ֔וּן מְשָׁרֵ֥ת מֹשֶׁ֖ה לֵאמֹֽר: ב מֹשֶׁ֥ה עַבְדִּ֖י מֵ֑ת וְעַתָּה֩ ק֨וּם עֲבֹ֜ר אֶת־הַיַּרְדֵּ֣ן הַזֶּ֗ה אַתָּה֙ וְכָל־הָעָ֣ם הַזֶּ֔ה אֶל־הָאָ֕רֶץ אֲשֶׁ֧ר אָנֹכִ֛י נֹתֵ֥ן לָהֶ֖ם לִבְנֵ֥י יִשְׂרָאֵֽל: ג כָּל־מָק֗וֹם אֲשֶׁ֨ר תִּדְרֹ֧ךְ כַּֽף־רַגְלְכֶ֛ם בּ֖וֹ לָכֶ֣ם נְתַתִּ֑יו כַּֽאֲשֶׁ֥ר דִּבַּ֖רְתִּי אֶל־מֹשֶֽׁה: ד מֵֽהַמִּדְבָּר֩ וְהַלְּבָנ֨וֹן הַזֶּ֜ה וְעַד־הַנָּהָ֧ר הַגָּד֣וֹל נְהַר־פְּרָ֗ת כֹּ֚ל אֶ֣רֶץ הַֽחִתִּ֔ים וְעַד־הַיָּ֥ם הַגָּד֖וֹל מְב֣וֹא הַשָּׁ֑מֶשׁ יִֽהְיֶ֖ה גְּבֽוּלְכֶֽם: ה לֹֽא־יִתְיַצֵּ֥ב אִישׁ֙ לְפָנֶ֔יךָ כֹּ֖ל יְמֵ֣י חַיֶּ֑יךָ כַּֽאֲשֶׁ֨ר הָיִ֤יתִי עִם־מֹשֶׁה֙ אֶֽהְיֶ֣ה עִמָּ֔ךְ לֹ֥א אַרְפְּךָ֖ וְלֹ֥א אֶֽעֶזְבֶֽךָּ: ו חֲזַ֖ק וֶֽאֱמָ֑ץ כִּ֣י אַתָּ֗ה תַּנְחִיל֙ אֶת־הָעָ֣ם הַזֶּ֔ה אֶת־הָאָ֕רֶץ אֲשֶׁר־נִשְׁבַּ֥עְתִּי לַֽאֲבוֹתָ֖ם לָתֵ֥ת לָהֶֽם: ז רַ֠ק חֲזַ֨ק וֶֽאֱמַ֜ץ מְאֹ֗ד לִשְׁמֹ֤ר לַֽעֲשׂוֹת֙ כְּכָל־הַתּוֹרָ֗ה אֲשֶׁ֤ר צִוְּךָ֙ מֹשֶׁ֣ה עַבְדִּ֔י אַל־תָּס֥וּר מִמֶּ֖נּוּ יָמִ֣ין וּשְׂמֹ֑אול לְמַ֣עַן תַּשְׂכִּ֔יל בְּכֹ֖ל אֲשֶׁ֥ר תֵּלֵֽךְ: ח לֹֽא־יָמ֡וּשׁ סֵפֶר֩ הַתּוֹרָ֨ה הַזֶּ֜ה מִפִּ֗יךָ וְהָגִ֤יתָ בּוֹ֙ יוֹמָ֣ם וָלַ֔יְלָה לְמַ֨עַן֙ תִּשְׁמֹ֣ר לַֽעֲשׂ֔וֹת כְּכָל־הַכָּת֖וּב בּ֑וֹ כִּי־אָ֛ז תַּצְלִ֥יחַ אֶת־דְּרָכֶ֖ךָ וְאָ֥ז תַּשְׂכִּֽיל: ט הֲל֤וֹא צִוִּיתִ֨יךָ֙ חֲזַ֣ק וֶֽאֱמָ֔ץ אַֽל־תַּֽעֲרֹ֖ץ וְאַל־תֵּחָ֑ת כִּ֤י עִמְּךָ֙ יְהוָ֣ה אֱלֹהֶ֔יךָ בְּכֹ֖ל אֲשֶׁ֥ר תֵּלֵֽךְ: (כאן מסיימין הספרדים) י וַיְצַ֣ו יְהוֹשֻׁ֔עַ אֶת־שֹֽׁטְרֵ֥י הָעָ֖ם לֵאמֹֽר: יא עִבְר֣וּ | בְּקֶ֣רֶב הַֽמַּֽחֲנֶ֗ה וְצַוּ֤וּ אֶת־הָעָם֙ לֵאמֹ֔ר הָכִ֥ינוּ לָכֶ֖ם צֵדָ֑ה כִּ֞י בְּע֣וֹד | שְׁלֹ֣שֶׁת יָמִ֗ים אַתֶּם֙ עֹֽבְרִים֙ אֶת־הַיַּרְדֵּ֣ן הַזֶּ֔ה לָבוֹא֙ לָרֶ֣שֶׁת אֶת־הָאָ֔רֶץ אֲשֶׁר֙ יְהוָ֣ה אֱלֹֽהֵיכֶ֔ם נֹתֵ֥ן לָכֶ֖ם לְרִשְׁתָּֽהּ: יב וְלָרֽאוּבֵנִי֙ וְלַגָּדִ֔י וְלַֽחֲצִ֖י שֵׁ֣בֶט הַֽמְנַשֶּׁ֑ה אָמַ֥ר יְהוֹשֻׁ֖עַ לֵאמֹֽר: יג זָכוֹר֙ אֶת־הַדָּבָ֔ר אֲשֶׁ֨ר צִוָּ֥ה אֶתְכֶ֛ם מֹשֶׁ֥ה עֶֽבֶד־יְהוָ֖ה

[952]

The Conquest of Canaan

Joshua knew that it would be very hard to defeat the Canaanites; and in fact he never succeeded in overcoming them all. Nevertheless the reputation of the Children of Israel, and how God had delivered them from Egypt, had gone before them. Joshua sent two spies to Jericho, the first city he wished to conquer. The spies reported back to him that even though Jericho was well fortified and the Canaanites were armed with spears tipped with iron, the Israelites would succeed (The Children of Israel were backward in technology and did not learn how to use iron until very many years later.) The story of how the wall of Jericho came tumbling down has been retold through the ages.

Joshua succeeded in subduing some other fortified cities, but many were not conquered until very much later: Jerusalem, which at that time was a Jebusite fortress in the mountains of Judah, was only captured by King David. The Israelite tribes were just not strong enough to overcome many of their better armed and more sophisticated foes.

THE SANCTUARY AT SHILOH

Joshua set up a central sanctuary at Shiloh, where the Ark of the Covenant was kept, in order to keep the twelve tribes united. It was to Shiloh that all the people made pilgrimages, brought their sacrifices and prayed together. The sanctuary in Shiloh was tended by Aaron's son Elazar and his grandson Pinhas, assisted by the Levites.

What did the Ark of the Covenant contain?

The worst threat facing the Israelites was not the superiority of enemy weapons, nor even the strong walls around the cities. It was a threat far more difficult to avoid and overcome. The Israelites found themselves mingling with people of the land who worshipped idols, because Joshua had not succeeded in destroying the places of idol worship, as he had been commanded by God.

Fearing that his people would fall into the ways of the idol worshippers, Joshua, now an old man and knowing that he was soon to die, called the twelve tribes together for a great assembly at Shechem, near Shiloh. Gathered together before their leader, the people heard Joshua impress upon them the importance of remaining united and faithful to the laws of the one God. The people made a solemn promise to Joshua that they would put away all idols and hold steadfast to God's laws. With one voice they cried 'We will serve The Lord our God, and will obey his voice'. Thus the Israelites renewed their covenant with the one God and returned to their homes with fresh courage, determined to keep to their own way of life despite the attractions of the idol-worshippers around them.

Did the people keep their promise?

No, they did not! The following generations, who had not experienced the wonders God did for Israel, forsook the God of their fathers who had delivered them from Egypt. They abandoned the Lord and worshipped the gods of their Canaanite neighbours.

God withdrew his help as a consequence of that betrayal and the Israelite tribes were badly oppressed by the Canaanites. The Israelites were very backward in technology: they had only bronze weapons which were no match for the iron weapons of their neighbours. The Canaanites, the Philistines in particular, had mastered the use of iron which was a closely guarded state secret. The Israelites could not stand up to their iron swords and wheeled chariots, nor to their iron-tipped arrows and spears. Without God's help, the Israelites could not prevail in battle and were dominated and oppressed by the Canaanites. (When, later, Saul went into battle with the Philistines, only he and his son in the entire army of Israel were equipped with iron swords.)

THE JUDGES

After the death of Joshua each tribe ruled itself through a series of charismatic leaders, known as Judges. They were consulted by all the people and were followed, especially in times of trouble. The tribes only came together during periods of warfare with their neighbours.

The book of Judges contains many famous stories of bravery and heroism, such as that of Samson.

What happened to Samson?

DEBORAH

During this period there also lived a wise woman called Deborah who lived in the hill country of Ephraim. Her fame as a Judge spread far and wide, and people came from all over Israel (as the Promised Land was now called) to consult her. Deborah would sit under a palm tree near her home at a place between Ramah and Bethel, and help people with their problems.

The Israelites, for 40 years desert nomads, quickly changed to become farmers, shepherds, artisans and town dwellers. Their lives were beset with danger for Canaanite soldiers often raided their farms. Though the Israelites successfully fought off many of these raids, their efforts were futile against the armed might of King Jabin of the Canaanites. The soldiers of Jabin were commanded by his great general, Sisera. They were well-trained and equipped with heavy iron chariots and weapons; and they terrorised the Israelites for 20 years.

Deborah resolved that King Jabin must be defeated. She gathered her allies, and summoned Barak, an able warrior from the tribe of Naphtali. Deborah ordered Barak to gather together every available

Israelite soldier and prepare them to make a mass attack upon the Canaanites. Warriors from the tribes of Zebulun and Naphtali answered the call to battle. After Deborah had sent further messages of encouragement, more soldiers joined Barak's army from the tribes of Ephraim, Benjamin and Issachar.

Deborah and Barak decided on a plan to outwit the superior numbers and weapons of the enemy. They led their army up the sides of Mount Tabor, which looks over the plain of Jezreel, near the River Kishon. King Jabin and Sisera assembled their heavily armed troops below and waited for the Israelites to strike, thinking that they would easily repulse them.

Shouting their battle cry, the Israelites swooped down from the mountain upon the Canaanites. In the midst of the battle, miraculously the sky above opened and rain poured down. The River Kishon, normally a peaceful little stream, became a raging torrent, and flooded across the plain. The heavy iron wheels of the Canaanite chariots stuck in the thick, slippery mud. Weighed down by their heavy wet armour, the Canaanite soldiers were no match for the lightly armed Israelites, who seemed to be everywhere at once with lightening speed, cutting down the enemy with their spears and sling shots.

The Canaanites fled in confusion. Sisera, their general sought refuge in the tent of a Kenite woman called Jael. He begged her for water to quench his thirst. Jael gave the warrior a dry cloak and some milk and then stood guard at the door of her tent. Thinking that he was safe, Sisera fell into a deep sleep. And Jael slew him while he slept.

Was Jael justified in betraying her trust?

As a result of this great victory, Deborah led her people in a song of praise of God. This song is read as a Haftarah on Shabbat Shirah when in the Parasha of the day (Beshallah) we also read the Song of Moses (commonly called the 'Shirah').

Can you name any other of the Judges?
Gideon, Jair, Samson, Eli, Samuel and eight more

MATERIAL FOR LESSON 5

MAP
Conquest of the Land

PHOTOCOPY
Haftarah Beshallah

TEACHER'S BACKGROUND NOTES 1. Judges 4

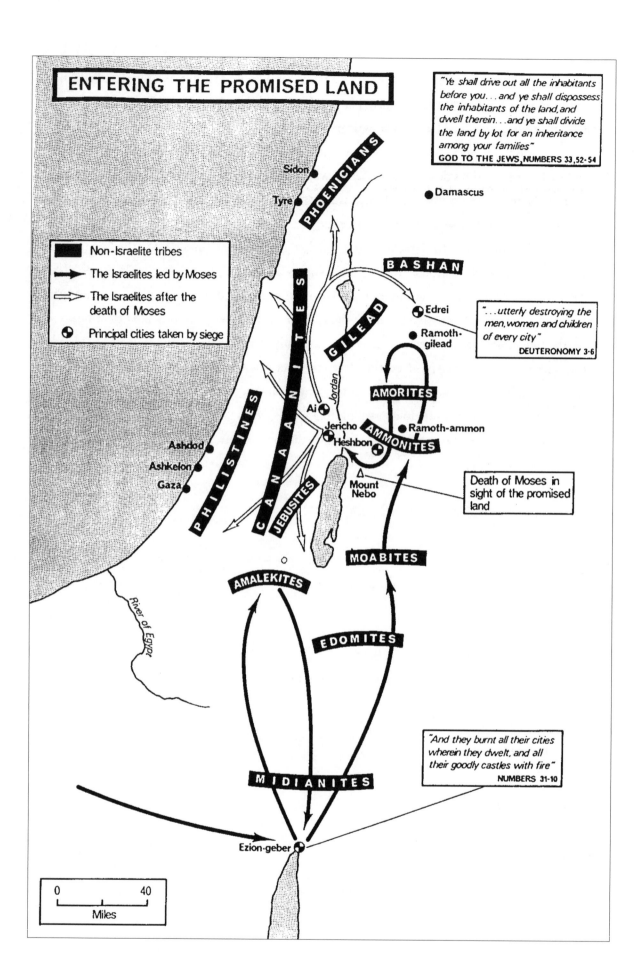

ENTERING THE PROMISED LAND

"Ye shall drive out all the inhabitants before you...and ye shall dispossess the inhabitants of the land, and dwell therein...and ye shall divide the land by lot for an inheritance among your families"
GOD TO THE JEWS, NUMBERS 33, 52-54

Sidon

Tyre

PHOENICIANS

Damascus

BASHAN

GILEAD

Edrei

Ramoth-gilead

"...utterly destroying the men, women and children of every city"
DEUTERONOMY 3-6

Non-Israelite tribes

The Israelites led by Moses

The Israelites after the death of Moses

Principal cities taken by siege

CANAANITES

Jordan

AMORITES

Ai

Jericho

Heshbon

AMMONITES

Ramoth-ammon

PHILISTINES

Ashdod

Ashkelon

Gaza

JEBUSITES

Mount Nebo

Death of Moses in sight of the promised land

MOABITES

River of Egypt

AMALEKITES

EDOMITES

"And they burnt all their cities wherein they dwelt, and all their goodly castles with fire"
NUMBERS 31-10

MIDIANITES

Ezion-geber

0   40
Miles

LESSON 5   THE CONQUEST OF CANAAN

274

HAFTORAH BESHALLACH הפטרת בשלח

JUDGES IV, 4–V, 31

CHAPTER IV

4. Now Deborah, a prophetess, the wife of Lappidoth, she judged Israel at that time. 5. And she sat under the palm-tree of Deborah between Ramah and Beth-el in the hill-country of Ephraim; and the children of Israel came up to her for judgment. 6. And she sent and called Barak the son of Abinoam out of Kedesh-naphtali,

CAP. IV. ד

4 וּדְבוֹרָה אִשָּׁה נְבִיאָה אֵשֶׁת לַפִּידוֹת הִיא שֹׁפְטָה אֶת־
5 יִשְׂרָאֵל בָּעֵת הַהִיא: וְהִיא יוֹשֶׁבֶת תַּחַת־תֹּמֶר דְּבוֹרָה
בֵּין הָרָמָה וּבֵין בֵּית־אֵל בְּהַר אֶפְרָיִם וַיַּעֲלוּ אֵלֶיהָ בְּנֵי
6 יִשְׂרָאֵל לַמִּשְׁפָּט: וַתִּשְׁלַח וַתִּקְרָא לְבָרָק בֶּן־אֲבִינֹעַם

ע. 4. יש מתחילין ותשר דבורה

In both Sedrah and Haftorah we have the story of a deliverance from oppression celebrated in a Song of triumph and praise.

These chapters of the Book of Judges take us back to an early period in Israel's history, the days after the death of Joshua, when the tribes were compelled to wage a hard and often desperate struggle against the remaining warlike Canaanites. It was a barbaric period, without national unity and devoid of religious authority. 'In those days there was no king of Israel: every man did that which was right in his own eyes.' But God does not utterly forsake His people. An overwhelming national calamity, or foreign oppression, would bring forth a Champion, who would repel or destroy the foe, or rescue the people from the threatened calamity. Such Champions, known as *Shofetim* ('Judges'), were Gideon, Jephthah, Samson, and the most remarkable of all, Deborah. The story of her achievement has come down to us in two versions, in prose and in verse. From them we can reconstruct the mortal danger from which her victory saved Israel. That victory was one of the 'decisive battles' of the world. It settled the destiny of Palestine, and a great many other things, for all time. Moreover, under the inspiration of Deborah's lofty patriotism, most of the tribes for the first time combined in face of a common danger. Those wild years forged the bonds of a nationality that has survived unprecedented shocks throughout the ages.

4. *prophetess.* Although she did not foretell the future, she is described as a prophetess, because she was inspired to grapple with the great difficulties of the hour (Kimchi).

5. *sat.* To decide disputes brought to her for judgment.

6. *Kedesh-naphtali.* About four miles from the north end of the 'waters of Merom'.

mount Tabor. The conical shaped hill commanding the Plain of Esdraelon. The Plain runs like a wedge from the coast to within 10 miles of the Jordan, and is dominated by hills on all sides. It is to-day known as 'the Emek'.

of Naphtali . . . Zebulun. These two tribes bordering on the Plain suffered most under the oppression of the heathens.

and said unto him: 'Hath not the Lord, the God of Israel, commanded, saying: Go and draw toward mount Tabor, and take with thee ten thousand men of the children of Naphtali and of the children of Zebulun? 7. And I will draw unto thee to the brook Kishon Sisera, the captain of Jabin's army, with his chariots and his multitude; and I will deliver him into thy hand.' 8. And Barak said unto her: 'If thou wilt go with me, then I will go; but if thou wilt not go with me, I will not go.' 9. And she said: 'I will surely go with thee; notwithstanding the journey that thou takest shall not be for thy honour; for the Lord will give Sisera over into the hand of a woman.' And Deborah arose, and went with Barak to Kedesh. 10. And Barak called Zebulun and Naphtali together to Kedesh; and there went up ten thousand men at his feet; and Deborah went up with him. ¶ 11. Now Heber the Kenite had severed himself from the Kenites, even from the children of Hobab the father-in-law of Moses, and had pitched his tent as far as Elon-bezaanannim, which is by Kedesh. ¶ 12. And they told Sisera that Barak the son of Abinoam was gone up to mount Tabor. 13. And Sisera gathered together all his chariots, even nine hundred chariots of iron, and all the people that were with him, from Harosheth-goiim, unto the brook Kishon. 14. And Deborah said unto Barak: 'Up; for this is the day in which the Lord hath delivered Sisera into thy hand; is not the Lord gone out before thee?' So Barak went down from mount Tabor, and ten thousand men after him. 15. And the Lord discomfited Sisera, and all his chariots, and all his host, with the edge of the sword before Barak; and Sisera alighted from his chariot, and fled away on his feet. 16. But Barak pursued after the chariots, and after the host, unto Harosheth-goiim; and all the host of Sisera fell by the edge of the

מִקֶּדֶשׁ נַפְתָּלִי וַתֹּאמֶר אֵלָיו הֲלֹא־צִוָּה ׀ יְהֹוָה אֱלֹהֵי
יִשְׂרָאֵל לֵךְ וּמָשַׁכְתָּ בְּהַר תָּבוֹר וְלָקַחְתָּ עִמְּךָ עֲשֶׂרֶת

7 אֲלָפִים אִישׁ מִבְּנֵי נַפְתָּלִי וּמִבְּנֵי זְבֻלוּן: וּמָשַׁכְתִּי אֵלֶיךָ
אֶל־נַחַל קִישׁוֹן אֶת־סִיסְרָא שַׂר־צְבָא יָבִין וְאֶת־רִכְבּוֹ

8 וְאֶת־הֲמוֹנוֹ וּנְתַתִּיהוּ בְּיָדֶךָ: וַיֹּאמֶר אֵלֶיהָ בָּרָק אִם־תֵּלְכִי

9 עִמִּי וְהָלָכְתִּי וְאִם־לֹא תֵלְכִי עִמִּי לֹא אֵלֵךְ: וַתֹּאמֶר הָלֹךְ
אֵלֵךְ עִמָּךְ אֶפֶס כִּי לֹא תִהְיֶה תִּפְאַרְתְּךָ עַל־הַדֶּרֶךְ אֲשֶׁר
אַתָּה הוֹלֵךְ כִּי בְיַד־אִשָּׁה יִמְכֹּר יְהֹוָה אֶת־סִיסְרָא וַתָּקָם

10 דְּבוֹרָה וַתֵּלֶךְ עִם־בָּרָק קֶדְשָׁה: וַיַּזְעֵק בָּרָק אֶת־זְבוּלֻן
וְאֶת־נַפְתָּלִי קֶדְשָׁה וַיַּעַל בְּרַגְלָיו עֲשֶׂרֶת אַלְפֵי אִישׁ וַתַּעַל

11 עִמּוֹ דְּבוֹרָה: וְחֶבֶר הַקֵּינִי נִפְרָד מִקַּיִן מִבְּנֵי חֹבָב חֹתֵן

12 מֹשֶׁה וַיֵּט אָהֳלוֹ עַד־אֵלוֹן בְּצַעֲנַנִּים אֲשֶׁר אֶת־קֶדֶשׁ: וַיַּגִּדוּ

13 לְסִיסְרָא כִּי עָלָה בָּרָק בֶּן־אֲבִינֹעַם הַר־תָּבוֹר: וַיַּזְעֵק
סִיסְרָא אֶת־כָּל־רִכְבּוֹ תְּשַׁע מֵאוֹת רֶכֶב בַּרְזֶל וְאֶת־כָּל־

14 הָעָם אֲשֶׁר אִתּוֹ מֵחֲרֹשֶׁת הַגּוֹיִם אֶל־נַחַל קִישׁוֹן: וַתֹּאמֶר
דְּבֹרָה אֶל־בָּרָק קוּם כִּי זֶה הַיּוֹם אֲשֶׁר נָתַן יְהֹוָה אֶת־
סִיסְרָא בְּיָדֶךָ הֲלֹא יְהֹוָה יָצָא לְפָנֶיךָ וַיֵּרֶד בָּרָק מֵהַר

15 תָּבוֹר וַעֲשֶׂרֶת אֲלָפִים אִישׁ אַחֲרָיו: וַיָּהָם יְהֹוָה אֶת־
סִיסְרָא וְאֶת־כָּל־הָרֶכֶב וְאֶת־כָּל־הַמַּחֲנֶה לְפִי־חֶרֶב לִפְנֵי

16 בָרָק וַיֵּרֶד סִיסְרָא מֵעַל הַמֶּרְכָּבָה וַיָּנָס בְּרַגְלָיו: וּבָרָק
רָדַף אַחֲרֵי הָרֶכֶב וְאַחֲרֵי הַמַּחֲנֶה עַד חֲרֹשֶׁת הַגּוֹיִם וַיִּפֹּל

---

v. 11. הר' בקמץ ibid. בצעננים קרי

---

7. *Jabin.* The king of Canaan who oppressed Israel. He had 900 chariots of iron; and against these 'armoured cars', the Israelite peasants were powerless.

8. *if thou wilt go with me.* Indicates the remarkable confidence that Deborah's wisdom and work had inspired.

9. *for thy honour.* The word *thy* is emphatic: the chief glory of the victory shall not be his. *give.* Deliver.

10. *went up. i.e.* to Mount Tabor.

11. *the Kenites.* A nomadic tribe in close league with Israel; see Num. XXIV, 22. Heber had branched off from the main clan, in Southern Palestine, and wandered as far north as Kedesh. This information is necessary for the understanding of *v.* 17.

13. *Harosheth-goiim.* Near Megiddo. *Kishon.* The river rises in the S.E. of the Plain of Esdraelon, and flows through it into the sea near Haifa. It is the second river of Palestine.

14. *went down.* From Mt. Tabor; the Israelites dashed down, and drove the Canaanites back upon the banks of the river Kishon. Its overflowing waters, swollen by a rain-storm, had turned the Plain into a morass, rendering any use of the chariots impossible.

15. *discomfited.* Confused, threw into a panic; cf. the Sedrah, XIV, 24.

LESSON 5   THE CONQUEST OF CANAAN

sword; there was not a man left. ¶ 17. How-beit Sisera fled away on his feet to the tent of Jael the wife of Heber the Kenite; for there was peace between Jabin the king of Hazor and the house of Heber the Kenite. 18. And Jael went out to meet Sisera, and said unto him: 'Turn in, my lord, turn in to me; fear not.' And he turned in unto her into the tent, and she covered him with a rug. 19. And he said unto her: 'Give me, I pray thee, a little water to drink; for I am thirsty.' And she opened a bottle of milk, and gave him drink, and covered him. 20. And he said unto her: 'Stand in the door of the tent, and it shall be, when any man doth come and inquire of thee, and say: Is there any man here? that thou shalt say: No.' 21. Then Jael Heber's wife took a tent-pin, and took a hammer in her hand, and went softly unto him, and smote the pin into his temples, and it pierced through into the ground; for he was in a deep sleep; so he swooned and died. 22. And, behold, as Barak pursued Sisera, Jael came out to meet him, and said unto him: 'Come, and I will show thee the man whom thou seekest.' And he came unto her; and, behold, Sisera lay dead, and the tent-pin was in his temples. 23. So God subdued on that day Jabin the king of Canaan before the children of Israel. 24. And the hand of the children of Israel prevailed more and more against Jabin the king of Canaan, until they had destroyed Jabin king of Canaan.

17 כָּל־מַחֲנֵה סִיסְרָא לְפִי־חָרֶב לֹא נִשְׁאַר עַד־אֶחָד: וְסִיסְרָא נָס בְּרַגְלָיו אֶל־אֹהֶל יָעֵל אֵשֶׁת חֶבֶר הַקֵּינִי כִּי שָׁלוֹם בֵּין

18 יָבִין מֶלֶךְ־חָצוֹר וּבֵין בֵּית חֶבֶר הַקֵּינִי: וַתֵּצֵא יָעֵל לִקְרַאת סִיסְרָא וַתֹּאמֶר אֵלָיו סוּרָה אֲדֹנִי סוּרָה אֵלַי אַל־תִּירָא

19 וַיָּסַר אֵלֶיהָ הָאֹהֱלָה וַתְּכַסֵּהוּ בַּשְּׂמִיכָה: וַיֹּאמֶר אֵלֶיהָ הַשְׁקִינִי־נָא מְעַט־מַיִם כִּי צָמֵאתִי וַתִּפְתַּח אֶת־נֹאוד הֶחָלָב

כ וַתַּשְׁקֵהוּ וַתְּכַסֵּהוּ: וַיֹּאמֶר אֵלֶיהָ עֲמֹד פֶּתַח הָאֹהֶל וְהָיָה אִם־אִישׁ יָבֹא וּשְׁאֵלֵךְ וְאָמַר הֲיֵשׁ־פֹּה אִישׁ וְאָמַרְתְּ אָיִן:

21 וַתִּקַּח יָעֵל אֵשֶׁת־חֶבֶר אֶת־יְתַד הָאֹהֶל וַתָּשֶׂם אֶת־הַמַּקֶּבֶת בְּיָדָהּ וַתָּבוֹא אֵלָיו בַּלָּאט וַתִּתְקַע אֶת־הַיָּתֵד בְּרַקָּתוֹ

22 וַתִּצְנַח בָּאָרֶץ וְהוּא־נִרְדָּם וַיָּעַף וַיָּמֹת: וְהִנֵּה בָרָק רֹדֵף אֶת־סִיסְרָא וַתֵּצֵא יָעֵל לִקְרָאתוֹ וַתֹּאמֶר לוֹ לֵךְ וְאַרְאֶךָּ אֶת־הָאִישׁ אֲשֶׁר־אַתָּה מְבַקֵּשׁ וַיָּבֹא אֵלֶיהָ וְהִנֵּה סִיסְרָא

23 נֹפֵל מֵת וְהַיָּתֵד בְּרַקָּתוֹ: וַיַּכְנַע אֱלֹהִים בַּיּוֹם הַהוּא אֵת

24 יָבִין מֶלֶךְ־כְּנָעַן לִפְנֵי בְּנֵי יִשְׂרָאֵל: וַתֵּלֶךְ יַד בְּנֵי־יִשְׂרָאֵל הָלוֹךְ וְקָשָׁה עַל יָבִין מֶלֶךְ־כְּנָעַן עַד אֲשֶׁר הִכְרִיתוּ אֵת יָבִין מֶלֶךְ־כְּנָעַן:

17. *Jael the wife of Heber.* This family had taken no part in the battle.

21. *tent-pin.* On the morality of the action, see note on *v.* 24 of next chapter.

24. *prevailed more and more.* This staggering success was the beginning of a series of crushing victories over Jabin.

CHAPTER V. DEBORAH'S SONG OF DELIVERANCE AND PRAISE

'The Song of Deborah holds a high place among Triumphal Odes in the literature of the world. It is a work of that highest art which is not studied and artificial, but spontaneous and inevitable. It shows a development and command of the resources of the language for ends of poetical expression, which prove that poetry had long been cultivated among the Hebrews' (Moore).

2. *when men let grow their hair in Israel. i.e.* when men took the vow and consecrated themselves to the war of liberation. 'Wearing the hair long was the mark of a vow not to do certain things until a specified object had been attained' (Cooke); cf. Num. vi, 5.

4 The Israelites again did what was offensive to the LORD—Ehud now being dead. ²And the LORD surrendered them to King Jabin of Canaan, who reigned in Hazor. His army commander was Sisera, whose base was Harosheth-goiim. ³The Israelites cried out to the LORD; for he had nine hundred iron chariots, and he had oppressed Israel ruthlessly for twenty years.

⁴Deborah, wife of Lappidoth, was a prophetess; she led Israel at that time. ⁵She used to sit under the Palm of Deborah, between Ramah and Bethel in the hill country of Ephraim, and the Israelites would come to her for decisions.

⁶She summoned Barak son of Abinoam, of Kedesh in Naphtali, and said to him, "The LORD, the God of Israel, has commanded: Go, march up to Mount Tabor, and take with you ten thousand men of Naphtali and Zebulun. ⁷And I will draw Sisera, Jabin's army commander, with his chariots and his troops, toward you up to the Wadi Kishon; and I will deliver him into your hands." ⁸But Barak said to her, "If you will go with

˙ *Meaning of Heb. uncertain*

me, I will go; if not, I will not go." 9"Very well, I will go with you," she answered. "However, there will be no glory for you in the course you are taking, for then the LORD will deliver Sisera into the hands of a woman." So Deborah went with Barak to Kedesh. 10Barak then mustered Zebulun and Naphtali at Kedesh; ten thousand men marched up a-after him;-a and Deborah also went up with him.

11Now Heber the Kenite had separated b-from the other Kenites,-b descendants of Hobab, father-in-law of Moses, and had pitched his tent at Elon-bezaanannim, which is near Kedesh.

12Sisera was informed that Barak son of Abinoam had gone up to Mount Tabor. 13So Sisera ordered all his chariots—nine hundred iron chariots—and all the troops he had to move from Harosheth-goiim to the Wadi Kishon. 14Then Deborah said to Barak, "Up! This is the day on which the LORD will deliver Sisera into your hands: the LORD is marching before you." Barak charged down Mount Tabor, followed by the ten thousand men, 15and the LORD threw Sisera and all his chariots and army into a panic c-before the onslaught of Barak.-c Sisera leaped from his chariot and fled on foot 16as Barak pursued the chariots and the soldiers as far as Harosheth-goiim. All of Sisera's soldiers fell by the sword; not a man was left.

17Sisera, meanwhile, had fled on foot to the tent of Jael, wife of Heber the Kenite; for there was friendship between King Jabin of Hazor and the family of Heber the Kenite. 18Jael came out to greet Sisera and said to him, "Come in, my lord, come in here, do not be afraid." So he entered her tent, and she covered him with a blanket. 19He said to her, "Please let me have some water; I am thirsty." She opened a skin of milk and gave him some to drink; and she covered him again. 20He said to her, "Stand at the entrance of the tent. If anybody comes and asks you if there is anybody here, say 'No.'" 21Then Jael wife of Heber took a tent pin and grasped the mallet. When he was fast asleep from exhaustion, she approached him stealthily and drove the pin through his temple till it went down to the ground. Thus he died.

22Now Barak appeared in pursuit of Sisera. Jael went out to greet him and said, "Come, I will show you the man you are looking for." He went inside with her, and there Sisera was lying dead, with the pin in his temple.

23On that day God subdued King Jabin of Hazor before the Israelites. 24The hand of the Israelites bore harder and harder on King Jabin of Canaan, until they destroyed King Jabin of Canaan.

a-a Lit. "at his feet."

Israel's First King

The Israelites tribes suffered defeat after defeat, particularly at the hands of the Philistines who lived at the southern end of the coast of the country that would later be called Palestine after them.

They were an advanced sea-going people who had mastered the technology of iron working, which they preserved as a closely guarded state secret. The twelve fiercely individualistic Hebrew tribes with their bronze-age implements were no match for the iron weapons, chariots and archers of their better organised and more sophisticated foe. They longed for a hero under whom they could unite to regain their freedom.

The Israelite tribes clamoured for a king to lead them in their unrelenting struggle against Philistine domination. Samuel, who served as their judge and leader, was deeply troubled by this demand, for he thought that the tribes were rejecting the rule of God. However, God told Samuel to give in to their demands. But he was instructed to warn the people what it would mean to have a king to rule over them. So Samuel told them that the king would demand taxes from the people to maintain a grand style of living, and that he would take their children from them, to work his fields and fight in his army. One by one, Samuel presented these arguments against the establishment of a kingdom – but the Elders refused to be discouraged. The people had set their hearts on having a king and Samuel had to agree.

After much hesitation, Samuel yielded to popular pressure and chose a tall and handsome young man from a leading family of the smallest tribe, Benjamin. Saul was solemnly anointed by Samuel and declared king in the name of the Lord God of Israel.

> *Do you think the tribes were right in demanding a king to unite them and defend them from their enemies?*

> *What future do you think that twelve small, independent tribes would have had?*

Saul immediately proved himself a forceful leader by defeating one of the enemies of Israel, the Ammonites. He was an able soldier and, helped by his son Jonathan, Saul also defeated the Philistines in battle. But Samuel was disappointed in the new king, for Saul did not always obey God's commands fully. Saul defended himself by saying that he had sacrificed much of the booty of war to God but Samuel answered that God prefers obedience to sacrifices upon an altar. Samuel warned Saul that God would give his kingdom to another and more worthy person.

The Philistine army, encouraged by news of King Saul's decline, prepared again for all-out attack. At the foot of Mount Gilboa, a bloody battle took place, which resulted in a terrible defeat for the

Israelites. Many thousands were killed, among them the sons of Saul, including Jonathan. King Saul, dreading being taken captive by the Philistines, fell on his own sword and died. The Philistines carried the bodies of Saul and his sons in triumph to their temple at Beth Shan, and hung them up on the temple walls. Some of Saul's followers removed the bodies in the dark of the night and buried them.

David was overcome with grief when he heard of the death of Saul and his best friend Jonathan. He composed a song of mourning, extolling the courage of the two great warriors and lamenting their fall in battle. This is one of the great poems of the Bible.

The twenty-years long reign of the first king of Israel was the first step towards the establishment of a kingdom which would be looked back to in future ages as ideal. Before Saul, the tribes had in common only their shared history and their belief in God and his prophets. Because of Saul, their brilliant warrior king, they gained the institution of monarchy from which central government would later develop. They also acquire their first trained standing army, which eventually was able to defeat neighbouring tribes, maintain an uneasy balance of power with the Philistines and liberate most of their territory.

How did the tribes fight their battles before they had a standing army, led by the king?

MATERIAL FOR LESSON 6

PHOTOCOPY

David's lament for Saul and Jonathan (Book of Samuel)

[17]And David intoned this dirge over Saul and his son Jonathan—[18a-]He ordered the Judites to be taught [The Song of the] Bow.[-a] It is recorded in the Book of Jashar.[c]

[19]Your glory, O Israel,
Lies slain on your heights;
How have the mighty fallen!
[20]Tell it not in Gath,
Do not proclaim it in the streets of Ashkelon,
Lest the daughters of the Philistine rejoice,
Lest the daughters of the uncircumcised exult.

[21]O hills of Gilboa—
Let there be no dew or rain on you,
[d-]Or bountiful fields,[-d]
For there the shield of warriors lay rejected,
The shield of Saul,
Polished with oil no more.

[22]From the blood of slain,
From the fat of warriors—
The bow of Jonathan
Never turned back;
The sword of Saul
Never withdrew empty.

[23]Saul and Jonathan,
Beloved and cherished,
Never parted
In life or in death!
They were swifter than eagles,
They were stronger than lions!

[24]Daughters of Israel,
Weep over Saul,

[c] See note at Josh. 10.13.
[d] Meaning of Heb. uncertain. Emendation yield...

Who clothed you in crimson and finery,
Who decked your robes with jewels of gold.

25How have the mighty fallen
In the thick of battle—
Jonathan, slain on your heights!
26I grieve for you,
My brother Jonathan,
You were most dear to me.
Your love was wonderful to me
More than the love of women.

27How have the mighty fallen,
The c-weapons of war-c perished!

David

David, youngest child of Jesse from Bethlehem in Judah, was a good looking young shepherd with bright eyes and red cheeks when Samuel sought him out in secret and anointed him as the future ruler of the nation. He entered the king's service and rose through the ranks to become a successful army commander and popular hero. Not content with inspiring the king's affection – for Saul came to love him dearly – David consolidated his position at court by cultivating an intense loving relationship with the king's eldest son Jonathan; and that friendship endured through the troubled times that followed. The king's younger daughter Michal also fell in love with David. She was married to him after David had provided her father with twice the specified bride price in slain Philistine soldiers.

Saul eventually came to fear David as a dangerous rival, especially after Samuel's declaration that God would tear his kingdom from him and bestow it on another more worthy, David was forced to flee for his life. He became the leader of an armed band of outcasts, existing first by freebooting against the Philistines, then by protecting the edges of the settled land from nomads, and finally by raiding and plundering the neighbouring pagan tribes.

On Saul's death David was acclaimed king by his own tribe of Judah, and anointed in Hebron. Bitter warfare then broke out between Judah and the other Hebrew tribes which acknowledged Saul's son Ish-Bosheth as king. David's side grew steadily stronger at the expenses of the House of Saul.

After the murder of King Ish-Bosheth, the tribal elders visited David in Hebron. They made their peace with him and anointed him king over Israel and Judah.

David's character is described in the biblical Book of Samuel, in which frank accounts of his failings and virtues convey an unmistakable sense of authenticity. An outstanding warrior, diplomat and empire builder, David was also a fine poet and musician. He was engagingly impetuous in his personal behaviour. Ignoring the sneers of his aristocratic wife, he uninhibitedly danced for joy in the streets of Jerusalem when bringing the Ark of the Covenant into the city. Though eager for the throne and sorely provoked by Saul, he preferred to wait until the natural end of Saul's reign before making his bid for power. Once he had attained his aim, David showed respect for the former royal house and did his best to reconciled Saul's supporters.

Where can we find David's poems in the Bible?

On occasion David displayed a cruel and vindictive side to his nature. He did not scruple to seduce the lovely Bathsheba and then ruthlessly dispose of her uncooperative husband. He had seven of Saul's direct descendants put to death on what seems a flimsy pretext. And on his deathbed he used his last charge to his son Solomon to settle scores with old enemies, even though he had previously sworn not to exact vengeance.

David was a man chosen by God and anointed for his service. Throughout his life he expressed deep devotion to the Lord God of Israel and tried to walk in his ways. His faith was absolute; and once in desperate plight he prayed that he might fall into the hands of God 'whose mercy is great', and not fall into the hands of man. Being human, he sometimes lapsed from the high standards demanded of him; but when that happened, he accepted the rebukes of God's prophets with humility and expressed genuine remorse. His conduct should not be judged in present-day terms, but rather in comparison with that of the absolute monarchs of his own time. It then becomes clear why David made such an impact, and why he came to be regarded as a model by future generations.

David paid a bitter personal price for his several unconventional marriages; for though a gifted politician, he failed dismally with his own children. David's eldest son Amnon was murdered by his half-brother Absalom. Absalom led a revolt against his father, and very nearly managed to seize the kingdom before being slain by one of David's army generals. Adonijah, who then became the king's rightful heir, attempted to usurp the throne in David's old age; but he was thwarted by the wily Bathsheba who secured the succession for her own son Solomon.

One of David's first acts as king of all Israel was to establish his capital in a neutral city, one which had not previously belonged to any of the twelve tribes. He conquered Jerusalem from the Jebusites for that purpose. David attempted to weld the autonomous tribes into a single nation by creating a central administration and a new focus for religious worship in Jerusalem. He strongly fortified his 'City of David', to which he brought the Ark of the Covenant. He built an altar there for the Lord and prepared a site for the future Temple. In that way he hoped to reconcile the northern tribes of Israel with his own dominant southern tribe of Judah.

The Philistines, rightly sensing a serious challenge to their authority, marched on Jerusalem but were defeated. During David's reign the Philistines were finally conquered and other neighbouring nations subdued. Israel became a powerful empire, stretching from modern Eilat on the Red Sea up through Syria to the River Euphrates, and from the Mediterranean coast to key desert oases on the caravan route to Mesopotamia. Only the Phoenicians under Hiram King of Tyre, who occupied the coastal strip of modern Lebanon, remained undisturbed; but they were firm friends of Israel who helped repeatedly with advanced technology and with their merchant navy, unrivalled in the ancient world.

King David had wanted to build the Temple in Jerusalem. He said: 'I live in a house of cedar but the Ark of God dwells within curtains'. But the Prophet Nathan told him that his wish would not be granted, and that his son Solomon would build the Temple instead.

Why did God refuse David's request?

MATERIAL FOR LESSON 7

MAP

The kingdom of David & Solomon

TEACHER'S NOTE

Saul, David and Solomon

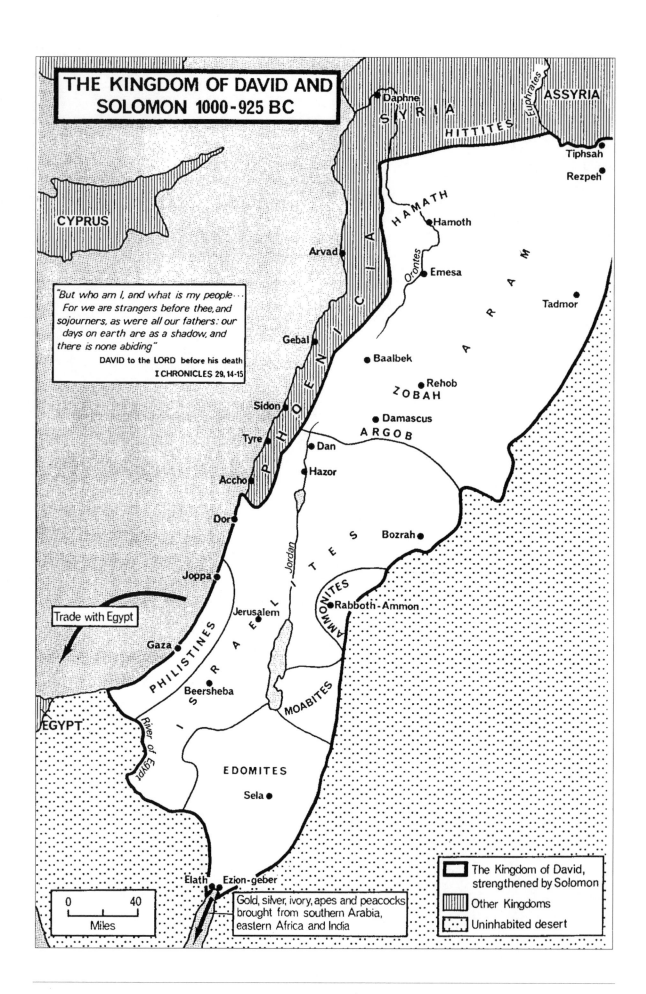

THE KINGDOM OF DAVID AND SOLOMON 1000-925 BC

CYPRUS

"But who am I, and what is my people...
For we are strangers before thee, and
sojourners, as were all our fathers: our
days on earth are as a shadow, and
there is none abiding"

DAVID to the LORD before his death
I CHRONICLES 29, 14-15

Daphne

SYRIA

ASSYRIA

HITTITES

Euphrates

Tiphsah

Rezpeh

HAMATH

Hamoth

Arvad

Orontes

Emesa

ARAM

Tadmor

Gebal

Baalbek

Rehob

ZOBAH

Sidon

Damascus

Tyre

ARGOB

Dan

Accho

Hazor

Dor

Bozrah

Joppa

Jordan

Trade with Egypt

Jerusalem

Rabboth-Ammon

AMMONITES

Gaza

PHILISTINES

ISRAEL

Beersheba

MOABITES

EGYPT

River of Egypt

EDOMITES

Sela

Elath   Ezion-geber

| | 0 | 40 | |
Miles

Gold, silver, ivory, apes and peacocks
brought from southern Arabia,
eastern Africa and India

	The Kingdom of David, strengthened by Solomon
	Other Kingdoms
	Uninhabited desert

On Saul's death David was acclaimed king by his own tribe of Judah, and anointed in Hebron. Bitter warfare then broke out between Judah and the other Hebrew tribes which acknowledged Saul's son Ish-Bosheth as king. David's side grew steadily stronger at the expense of the House of Saul. A poignant episode in the civil war occurred when Ish-Bosheth complied with David's demand to return his abandoned wife Michal, to whom he had been betrothed for the price of a hundred Philistine foreskins. Michal was taken away from her new husband Paltiel – and while her feelings can only be guessed at, it is recorded that the unfortunate Paltiel followed her weeping most of the way to Hebron before being ordered back home. After the murder of King Ish-Bosheth, the tribal elders visited David in Hebron. They made their peace with him and anointed him king over Israel and Judah.

David's character is described in the biblical Book of Samuel, in which frank accounts of his failings and virtues convey an unmistakable sense of authenticity. An outstanding warrior, diplomat and empire builder, David was also a fine poet and musician. He was engagingly impetuous in his personal behaviour. Ignoring the sneers of his aristocratic wife, he uninhibitedly danced for joy in the streets of Jerusalem when bringing the Ark of the Covenant into the city. Though eager for the throne and sorely provoked by Saul, he preferred to wait until the natural end of Saul's reign before making his bid for power. Once he had attained his aim, David showed respect for the former royal house and did his best to reconcile Saul's supporters.

On occasion David displayed a cruel and vindictive side to his nature. He did not scruple to seduce the lovely Bathsheba and then ruthlessly dispose of her uncooperative husband. He had seven of Saul's direct descendants put to death on what seems a flimsy pretext. And on his deathbed he used his last charge to his son Solomon to settle scores with old enemies, even though he had previously sworn not to exact vengeance.

David was a man chosen by God and anointed for his service. Throughout his life he expressed deep devotion to the Lord God of Israel and tried to walk in his ways. His faith was absolute; and once in desperate plight he prayed that he might fall into the hands of God 'whose mercy is great', and not fall into the hands of man. Being human, he sometimes lapsed from the high standards demanded of him; but when that happened, he accepted the rebukes of God's prophets with humility and expressed genuine remorse. His conduct should not be judged in present-day terms, but rather in comparison with that of the absolute monarchs of his own time. It then becomes clear why David made such an impact, and why he came to be regarded as a model by future generations.

David paid a bitter personal price for his several unconventional marriages; for though a gifted politician, he failed dismally with his own children. David's eldest son Amnon was murdered by his half-brother Absalom after raping Absalom's sister Tamar. Absalom led a revolt against his father, and very nearly managed to seize the kingdom before being slain by one of David's army generals. Adonijah, who then became the king's rightful heir, attempted to usurp the throne in David's old age; but he was thwarted by the wily Bathsheba who secured the succession for her own son Solomon.

★　　★　　★

One of David's first acts as king of all Israel was to establish his capital in a neutral city, one which had not previously belonged to any of the twelve tribes. He conquered Jerusalem from the Jebusites for that purpose. David attempted to weld the autonomous tribes into a single nation by creating a central administration and a new focus for religious worship in Jerusalem. He strongly fortified his 'City of David', to which he brought the Ark of the Covenant. He built an altar there for the Lord and prepared a site for the future Temple. In that way he hoped to reconcile the northern tribes of Israel with his own dominant southern tribe of Judah.

The Philistines, rightly sensing a serious challenge to their authority, marched on Jerusalem but were defeated. During David's reign the Philistines were finally conquered and other neighbouring nations subdued. Israel became a powerful empire, stretching from modern Eilat on the Red Sea up through Syria to the River Euphrates, and from the Mediterranean coast to key desert oases on the caravan route to Mesopotamia. Only the Phoenicians under Hiram King of Tyre, who occupied the coastal strip of modern Lebanon, remained undisturbed; but they were firm friends of Israel who helped repeatedly with advanced technology and with their merchant navy, unrivalled in the ancient world.

David's military conquests were consolidated by a shrewd network of alliances started by him and extended by his son Solomon. The pacification of so large an area, containing the main trade routes between Egypt and Mesopotamia as well as ports on the Mediterranean and the Red Sea, caused an unprecedented expansion of trade. This was responsible for the spectacular affluence of the kingdom, especially during King Solomon's reign. The magnificent Temple was erected in Jerusalem by Solomon; and that endowed David's city with an aura of sanctity which it retains to this day. In the middle of the tenth century B.C., the Kingdom of Israel reached a peak of influence and material splendour which would not be seen again. It was a truly golden age.

King Solomon's closing years were marred by growing discontent within the nation as well as in the empire. Two of the subject peoples succeeded in re-establishing their independence after a bitter struggle. After the death of King Solomon in 928 B.C., the northern tribes refused to accept the authority of his stupidly tactless son,

King Rehoboam. They rebelled against the continuing rule of the House of David in Jerusalem and the dominance of the tribe of Judah; and established their own separate state, centred on Shechem. The united kingdom was thus replaced by the two rival and often mutually hostile kingdoms of Judah and Israel – no match for Egypt, Assyria and Babylonia, the super-powers of the region.

The Kingdom of Israel finally collapsed under the onslaught of the Assyrians in 720 B.C. Its population, known thereafter as the 'lost' Ten Tribes of Israel vanished for ever – though their memory persisted in popular legend, as shown by the account of one of their ships taking shelter from a storm in the port of Aberdeen over two thousand years later. The Kingdom of Judah, ruled by kings of the Davidic line, survived the Kingdom of Israel by one hundred and thirty-five years. Jerusalem and the Temple were then destroyed by the Babylonians; and the people carried off to Babylon in captivity. It seemed like the end of a glorious dream.

★　　★　　★

In David's last charge to his son Solomon, he assured him that

'If your descendants take care to walk faithfully in my sight with all their heart and with all their soul you shall never lack a successor on the throne of Israel . . .'

The belief that David and his descendants would rule over Israel to the end of time originated during David's reign, possibly when Nathan the prophet first transmitted God's message:

'Tell David: your family shall be established and your kingdom shall stand for all time in my sight, and your throne shall be established for ever'.

The inhabitants of Judah – or the Jews as they came to be known – did not willingly accept the secession of the northern tribes from the rule of the House of David. This they regarded as sinful and contrary to the will of God.

In the turbulent centuries that followed the break-up of the united kingdom, the Jews looked back to their golden age of power and influence with increasing nostalgia. They developed the doctrine that one day Israel and Judah would again be united by a descendant of King David, under whom they would regain their former glory. Coupled with this idea was the parallel belief in the special sanctity of David's city of Jerusalem – and especially of its Temple, uniquely blessed by God's indwelling presence. Even the Hebrew prophets, who in their ceaseless quest for righteousness fiercely denounced the Davidic kings of their own times, never doubted that a saviour would arise from the stock of David.

The Kingdom of David and Solomon

David's military conquests were consolidated by a shrewd network of alliances started by him and extended by his son Solomon. The pacification of so large an area, containing the main trade routes between Egypt and Mesopotamia as well as ports on the Mediterranean and the Red Sea, caused an unprecedented expansion of trade. This was responsible for the spectacular affluence of the kingdom, especially during King Solomon's reign.

Until then, Israel had worshipped God in a simple sanctuary that housed the Ark of Covenant. Solomon wanted (just as his father David had wanted) a more fitting House of God – a magnificent Temple that would be the grandest building in all Jerusalem, indeed in all the land of Israel.

From his friend and ally, King Hiram of Tyre, Solomon obtained the cedar wood of Lebanon for the building of the Temple. Solomon chose the most gifted architects to design the Temple. It was built of stone and precious wood, with great pillars and spacious inner courts, with special places appointed for various rites of the Services. No iron tools were used in the building of the Temple, for iron was associated with violence and war – while the Temple was the House of God, who wants all men to live in peace.

When the work was completed, Jerusalem was thronged with jubilant people. Many came merely to marvel, but many others came to rejoice and re-dedicate themselves to their faith.

One can image the hush that fell on the crowds as the priest carried the Holy Ark into the holiest part of the Temple, the Holy of Holies. The outer courts were crowded with worshippers. The Cohanim offered sacrifices on the altars. The Levites sang psalms and played their instruments.

The splendour of the Temple and the riches of the Kingdom soon attracted many visitors who came to marvel at Solomon's court. Among them was the Queen Sheba. The Temple endowed Jerusalem with an aura of sanctity which it retains to this day – three thousands years later.

In the middle of the tenth century B.C., the Kingdom of Israel reached a peak of influence and material splendour which would not be seen again. It was a truly golden age.

King Solomon had a huge household with many wives. In the manner of the great monarchs of his time, Solomon kept a luxurious harem, a palace where these wives lived. Many of them were foreign princesses, whom he had married in order to cement treaties with foreign kings. The foreign princesses often brought their own priests and their idols with them. It may be that Solomon, in spite of his great wisdom, dismissed these idols as the harmless toys of foolish women, little realising the danger they presented to the very foundation of his country.

Along with new technology, the foreigners who came to Solomon's court introduced their own gods, and some of the Israelites at court also adopted foreign habits. Although Solomon brought great riches to his Kingdom, not all the people benefited. For the first time in Israel's history the people were divided into two classes – the rich and the poor.

The Prophet Samuel had warned that a king would be a very heavy burden. Certainly Solomon proved such, for he imposed heavy burdens on his people. The rich were taxed to pay for the highways and the building projects. The poor who could not pay the taxes had to contribute their services to the king as labourers and soldiers just as Samuel had foretold.

Some of the lands conquered by David became restless under Solomon's rule and began to revolt. Solomon did not march against them as his father would have done, and so they began to break away. The seeds of rebellion were also sown among Solomon's own people. Ten northern tribes, unhappy because of heavy taxes, felt that they were not benefiting from Solomon's rule. Jeroboam, a young soldier from the tribe of Ephraim, led and unsuccessful revolt against the King and then escaped to Egypt to take refuge with Pharaoh Shishak.

Which two remained loyal to Solomon?

Solomon continued to reap a golden harvest, but discontent was spreading uncomfortably close to the throne. Many nobles at court strongly disapproved of the king's tolerance of the priests and servants of his foreign wives who prayed to their idols under Solomon's own roof.

What books of the Bible are attributed to Solomon?
1. Song of Songs (Shir Ha Shirim in Hebrew)
2. Proverbs (Mishlei in Hebrew)
3. Ecclesiastes (Kolelet in Hebrew).

MATERIAL FOR LESSON

BOOK

English Bible – for Psalms, Ecclesiastes, etc.

MAP

Kingdom of David and Solomon

TEACHER'S BACKGROUND

See Lesson 7 for this background note

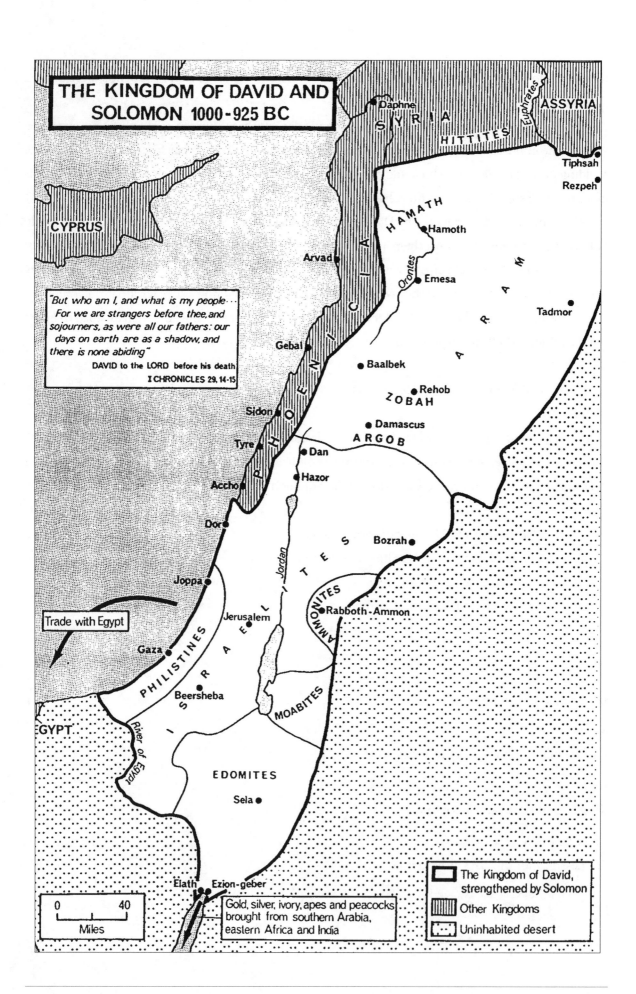

THE KINGDOM OF DAVID AND SOLOMON 1000-925 BC

CYPRUS

ASSYRIA

SYRIA

HITTITES

Euphrates

Daphne

Tiphsah

Rezpeh

HAMATH

Hamoth

Arvad

Orontes

Emesa

ARAM

Tadmor

"But who am I, and what is my people···
For we are strangers before thee, and
sojourners, as were all our fathers: our
days on earth are as a shadow, and
there is none abiding"

DAVID to the LORD before his death
I CHRONICLES 29, 14-15

Gebal

Baalbek

Rehob

ZOBAH

Sidon

Damascus

Tyre

ARGOB

Dan

Hazor

Accho

Dor

Bozrah

PHOENICIA

ISRAELITES

Jordan

Joppa

Trade with Egypt

Rabboth-Ammon

AMMONITES

Jerusalem

Gaza

PHILISTINES

Beersheba

MOABITES

EGYPT

River of Egypt

EDOMITES

Sela

	The Kingdom of David, strengthened by Solomon
	Other Kingdoms
	Uninhabited desert

0   40
Miles

Elath   Ezion-geber

Gold, silver, ivory, apes and peacocks
brought from southern Arabia,
eastern Africa and India

Defeat and Exile

King Solomon's closing years were marred by growing discontent within the nation as well as in the empire. Two of the subject peoples succeeded in re-establishing their independence after a bitter struggle. After the death of King Solomon in 928 B.C.E., the northern tribes refused to accept the authority of his stupidly tactless son, King Rehoboam.

The leaders of the ten northern tribes asked Rehoboam at Shechem to lighten their taxes and ease their burden. Rehoboam angered them by keeping them waiting for three days for his answer. He then refused to grant their request, despite the advice of Solomon's old advisers. The ten tribes then refused to accept Rehoboam as their king, and instead chose Jeroboam, the veteran rebel of the northern tribe of Ephraim.

Jeroboam was declared king of the northern Kingdom of Israel, while only two tribes – Judah and Benjamin – remained loyal to Rehoboam, king of the southern Kingdom of Judah. Jeroboam established his capital at Samaria. In order to discourage his people from making pilgrimage to the Temple in Jerusalem (for fear that they would become loyal to King Rehoboam), he built two sanctuaries – one in Bethel and the other at Dan.

The glorious united kingdom of David and Solomon was no more and the empire disappeared. The two weak successor kingdoms – Judah in the south and Israel (or Ephraim, as it was often called) in the north – existed side by side for over two hundred years. They often fought each other until Judah eventually accepted the existence of the northern Kingdom.

These two tiny states were no match for the superpowers of the region – Egypt, Assyria and Babylonia – and they struggled hard to maintain a kind of independence.

Without a king from the House of David to unite them, there was a constant power struggle between the ten tribes that made up the northern Kingdom of Israel. As a result, Israel was ruled by different dynasties. After two centuries, the kingdom of Israel was conquered by an Assyrian army in 720 B.C.E. Its people, known thereafter as the Lost Ten Tribes of Israel, were deported and disappeared from the stage of world history. The Bible records many of the events that took place during Israel's existence and tells of its prophets – including Elijah, Elisha, Amos and Hosea.

The Kingdom of Judah fared rather better than its sister kingdom. It was ruled by kings from the House of David throughout its history.

In 701 B.C.E. Sennacherib, King of Assyria, besieged Jerusalem. He did not succeed in capturing the city, but imposed heavy taxes on King Hezekiah, and later on his son Manasseh.

Later, when Assyria's power had weakened, King Josiah (Manasseh's grandson) found a Sepher

Torah hidden away. He ordered that Pesah, which had not been observed for very many years, should be kept properly. As a result, King Josiah's reign witnessed a remarkable religious and national recovery. This however was short lived for a new and aggressive super-power, Babylonia, was rising in the east to replace Assyria.

Judah became a vassal kingdom, paying tribute to Babylon; but its foolish King Jehoiakim tried to revolt against the Babylonian rule. This caused Nebuchadnezzar, King of Babylonia, to besiege Jerusalem in 598 B.C.E. Jehoiakim was killed, and his son Jehoiakim was deported to Babylon together with over 10,000 men from the leading families of Judah.

> And Nebuchadnezzar king of Babylon..carried away all Jerusalem, and all the princes, and
> all the mighty men of valour, even ten thousand captives, and all the craftsmen and smiths:
> none remained, save the poorest sort of people of the land.
> (2 King 24:14)

Zedekiah was made king of those remaining in Judah. Twelve years later, he too rashly rebelled against his Babylonian masters. That time King Nebuchadnezzar made no mistake. Jerusalem fell to his army in 586 B.C.E. Zedekiah tried to escape but was caught and brought to Nebuchadnezzar. His sons were killed in front of him, and his own eyes were put out. Blind and in chains, the last king of Judah was led away to captivity in Babylon. The Temple which Solomon had built was destroyed on the 9th of Ab. and a large part of the population of Judah was also carried off into captivity. A new era began for the people of Judah -The Babylonian Exile!. It seemed like the end of a glorious dream.

MATERIAL FOR LESSON 9

MAPS

The destruction of Jewish independence

The Exile

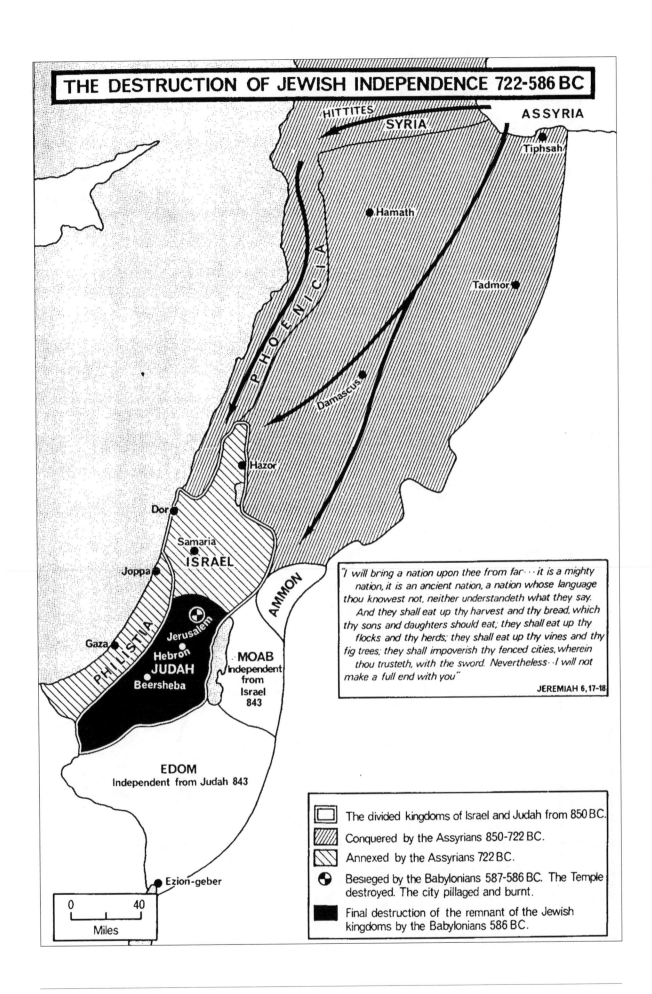

THE DESTRUCTION OF JEWISH INDEPENDENCE 722-586 BC

ASSYRIA

HITTITES

SYRIA

• Tiphsah

• Hamath

P H O E N I C I A

• Tadmor

• Damascus

• Hazor

Dor •

Samaria
•
ISRAEL

Joppa •

AMMON

"I will bring a nation upon thee from far···it is a mighty
nation, it is an ancient nation, a nation whose language
thou knowest not, neither understandeth what they say.
    And they shall eat up thy harvest and thy bread, which
thy sons and daughters should eat; they shall eat up thy
    flocks and thy herds; they shall eat up thy vines and thy
fig trees; they shall impoverish thy fenced cities, wherein
    thou trustest, with the sword. Nevertheless···I will not
make a full end with you"

JEREMIAH 6, 17-18

Gaza •

Jerusalem

Hebron •

JUDAH

Beersheba •

MOAB
Independent
from
Israel
843

P H I L I S T I A

EDOM
Independent from Judah 843

Ezion-geber •

0   40
Miles

☐ The divided kingdoms of Israel and Judah from 850 BC.

▨ Conquered by the Assyrians 850-722 BC.

▧ Annexed by the Assyrians 722 BC.

◉ Besieged by the Babylonians 587-586 BC. The Temple
destroyed. The city pillaged and burnt.

■ Final destruction of the remnant of the Jewish
kingdoms by the Babylonians 586 BC.

LESSON 9   DEFEAT AND EXILE

297

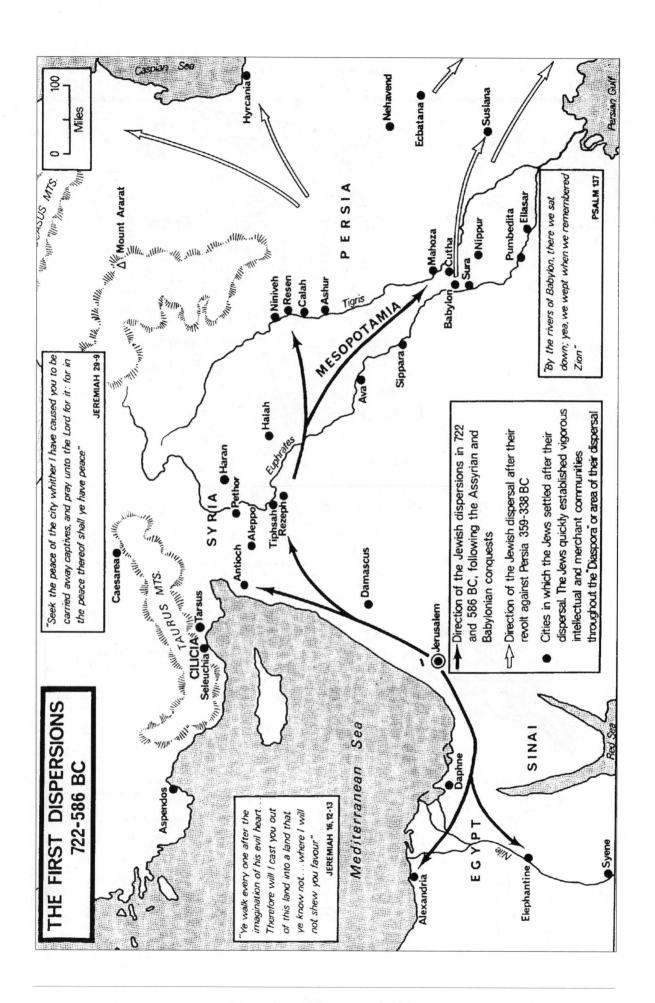

THE FIRST DISPERSIONS
722–586 BC

"Ye walk every one after the imagination of his evil heart... Therefore will I cast you out of this land into a land that ye know not... where I will not shew you favour"
JEREMIAH 16.12-13

"Seek the peace of the city whither I have caused you to be carried away captives, and pray unto the Lord for it: for in the peace thereof shall ye have peace"
JEREMIAH 29.9

"By the rivers of Babylon, there we sat down; yea, we wept when we remembered Zion"
PSALM 137

→ Direction of the Jewish dispersions in 722 and 586 BC, following the Assyrian and Babylonian conquests

⇨ Direction of the Jewish dispersal after their revolt against Persia 359-338 BC

● Cities in which the Jews settled after their dispersal. The Jews quickly established vigorous intellectual and merchant communities throughout the Diaspora or area of their dispersal

The Babylonian Exile

With the return of the Jewish people to its place of origin, the wheel of destiny appeared to have turned full circle.

What do we mean by this?

Abraham travelled from Ur of the Chaldees to Canaan.His descendants went from Canaan to Egypt. They went from Egypt to the wilderness where they were given the Torah at Mount Sinai.. They conquered the Promised Land and formed the united kingdom of David and Solomon, which later split into the separate kingdoms of Israel and Judah. Israel was conquered by Assyrians and its people deported – some to Babylon. Judah was conquered by Babylonians and most of its people deported to Babylon. But it was not so; for far from turning their backs on their faith, the exiles deepened their understanding of its teachings under the guidance of the Hebrew Prophets.

Many important developments in early Judaism, such as the institution of the Synagogue and the square Hebrew script still in use, can be traced back to the Babylonian Captivity.

How did the Jews write before they came to use the square Aramaic script?

Why did the Jewish exiles need synagogues when they had not needed them before?.

Which prophets were active during the Babylonian Exile?

After the first bitterness, the deportees were treated with tolerance by their new masters. Eventually they were even able to exercise a degree of local autonomy. The captive King Jehoiachin of Judah was released from prison in the year 561 B.C.E. and raised to a position of dignity in Babylon – exalted above all the other exiled kings there. And there is evidence to suggest that some of the sons of the Jewish nobility were groomed for service at the Babylonian court. The family and clan structure of the exiles was preserved; and communal leaders, known as Elders of the Exile, maintained traditional authority.

Mesopotamia had by then become the core of the mighty Persian Empire which included Egypt. Its capital city, Babylon – with the massive walls, high towers and rectangular grid of streets revealed by the archaeologists – must have been the most important city in the world.

A fascinating glimpse into the lives of those early exiles was provided by the discovery of the records

– written on clay tablets and stored in huge earthenware jars sealed with bitumen – of what must have been a leading business venture of the time.

Founded in 587 B.C.E. the firm of Murashu and Sons lasted for at least one hundred and fifty years. It head office was in Nippur and it claimed to have branches everywhere. It was an international bank which also dealt with personal loans at the then prevailing rate of interest of twenty per cent. The bank itself held the securities of those imprisoned for debt. It handled insurance and all kinds of legal transactions. Amongst the many deeds discovered was the conveyance of a large herd of cattle from a Jew to a Babylonian. Another was a twenty-year guarantee from two jewellers that the emerald would not fall out of a ring they had just sold to a customer.

Advised by the prophet Jeremiah to work for the welfare of the country of their captivity and settle down and increase in number, many did just that. Though some of the exiles eventually returned to Zion to restore their mother country, others remained behind and built up the leading community of the Jewish dispersion.

On the whole, conditions for the Jews remained favourable throughout the centuries, enabling, the community to strike deep roots in its adopted land and perform useful service throughout the Empire. Persian tolerance of the Jews and their religion is illustrated by a surviving letter of instruction to the Jewish garrison of Elephantine (Aswan) in Upper Egypt, instructing how Passover of the year 419 B.C.E. was to be celebrated. The letter was issued in the name of King Darius II.

By the time of the Bar Kochba revolt of 132 C.E. against the Roman occupation of the Holy Land, the Jewish community of Babylon had become largely self-governing with its own courts of law and central administration. At its head was the Resh Galuta (Head of the Exile, Exilarch, or more grandly, Prince of the Captivity), always chosen from descendants of the royal House of David. Such was the respect shown to the Resh Galuta that when he was 'called' to the reading of the Torah in synagogue, the scroll was brought to him instead of his having to go to the reading desk.

There is a rabbinic tradition to the effect that the office of Exilarch existed from the earliest days of the captivity, starting with King Jehoiachin; but there is no independent confirmation.

The Exilarch was accorded semi-royal honours by the kings of the country and he governed the secular affairs of the community. The Babylonian community looked to the rabbis of the Holy Land for its reli¬gious leadership.

Little is known about the culture of the mass of the people, mostly engaged in agriculture; but we do have some evidence of an established Jewish nobility, well assimilated to the style and manners of the local aristocracy. Prominent Jews also participated in international commerce, particularly in the lucrative silk trade between China and Roman Empire.

Why did it suit the Persians to allow the Jews to govern themselves within their empire?

What was the advantage for the Jews?

Could such a situation happen in England today?

MATERIAL FOR LESSON 10

PHOTOCOPIES

1. Development of Hebrew Script

2. Modern and ancient Hebrew Scripts

3. Psalm 137

Name	Numerical value	Pronunciation	Ancient Hebrew	Final form	Primary form
Aleph	1	–			א
Bet	2	b,v			ב
Gimel	3	g			ג
Daled	4	d			ד
He	5	h			ה
Vav	6	v			ו
Zayin	7	z			ז
Het	8	h (kh)			ח
Tet	9	t			ט
Yod	10	y			י
Kaph	20	k,kh		ך	כ
Lamed	30	l			ל
Mem	40	m		ם	מ
Nun	50	n		ן	נ
Samekh	60	s			ס
Ayin	70	–			ע
Pe	80	p,f		ף	פ
Tsade	90	ts		ץ	צ
Koph	100	k			ק
Resh	200	r			ר
Shin	300	sh,s			ש
Tav	400	t (t,s)			ת

The Paleo-Hebrew Script.

The Paleo-Hebrew Script. The Hebrew script did not cease to exist after the Babylonian capture of Judah, when most of the nobles were taken into exile. It was used by the people who remained to work the fields; the sixth-century inscribed jar handles from Gibeon, on which the names of winegrowers are listed, are an example. However, from the fifth century onward, when the Aramaic language and used in the time of the Second Temple) was used for writi Hebrew both in Judah and Samaria. It was preserv mainly as a biblical book hand by a coterie of erud scribes (presumably of the Zadokite priesthood; cf. t Paleo-Hebrew Pentateuch fragments found among t *Dead Sea Scrolls). The vast majority of the *Hasmone coinage as well as the coins of the First and Second Jew Revolts bears Paleo-Hebrew legends. Although this scrip

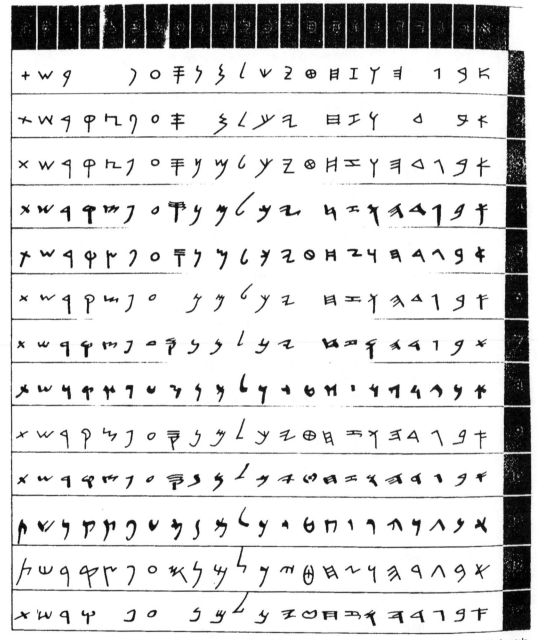

Figure 10. (1) Aḥiram sarcophagus, c. 1000 B.C.E., Phoenician; (2) Gezer Calendar, late tenth century B.C.E., Hebrew; (3) Mesha stele, mid-ninth century B.C.E., Moabite; (4) Samaria ostraca, eighth century B.C.E., Hebrew; (5) Bar-Rekub stele, late eighth century B.C.E., Aramaic; (6) Siloam inscription, c. 700 B.C.E., Hebrew; (7) Meẓad Ḥashavyahu ostracon, late seventh century B.C.E., Hebrew; (8) Saqqara papyrus, c. 600 B.C.E., Aramaic; (9) Hebrew seals, late seventh–early sixth century B.C.E.; (10) Lachish ostraca, early sixth century B.C.E., Hebrew; (11) Elephantine papyrus, late fifth century B.C.E., Aramaic; (12) Eshmun'azor inscription, fifth century B.C.E., Phoenician; (13) Exodus scroll fragment, second century B.C.E., Paleo-Hebrew. Copyright Joseph Naveh.

By the rivers of Babylon,
　　there we sat,
　　sat and wept,
　　as we thought of Zion.
²There on the poplars
　　we hung up our lyres,
　　　³for our captors asked us there for songs,
　　our tormentors,ᵃ for amusement,
　　"Sing us one of the songs of Zion."
⁴How can we sing a song of the LORD
　　on alien soil?
⁵If I forget you, O Jerusalem,
　　let my right hand wither;ᵇ
　　　⁶let my tongue stick to my palate
　　if I cease to think of you,
　　if I do not keep Jerusalem in memory
　　even at my happiest hour.

⁷Remember, O LORD, against the Edomites
　　the day of Jerusalem's fall;
　　how they cried, "Strip her, strip her
　　to her very foundations!"
⁸Fair Babylon, you predator,ᶜ
　　a blessing on him who repays you in kind
　　what you have inflicted on us;
　　　⁹a blessing on him who seizes your babies
　　and dashes them against the rocks!

ᵃ *Meaning of Heb. uncertain.*
ᵇ *Others "forget its cunning."*
ᶜ *With Targum; others "who are to be destroyed."*

The Prophets

Though the entire content of Five Books of Moses (The Torah) is read out in synagogue during the course of each year, only extracts from the Books of the Prophets are included in the weekly reading of the Haphtarah. In practice, therefore, there is a lack of emphasis on the prophets.

WHAT IS PROPHESY

God made his will known to the Jewish people through a series of prophets. Prophesy was not something to be learned, not something for which a man trained. The ability to receive divine messages and pass them on to others was a gift from God that simply had to be accepted, however unwillingly. No man ever chose to become a prophet and many were reluctant to accept God's calling. Moses, Jeremiah and Isaiah all pleaded with the Almighty to spare them because of their unworthiness. Jonah actually fled across the sea in an unsuccessful attempt to escape the divine command.

DIVINE REVELATIONS

The experience of receiving a divine communication was awe-inspiring and accompanied by fear and trembling. The prophet's life could be hard: he was often an unpopular, solitary, figure. "I sat alone because your hand was upon me", Jeremiah complained to God. Prophets were often ridiculed, sometimes hated and occasionally imprisoned.

God generally communicated to prophets in dreams or visions. Only to Moses 'the man of God' did God reveal himself plainly and directly – mouth to mouth, so to speak. Moses is therefore considered to be the greatest of the prophets. To quote the Yigdal, sung in synagogue at the end of the service on Friday nights,

There never arose in Israel a prophet, who like Moses, did see the likeness of God.

THE EARLY PROPHETS

The early prophets rarely acted independently and were simply agents through whom God spoke to the people. They had no choice but to obey God's command, whether or not they agreed with the message, whether or not anyone was prepared to listen – and sometimes such messages were received with hostility . It was no easy thing to rebuke kings and the great men of the world, even in God's name; and it could be dangerous to transmit threats of divine punishment and messages of doom.

Some of the early prophets were men of affairs with key positions at the king's court. Samuel, who had the ability to foresee the future, started as a ruler in his own right (a 'Judge') before annointing

Saul as the first king of Israel: even then, he retained sufficient authority to choose David to succeed Saul as king. Nathan had the unenviable task of rebuking the mighty King David for seducing Bathsheba - and then of recalling him to God's service. In another extraordinary act of courage, Elijah rebuked King Ahab for being an accessory to murder. Elijah and Elisha were credited with many miracles, such as dividing the waters of the river and reviving the dead: they were both described as 'madmen' for communing with God in ecstatic trances, sometimes induced by music.

THE LATER PROPHETS

Some of later prophets also went into ecstatic trances and were called madmen. They too were influential in state affairs and were asked to foretell the outcome of battles and ascertain God's will in other matters. Commencing with the shepherd Amos (8th century B.C.E.), the line of prophets turned into one of great religious teachers who added another vital dimension to the Jewish faith. It is claimed that it was they who invented the ideal of universal peace as a goal towards which all men should strive - another 'first' in the history of religion.

Jeremiah's injunction (Jeremiah 29:7)

Seek the peace of the city to which you have been exiled. Pray to God on its behalf, for in its peace you will find peace.

was crucial advice to the embittered exiles in Babylon and has been followed by the Jewish people since that time.

The major prophets of this period were Ezekiel, Jeremiah and Isaiah. Though in no way rejecting the developed rituals of Judaism, they placed more urgent emphasis on righteousness - the supreme law of the universe and one of God's attributes. To them, morality and social justice were the decisive factors in determining the future of the nation; and they pleaded repeatedly for Israel to repent and return to God's ways. Towards the end of the prophetic period, Jeremiah's vision of Israel's mission to bring all peoples to the knowledge and worship of the one true God received powerful expression in Isaiah's message of salvation for the whole of mankind.

The Hebrew prophets, with their stress on the personal relationship of each individual to God, and their message of hope, helped the Jewish people to survive the destruction of the Temple and the rigours of exile in Babylon and elsewhere. Their influence enabled Jews in exile to deepen their faith and to develop Judaism into the universal faith it is today.

INFLUENCE OF THE PROPHETS IN ENGLAND

Medieval Europe was firmly in the grip of the Catholic Church, which strongly discouraged ordinary people to read the Bible. This was available only to the clergy - and only in Latin (and in Greek for the New Testament). Until King Henry VIII's quarrel with the Pope in 1535, possession of an English translation of any part of the Bible was a criminal offense, subject to dire penalties. In 1530, copies of translations of the New Testament, made and printed in Europe, were seized by the authorities and burned in a public ceremony in St. Paul's churchyard.

In 1538, King Henry VIII had the Bible freshly translated into English. He then ordered a copy to be placed in a prominent position in every church in the country so that all could read it for themselves. People everywhere rushed to read the Bible; and the large crowds caused public disorder in several places.

The effect of the Hebrew Bible on the people of England was revolutionary. For the very first time, they were able to read the word of God for themselves in their own language. They learned of the struggles of the ancient Jewish people against oppression and of their efforts to establish on earth the rule of freedom and justice for all. They too heeded the words of the prophets and wanted to establish righteousness and social justice for themselves in England.

Inspired by the Hebrew prophets, the people of England increasingly identified with ancient Israel. They saw themselves as the New Israel, striving to build a New Jerusalem in England's green and pleasant land. The English Bible became their own book, one of the greatest ever written in their own language. To Englishmen of the time, the names and the exploits of the kings of ancient Israel became more familiar than those of many of their own kings and queens. They called their children after the heroes of the Bible; and the geography of the Holy Land became their own geography.

The newly awakened religious enthusiasm, coupled with the thirst for righteousness on earth inspired by the Hebrew prophets, led directly to the Puritan reformation and to the civil war. King Charles I was executed. Oliver Cromwell eventually emerged as the Lord Protector of England.

That great change of religious perception also formed the background to the first fruitful encounter between Englishmen and Jews since the Middle Ages.

It was in 1656 that Jews were again permitted to settle in England – a country barred to them since the year 1290. In the following year, what is now the Spanish and Portuguese Jews' Congregation opened its first synagogue in the City of London, bought a plot of land in which to bury their dead with dignity and began to trade openly as Jews on the London Exchange. London then joined Amsterdam and Livorno as almost the only places in Western Europe where the presence of Jews was welcomed and where they could enjoy what we now consider to be basic human rights

The Return to Zion

Eventually a benevolent conqueror of Babylon, King Cyrus the Great of Persia, encouraged some of the exiles to return to Jerusalem and rebuild their ruined land and its Temple.

The hardship involved in that enterprise did not appeal to all of them, for most were by then well established and enjoying life in one of the most luxurious centres of the world. However, many of the more idealistic did seize the opportunity of returning to Zion between the years 528 and 428 B.C.E.

Under the leadership of Nehemiah and Ezra, Judah was slowly and painfully restored – this time not as an independent kingdom but as a semi-autonomous province of the mighty Persian Empire. The Temple was rebuilt in Jerusalem and, profiting from lessons learnt in exile, the Jewish religion was further consolidated and developed by the Scribes and their successors.

The next three hundred years passed in a relatively tranquil manner. Alexander the Great's conquest of the Persian Empire caused little hardship; and Alexander confirmed the special privileges enjoyed by Jerusalem's inhabitants. Conditions worsened after Alexander's death, with Judah becoming a self-governing province of his two successor empires in turn.

In the year 175 B.C.E. Antiochus IV ascended the throne of the ruling Syrian-Greek empire and promptly attempted to unify his realm by banning the practice of Judaism on pain of death. The Jews of Judah revolted against their Greek masters and, under the leadership of the remarkable Maccabean family, eventually succeeded in gaining full independence from foreign rule.

The revolt against the Greeks was also accompanied by a very bitter civil war in which Jews who had assimilated to Greek culture fought desperately against those who had remained true to a Jewish way of life uncontaminated by alien culture.

Where would most of us today have been placed in the conflict?

What festival celebrates the success of the Jewish revolt against the Greeks?

The Jewish state established as the result of the Maccabean revolt expanded its borders; and many pagan inhabitants of the land were incorporated into the nation by mass conversion to Judaism. Judea, as the new state was called, managed to preserve its independence for eighty years.

In 63 B.C.E., two rival claimants to the throne of Judea made the disastrous mistake of appealing for help to a Roman army recently arrived in neighbouring Syria. Its general, Pompey, did not need to be asked twice. He promptly invaded the country and entered Jerusalem at the head of his troops. Temple

Mount was besieged for three months before it was finally taken and thousands of its defenders killed. The Temple was sacked; and Pompey committed the ultimate sacrilege of entering its sanctuary, the Holy of Holies.

Judea was stripped of most of its territory and firmly incorporated into the Roman Empire. The truncated country was allowed a measure of local autonomy under its former king, who lost his royal title. Life was hard and taxation heavy under the Romans. Having enjoyed freedom for the past eighty years, the Jews did not take kindly to foreign rule. They proved turbulent subjects and they rebelled against their new masters again and again – but to no avail.

Conditions improved for a while when Judea became a vassal Kingdom under Herod the Great, a trusted friend of Rome. But the country was fragmented again after Herod's death and the bad times returned once more.

Eventually, goaded beyond endurance, the Jews of Roman Palestine rose in armed revolt against the Romans. The war lasted for four years and cost Rome dear. But in the year 70 C.E., Jerusalem was totally destroyed. Its inhabitants were either killed or enslaved and the Temple was burned to the ground.

The Temple had stood in Jerusalem with only one interruption of seventy years since the days of King Solomon, a thousand years before. For Jews it had become the centre of their national existence, the focus of their faith. God's presence had hovered in its sanctuary – a bare room considered so sacred that entry was restricted to the High Priest, and then only once a year at the climax of the service on the Day of Atonement. The destruction of the Temple was a catastrophe – a disaster so keenly felt that, almost two thousand years later, Jews still fast on each anniversary.

What is the name of that fast?

Yet for Judaism itself, seeds of renewal in a more vital form were also present at that terrible event. At the height of the siege of Jerusalem a leading Pharisee, Rabbi Yohanaan ben Zakkai, had his disciples declare that he had died of the plague. With great show of grief, they carried him in a sealed coffin for burial outside the city walls. Once beyond the ring of determined defenders, the rabbi emerged from his coffin and demanded to be taken to the Roman commander, General Vespasian. By some miracle Ben Zakkai persuaded Vespasian to give him permission to start a religious college in a small town remote from the fighting. Just why Vespasian, who became Emperor shortly afterwards, agreed to so bizarre a request in the middle of a brutal war will never be known. But Rabbi Yohanaan ben Zakkai did found his famous academy at Yavneh. From that new beginning, Judaism developed into a progressive and universal religion, no longer dependent on the Temple and the Holy Land for its continuation.

And that was just as well, for conditions in the Holy Land never completely recovered after the war, though they did improve for a while.

The next major setback occurred in the year 132 C.E., when the Jews under their messianic leader

Bar Kochba again rose up in furious rebellion and were again vanquished by the power of Rome. A period of harsh repression followed the defeat of that revolt; but better times came later, during the long and relatively peaceful patriarchate of Rabbi Judah the Prince, who was a personal friend of the Roman Emperor Marcus Aurelius. Rabbi Judah, in his Mishnah, for the very first time sifted and organised the almost incoherent mass of oral law and tradition which had accumulated over the ages. This formed the core of both the Palestinian Talmud and the Babylonian Talmud.

The death of Rabbi Judah in about the year 220 precipitated the declined of the Holy land as the prime centre of Jewish learning. Mesopotamia then gradually took over as the religious and cultural centre of the Jewish people, a position which it continued to occupy without challenge for the next seven hundred years.

MATERIAL FOR LESSON 12

MAP

Hasmonean Kingdom

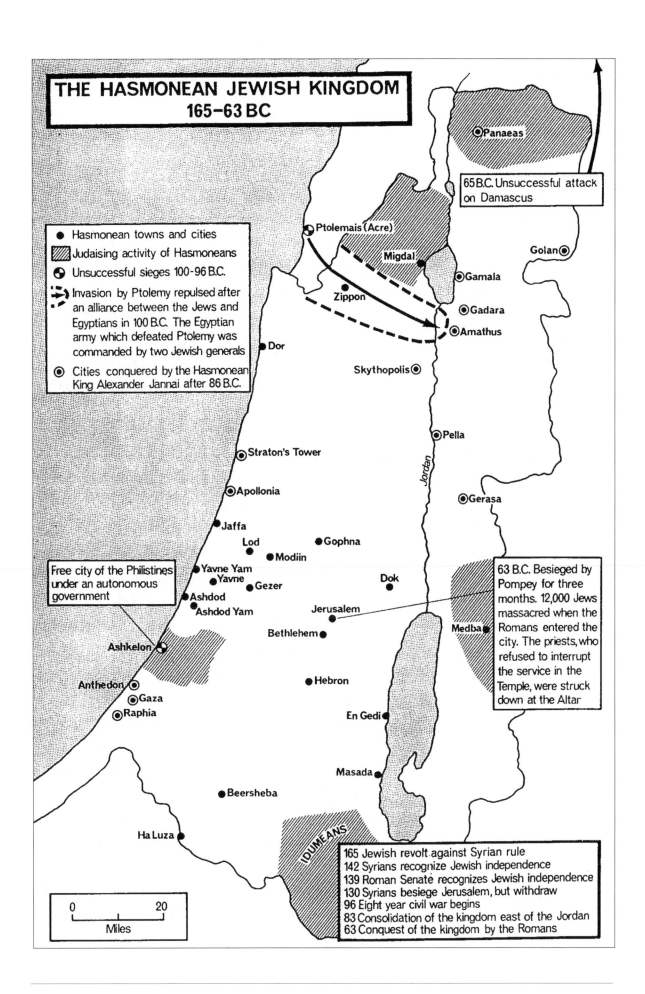

THE HASMONEAN JEWISH KINGDOM 165–63 BC

- ● Hasmonean towns and cities
- ▨ Judaising activity of Hasmoneans
- ✪ Unsuccessful sieges 100-96 B.C.
- ⇢ Invasion by Ptolemy repulsed after an alliance between the Jews and Egyptians in 100 B.C. The Egyptian army which defeated Ptolemy was commanded by two Jewish generals
- ◉ Cities conquered by the Hasmonean King Alexander Jannai after 86 B.C.

●Panaeas

65 B.C. Unsuccessful attack on Damascus

Ptolemais (Acre)

Migdal

Golan◉

●Gamala

Zippon

●Gadara

●Amathus

●Dor

Skythopolis◉

◉Straton's Tower

◉Pella

◉Apollonia

◉Gerasa

●Jaffa

●Gophna

Lod

●Modiin

Free city of the Philistines under an autonomous government

Yavne Yam
Yavne

●Gezer

●Dok

Ashdod

Jerusalem

Ashdod Yam

Bethlehem●

Medba●

63 B.C. Besieged by Pompey for three months. 12,000 Jews massacred when the Romans entered the city. The priests, who refused to interrupt the service in the Temple, were struck down at the Altar

Ashkelon◉

●Hebron

Anthedon◉

◉Gaza

◉Raphia

En Gedi●

●Masada

●Beersheba

IDUMEANS

Ha Luza●

165 Jewish revolt against Syrian rule
142 Syrians recognize Jewish independence
139 Roman Senate recognizes Jewish independence
130 Syrians besiege Jerusalem, but withdraw
96 Eight year civil war begins
83 Consolidation of the kingdom east of the Jordan
63 Conquest of the kingdom by the Romans

Jordan

0   20
Miles

LESSON 12   THE RETURN OF ZION

311

Babylon Takes Over

Refugees from Judea were eagerly welcomed by the Jewish community of Babylon. Those with learning were recruited into its courts and administration; and former pupils of Rabbi Judah the Prince founded religious academies near Babylon at Sura, Nehardea and Pumbeditha. The veritable explosion of Jewish learning that followed was centred on those famous schools. It was in them that the Babylonian Talmud, the underlying structure of modern Judaism, was compiled and written down between the years 200 and 500.

The rapid decline of the Jewish institutions of Roman Palestine from the early years of the third century did not leave an irreplaceable void; for the leadership of world Jewry was simply transferred to the worthy hands of the by then ancient community of exiles in Babylon – where it remained until the rise of new centres of Jewish learning and culture in North Africa and Europe.

The Jewish community of Mesopotamia was already well over a thousand years old when, in the seventh century, the Arabs burst out of Arabia with tremendous vigour. One result of their spectacular swathe of conquest, stretching from Spain to the borders of India, was that the great majority of the Jews then found themselves living in an united Islamic world.

Baghdad, close to the site of ancient Babylon, became the seat of the Caliphs in the year 762. It reached the peak of its prosperity under the rule of Harun al-Rashid in the early years of the following century when the city attracted to itself many of the riches and much of the learning of the known world. As described by travelers from comparatively barbarous Europe, it must have been truly splendid – with its pleasure gardens, peacock-blue tiled mosques and ornate buildings. It was also a great centre of commerce as well as of scholarship, science and the arts. For a time, Baghdad was unequaled in its wealth and culture.

After a decline immediately following the Arab conquest of the eight century, the condition of the Jewish population of Mesopotamia improved. The heads of the two great centres of Jewish learning, the colleges of Sura and Pumbeditha, were each addressed as Gaon (Excellency). The Geonim (plural of Gaon) helped the Exilarch to govern the community.

Because of the importance of Baghdad, the authority of the Geonim was accepted without question in all the lands conquered by Islam, from India in the East to Spain in the West. Copies of the Talmud were dispatched to Jewish communities as far away as Spain; and scholars flocked to Sura and Pumbeditha from many distant places. The first legal codes to aid understanding and observance were developed in Baghdad and circulated; and the first complete prayer books were prepared specially for Jewish communities in Spain and Cairo.

Sa'adia ben Yusef was born in Cairo in 882. Summoned to Baghdad to become Gaon of the Academy of Sura, he soon proved to be as independent of mind as he was brilliant as a scholar. He disagreed with the Exilarch on an important matter of principle, and unlike the Gaon of Pumbeditha, he refused to be cowed. Sa'adia was sacked by the Exilarch and he promptly retaliated by deposing the Exilarch in favour of his younger brother. Though this painful conflict was resolved eventually, his period of forced retirement enabled Sa'adia to concentrate on his writing.

In many ways the greatest of the Geonim, Sa'adia attempted to persuade the doubters of his age that the validity of divinely revealed religious truth can be confirmed by pure reason – also God-given. To him, there was no contradiction between revelation and reason. Both come from God.

What arguments can you find that divine revelation cannot be 'proved' by logical argument?

Perhaps an even more important achievement of the Geonic period was the development of the method of extending the religious learning of the Talmud which is still in use today. The Geonim enlarged understanding of their faith by means of a long series of reasoned judgments on law and practice. These were called Responsa – for each one was written in response to a query from a Jewish scholar, sometimes from a far away country.

The Babylonian academies began to decline after the death of Sa'adia in 942; and Baghdad's position of pre-eminence in Jewish scholarship passed to rising new centres of learning elsewhere. However, the material well-being of Mesopotamia's Jews continued almost undiminished until the country was devastated by Mongol invaders in the thirteenth century.

Can you think of modern examples of important rulings in Judaism established by means of rabbinic responsa?

Benjamin of Tudela gave the following account of his visit to Baghdad in 1170.

There are in Baghdad some 40,00 Jews of the People of Israel (this is a wild exaggeration, 4,000 is more likely). They live in peace, tranquility, and honour under the great Caliph. Among them are great scholars and heads of Yeshivot who are engaged in the study of Torah. There are ten Yeshivot in the city.

Over all of them is Daniel b. Hasday, who is called the "Exilarch of All Israel". He has a written pedigree going back to David, King of Israel. The Jews address him as Our Lord the Exilarch, and the Muslims as Our master, the son of David. He has been invested with supreme authority over all the congregations of Israel by the Lord of the Muslims who ordered that every individual, be he Muslim or Jew, should rise up before him and salute him, and that whoever does not rise up before him should receive one hundred stripes. Every

Thursday, when he goes to behold the countenance of the great Caliph, he is accompanied by Gentile and Jewish horsemen, and heralds cry out before him. "Make way for our Lord, the scion of David, as is due to him!"

He rides on horseback, wearing garments of embroidered silk with a large turban on his head. Over the turban is a large white shawl upon which is a chain.

When he comes before the Caliph, he kisses his hand. Then the Caliph rises before him, seats him upon a throne and all of the Muslim princes who have come to behold the countenance of the Caliph rise altogether before him.

The Exilarch grants all communities the right to appoint rabbis and hazanim for each and every congregation from Iraq to Persia and Yemen and Mesopotamia, from Armenia to Georgia, and from Siberia and the land of the Turks as far as Tibet and India. These men come to him to be ordained and to receive authority from him. They bring him offerings and gifts from the ends of the earth.

He owns hospices, gardens and orchards in Baghdad, as well as many plots of land inherited from his forefathers. No man can take anything from him by force. He receives a fixed revenue every week from the Jewish hospices, markets, and local merchants, exclusive of that which is brought to him from distant lands. He is an extremely wealthy man and is learned in both Scriptures and Talmud. Many Jews eat at his table each day.

Whenever a new Exilarch is appointed, he must expend a great deal of wealth upon the Caliph, the ministers, and the officials. On the day when the Caliph bestows the writ of authority upon him, he rides in the litter of viceroy. He is conducted from the Caliph's palace to his home to the accompaniment of tambourines and dancing.

He (the Exilarch) performs the ordination of the Head of the Yeshiva. The Jews in this city are very learned and wealthy. There are in Baghdad twenty-eight synagogues.

MATERIAL FOR LESSON 13

Map showing the area of Jewish settlement controlled by the Geonim of the 8th century.

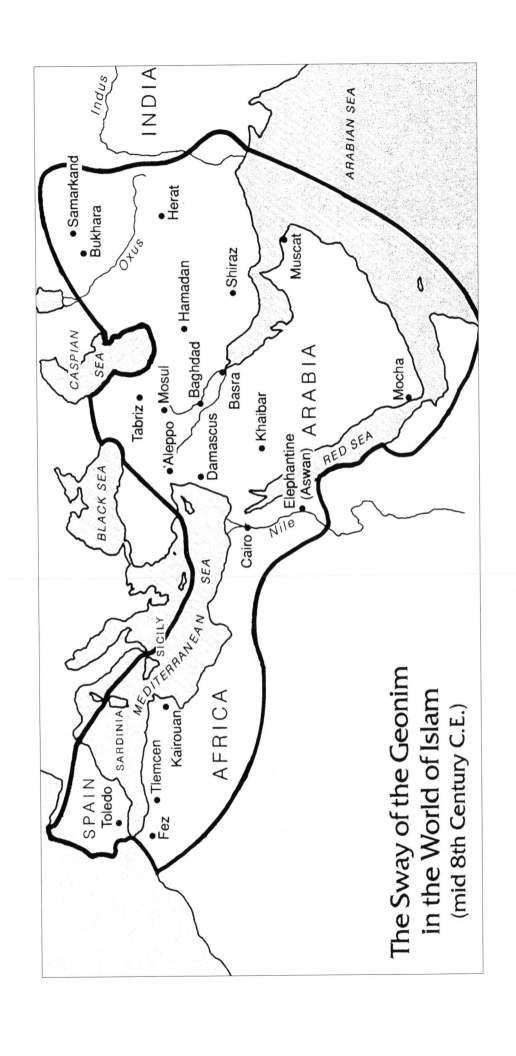

The Sway of the Geonim
in the World of Islam
(mid 8th Century C.E.)

The Cairo Geniza

RECORDING HISTORY

The great problem confronting anyone attempting to picture the conditions in which Jews lived in the centuries before the coming of Islam in the 7th century, and in Islam's early years, is the almost complete lack of Jewish records, other than religious writings that ignored contemporary events.

What little we do know has been gleaned from fragmentary mentions in mainly unfriendly sources such as Christian decrees against the Jews. Sad though it may be to accept, the barest outline of the Jewish story can only be pieced together with the help of the spiteful comments of sworn enemies.

For example, we know of the part played by the Jews of Arabia in the drama accompanying the rise of Islam and its Prophet only from later and distinctly hostile Arab accounts.

Even earlier, our knowledge of the continued existence of the great Babylonian Jewish community after the return to Zion of some of its members in the 5th century BCE comes only from occasional references in Palestinian writings and from the much later Roman-Jewish historian Josephus (1st century CE).

History, as we now understand the term, was considered a sheer waste of time by the rabbis; and it is clear that the Jews of that period displayed no interest at all in recording and preserving accounts of the times through which they were living.

Historical writing, so brilliant in the Biblical era, ceased altogether with Josephus in the 1st century CE; and even his works were promptly forgotten by Jews. Attention to history only resumed, falteringly, in the 16th century after the expulsion of the Jews from Spain. This striking indifference to history was probably due to the Jewish view of the Bible solely as a record of the nation's encounters with God – God's challenges and its responses.

For Jews, eagerly awaiting the end of the historical process by redemption at the hands of the Messiah, the Bible with its prophesies was the divinely revealed pattern of what had been and what was still to come. Nothing else mattered. The rise and fall of mighty empires, as well as daily events of lesser consequence, could all be clearly understood in the light of the prophesies, and then related directly to the underlying pulse of history described in the Bible. Their actual details must have seemed so unimportant as not even to be worth noting.

The first 200 years after the Arab conquest, from about 650 to 850, are the most obscure in the whole of Jewish history. The Arabs were far too busy to interest themselves in a small and non-threatening minority and the Jews themselves wrote nothing. As a result we have few clues concerning the everyday lives of the Jews of the early Islamic empire.

Later, the picture clears. By the 9th century, Arab historians were busily at work; and as their wide-ranging interests encompassed the affairs of their Christian and Jewish minorities, a steady trickle of valuable information about the Jews of the Empire began to emerge from Arab sources.

There were also some chinks in the heavy curtain of Jewish indifference to the recording of history. Lists of names of the sages of the Talmudic era, and then of those of the later Exilarchs and Geonim were prepared in the 10th century. The most valuable were contained in two letters, one from Nathan ha-Babli and the other from Gaon Sherira of Pumbeditha in response to an inquiry from the Jews of Kairouan in North Africa. Though now known to contain errors, those documents were of crucial importance to later historians.

Ancient legends, whether based on fact or otherwise, were also useful in trying to build up the picture of an age.

It was however the discovery of the Cairo Geniza at the end of the 19th century that did most to give us a clear picture of Jewish life in the Middle Ages.

WHAT IS A GENIZA?

Such is the veneration accorded by Jews to the Almighty that papers, letters, manuscripts or printed books in which the name of God appears are not destroyed after use like other waste paper, but are either buried reverently in a cemetery or else deposited in a store called a Geniza (usually attached to a synagogue) for future burial. This practice continues to the present day.

The present Geniza at Lauderdale Road consists of a black plastic sack next to the photocopier. When the sack is full, its contents are buried in a special grave in the cemetery.

THE CAIRO GENIZA

The Geniza of the Palestinian synagogue of Fustat (Old Cairo) remained undisturbed for very many hundreds of years. It was found to contain pages and fragments of documents dating from the 8th to the 15th centuries, with the bulk deriving from the 11th century onwards.

There are now over 140,000 such pages and fragments in Cambridge alone, with many others scattered in other learned institutions throughout the world.

This random deposit of papers and parchments ranges in content from ancient manuscripts and autograph letters of famous rabbis to records of business transactions and ordinary family gossip.

In the Middle Ages it would have been hard to write any kind of letter, even on a matter of business, without mentioning God at least once – either in thanks for favours received or in invoking a blessing on the person addressed.

Cairo, being the pivot of communications between the eastern and western wings of the Islamic world, thus generated a great deal of commercial and other correspondence, which ended up in the Geniza. This was invaluable to scholars attempting to reconstruct a realistic model of the everyday life of Jews of the period.

It is difficult to exaggerate the importance of the Geniza in our understanding of the condition of the Jews of the Mediterranean basin in the Middle Ages. Before its discovery we knew very little indeed about the period.

Indeed, the absence of similar sources of information prior to the 8th century is far more keenly felt because of the Geniza's revelations.

THE CAMBRIDGE TAPE

This should be reviewed by the teacher in advance of the lesson, for not all of it is suitable for children, who are easily bored.

Part of Prof. Reif's introduction on side A is of much interest, as is most of Mrs Reif's section also on side A. There may also be some interest in the part of Mrs Wilson's section on women on side B.

Dr Shivtiel's section and Mr Weinberger's section on side B will probably not be of interest to children.

MATERIAL FOR LESSON 14:

Tape entitled 'Cambridge Geniza Collection' obtainable from the Geniza Section, the Library of the University of Cambridge

The MediterraneanWorld

The period discussed in this lesson covers the three centuries roughly between 950 and 1250. The great majority of the Jews of the world then lived within the vast Muslim Empire, with comparatively few in Christian Europe.

Widespread changes in the Islamic world were reflected by mass migrations of Jews within it.

Babylonian Jews first started to move westwards in appreciable numbers at the beginning of the 10th century because of the declining prosperity of Baghdad. Syrian and Egyptian Jews also moved west to Kairouan (Tunisia) and to Sicily, North Africa and Spain because of economic opportunities there.

Later the flow was reversed – with Egypt becoming the magnet for migrants. This migration of Jews increased towards the end of our period when Jews from Spain and Morocco fled to Egypt and beyond to escape their persecutors.

It is only because of the treasure-trove of contemporary documents discovered in the Geniza of the Palestinian synagogue of Fustat (Old Cairo) that we now have information on the everyday lives of the Jews of the period.

FREEDOM OF MOVEMENT

The most remarkable feature of the time was the almost complete freedom of travel, communications and trade throughout the wide expanse of the Islamic realm. It was as if political boundaries between the sometimes bitterly hostile Muslim states did not exist as men, books, money and goods flowed everywhere almost without restriction.

TRAVEL

Travel was slow, hazardous and costly, with journeys sometimes involving several years away from home.

Sea voyages were always preferred to journeys overland; but even then, depending on where the ship called on route and the length of its stay there, it could take a very long time to reach its destination.

Starting from Alexandria in Egypt, some typical journey times recorded in the Geniza were 65 days to Almeria in Spain, 25 days to Marseilles in France, 72 days to Amalfi in Italy, 29 days and 50 days to Palermo in Sicily.

No sea voyage was ever undertaken in winter, when the Mediterranean was too rough for the ships of the time.

Journeys by land, even short ones, were always made in organised caravans on regular routes for safety – either on foot or by donkey or mule. As it was inconceivable for a Jew to travel on the Sabbath, Jews either had to pay large sums to halt the entire caravan for the duration of each Sabbath, or else would have to ride on ahead in order to be able to observe their day of rest.

Travel by land took even longer than travel by sea. An illustration of this is the regular caravan that left Kairouan (Tunisia) at the end of January each year and did not reach Cairo until mid summer.

JEWISH UNITY

The unity of the world of commerce was mirrored by that of Islam's many Jewish communities.

Not only was each Jewish community self-governing within its own country, but it also formed part of the larger Jewish community that transcended the boundaries between individual states.

Though a network of spies and secret police kept close watch on the minorities, Islam's treatment of Jews was remarkably liberal for most of the period. The loyalty of Jews to their own supreme authorities in Baghdad or Jerusalem was considered normal and not in any way threatening.

Sura and Pumbeditha, the two great academies of Jewish learning in Baghdad, as well as the Jerusalem academy, were maintained by contributions from Jews all over the world, including from countries that were sworn enemies of Baghdad. Even some Jewish communities in Christian Europe contributed to the upkeep of the academies.

THE ACADEMIES

All Jews everywhere submitted their questions on religion, ritual and civil law to the academies; and thus it was not unusual for complex litigation originating in Kairouan (Tunisia) to be judged and settled in Baghdad. Furthermore most Jewish communal leaders and higher officials, such as judges, were appointed or at least confirmed in office by the Geonim of Baghdad – and sometimes, to make quite sure, also by the authorities in the Holy Land.

TALMUDIC JUDAISM

Baghdad took advantage of the freedom of communication to impress its permanent stamp on Judaism.

Copies of the Talmud were sent out to distant communities, as were model prayer books and the beginnings of a legal code.

Jewish scholars travelled to the academies in Baghdad and then on to other centres of learning to study or meet and confer with respected colleagues. We know from the Geniza that Hai Gaon in 10th century Baghdad was teaching students from (Christian) Constantinople and several towns in southern Italy as well as from all over the Muslim world.

The main result of this centralisation of religious authority, knowledge and resources is that Jewish faith and practice became and has since largely remained remarkably uniform despite the wide dispersion of its adherents and the diversity of their cultural environments.

It is hardly surprising therefore that, by the end of the 12th century, the rite of the Babylonian Jews (what we now call 'Sephardi') had superseded that of the Palestinians almost everywhere in the Islamic world. It was several centuries before the large increase in numbers of Europe's Ashkenazi Jews restored a mass following to the Palestinian tradition.

RELIGIOUS TOLERATION

Though the Muslim attitude to non-believers was negative, religious toleration was accepted as the way of life, providing Muslims were always on top. There was little sign of the deep-rooted emotional hostility to Jews found under Christian rule.

INTEGRATION

Jews in all walks of life appear to have been well integrated with their neighbours.

They lived and worked together with very little conflict; and this is confirmed by the many accounts in the Geniza of small loans, commercial partnerships and Jewish and Muslim doctors studying under each other.

In the heartland of Islam, there were no restrictions on where Jews lived or the profession they followed – but Jews did tend to live together by choice, as did Christians. However Jews and Muslims were often neighbours; and members of one faith did not hesitate to rent rooms in the houses of the other.

OCCUPATIONS

Jews were heavily engaged in professions such as trade and finance, disdained by the Muslim ruling class.

Jews also specialised in occupations shunned by observant Muslims, such as diplomacy and interpreting – which involved contact with non-believers – and the working of gold and silver.

Only sometimes, on the edges of the Islamic world – Morocco, Yemen and Central Asia – were Jews concentrated in 'dirty' occupations such as cesspool cleaners, tanners, butchers and hangmen.

SOCIAL INEQUALITY

The very class-conscious population accepted social inequality without question.

High officials such as chief judges, leading physicians and bankers – all close to the government – were the highest in rank. Next came members of the upper middle class of merchants and professionals. Below them, in order, followed the master craftsmen, ordinary urban craftsmen, artisans and labourers – with peasants at the very bottom.

A man normally followed in the profession of his father; but it was not unusual for someone with luck and ability to move up the ladder.

Paid employment of any kind was considered demeaning – almost a form of slavery – and a system of partnerships, sometimes very unequal, was substituted. A shipwrecked Tunisian merchant, who having lost everything at sea was forced to enter into employment on his arrival in Egypt, wrote movingly of his plight:

> *I eat bread in the service of others. Every minute of the day I gulp the cup of death because of my degradation and that of my children ...*

SLAVES

Slavery as practised by the Jews of the period was quite different from the agricultural slavery of the American plantations or the industrial slavery of other societies.

Slaves were the personal possessions of the individuals who owned them. As they were imported from distant countries and commanded high prices, they were much valued. The purchase of a male slave was an occasion for congratulation, almost as if the family had acquired a new son.

A slave was a full member of the household, with all the trust and affection that implied. The Geniza contains many references to slaves being freed by their masters, but very few indeed of their running away.

In Jewish houses slaves were required to observe a modified form of Judaism, including keeping the Sabbath. According to law, they had to be sold if they had not agreed to convert to Judaism within a year of purchase; but once converted, they became full Jews in every respect.

The Biblical account of Abraham's slave Eliezer, who ran his master's household and travelled to Mesopotamia to choose a wife for his son Isaac, illustrates the best type of master-slave relationship in the Geniza period.

The slave was often required to act as the trusted agent of his master, almost as a partner in his business; and the slave of a high-ranking man thus participated to some extent in status of his master.

Female slaves were only used for domestic help and care of children. They enjoyed substantial protection from molestation.

WOMEN

In contrast to Muslim women, Jewish women did attend synagogue where they sat in galleries with separate entrances. As today, there was general mingling in the synagogue courtyard after the end of the service.

Though segregated in public, Jewish women were far freer than Muslims in the privacy of their own homes. There is an example in the Geniza of problems caused in a house shared by a Christian family and a Jewish family when the Christian woman converted to Islam and then had to be fully segregated.

All Jewish women, even the well to do, were expected to work in some way as well as run their households. Marriage contracts sometimes stipulated whether a wife's earnings belonged to her or to her husband; and if to her, whether they were reserved for clothing or could be spent at will.

Working with textiles was the main occupation of women; but it is not clear whether this always took place at home or whether sometimes in small workshops. Even upper class women sent their needlework products to the market for sale.

Women also worked in occupations such as teaching, organising wedding preparations and celebrations, preparing for burials, professional mourning, as well as midwives and nurses.

There is a query recorded in the Geniza from a Muslim family concerning the kasher meat required to enable their Jewish nurse to eat with them.

Jewish women were often skilled in traditional (non-scientific) medicine; and there is even mention in the Geniza of a female oculist.

Female brokers visited houses to collect items of work for sale in the markets. One instance mentioned in a Geniza document is of a man who entrusted two Bibles to a woman broker for sale. Finding no buyer among the Elders of the community, she sold them to her own son for seven and a half dinars, from which she deducted her commission of one-third of a dinar. Six years later, the original owner discovered that the true value of each book was twenty dinars. He brought the case to court – and thus to our knowledge.

Polygamy, though allowed by Jewish law (it was only forbidden to Ashkenazim by Rabbenu Gershom in the 10th century), was strongly discouraged by public opinion. However second wives were taken without much disapproval in cases where the first wife had not produced children – or male children – within a ten-year period. The second wife usually fitted quite happily into the extended family structure.

MATERIAL FOR LESSON 15

MAP

The World of Islam

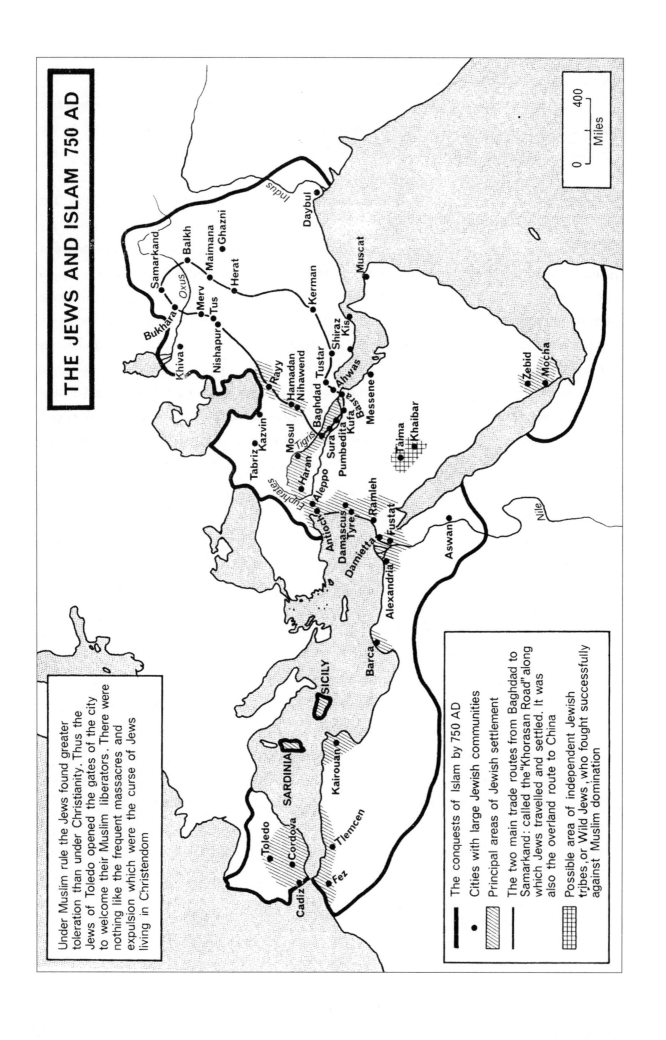

THE JEWS AND ISLAM 750 AD

Under Muslim rule the Jews found greater toleration than under Christianity. Thus the Jews of Toledo opened the gates of the city to welcome their Muslim liberators. There were nothing like the frequent massacres and expulsion which were the curse of Jews living in Christendom

	The conquests of Islam by 750 AD
•	Cities with large Jewish communities
	Principal areas of Jewish settlement
	The two main trade routes from Baghdad to Samarkand: called the "Khorasan Road" along which Jews travelled and settled. It was also the overland route to China
	Possible area of independent Jewish tribes, or Wild Jews, who fought successfully against Muslim domination

0 ___ 400 Miles

The Rise of the Ashkenazi Tradition

Though religious rulings from Babylon eventually came to be accepted as binding by all Jews everywhere, scholastic activity did not cease in the Land of Israel after the rise of the Babylonian academies. Its heroic rabbis laboured on for as long as they could. Despite relentless Christian persecution, they managed to complete their own masterwork, the Palestinian Talmud, about a century before its longer and more authoritative Babylonian counterpart.

In Roman times, the Jews of Palestine had naturally gravitated westwards towards Europe – for Babylon and the East were then in the hands of Rome's great enemy the Persian Empire, and something like an 'iron curtain' divided the two rival spheres of influence. Later, in the Islamic era, the Jews of Babylon readily travelled backwards and forwards along the established trade routes within the Islamic world – which included North Africa and Spain; but Christian Europe was still remote because of its alien rule and culture.

The Jews of Northern Europe, who had originated in the Roman Empire, naturally adopted Palestinian customs and attitudes where those differed from the Babylonian. The Palestinian influence was reinforced by Italian Jews, invited by the Emperor Charlemagne to apply their economic skills north of the Alps. Those around the southern shores of the Mediterranean remained loyal to their own Mesopotamian heritage with which they were in close contact. In some places, such as Egypt, tensions between the rival Babylonian and Palestinian traditions led to the establishment of separate congregations, each with its own synagogue.

The final development of the distinct Palestinian tradition occurred in Ashkenaz – the Rhine Valley and Northern France. There, at the edge of Christian Europe, the Exilarchs and Geonim of Babylon were far distant. Though communication did take place from time to time, no real leadership could be derived from the far-away heart of the Islamic world. Also, the lack of a local Jewish aristocracy with ready access to the Christian rulers caused a vacuum in the secular as well as in the religious direction of the community.

It was in the city of Mainz that an independent intellectual leadership arose for the first time in Christian Europe. Great luminaries such as Rabbenu Gershom of Mainz (c. 960-1028) – called the 'Light of the Exile' – and several of his contemporaries laid the foundations for what developed into the Ashkenazi branch of Judaism. They achieved this by sheer force of personality and by the authority that flowed naturally from their scholarship. Rabbi Gershom was followed by an even more brilliant scholar, Rabbi Shelomo Itzhaki – 'Rashi'; and from that time on the new path was firmly established.

The leadership in Ashkenaz still accepted the authority of the Babylonian Talmud; but it looked back more directly to the Land of Israel as the source of many of its traditions. Nor were its rabbis afraid to strike out on their own. Rabbenu Gershom, for example, issued the famous ruling that departed from Talmudic law by forbidding polygamy – but only to Ashkenazim of course, for Sephardim lived in Islamic lands where limited polygamy was sanctioned. In similar manner, he ruled that no woman could be divorced from her husband without her consent.

Though there are only small differences in the principal prayers of the Ashkenazi and Sephardi rites, Ashkenazi prayer books depend heavily on the poetry of Kallir and others who were active in Palestine in the sixth and seventh centuries. They ignore completely the compositions of the poets of the Spanish Golden Age, such as Ibn Gabirol and Yehuda Halevi, which so enrich the Sephardi liturgy.

Migrating Ashkenazi Jews carried their culture with them into Central Europe. Jews were then invited by Polish kings to colonise the empty lands in the East. They enjoyed their own Golden Age of learning and culture in Poland and Lithuania between the twelfth and the seventeenth centuries, by which time the Ashkenazi branch of Judaism had become the norm in most of Europe except for the Mediterranean basin. It later spread further east to Russian and then west to the Americas.

The attitudes and traditions of Ashkenazi Jews were forged first in the cramped and hostile environment of Roman Palestine, and then under the harshly repressive regimes of mediaeval Christianity.

Sephardim, on the other hand, developed their way of life in the comparative freedom and prosperity of Babylon, and then later under the usually benevolent rule of Islam. Rarely excluded from participation in the affairs of their host countries, they were able to accommodate their own intense Jewish consciousness to the intellectual, cultural and political activities of their neighbours.

This ease and breadth of living became the hallmark of the Sephardim. It resulted in greater leniency and tolerance in Halacha (Jewish 'law') than that of the Ashkenazim; but it also contributed to their eventual decline.

A good example of this difference in emphasis is the famous ruling of Samuel (circ 200 C.E.) that 'The Law of the land is the law' – meaning that Jews are obliged to obey the just laws of their particular countries of residence. This appeared in the Babylonian Talmud but, significantly, not in the Palestinian Talmud. In other words, the Sephardim were influenced by the good relations that often existed between Jew and gentile in their own experience, while the Ashkenazim had no choice other than to react to the prevailing hostility which surrounded them.

This fundamental difference in attitude can best be expressed by the two words 'accommodation' and 'confrontation'.

The preoccupation of Sephardim with secular pursuits prevented them from spending as much time as Ashkenazim in the study of the Talmud. Hence the Spanish period saw a rapid development of the codification of Jewish law, designed as an alternative to the vast and unsystematic legal structure of the Talmud. The codification was both accurate and precise – though always biased towards the opinion of Sephardi scholars. This clear-cut method persisted throughout the centuries. It became a characteristic of later Sephardi Responsa, which rarely indulged in the hair-splitting arguments common to rabbis of German and East-European origin.

What differences can you find between Ashkenazim and Sephardim today?

Chart of Ashkenazi and Sephardi Traditions

MAPS

Jews of Germany 500–1000

Expulsion 1000–1500

Ghettoes 1215–1870

The Babylonian/Sephardi and the Ashkenazi traditions

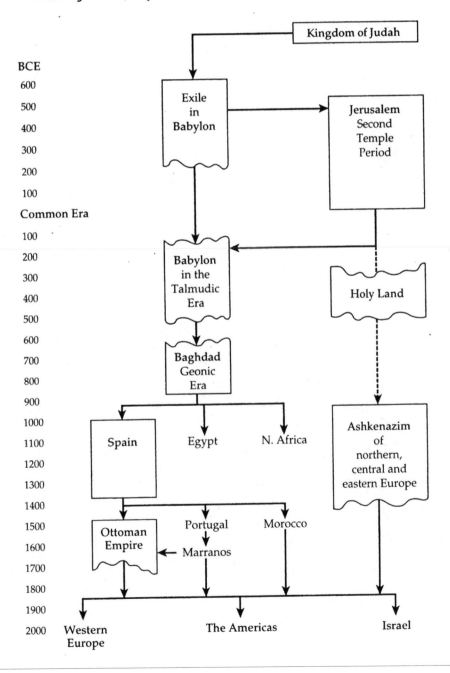

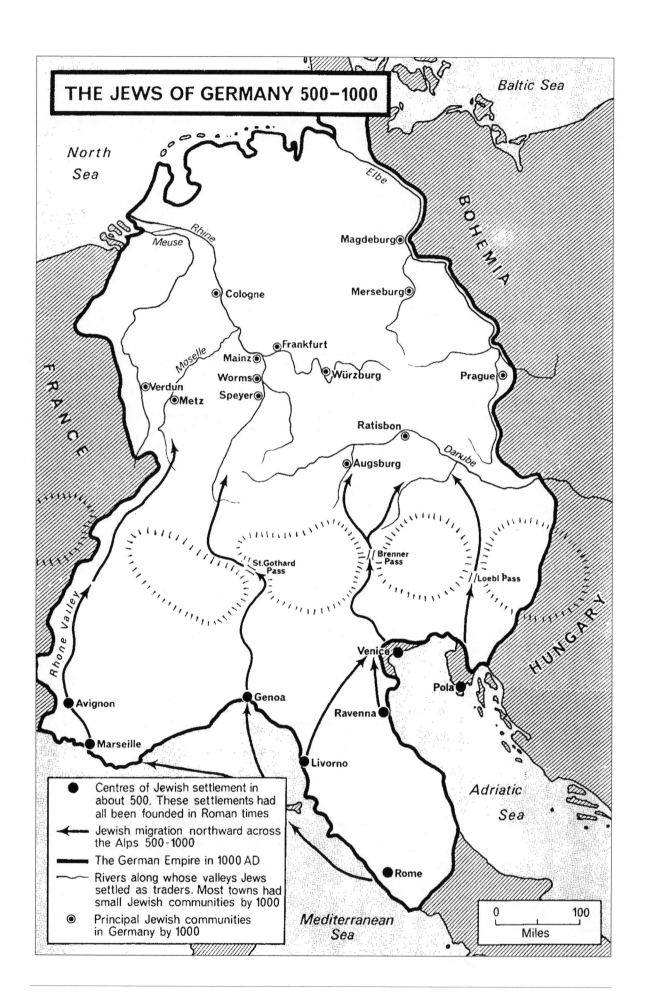

THE JEWS OF GERMANY 500-1000

Baltic Sea

North Sea

BOHEMIA

Elbe

Rhine

Meuse

Magdeburg⊙

Merseburg⊙

Cologne⊙

Moselle

Frankfurt⊙

Mainz⊙

Würzburg⊙

Prague⊙

Worms⊙

Verdun⊙

Speyer⊙

Metz⊙

FRANCE

Ratisbon⊙

Augsburg⊙

Danube

St.Gothard Pass

Brenner Pass

Loebl Pass

HUNGARY

Rhone Valley

Venice

Pola

Avignon

Genoa

Ravenna

Marseille

Livorno

Adriatic Sea

● Centres of Jewish settlement in about 500. These settlements had all been founded in Roman times

← Jewish migration northward across the Alps 500-1000

━━ The German Empire in 1000 AD

── Rivers along whose valleys Jews settled as traders. Most towns had small Jewish communities by 1000

⊙ Principal Jewish communities in Germany by 1000

Rome

Mediterranean Sea

0   100
Miles

LESSON 16   THE RISE OF THE ASHKENAZI TRADITION

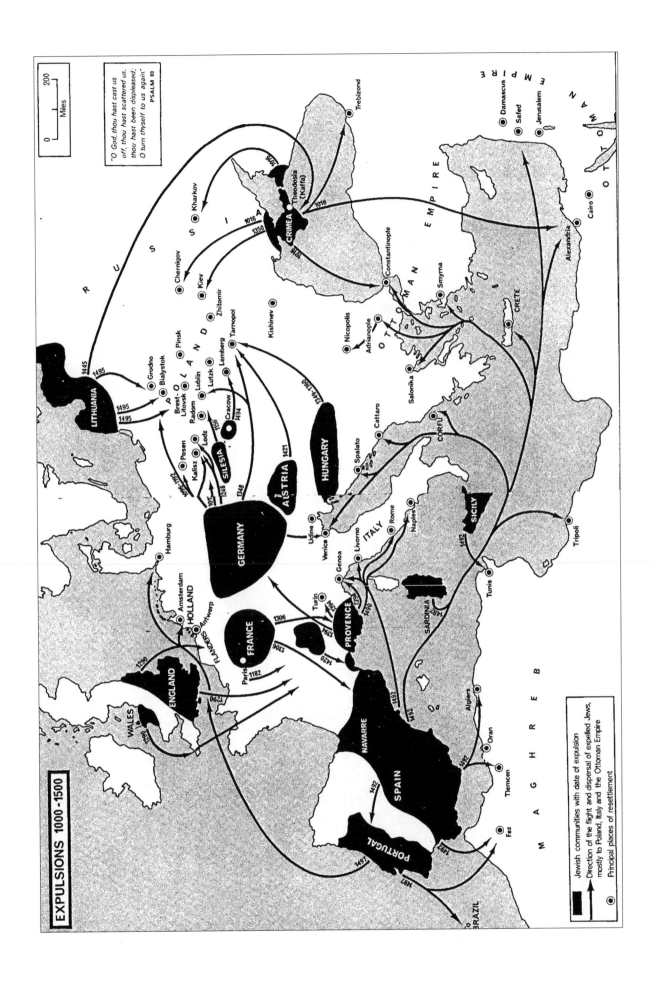

EXPULSIONS 1000-1500

"O God, thou hast cast us off, thou hast scattered us; thou hast been displeased; O turn thyself to us again"
PSALM 60

0   200
Miles

Jewish communities with date of expulsion

Direction of the flight and dispersal of expelled Jews, mostly to Poland, Italy and the Ottoman Empire

Principal places of resettlement

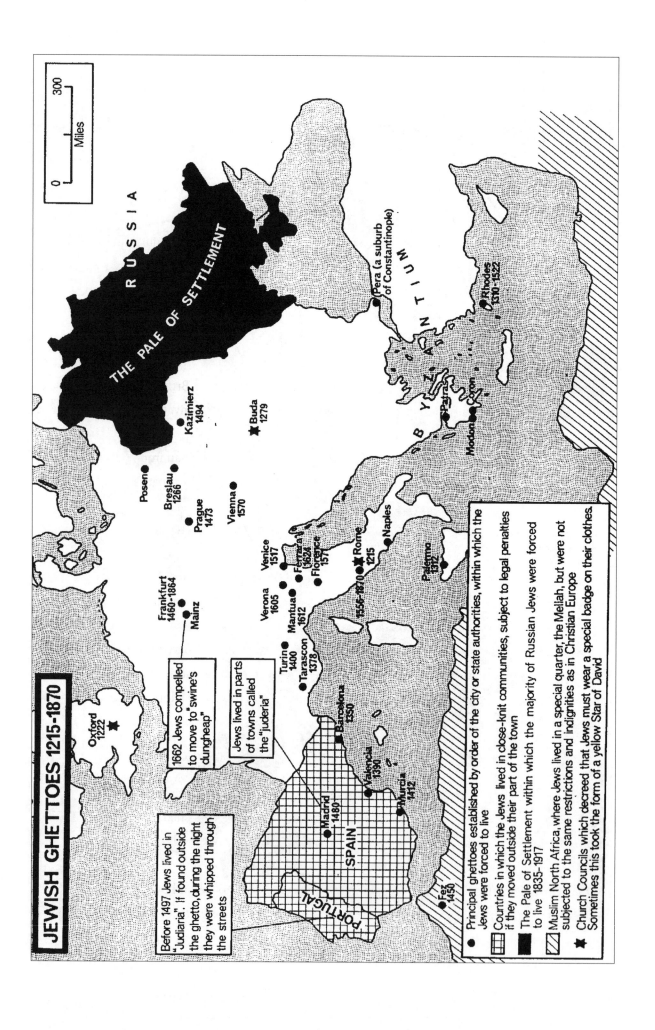

JEWISH GHETTOES 1215-1870

RUSSIA

THE PALE OF SETTLEMENT

BYZANTIUM

Oxford
1222

Before 1497 Jews lived in
"Judiaria". If found outside
the ghetto, during the night
they were whipped through
the streets

Posen

Breslau
1266

Kazimierz
1494

Buda
1279

Frankfurt
1460-1864

Mainz

Prague
1473

Vienna
1570

1662 Jews compelled
to move to "swine's
dungheap"

Jews lived in parts
of towns called
the "juderia"

Turin
1400

Verona
1605

Venice
1517

Mantua
1612

Ferrara
1624

Florence
1571

Tarascon
1378

Rome
1215

1556-1870

Naples

Barcelona
1350

Valencia
1390

Madrid
1480

SPAIN

PORTUGAL

Churca
1412

Palermo
1312

Modon & Coron

Pera (a suburb
of Constantinople)

Rhodes
1310-1522

Fez
1450

Miles

300

- ● Principal ghettoes established by order of the city or state authorities, within which the
  Jews were forced to live

- ▦ Countries in which the Jews lived in close-knit communities, subject to legal penalties
  if they moved outside their part of the town

- ■ The Pale of Settlement within which the majority of Russian Jews were forced
  to live 1835-1917

- ▨ Muslim North Africa, where Jews lived in a special quarter, the Mellah, but were not
  subjected to the same restrictions and indignities as in Christian Europe

- ★ Church Councils which decreed that Jews must wear a special badge on their clothes.
  Sometimes this took the form of a yellow Star of David

Northern Europe and the Crusades

WHERE DID THE JEWS OF EUROPE COME FROM?

The pagan Roman emperors regarded Judaism as a legally tolerated religion — quite unlike Christianity, which they persecuted and tried to stamp out.

Many Jews therefore became Roman citizens. They were free to practice their religion throughout the Empire and were exempted from military service, as that conflicted with religious requirements. Jewish law was used freely to settle disputes between Jews.

The Jews followed the Roman legions into Northern Europe as well as into Spain and Northern Italy. They established settlements in all parts of the Roman Empire, except for Britain. By the year 300 CE, Jews were living in Northern France and along the Rhine valley in Germany. Cologne was one of the leading centres.

The Jews of Northern Europe were mostly traders — slaves were then an important commodity. Jews also seemed to have been active in the clothing industry and similar occupations.

HOW WERE THE JEWS OF NORTHERN EUROPE AFFECTED BY THE RISE OF CHRISTIANITY AND THE COLLAPSE OF THE ROMAN EMPIRE?

Life became progressively more difficult for Jews after the Roman Empire adopted Christianity as its state religion. However, Judaism remained a licit religion and Jewish life was not at first very badly affected by the hostility of the Church.

We know almost nothing about what happened to the Jewish settlements of Northern Europe after the collapse of the Roman Empire, but must assume that most of them survived in some form under the rule of the barbarian invaders who eventually abandoned paganism and adopted Christianity themselves.

THE DAWN OF THE MIDDLE AGES

Some of the original Roman Jewish settlements must have survived in France and along the Rhine valley from the 5th to the 10th centuries; and new ones were gradually established in the rest of Germany. Although tiny Jewish trading communities had existed in Europe for hundreds of years, it was not until the tenth century that more important centres appeared.

Jewish settlements were usually encouraged to start and then to expand by kings and other local rulers who valued Jewish traders with their contacts with Jews in other parts of the known world.

For example, the Emperor Charlemagne employed Jewish traders as diplomats to handle his relations with the Muslim world. Jews also became useful to the Christian rulers in the role of bankers; for banking or money-lending of any kind, was strictly forbidden to Christians.

There was no place for Jews in the feudal society of medieval Europe, where each man owed allegiance to a noble; and so Jews came under the protection of the king and acted as his agents and tax collectors.

The Jewish communities of Northern Europe were very small and poor compared to those of the Islamic world. But, as described in the lesson on the Ashkenazi Tradition, great intellectual leaders such as Rabbenu Gershom and Rashi began to appear in the 11th century; and it was they who laid the foundation of a great new tradition in Jewry — that of the Ashkenazim.

So far as we know, these early medieval Jewish communities of Christian Europe managed to exist in reasonable harmony with their neighbours, or at least without much conflict, until the time of the Crusades.

THE CRUSADES

Pope Urban II probably had little idea of the forces he was releasing when he launched the first crusade in his famous address to the assembled clergy and nobility of France in the year 1095. Though the declared aim of the crusade was to liberate Jerusalem and its holy places from Muslim rule, the Pope also had other objectives in mind.

The first was to re-unite Christendom by forcing the independent Eastern Church to submit to the authority of Rome.

And the second was to divert the land-hungry lords of western Europe from their petty wars by providing them with the prospect of rich pickings in the fertile countries of the Near East.

Attractive too was the Pope's promise that the burden of sin would be partly removed from those who took part in the sacred enterprise, and completely lifted from those who died in battle for the Cross.

The effect of Urban's eloquence on the members of his audience at Clermont was immediate. A wave of intense religious emotion swept over them. 'It is God's will' they cried in unison as they knelt trembling and weeping before the Pope, confessing their sins and pledging themselves to join in the holy work. Those swept along that day by overwhelming love of Christ and willingness to serve him did not realise that the holy war proclaimed by Urban would result in two centuries of slaughter on the battlefield. It also involved the plunder, rape and mass murder of non-combatants Muslim, Jew and Christian alike – and outbreaks of cannibalism.

Pope Urban's crusade was crowned with success. Jerusalem fell to the Frankish armies in 1099. This was followed by the massacre of every Muslim man woman and child found alive, except for the governor and his entourage who were allowed to buy their freedom at huge cost. The Jews of Jerusalem, who had helped the Muslims to defend the city, were all burnt alive in their largest synagogue.

Particularly horrifying is the satisfaction expressed by a contemporary historian who witnessed the event. He described with relish how the soldiers had to wade through the blood and corpses of blasphemous non-believers, which at times reached as high as the bridles of their horses, before proceeding to the Church of the Holy Sepulchre to give thanks for the triumphant vindication of their faith.

Christian grip on the Holy Land and on the other crusader states of the Near East weakened soon after the capture of Jerusalem by the armies of the first crusade; and Saladin re-conquered the city for Islam in 1187.

During the course of the following two centuries, another seven major military expeditions, and several minor ones, were dispatched from Europe in a vain attempt to wrest Jerusalem back from Saladin.

The third crusade, launched in 1189, was led by the three greatest kings of the West, including King Richard of England, known as Coeur de Lion. The fourth crusade did not even reach the Holy Land. Its rapacious participants achieved their purpose en route by first storming and then greedily plundering Constantinople, capital of the Byzantine Empire, seat of the Eastern Church and the most splendid Christian city in the world.

The preaching of the first crusade by Pope Urban II stimulated two parallel but separate responses. The princes of Western Europe formed regular armies, properly equipped to sustain the rigours of the long journey to the East. But several months before the official armies were ready to start, large numbers of the poor were already on the move in Northern France and Germany. Aroused by venerated popular preachers, they were quick to abandon all means of livelihood, sell their possessions to buy arms and march towards the Promised Land. The motley hordes included men, women and children – the credulous, the pious and those intent on adventure and plunder. They formed themselves into wild undisciplined bands, impatiently urged forward to ultimate destruction by fanatical leaders, among whom Peter the Hermit was the most prominent.

Unfortunately for them, few poor crusaders survived to glimpse Jerusalem, for most perished on the journey. Only a remnant of the original hordes reached the Holy Land and participated in the capture of Jerusalem. And one particularly ferocious band of fanatics, dressed in tatters, was feared by fellow crusaders almost as much as by the Muslims for its record of rape, massacre and destruction, as well as for the horrible practice of feasting on the roasted corpses of its enemies.

In another particularly sad expedition, thousands of children from France and Germany overcame all manner of obstacles to make their way down to the Mediterranean coast. They fondly believed that the waters would part to enable them to cross to Jerusalem on dry land, just as had the Red Sea for the Children of Israel fleeing from Egypt. It did not happen as they expected. The only result of their credulity was that prices in the slave markets of North Africa were depressed by the sudden glut caused by the offer for sale of many children who had not been slaughtered or drowned.

THE EFFECT OF THE CRUSADES ON EUROPE'S JEWS

Jews had been established in small communities throughout Europe for hundreds of years, and in some places even since Roman times. During this long period, they had lived alongside their Christian neighbours and had rarely suffered persecution. However, in the eleventh century, with the advent of the crusades, the climate changed dramatically.

The religious fervour stirred up by the Pope's call brought dire consequences for the Jews, not only in the Holy Land but in the many European Jewish communities on the crusaders' route to Palestine.

In 1096, the first crusading masses on their way to the Mediterranean Sea attacked and destroyed Jewish communities in the Rhineland and massacred large numbers of Jews. The crusaders' argument was that, before they went to fight the Muslims abroad, they ought to deal with the infidels in their midst.

The local nobles and the bishops usually tried their best to protect the Jews, sometimes sheltering them in their castles, but in most cases, they found it impossible to thwart the fanaticism of the crusaders.

These small communities in France and Germany, led by scholars such as Rashi, were highly advanced in Jewish education and social welfare; and it was those along the River Rhine that suffered the worst of the anti-Jewish excesses that soon became part of medieval European life.

The tide was also changing within the Church itself as the preaching of the newly formed monastic orders began to reach the masses and fuel anti-Jewish feeling. Henceforth, the Jew, as an alien element in Christendom, was subject to continual and varied forms of oppression and attack.

Starting with the First Crusade in 1096, attacks against Jews began to be commonplace. Based on a variety of false accusations, from poisoning of wells to ritual murder, these attacks continued into the sixteenth century and beyond.

In England, in 1144, an accusation was made that the Jews of Norwich had killed a Christian child (William of Norwich) for ritual purposes. His blood was allegedly used in making the matzah for the Jewish Passover. Although the English Jews were then protected by the king, this preposterous charge, later known as the blood libel, soon gained wide credence. Since then, such libels have been repeated

A common pattern emerged. Jewish communities would be encouraged by a local ruler to settle in his territory and act as his agents. They would frequently prosper, but their very prosperity ultimately led to attacks. It mattered little whether such attacks were motivated by religion or economic resentment or were merely the result of the Jews no longer being of use to the ruler. The end result was often the same: the destruction of the community and the migration of its survivors elsewhere.

Expulsion was the fate of many Ashkenazi Jewish communities in western and central Europe during this period, especially when they ceased to be of economic value to the ruler.

England provided the earliest example. William the Conqueror invited Jews from France to settle in England. Some two centuries later, in 1290, the Jews, having been impoverished by the King's taxes, were expelled. Southern Italy followed in 1294 and France in 1306. Jewish life in France was again devastated by the massacres of 1348.

THE LATER PERIOD

The Reformation in the sixteenth century, and the religious wars between Catholics and Protestants that followed, relieved the Jewish population of much of the previous physical persecution. Nevertheless, the oppressive legal and social measures against Jews adopted by both sides continued in central Europe, in some cases well into the nineteenth century.

In Western Europe, where from the thirteenth to the fifteenth century the Jews had been subjected to wholesale expulsions, Jewish centres began to be re-established from the seventeenth century onwards. This resettlement, for example in London and Amsterdam, was largely effected through the migration from Spain and Portugal of Marranos, or secret Jews, who had managed to escape the terrors of the Spanish Inquisition and had retained their clandestine Judaism, frequently over many generations.

One country from which Jews were not expelled, and which maintained an unbroken Jewish presence for more than two millennia, was Italy – first during the Roman Republic, and then through the Empire and in various of its successor states.

Eastern Europe, to which Jews had fled in increasing numbers from persecution in Northern and Central Europe, contained something like 60% of world Jewry by the end of the eighteenth century. Beginning in the fourteenth century and continuing to the seventeenth century, economic prosperity allowed the Jews of Poland and Lithuania to create a centre of learning which some of them claimed to have almost equalled that of Babylon.

But this centre too was viciously attacked and seriously weakened in 1648 by Ukrainian Cossacks, rising up against their Polish landlords and the Jews who acted as their agents. Poland gradually declined during the following century until its territory was partitioned between its stronger neighbours. Various parts, together with their resident and increasingly vulnerable Jewish populations, were incorporated into Prussia, Austria and Tsarist Russia.

MATERIAL FOR LESSON 17

MAPS

The Jews of the Roman Empire

The Jews of France 800 – 1500

The Jews of Germany 500 – 1000

The Jews of Central Europe 1000 – 1500

The Jews of Poland and Lithuania 1000 – 1500

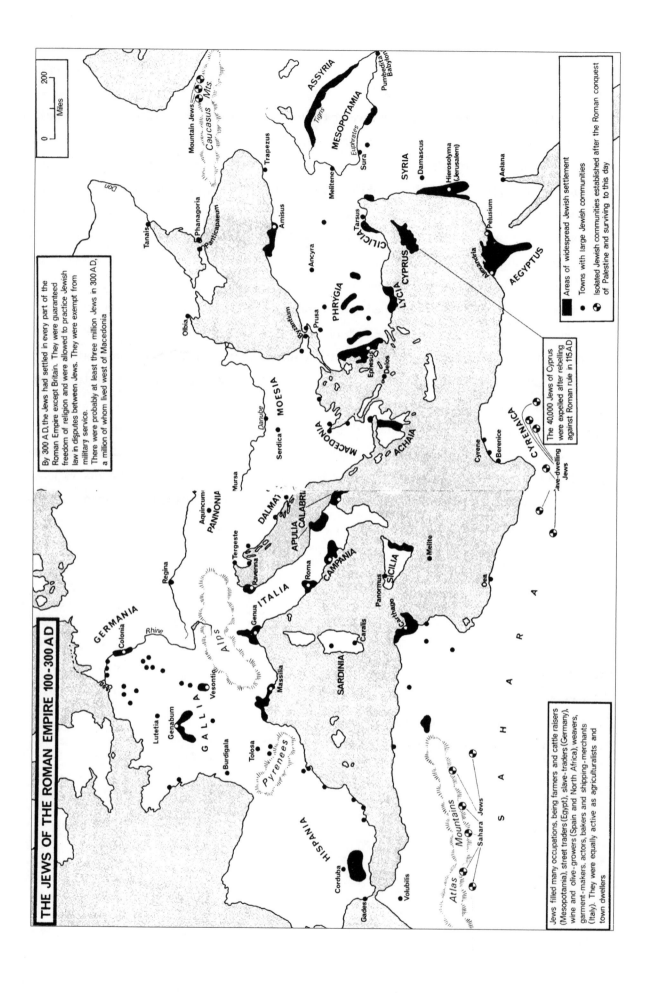

THE JEWS OF THE ROMAN EMPIRE 100-300 AD

By 300 A.D. the Jews had settled in every part of the Roman Empire except Britain. They were guaranteed freedom of religion and were allowed to practice Jewish law in disputes between Jews. They were exempt from military service.

There were probably at least three million Jews in 300 A.D., a million of whom lived west of Macedonia

The 40,000 Jews of Cyprus were expelled after rebelling against Roman rule in 115 AD

■ Areas of widespread Jewish settlement
• Towns with large Jewish communities
◉ Isolated Jewish communities established after the Roman conquest of Palestine and surviving to this day

Jews filled many occupations, being farmers and cattle raisers (Mesopotamia), street traders (Egypt), slave-traders (Germany), wine and olive-growers (Spain and North Africa), weavers, garment-makers, actors, bakers and shipping-merchants (Italy). They were equally active as agriculturalists and town dwellers

0   200
Miles

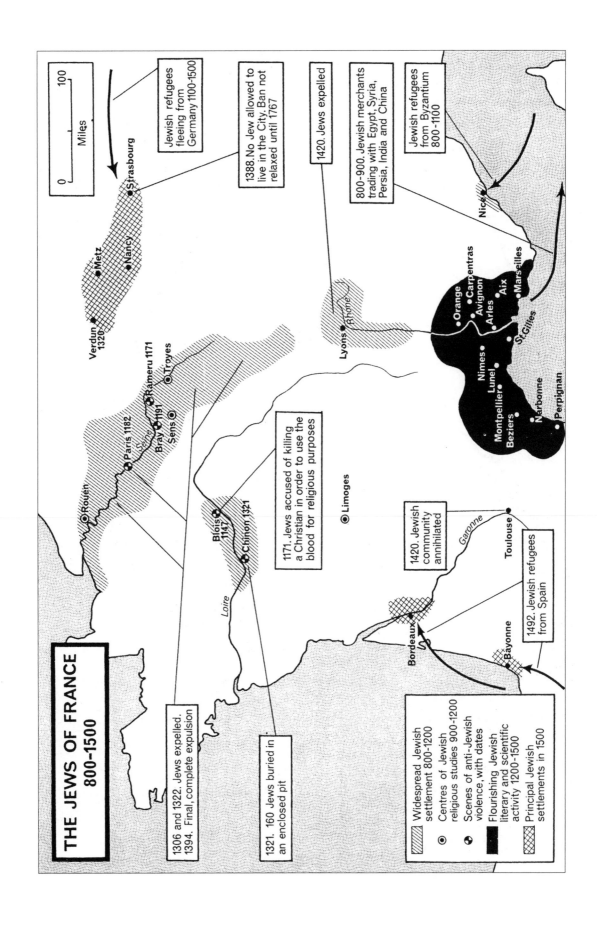

THE JEWS OF FRANCE 800-1500

Miles
0 _____ 100

Jewish refugees fleeing from Germany 1100-1500

1388. No Jew allowed to live in the City. Ban not relaxed until 1767

1420. Jews expelled

800-900. Jewish merchants trading with Egypt, Syria, Persia, India and China

Jewish refugees from Byzantium 800-1100

Strasbourg

Metz

Nancy

Verdun 1320

Rameru 1171

Troyes

Paris 1182

Bray 1191

Sens

Rouen

Blois 1147

Chinon 1321

Loire

Limoges

Lyons

Rhône

Orange

Carpentras

Avignon

Arles

Aix

Marseilles

St-Gilles

Nîmes

Lunel

Montpellier

Béziers

Narbonne

Perpignan

Nice

1171. Jews accused of killing a Christian in order to use the blood for religious purposes

1306 and 1322. Jews expelled. 1394. Final, complete expulsion

1321. 160 Jews buried in an enclosed pit

1420. Jewish community annihilated

Garonne

Toulouse

Bordeaux

Bayonne

1492. Jewish refugees from Spain

Widespread Jewish settlement 800-1200

Centres of Jewish religious studies 900-1200

Scenes of anti-Jewish violence, with dates

Flourishing Jewish literary and scientific activity 1200-1500

Principal Jewish settlements in 1500

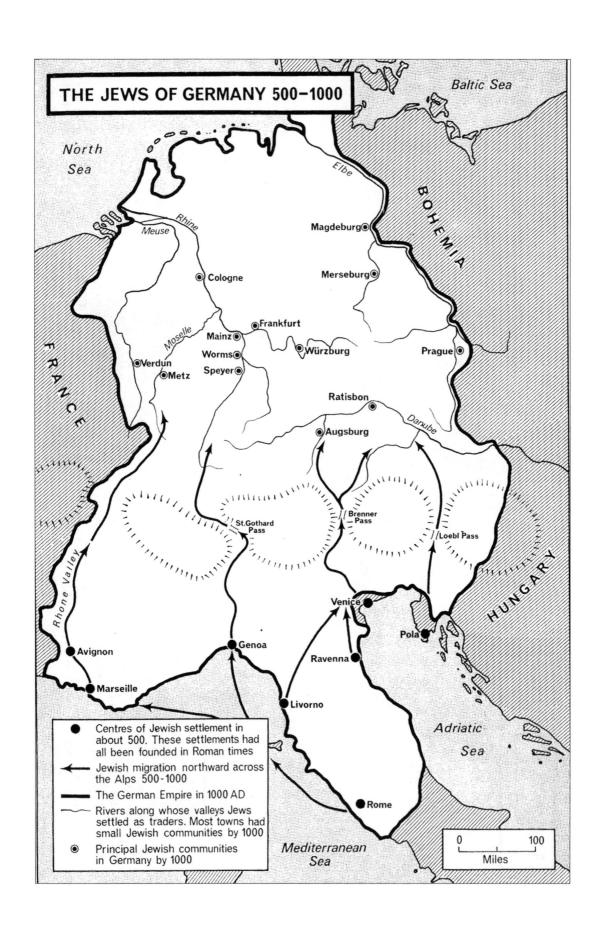

THE JEWS OF GERMANY 500–1000

Baltic Sea

North Sea

Elbe

BOHEMIA

FRANCE

Rhine

Meuse

Moselle

Magdeburg

Merseburg

Cologne

Frankfurt

Mainz

Würzburg

Worms

Prague

Verdun

Speyer

Metz

Ratisbon

Augsburg

Danube

HUNGARY

St.Gothard Pass

Brenner Pass

Loebl Pass

Rhone Valley

Venice

Pola

Avignon

Genoa

Ravenna

Marseille

Livorno

Adriatic Sea

Rome

- ● Centres of Jewish settlement in about 500. These settlements had all been founded in Roman times
- ← Jewish migration northward across the Alps 500–1000
- ▬ The German Empire in 1000 AD
- ～ Rivers along whose valleys Jews settled as traders. Most towns had small Jewish communities by 1000
- ⊙ Principal Jewish communities in Germany by 1000

Mediterranean Sea

0 ———— 100
Miles

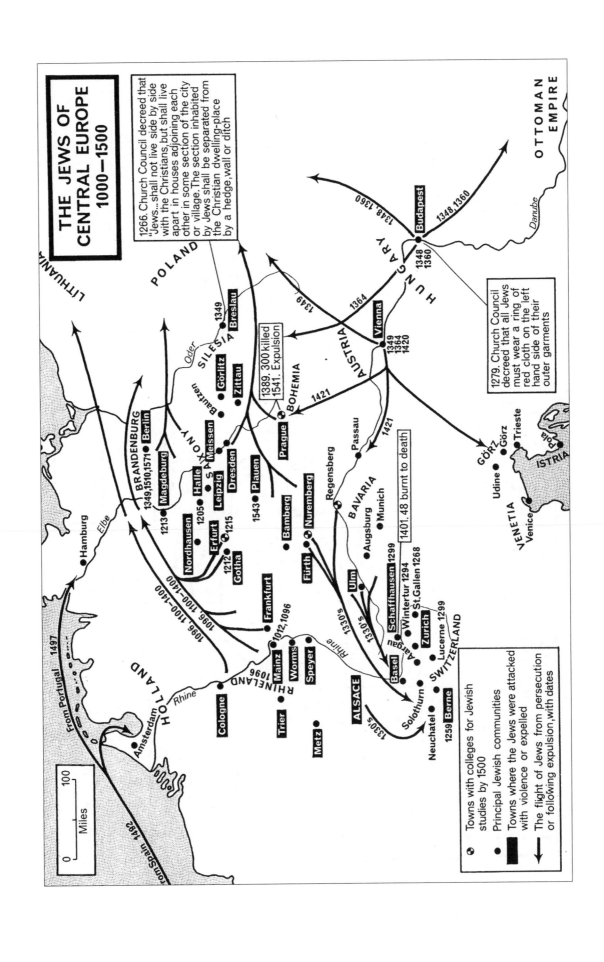

THE JEWS OF CENTRAL EUROPE 1000–1500

1266. Church Council decreed that "Jews...shall not live side by side with the Christians, but shall live apart in houses adjoining each other in some section of the city or village. The section inhabited by Jews shall be separated from the Christian dwelling-place by a hedge, wall or ditch

1279. Church Council decreed that all Jews must wear a ring of red cloth on the left hand side of their outer garments

LITHUANIA

POLAND

OTTOMAN EMPIRE

Danube

1348, 1360

Budapest
1348
1360

HUNGARY

1349

1364

Vienna
1349
1364
1420

AUSTRIA

1421

1421

Oder

SILESIA

Breslau 1349
Görlitz
Zittau

Bautzen

BOHEMIA

Prague

1389. 300 killed
1541. Expulsion

GÖRZ

Görz
Trieste

Udine

ISTRIA

VENETIA

Venice

Pola

Passau

Regensburg

BRANDENBURG

Berlin
1349,1510,1571

Magdeburg 1213

SAXONY

Meissen

Halle 1205

Leipzig

Dresden 1215

Plauen

1543

Nordhausen

Erfurt 1212

Gotha

Bamberg

Nuremberg

Fürth

BAVARIA

Munich

Augsburg

Ulm

1401. 48 burnt to death

Schaffhausen 1299

Wintertur 1294

St.Gallen 1268

Zürich

Lucerne 1299

SWITZERLAND

Aargau

Basel

Solothurn

Neuchatel

Berne 1259

1330's

1330's

1330's

ALSACE

Rhine

Hamburg

Elbe

1096, 1100–1400

1096, 1100–1400

HOLLAND

Amsterdam

From Portugal 1497

From Spain 1492

Rhine

RHINELAND

Cologne

Trier

Metz

Mainz 1012, 1096

Worms

Speyer 1096

Frankfurt

Miles
0   100

Towns with colleges for Jewish studies by 1500

Principal Jewish communities

Towns where the Jews were attacked with violence or expelled

The flight of Jews from persecution or following expulsion, with dates

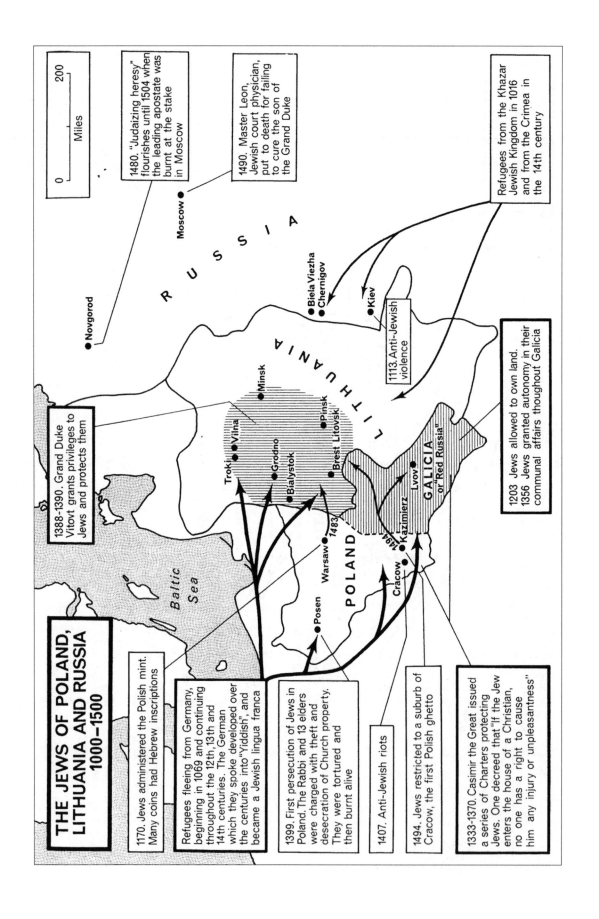

THE JEWS OF POLAND, LITHUANIA AND RUSSIA 1000–1500

1170. Jews administered the Polish mint. Many coins had Hebrew inscriptions

Refugees fleeing from Germany, beginning in 1069 and continuing throughout the 12th,13th and 14th centuries. The German which they spoke developed over the centuries into "Yiddish", and became a Jewish lingua franca

1399. First persecution of Jews in Poland. The Rabbi and 13 elders were charged with theft and desecration of Church property. They were tortured and then burnt alive

1407. Anti-Jewish riots

1494. Jews restricted to a suburb of Cracow, the first Polish ghetto

1333–1370. Casimir the Great issued a series of Charters protecting Jews. One decreed that "if the Jew enters the house of a Christian, no one has a right to cause him any injury or unpleasantness"

1388–1390. Grand Duke Vitovt grants privileges to Jews and protects them

1480. "Judaizing heresy" flourishes until 1504 when the leading apostate was burnt at the stake in Moscow

1490. Master Leon, Jewish court physician, put to death for failing to cure the son of the Grand Duke

Refugees from the Khazar Jewish Kingdom in 1016 and from the Crimea in the 14th century

1113. Anti-Jewish violence

1203 Jews allowed to own land.
1356 Jews granted autonomy in their communal affairs thoughout Galicia

R U S S I A

L I T H U A N I A

POLAND

GALICIA or "Red Russia"

Baltic Sea

• Novgorod
• Moscow

• Biela Viezha
• Chernigov
• Kiev

• Minsk
• Troki • Vilna
• Grodno
• Białystok
• Pinsk
• Brest Litovski

• Posen
• Warsaw 1483
• Cracow
• Kazimierz
• Lvov

0   200
Miles

Spain

The Jewish communities of North Africa, Spain and Christian Europe gradually took over the leadership that slipped from Baghdad. But it was in Spain that Jewish experience of exile acquired a new dimension. Jews had first come to Spain with the Romans. Some thought themselves descended from captives taken by Titus in his sack of Jerusalem in the year 70 C.E.

The Jews continued to live in peace under the Visigoths, who succeeded the Romans, until after their conversion from the Arian to the Roman Catholic form of Christianity early in the seventh century.

The beginning of what later historians described as 'the first evil' occurred in 616, when all Jews were ordered to become Christians or submit to the confiscation of their property and expulsion from the country. Many thousands succumbed and accepted baptism – but they became Christians in name only and lost no opportunity to revert openly to Judaism as soon as circumstances allowed.

It was not surprising therefore that the Jews warmly welcomed the Arab invaders who crossed into Spain in 711. They helped them wrest control of the cities from the Christians, and held them safe for the Arabs afterwards.

Once Spain was securely incorporated into the Islamic world, it did not take long for its Jews to establish close contact with their brethren in Baghdad. Books and scholars, ideas and inspiration, all rapidly flowed into Jewish Spain as they had already into North Africa. Spain soon became an integral branch of the Babylonian tradition, then still under the direction of the Geonim.

The Legend of the Four Captives illustrates well the transfer of scholars from Baghdad to North Africa and Spain. According to this story, four rabbis on a mission to collect funds for the Babylonian academies were captured by pirates after their ship had set sail from Bari in Southern Italy on one leg of their voyage. The rabbis were ransomed by the Jewish communities of Egypt, Tunisia and Spain – where each became the respected head of the community. (The identity of the fourth rabbi and his place of ransom was not related).

Spanish Jews participated to the full in the flowering of Arabic learning and culture that followed the conquest; and the Jewish community of Muslim Spain became the largest and most influential in Europe. Its leaders contributed much to the government and prosperity of the state; and its scholars, renowned for their piety and learning, took over the leadership of the Jewish world. It was indeed a Golden Age.

The very basis of Jewish life changed dramatically for the worse in 1148 when fanatical rulers from North Africa, who had been invited into Spain, reversed the previous attitude of tolerance and offered all non-believers the stark choice of Islam or the sword. Large numbers were massacred or sold as slaves. Others escaped by accepting Islam, by moving elsewhere in the peninsula, or by leaving for Algeria and other places overseas.

Like their forbears in Visigothic Spain, the new converts mostly cast off their assumed Islamic disguise as soon as they could, and were re-admitted to the Jewish fold. The most famous of these Anusim (Compelled Ones) may have been Rabbi Maimon ben Yusef, father of Maimonides, who fled from Cordova to Morocco with this family, where some scholars suspect they were compelled to live for a time as outward Muslims.

The Christians, in their gradual re-conquest of Spain, did not at first differentiate between Arabs and Jews. They treated them both as enemies and burned down mosques and synagogues with equal enthusiasm. However, experience soon tempered the initial distrust as the rough, uneducated Christian rulers came to appreciate the valuable contribution that talented and learned Jews could make to their kingdoms.

The Jewish communities of Christian Spain then entered into a second, though lesser, Golden Age – a period that was looked back to with nostalgia in the centuries that followed, and which is still remembered today.

The Jews continued to govern themselves in separate communities under Chief Rabbis and Chief Justices appointed by the Spanish kings; and devoted much energy to developing their own religion and culture. None of this however inhibited them from entering wholeheartedly into the secular life around them. Their leaders served as courtiers, financiers, administrators, diplomats and physicians to the Kings of the states into which Christian Spain was divided. The Jewish middle class earned its living from the land, from commerce and from manufacture; and lower down the social scale, Jews worked as skilled craftsmen and artisans.

The crowning glory of the Jewish community in its Golden Age was the contribution of its rabbis, scholars, philosophers and poets. Proficient in Arabic and other languages, Jewish scholars served as a channel through which the civilisation of the Arabs and that of the classical world before them, was transmitted to Christian Europe, just emerging from the Dark Ages.

The superb secular work of the Spanish Hebrew poets never lost its fascination for later generations; and is still being translated and published in other languages. Also their sublime liturgical compositions, many of which are now incorporated in Sephardi prayer books, remain unsurpassed.

The Talmud is a vast compendium of human wisdom and knowledge, embracing subjects as diverse as religion, civil and criminal law, morals, medicine and astronomy. The Babylonian sages, who compiled it, set little value on logical order or on clarity of expression. As a result, the Talmud is unsystematic in its arrangement and lacks ordered sequence. The same subject, for example, can be referred to in several different and sometimes unexpected places, and without cross-reference. Moreover it contains a bewildering welter of conflicting opinions – which the reader is left to sort out for himself without guidance. To make understanding more difficult, the deliberations of its many authors are expressed with extreme brevity, almost in a kind of shorthand. The Talmud cannot be mastered without the help of skilled teachers, and even then not before years of devoted study.

The process of attempting to summarise the contents of the Talmud for practical application started in the Baghdad of the Geonim. The first complete Code to appear outside Mesopotamia was written in Morocco by Rabbi Isaac of Fez (1013-1103), known as Alfasi. He simplified the Talmud by eliminating all argument and opinions with which he disagreed, and managed to produce a succinct summary of the law.

The work of codification was taken up eagerly by Jewish scholars in Spain, whose approach was dictated by the principles of reason. Rabbi Moses ben Maimon, known as 'the Rambam' to the Jews and Maimonides to the outside world was the outstanding codifier of the time and one of the most brilliant men of his age. He fled with his family from persecution in Spain and finally settled in Cairo, where he became a famous physician and the head of its Jewish Community.

Maimonides's monumental code, the Mishneh Torah, one thousand chapters long, was completed before 1184. Written with deep religious feeling and a clarity unusual for the period, it offered its readers an authoritative summary of developed Jewish law.

The most influential code of all was the Shulhan Aruch (The Prepared Table), first printed in Venice in 1565. Its author, Joseph Caro, was one of those forced to leave Spain in 1492. He finally settled in Safed in the Holy Land, where he wrote his masterwork, Beth Yosef, after twenty years of intensive study and comparison of previous codes. The Shulhan Aruch was written as a precis of that book. An Ashkenazi rabbi, Moses Isserles of Cracow, then prepared a Mappah (Tablecloth) for the Prepared Table, setting out all the Ashkenazi variations to Caro's rulings. The Mappah was printed alongside Caro's original text; and this modified version very soon became the definitive guide to Jewish law and practice that it still remains.

In Spain – both Muslim and Christian – Jews, for the first time in their history, managed to develop a genuine synthesis between their own religiously-based culture and the outside world around them. That synthesis was unique in the history of their exile. But the very success of the endeavour to live in both worlds nourished the seeds of its own destruction. The sight of the Jews enjoying all the fruits of secular Spanish life, whilst at the same time maintaining a separate identity as resident aliens living under their own law, excited the envy of the less fortunate of their Christian fellow subjects. And for many Jews, peace and prosperity had lessened their sense of exile and their attachment to the faith of their ancestors.

The disturbance of the Crusades in France and the rest of Europe had its repercussions in Spain, especially in the North. Sporadic outbreaks of popular violence took place with increasing frequency and severity; and in 1328, for example, many Jewish communities in Navarre were massacred. The Golden Age ended finally in 1391 when the pent-up jealousy of Christian mobs, whipped to fever pitch by determined priests, expressed itself in an outburst of public fury that at a stroke nullified the progress of centuries. The first pogrom broke out in Seville where, to quote a contemporary chronicler:

On 4th June thirteen hundred and ninety one, the Lord bent his bow like an enemy against

the community of Seville. They set fire to the gates of the Jewish quarter and killed many of
its people; and some of the women and children were sold as slaves... Some died to sanctify
God's name... but many others violated the holy covenant and changed their religion to
escape.

Jews were then massacred throughout Christian Spain and, one by one, their centres of population were destroyed.

Their persecutors offered the Jews the choice of baptism or death; and very large numbers chose to accept the Cross in preference to dying as martyrs – a few willingly, some with reluctance and most in sheer desperation. One third of all Spanish Jews perished or fled overseas in the decades that followed the first pogrom of 1391. A further third converted to Christianity; and only one third survived as openly professing Jews.

The glory and pride of the community departed, never to return. But the remaining Jews of the Iberian peninsula struggled on after the catastrophe, sustaining further losses through massacre and conversion, and also experiencing minor successes from time to time.

Finally, all openly professing Jews were expelled from Spain in 1492. At the end many opted for the Cross rather than leave their adopted homeland. It is estimated that fewer than two hundred thousand Jews actually quit Spain in 1492 – the remaining survivors being lost to the sword or to the Cross.

Typical perhaps was the behaviour of the two most prominent leaders of the community, one secular and the other religious. Don Abraham Seneor, Chief Justice of the Jews of Castile, was the courtier who had helped arrange the marriage between Ferdinand and Isabella which united Aragon and Castile and precipitated the decree of expulsion. Seneor accepted baptism – with the King, the Queen and the Cardinal of Spain standing as his godparents. On the other hand, his deeply religious and learned colleague in government, the great financier Don Isaac Abrabanel, had no hesitation in turning his back on Spain and going into exile.

It would be hard to exaggerate the impact on the entire Jewish people of the expulsion from Spain. The sudden end of the greatest, the best established and the most culturally assimilated Jewish community of Europe in the Middle Ages was a tragedy that seemed comparable only to the loss of their original homeland. In 1492, on the very anniversary of the destruction of the Temple by the Romans, the shattered and bewildered Spanish Jews entered into a further and deeper exile. Most found refuge in Portugal, only to meet an even worse fate in that country five year later. At roughly the same time, Jews were also expelled from Sicily, Sardinia and Provence.

A few exiles found temporary refuge in Naples and Venice. Others fled to Morocco, to other parts of North Africa, to Venetian colonies such as Crete and Cyprus, and above all to Turkey and the Ottoman Empire.

The refugees carried the culture of their beloved Spain with them into exile. They and their descendants long continued to cherish its customs, its music and its food. Proudly bearing Spanish or Portuguese family names, they carefully preserved the mediaeval Spanish language of their forbears and transformed it into Ladino – which still survives as a spoken language, though now only to a rather limited extent.

AN EPILOGUE

In October 1990 Crown Prince Don Felipe, son of King Juan Carlos of Spain, presented the Concorde Prize of the Prince of Asturias Foundation to a delegation of world Sephardi leaders including the Haham of this Congregation, Solomon Gaon. In his address, the prince expressed his deep regret and apologies for the actions of his ancestors in expelling the Jews from Spain. He praised the Sephardim for having spread Spanish culture in all the generation since the Expulsion; and voiced the hope that Spain would once again become a meeting place of the Spanish and Jewish traditions.

MATERIAL FOR LESSON 18

MAPS

Jews of Spain and Portugal

The Expulsions of 1492 – 1502

CHART

The Fate of the Jews of Christian Spain

THE JEWS OF SPAIN AND PORTUGAL 1000–1497

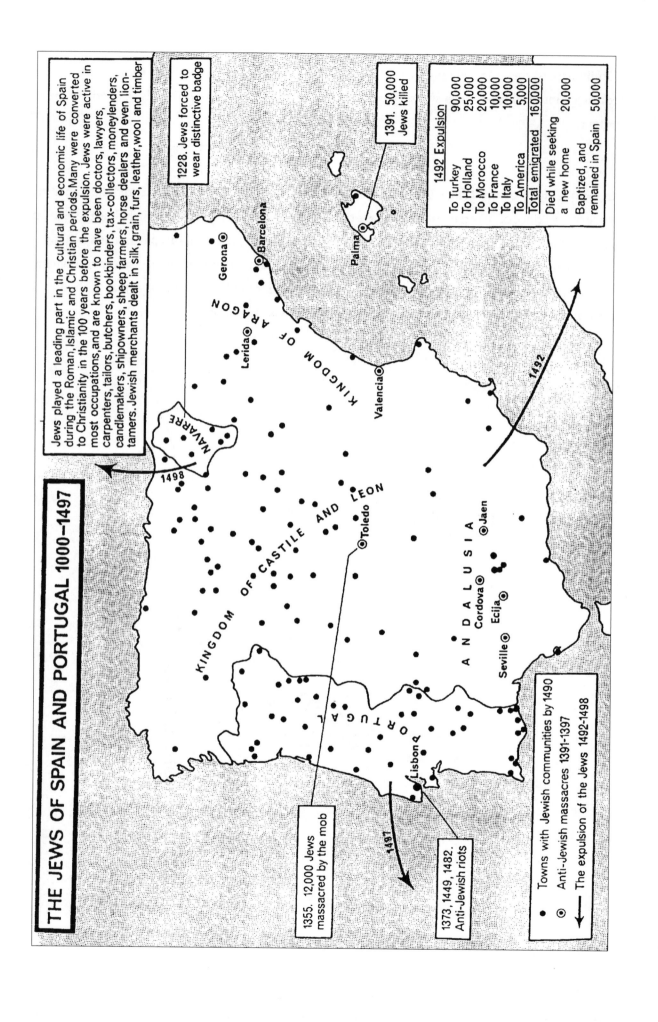

Jews played a leading part in the cultural and economic life of Spain during the Roman, Islamic and Christian periods. Many were converted to Christianity in the 100 years before the expulsion. Jews were active in most occupations, and are known to have been doctors, lawyers, carpenters, tailors, butchers, bookbinders, tax-collectors, moneylenders, candlemakers, shipowners, sheep farmers, horse dealers and even lion-tamers. Jewish merchants dealt in silk, grain, furs, leather, wool and timber

1228. Jews forced to wear distinctive badge

1391. 50,000 Jews killed

1492 Expulsion

To Turkey	90,000
To Holland	25,000
To Morocco	20,000
To France	10,000
To Italy	10,000
To America	5,000
Total emigrated	160,000
Died while seeking a new home	20,000
Baptized, and remained in Spain	50,000

Gerona

Barcelona

Lerida

KINGDOM OF ARAGON

Valencia

Palma

NAVARRE

1498

KINGDOM OF CASTILE AND LEON

Toledo

1492

Jaen

ANDALUSIA

Cordova

Ecija

Seville

PORTUGAL

Lisbon

1497

1355. 12,000 Jews massacred by the mob

1373, 1449, 1482. Anti-Jewish riots

- Towns with Jewish communities by 1490
- ⊙ Anti-Jewish massacres 1391-1397
- → The expulsion of the Jews 1492-1498

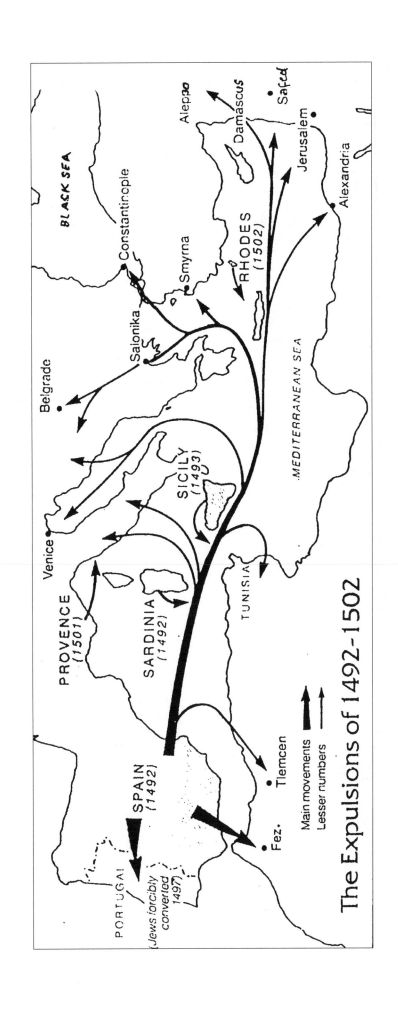

The Expulsions of 1492–1502

THE FATE OF THE JEWS OF CHRISTIAN SPAIN

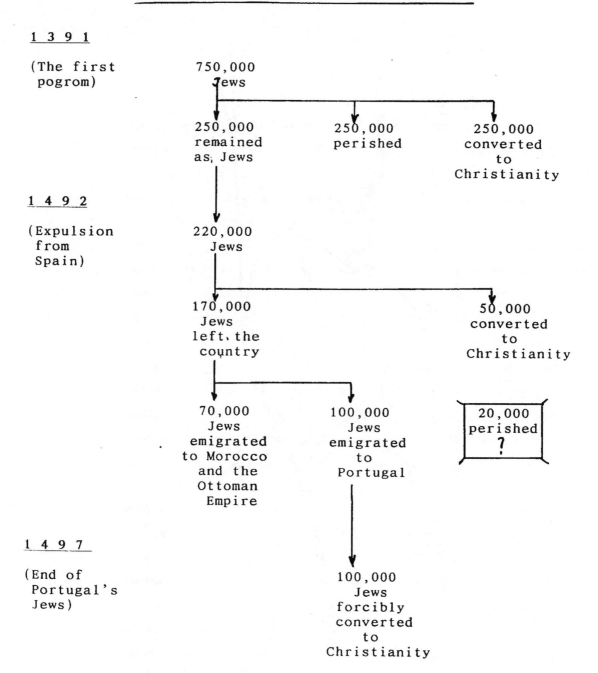

1 3 9 1

(The first pogrom)

750,000 Jews

250,000 remained as Jews

250,000 perished

250,000 converted to Christianity

1 4 9 2

(Expulsion from Spain)

220,000 Jews

170,000 Jews left the country

50,000 converted to Christianity

70,000 Jews emigrated to Morocco and the Ottoman Empire

100,000 Jews emigrated to Portugal

20,000 perished ?

1 4 9 7

(End of Portugal's Jews)

100,000 Jews forcibly converted to Christianity

Portugal

Significant numbers of Jews were living in Portugal as early as the year 300, long before the emergence of a separate Portuguese nation. It was not until the reign of King Affonso III in the twelfth century that Portugal attained full independence as a sovereign state.

Portugal's Jews enjoyed internal self-government under the rule of a Jewish court official known as the Arraby Mor (Chief Rabbi) who was appointed by the King. The community was divided into seven districts, each with its own judge selected by the Ar-raby Mor to hear civil and criminal cases. The selection of local rabbis was left to the people but the Crown paid all salaries and could veto any appointment. The Elders who governed day-to-day life in each community were also elected locally.

The Jews prospered. By the fifteenth century, much of the country's trade was in Jewish hands; and the closeness of the Ar-raby Mor to the court – he often served as the King's treasurer – gave Jews great political influence.

As in Spain, envy and jealousy increased over the years and Jews became more and more unpopular. Heavier taxes were imposed on them as well as humiliating disabilities, such as having to wear special badges on their clothing. Riots ensued; and in the Lisbon pogrom of 1449, a number of Jews were murdered by the mob intent on sacking their homes.

Nevertheless, conditions seemed less hopeless than those in Spain. Many Spanish New Christians moved to Portugal to escape the attentions of the Inquisition. And after the expulsion of 1492, over one hundred thousand Spanish Jews sought refuge across the Portuguese frontier.

The Spanish refugees were admitted after paying a heavy entry tax. One very large group, with little ready cash, was given permission to stay for eight months only – during which time King John II undertook to arrange the necessary shipping for them to leave.

The king broke his promise and many of the group were not able to embark before the deadline expired. They were then arrested and enslaved by royal command. In one horrific episode, seven hundred children were separated by force from their parents and sent to colonise the wild African island of St Thomas, where most of them perished.

The king died and was succeeded by Manoel the Fortunate, who promptly reversed his predecessor's policy and freed the newly created slaves. In 1496 however, the prospect of marriage to a daughter of the Catholic monarchs of Spain, Ferdinand and Isabella, caused King Manoel to change course once more and to devise a radical new policy.

In November 1496, all Portuguese Jews were given ten months notice to wind up their affairs and leave the country for good. In the event, the Jews were actually subjected to a far crueller fate and their expulsion never took place.

Guided by an apostate Jew, the king proceeded with cunning and ruthless efficiency. Despite opposition by the Council of State and leading churchmen, royal orders were suddenly issued requiring all Jewish children between the ages of four and fourteen to be presented for baptism the following Sunday. Those who did not appear were seized and marched to the nearest church. The king's officials were not too scrupulous about the age limit and youths of twenty were also forcibly baptised.

Manoel's order applied to all Jews regardless of position or rank; and Judah Abrabanel, the leading physician of the age, lost his son in that manner.

Scenes of indescribable horror accompanied the enforcement of the king's decree. Children were torn from the arms of their parents and distributed to Christian families as far away from their original homes as possible. Some Jews killed their own children rather than submit them for baptism. One such was the eminent Spanish scholar Isaac ben Abraham Zachin, who dispatched himself and his children for the Sanctification of the Name. Even some Christians were moved by the plight of the unfortunate Jews. The terrible scenes he had witnessed were vividly recalled by Bishop Coutinho more than thirty years later:

> *I saw many persons dragged by the hair to the font... Sometimes I saw a father, his head*
> *covered in sign of grief and pain, lead his son to the font, protesting and calling God to*
> *witness that they wished to die together in the law of Moses...*
> *Yet more terrible things that were done with them did I witness with my own eyes.*

As the deadline for departure approached, about twenty thousand surviving Jews were concentrated in Lisbon. They were imprisoned without food and drink for long periods, while priests endeavoured to persuade them to embrace the Cross. The weaker ones soon gave way under pressure. Much of the remaining resistance crumbled after the captives were declared slaves of the king. The process was not a gentle one, with an unknown number of Jews dying as martyrs for their faith. In the end, the remaining Jews had holy water sprinkled over them en-masse and were declared Christian, whether they liked it or not.

A remnant of the leadership led by Rabbi Simon Maimi, the last Arrabi Mor, continued openly to defy the triumphant priests. They were partly walled-up in a prison cell where Rabbi Maimi and two others died after a week of incarceration. Fewer than a dozen survivors were finally released by King Manoel and transported to North Africa in 1497.

Thus ended the smaller of the two Jewish communities of the Iberian Peninsula. But it was certainly not the end of the Portuguese Jews, who still had a strange but very significant part to play in the subsequent history of their people.

MATERIAL FOR LESSON 19

MAP

The Jews of Portugal

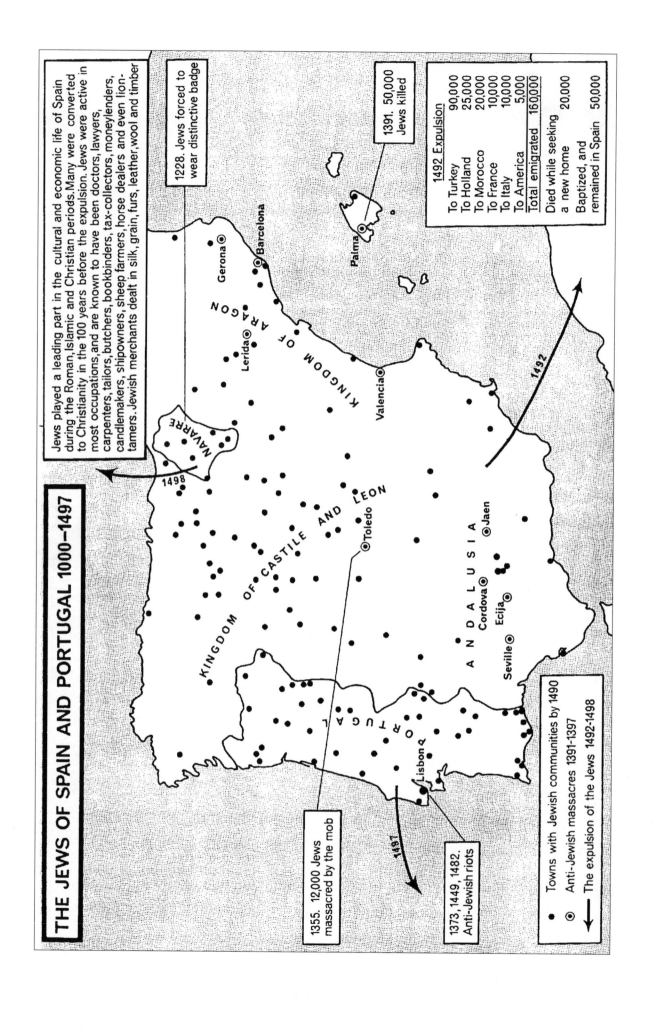

THE JEWS OF SPAIN AND PORTUGAL 1000–1497

Jews played a leading part in the cultural and economic life of Spain during the Roman, Islamic and Christian periods. Many were converted to Christianity in the 100 years before the expulsion. Jews were active in most occupations, and are known to have been doctors, lawyers, carpenters, tailors, butchers, bookbinders, tax-collectors, moneylenders, candlemakers, shipowners, sheep farmers, horse dealers and even lion-tamers. Jewish merchants dealt in silk, grain, furs, leather, wool and timber

1228. Jews forced to wear distinctive badge

1391. 50,000 Jews killed

1492 Expulsion	
To Turkey	90,000
To Holland	25,000
To Morocco	20,000
To France	10,000
To Italy	10,000
To America	5,000
Total emigrated	160,000
Died while seeking a new home	20,000
Baptized, and remained in Spain	50,000

Gerona

Barcelona

Palma

KINGDOM OF ARAGON

Lerida

Valencia

NAVARRE

1498

1492

KINGDOM OF CASTILE AND LEON

Toledo

ANDALUSIA

Jaen

Cordova

Ecija

Seville

PORTUGAL

Lisbon

1497

1355. 12,000 Jews massacred by the mob

1373, 1449, 1482. Anti-Jewish riots

- Towns with Jewish communities by 1490
- ⊙ Anti-Jewish massacres 1391-1397
- → The expulsion of the Jews 1492-1498

The Marranos

The forced conversion of Jews to Christianity or Islam was not new to Spain when the process started afresh in 1391. It had occurred before under the rule of the Visigoths in the seventh century and then again in 1148 when Muslims Spain fell under the sway of the fanatical Almohads from North Africa. In both periods, the 'Anusim' (Compelled Ones) were notoriously disloyal to their new religion and openly reverted to Judaism as soon as they could, whether in Spain or abroad.

In the fourteenth century, Jewish converts to Christianity were officially called Nuevos Christianos (New Christians), or simply 'conversos' (converts). They were also known as 'marranos' (pigs) by the coarser of their new brethren in Christ – a term chosen, no doubt, to indicate the contempt and even hatred with which they were regarded.

It is important to appreciate that the New Christians included sincere converts within their ranks, as well as those who were reluctant but basically indifferent. But many were secret Jews who maintained their old faith in private and yearned to reassert their true identity. It is these we now describe as Marranos, transforming the word into a name of honour.

Many conversos, and especially those who had accepted the religion of Jesus with willingness, lost no time in making the most of the opportunities created by their baptism. Also quick to benefit were those who had been convinced by philosophy to distrust all religion and who felt that they had simply exchanged one cloak of superstition for another.

Freed at last from the restrictive shackles of a hated minority faith, New Christians quickly rose to occupy many of the top positions of Church and state. Some married into the aristocracy and penetrated the highest ranks of Spanish society. Eventually it was claimed that as many as one in three of the inhabitants of several cities of Southern Spain were of New Christian descent; and few noble families in certain areas could claim that no Jewish blood flowed in their veins.

Some conversos went so far as to spearhead attacks on their former religion. But many, whilst punctiliously observing the outward ceremonies of the Catholic Church, remained Jewish in their hearts and in their private lives. They attached themselves to churches frequented by their own kind and confessed only to Marrano priests. They baptised their children; but then hurried home to wash the stain of baptism from their heads. They observed the Sabbath, the Jewish festivals and the dietary laws to the limited extent possible without arousing suspicion; and even the Church at first acquiesced in their aversion to eating pork. The Marranos gathered for a kind of abbreviated Jewish worship in the security of their own homes and in secret synagogues. They continued to maintain contact with openly professing Jews and, to some extent, married within their own group.

The conspicuous worldly success of the Marranos aroused the envy and hatred of the populace – for it was common knowledge that their Christianity was only assumed and their allegiance to the Church no more than skin-deep. Almost equally disliked were the converso intellectuals who believed in no religion at all.

This was not only a problem for Marranos and intellectuals: sincere New Christians suffered as well for the prejudice against them was too general and too deep to admit more than a few exceptions. The Spanish Church, and later that of Portugal, refused to accept that conversions undertaken under duress could later be repudiated. It strove hard to eradicate what it regarded as the heretical Judaising tendencies of New Christians. The Church came to regard the New Christians as a large and influential fifth column, dedicated to the subversion of its loyal following.

Concern over the problem increased with the years. In 1434, the Council of Tortosa pleaded for steps to be taken to check what was described as 'the blasphemous duplicity' of the New Christians. Fifteen year later, Toledo debarred all New Christians from holding public office or bearing testimony against Old Christians; and many highly respectable judges, Christian clerics and other officials lost their positions.

Riots directed against conversos spread; and these were sometimes accompanied by massacres. More and more decrees intended to separate New Christians from public life were promulgated in different parts of Spain from 1468 onwards; and only a few of the main centres of Marrano life – notably Seville – escaped without disturbance.

This time, there was no escape for secret Jews other than in flight. Having already been baptised, they could not take that way out again. Also the Church steadfastly refused to consider them other than heretics if they attempted to cast off Christianity on the ground that they had been compelled to accept baptism.

In 1480 Queen Isabella established an Inquisition in Seville and gave it unfettered jurisdiction over 'heretics and their accomplices'. Many New Christians, including some of the most eminent citizens were arrested, tried and condemned to death for heresy. Six men and women were burned alive at the first Auto-da-Fé (festival of faith) in February 1481. This was followed by many more atrocities as the whole region was gripped by an orgy of denunciation and terror. Even the bones of the dead were dug up and publicly burned after trial. By November of the same year, almost three hundred people had been burned at the stake and one hundred more condemned to perpetual imprisonment. Large numbers who confessed their error were heavily fined, debarred from holding public office and humiliated by being made to dress in coarse garments and parade as penitents through the streets.

Such ferocity on the part of the Church was unprecedented; and even the Pope wrote to Queen Isabella expressing his disapproval of the methods employed.

But the Inquisition was popular; and what is more, it was good business. Its tentacles soon spread all over the country. Many thousands fell under its sway, either losing all their property or else submitting to heavy fines. The Inquisition waxed fat on the proceeds; and there were few connected with it who did not benefit greatly.

(Note: The Inquisition could not touch 'open' Jews and had no authority over them.)

The Holy Inquisition with its widespread network of informers, imposed a reign of terror on the secret Jews as well as on less committed but genuine New Christians. It tracked the secret Jews relentlessly, devising ever more ingenious tests to discover them. Rooftops were scanned to see which chimneys were not smoking on Sabbaths and holydays. Even the act of changing the linen on a Friday (the eve of Sabbath), or of turning the head to the wall in prayer at the moment of death, was sufficient to bring the heavy hand of the Inquisition to bear on the unfortunate suspects and their families. When identified, truly or otherwise, every effort was made to torture the crypto-Jews into submission and they were put to death in large numbers.

Contrary to what might have been expected from their history, the determination of many Marranos to preserve their Jewish identity did not crumble under pressure but intensified with mounting persecution. They clung tenaciously to what they remembered of their ancestral faith, even when it had become so vestigial as to be barely recognisable. And many descendants of genuine apostates – those who had embraced Christianity of their own free will – tried hard to retrace their steps and return in secret to the religion of their people.

Many acts of great bravery were committed by victims of the Inquisition.

Quite padre que un palo a nadie salva (Take it away father for a piece of wood can save no one)

was the chilling response made by one Marrano, about to be burned to death in an Auto-da-Fé, when a priest snatched two pieces of wood from the kindling, made a rough cross and offered it to the condemned man as a last chance to save himself.

The more fortunate Spanish New Christians managed to leave the country.

Many Spanish New Christians moved to Portugal, where conditions were easier. In 1497 the entire surviving Jewish population of Portugal also became New Christians, having been suddenly and brutally forced to the baptismal font. Those bewildered Marranos knew nothing of Christianity and cared even less for it than their Spanish brothers in misfortune. Even King Manoel recognised that by granting them a general amnesty for religious offences already committed, and immunity from investigation of matters of faith for a period of twenty years. He also strictly forbad them to leave the country without royal license.

As in Spain, the Marranos flourished. They dominated the commercial life of the country and increasingly aroused the envy of the populace. In 1503, after a poor harvest which caused hardship, discontent against the Marranos led to a terrible massacre in Lisbon in which it is estimated that many thousands of New Christians were done to death.

An Inquisition was finally established in 1536; but it was not until 1540 that the first Auto-da-Fé was held in Lisbon. From that time on, there was no turning back; and the New Christians of Portugal were gripped progressively by an Inquisition which pursued its aims with even more rigour and cruelty than that of Spain. The story of those Marranos who succeeded in fleeing the country will be continued later.

In time, the Inquisitions of both Portugal and Spain gradually lost their fervour and increasingly allowed New Christians to live their lives undisturbed. Though the Inquisitions were not actually abolished until the early years of the nineteenth century, the last converso to be burned at the stake perished in Lisbon at an Auto- da-Fé in 1775. Eventually tolerance accomplished what persecution had failed to do and the New Christians melted away, merging into the general population.

Apart from a handful of surviving groups, the only traces of the Marranos that now remain are peculiar customs of undoubtedly Jewish origin, the meaning of which has long since been forgotten by those who observe them. Many of these survived in parts of Spain and Portugal until quite recently – and some still do today.

One such custom, described by a Majorcan, concerned his mother who always kept a side of bacon in her house – not to eat but to hang close to her window overlooking the street.

A similar kind of Portuguese practice involved the lighting of a candle by the woman of the house in the cellar, or at the bottom of a deep jar, every Friday night, the eve of the Sabbath.

The daughter of a good Spanish Catholic family, on learning the history of the Marranos for the first time wrote that this might account for her own grandmother's seemingly eccentric and previously inexplicable refusal ever to do housework or listen to music on Saturdays.

The Marranos did not quite disappear from history after the abolition of the Inquisition. Some few communities survived, partly due to their own stubborn tenacity and partly because of the distrust of their supposed fellow Christians.

A few hundred of them, remembering fragments of Jewish practice and still leading furtive double lives, were discovered in a remote part of Northern Portugal in 1917; and some were helped back to the faith of their ancestors. In 1989, thirty-two men of a Marrano community in Belmonte were circumcised in accordance with Jewish law, their leader declaring publicly that of several thousand Marrano families remaining in Northern Portugal, about two hundred were willing to return to Judaism. Curious too is the fact that, until the early years of this century, several thousand staunchly Roman Catholic Majorcans of converso descent were still maintaining a separate communal existence because of the dislike of their neighbours.

To this day, the members of this synagogue of Spanish and Portuguese Jews of London solemnly recite the following prayer in Kal Nidre, the first service for the Day of Atonement:

> *May he who blessed our fathers, Abraham, Isaac and Jacob, Moses and Aaron, David and*
> *Solomon, bless, preserve, guard and assist all our brethren imprisoned by the Inquisition.*
> *May the king of Kings bless them and make them worthy of his grace, hearken to the voice*
> *of their supplication and bring them forth from darkness to light. May such be thy divine*
> *will and let us say, Amen.*

Eventually perhaps, when Jews are no longer oppressed in any part of the world, that ancient prayer will at last be omitted.

MATERIAL FOR LESSON 20

MAP

The Marrano Diaspora

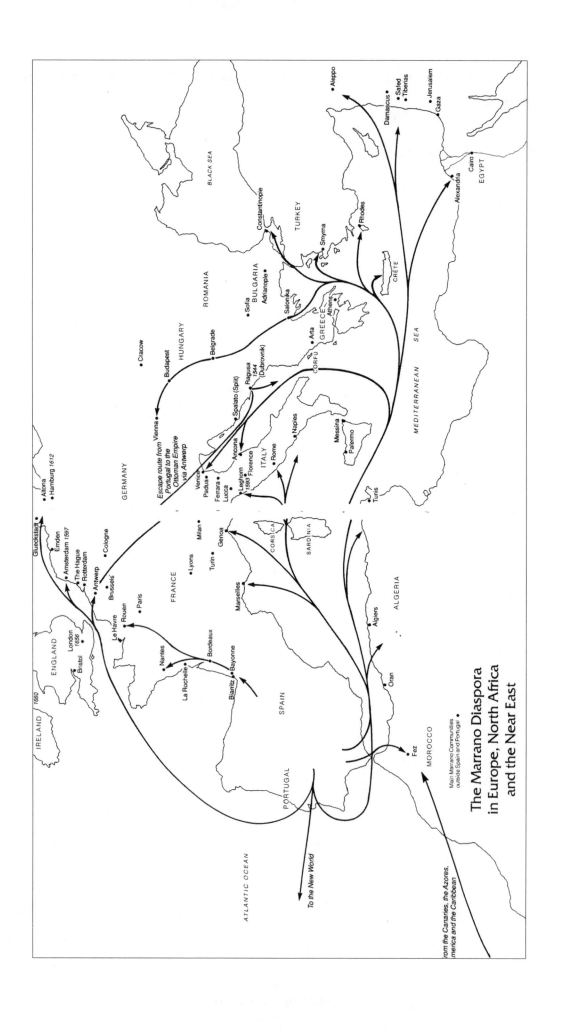

The Marrano Diaspora
in Europe, North Africa
and the Near East

Escape route from
Portugal to the
Ottoman Empire
via Antwerp

Main Marrano Communities
outside Spain and Portugal •

To the New World

from the Canaries, the Azores,
merica and the Caribbean

ATLANTIC OCEAN

IRELAND 1660

ENGLAND

Bristol 1656
London 1656

Glueckstadt
Altona
Hamburg 1612
Emden
Amsterdam 1597
The Hague
Rotterdam
Antwerp
Cologne
Brussels
Le Havre
Rouen
Paris
Nantes
La Rochelle
Bordeaux
Bayonne
Biarritz

GERMANY

FRANCE

Lyons
Milan
Turin
Genoa
Marseilles

PORTUGAL

SPAIN

MOROCCO

Fez

Oran

Algiers

ALGERIA

CORSICA

SARDINIA

Cracow

Vienna

Budapest

HUNGARY

Belgrade

BLACK SEA

ROMANIA

Sofia
BULGARIA
Adrianople
Salonika

Constantinople

TURKEY

Smyrna

Rhodes

CRETE

Ragusa
1544
(Dubrovnik)
Spalato (Split)
Ancona
Venice
Padua
Ferrara
Lucca
Leghorn
1593
Florence
ITALY
Rome
Naples
Messina
Palermo

CORFU
Arta
GREECE
Athens

MEDITERRANEAN SEA

Tunis

Aleppo
Damascus
Safed
Tiberias
Jerusalem
Gaza
Cairo
EGYPT
Alexandria

The New World

Christopher Columbus embarked on the first of his epoch-making voyages of discovery within a day of the deadline set for the final expulsion of the Jews from Spain in July 1492. Though there is no evidence that Columbus himself was of Jewish descent, as is sometimes claimed, it is thought that up to six of members of his crew may have been. Indeed the expedition's interpreter Luis de Torres – the first man actually to set foot in the New World – was a Jew who had accepted baptism shortly before his departure. Other Marranos must have followed the explorers, for one was brought back from Hispaniola to Seville in 1515 to face trial by the Inquisition.

Large scale Spanish settlements on the mainland of America started with Cortes's conquest of Mexico in 1521 and Pizarro's conquest of Peru eleven years later. Spanish colonies were then planted all over Central and South America – except for Brazil, which was left to the Portuguese. Some Marranos must have crossed the Atlantic with those early settlers, for we know that two of Cortes's own conquistadores were accused of heresy in Mexico City and burned at the stake in 1528. However numbers remained small at first, for both the King and the Pope did their utmost to prevent New Christians for settling in America.

Portuguese policy started rather differently. The first Auto-da-Fé to be held in Lisbon took place in 1540; and from 1548 onwards, penitent New Christians were actually deported to Brazil after trial for religious offences. The King of Spain took over Portugal thirty two years later, temporarily uniting the two kingdoms. The growing grip of the Inquisition, coupled with the coming of Spain rule, caused large number of New Christians to cross the Atlantic and seek haven in the Spain colonies, where the Inquisition's scrutiny of their beliefs and practice was less thorough. In fact King Phillip II of Spain even accepted a hefty bribe in 1601 in exchange for his consent for New Christians to emigrate freely to America.

Spanish control of Portuguese immigration to their colonies having slackened, it was not long before Marranos who had remained loyal to their ancestral faith were observing at least some of the practices of Judaism all over Central and South America – from Mexico to Argentina, and from Brazil to Chile and Peru Those Marranos, with close links to their brethren in Antwerp, Amsterdam, Livorno, Turkey and the Iberian Peninsula, dominated many aspects of European trade with the colonies; and they prospered accordingly.

It was when the Dutch invaded Brazil in 1624 and again in 1630, and offered freedom of conscience to all, that some local Marranos returned openly to the Jewish faith; and these were soon joined by professing Jews who came over from Holland. By 1638, it is thought that about half the total white population of twenty-two thousand in Dutch territory was of Jewish origin.

The Dutch evacuation of Brazil in 1654, under Portuguese pressure, was a disaster for its Jews; but the Portuguese did at least grant an amnesty for three months during which Jews could depart. Rather than submit to Portuguese rule, many returned to Holland. The remainder founded a series of settlements all over the West Indies. Curaçao was by far the largest; but Barbados, Jamaica and Martinique also hosted viable congregations, as did several of the smaller islands.

It was in 1654 that twenty-three Jews, fleeing from Recife in Brazil, first set foot in New Amsterdam – later to become New York. Peter Stuyvesant, the Dutch governor, wanted to turn them away but he was ordered to give them refuge after the intervention of the Jews of Amsterdam. From that small beginning grew the mighty Jewish community of the United States.

Forty-two Jews, including two Ashkenazi families, were sent by ship to Savannah by members of this synagogue, the London Sephardi Congregation, in 1733. The first Sephardi congregation of Charleston was established in 1750 and its synagogue, opened in 1795, was considered the most splendid in America. The Sephardi synagogue of Newport, Rhode Island, was founded in 1763 by families from Barbados, Curaçao and the Iberian Peninsula. And, in the same period, Sephardi communities were also established in Philadelphia and Richmond. Jews were granted citizenship of New Amsterdam in 1655: a synagogue was functioning by 1700 and the first purpose-built structure was opened thirty years later.

The community was able to appoint the American-born Gershom Mendes Seixas as its spiritual leader in 1768; and Seixas commanded sufficient respect to be invited to President George Washington's inauguration in 1798. The synagogue was rebuilt in 1818 with financial help from a number of overseas communities including those of Curaçao and Barbados.

From its early days, Ashkenazim formed a substantial part of the American Jewish community. They did however prove reluctant to start their own synagogues and preferred to join the Sephardim. Indeed Sephardi ways proved so attractive that Ashkenazim even founded a Sephardi synagogue in Baltimore, where no Sephardim lived. In time Ashkenazim came to outnumber Sephardim in most Sephardi synagogues, maintaining the Sephardi prayer book, services and music – but in an American rather than in a traditional Sephardi context.

These so-called Sephardim of the United States long enjoyed high prestige and formed themselves into a kind of Jewish aristocracy. They maintained their leadership of the Jewish community unchallenged until 1840 when they yielded their position to the by then far more numerous Ashkenazim.

Of the original Sephardi congregation of the United States, only those of New York and Philadelphia survive. Ashkenazim and those of mixed descent form a substantial part of their membership.

There was another wave of Sephardi immigration to Brazil after that country finally gained its independence from Portugal in the 1820s. This time the settlers came directly from Morocco, attracted by the economic opportunities of the rich new land.

Since those early days, a very substantial immigration of Ashkenazim has resulted in the Jewish community of United States of America becoming the largest in the world.

The Sephardi population of North, South and Central America increased sharply in the early years of the twentieth century because of a flood of new immigrants from the old Ottoman Empire and later, from Persia and the Arab world. In mid century, the final destruction of the ancient Jewish communities of the Near East provided what will probably be the last wave of Sephardi immigration to the New World. This fresh immigration certainly gave a new breath of life to the Sephardim of the United States.

Which Sephardi synagogue do you know of in America?

MATERIAL FOR LESSON 21

MAP

The Marrano diaspora in the New World

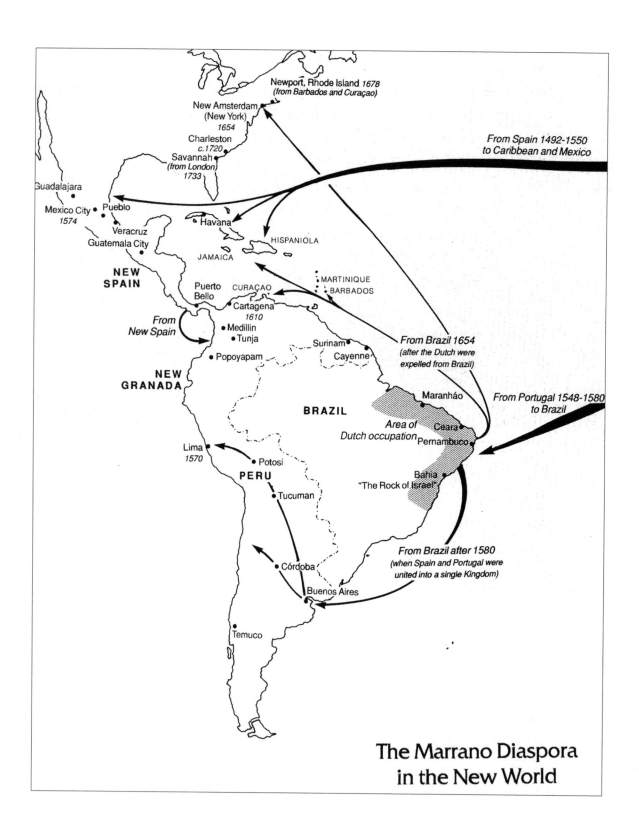

Newport, Rhode Island *1678*
(from Barbados and Curaçao)

New Amsterdam
(New York)
1654

Charleston
c.1720

Savannah
(from London)
1733

From Spain 1492-1550
to Caribbean and Mexico

Guadalajara

Mexico City
1574

Pueblo

Veracruz

Guatemala City

Havana

HISPANIOLA

JAMAICA

**NEW
SPAIN**

Puerto
Bello

CURAÇAO

MARTINIQUE

BARBADOS

*From
New Spain*

Cartagena
1610

Medillin

Tunja

Surinam

Cayenne

*From Brazil 1654
(after the Dutch were
expelled from Brazil)*

Popoyapam

**NEW
GRANADA**

BRAZIL

Maranháo

*Area of
Dutch occupation*

Ceara

Pernambuco

*From Portugal 1548-1580
to Brazil*

Lima
1570

Potosi

PERU

Bahia
"The Rock of Israel"

Tucuman

*From Brazil after 1580
(when Spain and Portugal were
united into a single Kingdom)*

Córdoba

Buenos Aires

Temuco

The Marrano Diaspora
in the New World

The Marranos of Western Europe

The Inquisition came much later to Portugal than to Spain. Taking advantage of the easier conditions there, many Spanish New Christians had crossed over the frontier into Portugal where their beliefs and religious practices were not at first subjected to close scrutiny. It must be remembered that the New Christians included sincere converts in their ranks; and that even those had to endure the same distrust and disabilities heaped on secret Jews.

Those who wished to return to Judaism moved even further afield to parts of Italy, North Africa and above all to the Ottoman Empire. From the end of the fourteenth century, many Mediterranean ports were sheltering forced converts who had fled from the Iberian peninsula.

Having been forcibly and brutally converted to Christianity within the space of a few months, the Marranos of Portugal were even more passionately devoted to their Jewish past than their brethren who had remained behind in Spain. It was not until forty years after this mass conversion that an Inquisition was established in Portugal; but once started on its course, it lost not time in gripping that country's New Christians with full intensity.

Strictly forbidden to leave without a royal licence, only comparatively few of Portugal's New Christians managed at first to slip away and seek refuge overseas. Antwerp, which though under Spanish rule had no Inquisition, attracted some who settled there under the protection of a safe-conduct issued by Emperor Charles V in 1526.

An escape route through Antwerp was established for Marranos who could obtain permission to leave Portugal for Flanders. They then proceeded overland – sometimes through Italy and the Balkans – until they could take ship for freedom in Turkey. A boatload of such refugees arrived in Ragusa (Dubrovnik) in 1544; and by 1564 it appears that there were few Italian cities in which Marranos could not be found. The Ottoman Empire remained the prime goal for those wishing to return to Judaism; and Rhodes, conquered by the Turks in 1522, became a transit destination for New Christians and a place in which many Marranos returned to their preferred religion.

Those among the New Christians who feared the Inquisition, but lacked the burning desire to renounce their baptism, sought asylum in other places where they might simply live in peace. They spread out from Antwerp into Germany, settling in Cologne, Hamburg, Emden, Altona and Glückstandt; and some penetrated to Scandinavia. At first they all continued to live as Christians though some eventually returned to Judaism.

Five prominent and wealthy New Christian families had settled in Cologne by 1578 and others joined them. It was partly due to their presence that Cologne first attained the status of an international financial centre in 1580s.

In 1612 some one-hundred and fifty Portuguese New Christians were given the right to remain in Hamburg for five years – but only as Christians. The first evidence of secret Jewish worship came five years later, when the Lutheran Church protested to the city's Burgomasters; and it was not until 1623 that a Jewish community was granted tacit toleration by the authorities. By 1646 numbers had grown to some five hundred strong; but opposition to Jewish settlement had also increased.

France was another country which attracted New Christian families, some arriving even before the expulsion from Spain. In the year 1475 King Louis XI granted extraordinary privileges to foreign merchants, including New Christians, who had settled in Bordeaux. These were confirmed by Henri II in his Letter Patent of 1550, after which New Christian settlement in France gained momentum.

It was not until well over one hundred years after the expulsion from Spain that larger numbers of Marranos began to find their way to Holland. The Union of Utrecht, which in 1579 had established the Protestant Dutch provinces in their independence from Spanish Catholic rule, included freedom of conscience as one of its terms. Once beyond the reach of the dreaded Inquisition, the Marranos lost no time in casting off their mask of Christianity and openly returning to Judaism. By that time they no longer knew any Hebrew, nor did they remember more than vestiges of Jewish practice; but they were eager to learn. Amsterdam became home to a flourishing Jewish community; and its fine synagogue and system of religious education were admired all over the world.

Amsterdam was the principal staging post for those Marranos who wished to revert to Judaism. It also served as the power-house of Western Sephardim through the efforts of its Jewish merchants who, participating to the full in the world-wide trading activity of the Dutch Republic, were able to maintain close but secret contact with the New Christian communities of Portugal, France, Northern Germany, Scandinavia and the New World.

The Jewish community of London, for example, owed much to its roots in Amsterdam. Its twenty or so Marranos families were helped by the celebrated Amsterdam rabbi Menasseh ben Israel to cast off their Catholic disguise and openly embrace Judaism. The Sephardim opened their first synagogue in London in the year 1656 (our own congregation); and Benjamin Disraeli, Queen Victoria's favourite Prime Minister, was the son of one of its members.

Livorno (Leghorn) in Italy was another of the very few towns of Christian Europe where Jews could live openly and without pretence; for in 1593 Grand Duke Ferdinand I issued a proclamation inviting all persecuted people to come and live freely in his new port. Many Marranos came direct from the Iberian Peninsula, and other Sephardi Jews flocked there from Venice and from parts of the Ottoman Empire when conditions there began to deteriorate. By 1645 it is estimated that there were more than two thousand Jews in Livorno out of a total population of nine thousand.

Portuguese remained for many years the day-to-day language of the Marrano diaspora; and Spanish, though still remembered, was used mainly for commercial dealings with the outside world and as a language of literature and prayer. The Marranos were proud to preserve their identity as a self-styled

Portuguese 'nation' in exile; and indeed, in most of Europe, Asia and the Americas the very word 'Portuguese' became synonymous with 'Jewish'.

The Marrano merchants, with their widespread but closely knit family businesses and their network of trusted contacts in most of the trading centres of the world, operated what amounted to an international credit system. This gave them a disproportionately large share of the world's commerce and virtual monopoly of products such as sugar, tobacco, coral and gem stones. In time, some of them also became prominent in the emerging financial system of Western Europe and on its exchanges.

Perhaps the greatest contribution of all to Jewish life in Western Europe was the part played by former Marranos in the re-establishment of Jewish communities in many of its countries. These Jews, though foreign and Portuguese-speaking, wore the same dress and had the same kind of manner as the upper classes of the lands of their adoption. Once they had been admitted and recognised as Jews, it became harder to exclude their Ashkenazi brethren- some of whom were far stranger and more uncouth in their habits and dress. Though, to their discredit, the Sephardim did not always do as much as they might to welcome the Ashkenazi immigrants who followed them – sometimes even the reverse – nevertheless they were the forerunners. It was they who paved the way for the acceptance of the very much larger Ashkenazi immigration into Western Europe that came after their own settlement.

MATERIAL FOR LESSON 22

MAP

The Marrano Diaspora of Western Europe

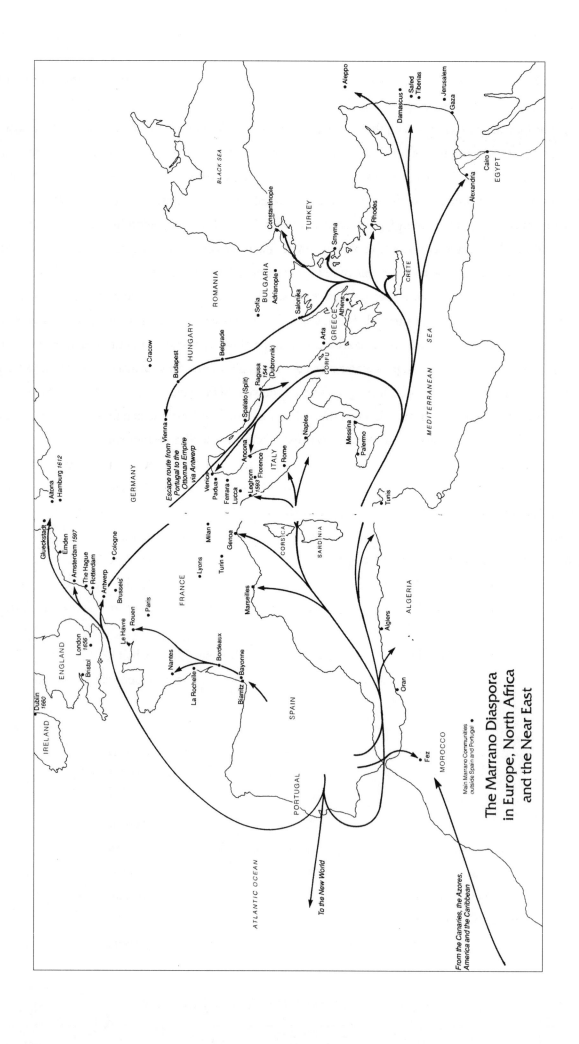

The Marrano Diaspora
in Europe, North Africa
and the Near East

The Ottoman Empire

The Ottomans were descended from one of the many clans of Turkish nomads which swept westwards from the steppes of Central Asia and decisively defeated the enfeebled Byzantine Empire in 1071. The tribesmen converted to Islam and then slowly expanded their territory.

The Ottoman Turks caused near panic in Christian Europe when their armies conquered Constantinople in 1453 and then, marching up through the Balkans, reached the gates of Vienna in 1529. Though unsuccessful in their siege of Vienna, the Turks remained a constant threat to the very heart of Europe for the next 150 years until their final attempt to capture Vienna ended in a decisive defeat at the hands of the Christians.

The existing Jewish communities of lands so far conquered by the Turks had for centuries suffered only humiliation, harassment and persecution at the hands of their Christian rulers. The Ottomans changed all that. They trusted the Jews, and valued the contribution they could make to the economic development of the Empire. Within the bounds of Islam law, they treated the Jews with fairness and justice; and the Jews responded with gratitude and loyalty.

Some Ashkenazi Jews found a haven in the Ottoman Empire. These included Jews expelled from Hungary in 1376, from France in 1394, from Sicily in the early 15th century, from Venetian-ruled Salonica and, in 1470, form Bavaria. In fact, shortly before the fall of Constantinople, the Turks seem to have actively encouraged Jewish immigration from Europe by offering conditions of tolerance and relative freedom.

The best known example of this is the famous letter from Rabbi Sarfati, Chief Rabbi of Edirne (formerly Adrianople), written in the first half of the 14th century and circulated in Central Europe, Northern France, the Rhineland and Hungary.

> *I too was born in Germany and studied Torah with the German rabbis. I was driven out of*
> *my native country and came to the Turkish land, which is blessed by God and filled with all*
> *good things ...*
> *Here in the land of the Turks we have nothing of which to complain. We possess great*
> *fortunes: much gold and silver are in our hands. We are not oppressed with heavy taxes and*
> *our commerce is free and unhindered. Everything is cheap and every one of us lives in peace*
> *and freedom. Here the Jew is not compelled to wear a yellow hat as a badge of shame, as is*
> *the case in Germany...*
> *Arise my brothers, gird up your loins, collect your forces and come to us. Here you will be*

free of your enemies. Here you will find rest...

Rabbi Capsali, Chief Rabbi of Istanbul, claimed that Sultan Bayesid II (1481 – 1512), who ruled at the time of the expulsion of the Jews from Spain, made even more urgent efforts to attract Sephardi Jews into his domains.

He wrote:

> *Sultan Bayesid, monarch of Turkey, heard of all the evil that the King of Spain inflicted on the Jews and he heard that they were seeking a refuge and a resting place. He took pity on them, wrote letters, sent messengers to proclaim throughout his kingdom that none of his city governors be wicked enough to refuse entry to Jews or to expel them. Instead they were to be given a gracious welcome, and anyone who did not behave in this manner would be put to death ... Thousands and tens of thousands of deported Jews came to the lands of the Turks and filled it...*

The Sultan is said to have remarked in conversation:

> *You call Ferdinand a wise king, he who impoverishes his country and enriches our own ... by expelling the Jews.*

Sephardi Jews fleeing from Spain and Portugal were welcomed with open arms by the Turks, who found it hard to believe their good fortune in acquiring so many talented, cultivated and useful subjects. Indeed Sultan Bayazid II even sent two of his own ships into Lisbon harbour to take off Jewish refugees in 1497.

The Ottoman Turks, it should be remembered, were a highly successful nation of warriors. It was beneath their dignity to engage in occupations other than the army, the government of the Mosque; and they despised commerce and crafts. They also disdained to colonise their far-flung empire or settle in its cities.

The Jews provided the Ottoman Empire with the nucleus of a new middle class – one that was free from political ambition and on which the Turks could rely for a degree of loyalty they were unable to obtain from the newly conquered subject people of their huge empire. To the Turks, the Jews were by far the most productive and stable non-Turkish minority in their domains.

As followers of the religion of Abraham, the People of the Book, Jews and Christians were accorded the status of dhimmis (protected persons) in all Islamic lands. This ensured state protection for their lives and property, freedom for them to follow their own religion on condition they did not insult Islam or attempt to convert Mohammedans, and exemption from military service. In return, dhimmis had to accept restrictions and humiliations as second-class subjects. They had to pay a special poll tax, wear distinctive clothes and refrain from building new synagogues and churches without permission. Their evidence in court was not accepted against that of a Mohammedan; not could a Mohammedan be put to death for killing a dhimmi. Fortunately many of the restrictions, except for the paying of the tax, were not always imposed – or if they were, not strictly. They served mainly to preserve the subservient status of the dhimmi in Islamic society.

As dhimmis, communities of Jews and Christians formed many separate millets (nations) in the Ottoman Empire. Each millet was largely self-governing, with its own laws and administration. It levied and collected its own taxes; and was ruled by a Chief Rabbi or Patriarch directly responsible to the Sultan. This system suited the Jews very well, especially in the early days when humiliating restrictions were not imposed on their lives.

Under the benevolent sway of the Sultan, Sephardim joined existing Jewish communities all over the Ottoman Empire. They settled around the shores of the Mediterranean, penetrating up through the Balkans towards central Europe, and eventually across Turkey to Baghdad and beyond. Usually superior in education and culture to the local Jews in whose midst they settled, the Sephardim at first jealously preserved their separate identity, forming themselves into a kind of aristocracy. In time though, they either succeeded in absorbing the older-established resident Jews or else merged into them.

The Sephardi Jews who found their way to the Land of Israel transformed that country's Jewish community. They soon became a majority in Jerusalem. In Tiberias they participated in a grand venture to rebuild the town as a refuge for oppressed Jews. Under the influence of the Sephardi rabbis, mystics and poets who settled there, Safed (in Galilee) became a spiritual centre of world Jewry – and, in particular, the focus of the Kabbalistic (mystical) movement which came to dominate Jewish thought after the Expulsion from Spain.

Turkey was then approaching the peak of its power as the leader of a vast Islamic civilisation. The Turks' kindly treatment of their own Jewish populations and their warm welcome to the refugees ensured that, from that time on, the fate of most Sephardim would be closely bound to that of their Islamic hosts. As Turkey prospered, so did its Jews. And Ottoman Jews soon became the financiers, the tax farmers, the merchants, the diplomats, the interpreters and the physicians of the Empire.

Nor did the Jews neglect industry and the crafts. Indeed the Christians of Europe were soon to complain bitterly that Spanish Jews had introduced the manufacture of cannon and gunpowder into Turkey and had taught the Turks the art of modern warfare. The textile industry in all its aspects, from raw materials to the making of garments, became a Jewish speciality – and, in places, a near monopoly. The great Jewish commercial houses, run as close family business with widespread networks of trusted contacts all over the world, dominated international trade to an extent difficult to visualise today.

Turkey eventually began to decay from within. The sultans who succeeded, Suleiman the Magnificent (1520-1566), generally lacked the ability of their brilliant predecessors. Spoilt by the wealth that seemed so effortlessly to flow in their direction, they grew increasingly decadent and devoted far more their energies to court and harem intrigue than to governing their empire. Their grip on government relaxed. Some of its important posts became hereditary; and others were openly sold to the highest bidder. Corruption and nepotism flourished as the huge bureaucracy became increasingly inefficient.

Taxation was increased to ruinous levels. Economic troubles and inflation followed, with large price increases. Crop yields fell sharply as more and more peasants moved into the towns from the countryside. Greater competition from Christian Europe, particularly in textiles, had a bad effect on trade. Military reverses lead to a progressive crumbling of the edges of the Empire; while within it, chaos and lawlessness gradually became usual.

In time not only did Turkey decline in wealth and power, but the relatively privileged position of its Jews was also eroded. This was partly the result of the weakening of central Ottoman control over the far-flung provinces of the Empire – which led to an increasing degree of autonomy for the local governors, who often proved lazy, greedy and corrupt. Another important factor was the failure of the Jews to maintain their own formerly high standards of education and culture in the decaying Islamic environment.

The Jews somehow seemed to lose the will to rise above the torpor that progressively paralysed a society that had lost confidence in its own worth. Eastern Sephardim shared in the decline of the Islamic world just as they had previously shared in its success; but they did even worse.

The condition of the Jews of the Ottoman Empire deteriorated steadily until its lowest point was reached in the first half of the nineteenth century, when their degradation was movingly described in many accounts written by European travellers to the Near East.

A very important factor in the improvement of the Jewish condition was the establishment in 1860 in Paris of the Alliance Israélite Universelle. The Alliance created a network of European-type Jewish schools throughout the Near East. It was those schools that enabled Jews to acquire the rudiments of a secular education for the first time, as well as some knowledge of French and English. Once again they were able to start competing with their Christian rivals; and for the first time they began to look to the West, not just with nostalgia but as the key to survival and worldly success.

Despite its splendid work, the Alliance was criticised in some religious quarters for alienating its pupils from their Jewish roots. In its enthusiasm for all things French and European, for the new world ahead, it was accused of failing to foster appreciation for the old, of tending to diminish respect for religion and of opening a gulf between secularly educated children and their more pious parents.

The Alliance schools certainly were very different from the traditional religious schools of the poverty-stricken Jewish areas of North Africa and Middle East. But it must be said that , as well as secular subjects, the study of Judaism and Jewish history always constituted an important part of the curriculum, both at local level and at the college for teachers established in Paris.

However part of the inevitable price paid for the Alliance's tremendous achievement in liberating so many Ottoman Jews from obscurity and poverty was that some of its graduates became vulnerable to assimilationist pressure when removed from their closely-knit communities.

A similar dilemma was faced by Shneur Zalman of Lyady, founder of the Lubavich Movement (Habad), when asked to support Napoleon's invasion of Russia in 1812. Zalman accepted that the French would bring emancipation and great material improvement to the oppressed and poverty-stricken Jews of Russia; but for the sake of religion, he opposed emancipation for the Jews and brought all his influence to bear in favour of the Czar and against Napoleon.

Not only did the Alliance schools help to bring the long isolated Sephardim of the Near East back within sight of the mainstream of European life, but its European-trained teachers and inspectors ensured that Jews could no longer be oppressed by local Turkish governors in secret. From the date of the Alliance's foundation in 1860, the full glare of international publicity was brought to bear on cases of wrong-doing, with beneficial result.

By that time, the Islamic world had started to open embassies in the capitals of Europe; and through those embassies, pressure by prominent European Jews and Christians could more easily be brought to bear on the Turkish authorities to counter anti-Jewish excesses.

It was therefore through secular European-style education and increasing contact with merchants from Europe – for whom Jews often acted as agents – that Sephardim of the Ottoman Empire began to trade and travel to the West. Some few of the leading families were helped by acquiring European nationality, but by no means all. The more energetic started moving to countries such as British India and cosmopolitan Egypt, where European influence was strong. Others migrated directly to Western Europe and to North, Central and South America.

Only a proportion of the Jews of the Ottoman Empire was exposed to the European influence of the Alliance school; and even then, most parents were not able to afford to keep their children there for more than three or four years of education. A small minority only of the children was able to proceed from the Alliance to higher French or other European schools, or else was educated wholly in foreign (usually Christian) schools.

The remainder, trained only in traditional religious schools (Talmud Torah), emerged with little secular knowledge and no command at all of French or of English. Unfortunately they were very ill-equipped to face the great migrations to which they were subjected after the collapse of the Ottoman Empire and the later thrust of modern Arab nationalism. On the positive side though, it must be said that however poor and however ignorant in a secular sense they may have been, they were mostly people of genuine piety untinged with fanaticism – modest folk, God-fearing and with a high standard of morality. Their like may not be seen again.

In the middle decades of the twentieth century the earlier emigrants were followed to Europe, to Israel and to the Americas by the remainder of their brethren, fleeing from the rising tide of Arab nationalism which culminated in the total destruction of their ancient communities. There are now very few Jews left in the Arab world; and the story of their subsequent wanderings will be told later.

Unfortunately those Sephardi Jews who remained in the European part of the former Ottoman Empire – mainly Salonika (Greece), Rhodes and the Balkans -fared far worse. They suffered horribly in

Hitler's Holocaust during the Second World War of 1939-45. They were not allowed to emigrate; and their communities were destroyed by deportation and mass-murder on a scale that even surpassed that endured by their ancestors in Spain and Portugal. It is a tragic story.

MATERIAL FOR LESSONS 23

MAPS

The Ottoman Empire at its peak.

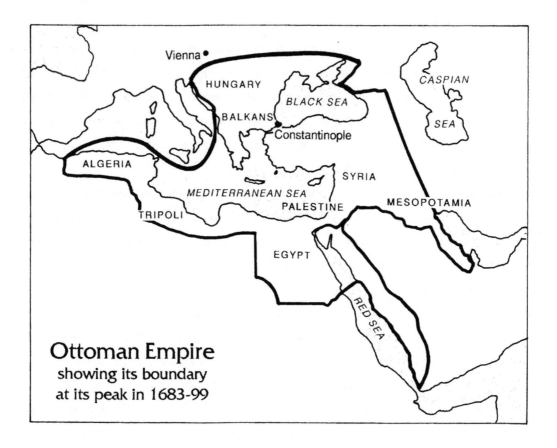

Ottoman Empire
showing its boundary
at its peak in 1683-99

The Sephardi Communities of the Exile

This lesson is reserved for a survey of those ancient communities of the Sephardi diaspora of most interest to the pupils. The teacher should balance the family origins of the children in each particular class with variety and interest when deciding on which to choose.

Baghdad and the Ottoman Empire were covered in general terms in earlier lesson packs. Amsterdam and London will follow in later lesson packs.

For information on other communities the teacher should refer to 'The Sephardim' by Gubbay and Levy, available from the Headmaster and also in the library of the Sephardi Centre.

Communities described in the book include:

Baghdad, Aleppo, Damascus, Calcutta, Bukhara, Meshed (Iran), Afghanistan, Egypt, Istanbul, Salonica, Rhodes, the Balkans, Algeria, Tunisia, Libya, Morocco, France, Gibraltar, Italy and other Sephardi communities in London today.

The book contains many pictures and maps to supplement its text and these should be photocopied for distribution as appropriate.

The Headmaster also has several interesting videos available on individual communities, including one on Djerba (Tunisia) which could be used with any lesson on a North African community and a video on the Baghdad community in the Middle Ages.

Poland & Lithuania

THE BEGINNING

Eastern Europe, remote and beyond the edge of the settled world, had not been influenced by the civilisations of Rome or Islam. It remained outside the mainstream of European culture until the 13th century. The land itself was covered by dense forests; and its few settled inhabitants were constantly harried by the incursions of wild tribesmen from the steppes of Central Asia.

It was only in the thirteenth century that the forests were cut down and a centralised system of law and order established by the (Roman Catholic) Polish kings. Large tracts of newly cleared but empty land in the east were then distributed to the Polish nobility and the Church.

Just as in the American West, many centuries later, there was then a great need for pioneers to settle the land and consolidate the rapidly expanding Polish kingdom.

SETTLEMENT OF THE EMPTY LAND

The kings of Poland therefore did all in their power to encourage settlers from central Europe and elsewhere to come and populate their empty country.

In 1264 and again in 1344, Polish kings issued charters of protection to the new settlers. Jews in particular were offered specific guarantees of safety and religious freedom as well as royal protection from the kind of persecution they had endured in Europe.

Jews then flocked to Poland in large numbers to find refuge from the ever-increasing massacres and expulsions to which they had been subjected in the rest of Europe. Poland was then a backward, under-populated country to which the Jews brought education, skills, trade, knowledge of languages and a network of connections abroad.

German merchants also came to Poland in considerable numbers. They settled mostly in the towns, to which they brought strong German cultural influence as well as the anti-semitism that would later result in increasing conflict with the Jews.

Poland merged with Lithuania; and the combined kingdom expanded steadily until it became the largest state in Europe. With the inclusion of the Ukraine, its territory extended from the Baltic Sea in the north to the Black Sea in the south.

THE MEDIAEVAL JEWISH COMMUNITY

The Jew, as elsewhere in feudal Europe, belonged to the king and enjoyed his direct protection. The Polish kings found the Jews, with their economic strength, a very useful ally in their constant struggle for power over the nobility and the Church.

The Jews were treated as a separate group and allowed to develop their own way of life, language, culture and even dress, which isolated them from their Christian fellow countrymen. The Polish rulers, with the sanction of the Church, encouraged such separation and granted the Jewish community extensive autonomy and local self-government. In 1564 the Jews were given their own parliament known as the Council of Four Lands, with sway over all Jewish affairs.

This cultural, physical and economic separation of the Jews from the rest of society had a unifying effect on the Jews themselves; and they developed a distinctive culture, based on the Ashkenazi rites, liturgy and customs brought with them from the west.

An essential element of this culture was the development of the Yiddish language, which produced a rich literature in the nineteenth and early twentieth centuries. Yiddish, which had originally evolved among the Jews of Germany, spread rapidly to become the common tongue of all Jews in eastern Europe.

In the early days of the settlement, Jews were granted royal monopolies for highly lucrative operations such as the running of the Royal Mint, the salt mines, customs offices and the collection of taxes. For example, most Polish coins of the 13th century were issued with Hebrew inscriptions. In later years, the Polish nobility struggled hard to prohibit these Jewish monopolies and, in the end, largely succeeded.

The Polish nobles themselves used Jews as their agents and entrusted them with the administration of their own economic affairs. Those favoured Jews would then deal exclusively with the peasants on a nobleman's vast estates, collecting and marketing agricultural products, running breweries and taverns, and collecting the rents and taxes

Prosperity caused the Jewish population of the Poland to increase dramatically. It is estimated that the 30,000 Jews in Poland and Lithuania in 1490 had become over 300,000 by the middle of the 17th century.

In the 1640s Nathan of Hanover wrote of Polish Jewry

> *In no country is the study of the Torah so widespread as amongst the Jews of the Kingdom of Poland. Every Jewish community maintains a yeshiva, paying its principal a large salary, to enable him to run the college without worry and to devote himself entirely to the pursuit of learning. Every Jewish community supports college students with a regular weekly grant of money. Each student has to instruct at least two other boys for the purpose of deepening his own studies and gaining experience in Talmudic dis¬cussion. The poor boys are fed in the public kitchen or by use of a special charitable fund.*

DISASTER

Some anti-Jewish outbreaks had occurred as early as the 15th century, caused mostly by the commercial rivalry of German burghers who had also settled in the towns. This was at a time when the rising power of the nobles and their allies in the Church had begun to encroach on the authority of the king and his ability to protect his Jewish subjects. But on the whole, the Jews continued to thrive.

The Jewish Golden Age in Poland came to an end in 1648 when the (Greek Orthodox) Cossacks of the Ukraine revolted against their (Roman Catholic) Polish overlords. The Jews, who served as the agents of the Polish nobles, and were therefore identified with them, bore the brunt of the terrible massacres that accompanied the uprising.

Many Jewish communities and centres of learning were totally destroyed during the Cossack advance and the death toll was truly appalling. The once prosperous and powerful Jewish Community of Poland was brought to its knees and never fully recovered.

The Polish Commonwealth itself gradually disintegrated over the next century or so. This was accompanied by a collapse of law and order, with the king losing his power to protect the Jews. All this exposed the Jews to further attacks by disgruntled peasants and others.

The Council of Four Lands was abolished in 1764; and not very long after that, Poland was partitioned between its more powerful neighbours – Russia, Austria and Prussia. It then ceased to exist as an independent state.

The Jewish population, by this time totalling some one and a half million, was thus divided between the three conquering states, with the majority in Russia.

RELIGIOUS CONSEQUENCES OF THE COLLAPSE

The internal life of Jewish communities deteriorated as the result of destruction and continuing privations. Economic hardships exacerbated the divisions between the rich and the poor. Institutions of self-government lost control and corruption became endemic.

Learning had always been a major part of religious life; but due to the continuing chaos, the yeshivot of the southern Poland and the Ukraine had not been re-established after their destruction by the Cossacks. The rabbis of Lithuania and northern Poland, which had escaped much of the destruction, formed an intellectual elite that despised the unlearned Jews of the south.

For most Jews of the south, learning was out of reach; and their communal institutions had failed them. They lacked all leadership at a time when it was particularly needed.

It was then that a powerful spiritual figure appeared in south-east Poland. Israel ben Eliezer (1700-1760), the Ba'al Shem Tov (known as the Besht) started life as a faith healer with little formal Jewish education.

He left very little in writing but his ideas were passed on by his disciples through simple folk-tales, parables and homilies. He preached a new doctrine to the depressed Polish Jews, which later became known as Hasidism. This was a message of hope and joy rather than of suffering and learning. God could be reached by devotion, by simple prayers and even by singing and dancing; it was not necessary to study to be a good Jew. This last claim was, of course, anathema to most rabbis and scholars of the time.

The followers of the Besht also created a new type of Jewish religious leader called the Zaddik (the Righteous) who, according to Hasidic thought, was close to God and served as a mediator between God and the believer.

It was the Zaddik's responsibility to mix with the common people in order to lift them up to his own exalted spiritual level. In return, they were expected to obey him in both spiritual and temporal matters and to support him financially. The Hasidim believed that the Zaddik's powers could be inherited by his sons or even by his sons-in-law; and dynasties of Zaddikim were formed, many of which have survived to the present day.

FURTHER HISTORY

The further turbulent history of the Jews of Eastern Europe and the eventual emigration of many of them to the United States of America and to countries in Western Europe is another large topic which is covered elswhere.

MATERIAL FOR CHAPTER 25

MAP

The Jews of Poland and Lithuania

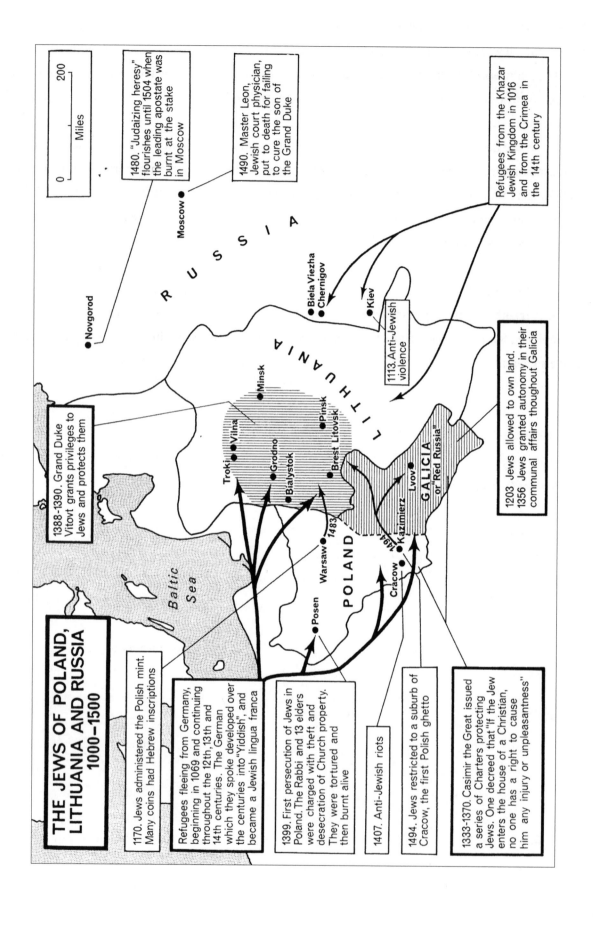

THE JEWS OF POLAND,
LITHUANIA AND RUSSIA
1000–1500

0   200
Miles

1480. "Judaizing heresy" flourishes until 1504 when the leading apostate was burnt at the stake in Moscow

1490. Master Leon, Jewish court physician, put to death for failing to cure the son of the Grand Duke

Refugees from the Khazar Jewish Kingdom in 1016 and from the Crimea in the 14th century

1388-1390. Grand Duke Vitovt grants privileges to Jews and protects them

1113. Anti-Jewish violence

1203 Jews allowed to own land. 1356 Jews granted autonomy in their communal affairs thoughout Galicia

1170. Jews administered the Polish mint. Many coins had Hebrew inscriptions

Refugees fleeing from Germany, beginning in 1069 and continuing throughout the 12th,13th and 14th centuries. The German which they spoke developed over the centuries into "Yiddish", and became a Jewish lingua franca

1399. First persecution of Jews in Poland. The Rabbi and 13 elders were charged with theft and desecration of Church property. They were tortured and then burnt alive

1407. Anti-Jewish riots

1494. Jews restricted to a suburb of Cracow, the first Polish ghetto

1333-1370. Casimir the Great issued a series of Charters protecting Jews. One decreed that "If the Jew enters the house of a Christian, no one has a right to cause him any injury or unpleasantness"

RUSSIA

LITHUANIA

POLAND

GALICIA or "Red Russia"

Baltic Sea

Novgorod

Moscow

Biela Viezha
Chernigov

Kiev

Minsk

Troki
Vilna
Grodno
Bialystok
Pinsk
Brest Litovsk

Posen

Warsaw
1483

1494

Cracow
Kazimierz

Lvov

The European Enlightenment

The story of how the Jews gained equal civil and political rights in central and western Europe, is not a simple one.

It happened in the eighteenth and nineteenth centuries as a direct result of the European Enlightenment, which transformed all aspects of European thought and resulted in the formation of entirely new social structures and political institutions.

The movement we call the Enlightenment started in the middle of the seventeenth century in a Europe weary of religious war. Europe then had just emerged from over a century of warfare between Catholics and Protestants that had brought unprecedented destruction in its wake. In central Europe, for example, the devastation was so great that on the site of previously important towns travellers reported that they could find only wolves. Fanatical religious conflict arising from the Reformation (when the monolithic Catholic Church split into Catholic and Protestant sections) had led to hatred, destruction and widespread ruin.

The Enlightenment marked a turning point in European culture by overturning the paralysing grip of the medieval Church on the thoughts of the people of Europe and inspiring a new confidence in the ability of human beings to understand and control the world for themselves.

The middle of the seventeenth century was a time of paradox. It was still an age of faith, with absolute belief in God ingrained in the pattern of everyday life to an extent hard to picture today. In contrast, it was also a time of unprecedented scientific discovery. Leading minds for the first time cast off the restrictive shackles imposed on them by the Church, and revelled in their newly found freedom to explore the nature of the physical world.

Galileo invented the telescope and used it to demonstrate that the sun rather than the earth is at the centre of the universe. Isaac Newton dealt decisively with the orbits of the earth and planets around the sun, and also formulated his law of universal gravitation.

The world was no longer to be explained in terms of Church dogma and accepted as an act of faith; but was suddenly seen to be a marvellously ordered structure of its own, obedient to laws which could be learnt by the application of logical thought to physical observation.

The Enlightenment promised a new era in which human beings would understand the world and themselves by means of their own reason. This is not to say that the Enlightenment was incompatible with religious belief. What the Enlightenment aimed at was a religion in accord with reason, one that had been purged of superstition, falsehood and legend.

This new confidence in human reason altered the balance of European culture by elevating science and philosophy at the expense of religion.

The leading thinkers of the time proposed to replace religious strife with toleration based on compromise. They suggested the idea of a 'natural religion'. All those who subscribed to three key ideas (the existence of God, the immortality of the soul and the principle of divine reward and punishment) would be acceptable to society.

Enlightenment thinkers also offered a similar notion in the realm of politics. The idea of 'natural law' suggested that people should be governed by laws to be formulated by reason. Such laws defined an individual's rights and duties, obligations and privileges, irrespective of religion or belief.

THE PLACE OF THE JEWS IN NORTHERN EUROPE

Jews in Europe had been subjected to special laws and restrictions since the time of the Roman Empire. There had been no Jews (officially at least) in England and France since the medieval expulsions. Central Europe had witnessed a wave of expulsions in the Reformation and post-Reformation period so great that it had virtually emptied the German states of Jews.

The seventeenth century brought a resettlement of Jews in central and western Europe. During the Thirty Years War (1618-1648) Jews found their way back into many German territories under the protection of invading armies. After the end of the war, they were often invited back by princes wanting to rebuild their states and their economies.

In Christian Europe Jews were outside society, unable to reside or work at will and denied most basic human rights. They were considered a degraded and useless people, undesirable outlaws speaking a foreign language. Jews were forced to live in segregated ghettos. Although physical attacks on them had more or less ceased, their day-to-day existence continued to be subjected to stringent limitations on residence, occupation and demographic expansion.

A good example of such restrictions is the edict issued by Frederick the Great of Prussia in 1750 concerning the Jews of Berlin:

> *We, Frederick, by God's grace, King of Prussia ... establish that no other Jews are to be tolerated except those named in the lists that are attached to the end of these regulations.*

> *A distinction is to be made between Regular Protected Jews and Special Protected Jews who are merely tolerated in their lifetimes.*

> *Foreign [non-Prussian] Jews are not allowed to settle in our land at all. However, if one should really have a fortune of ten thousand Reichstaler, and bring the same into the country and furnish authentic evidence of the fact, then we are to be asked about this and concerning the fee he is to pay.*

In order that in the future all fraud, cheating and secret and forbidden increase of the number of families may be more carefully avoided, no Jew shall be allowed to marry, nor will he receive permission to settle, in any manner, nor will he be believed, until a careful investigation has been made by the War and Domains Office together with the aid of the Treasury.

Male and female servants and other domestics, however, are not allowed to marry. Should they attempt to do this they are not to be tolerated any longer.

No Protected Jew can stay away from home for more than a year without authorization; otherwise his place will be given to another.

The Jews must not pursue any manual trade . Particularly are they enjoined not to brew beer nor to distil spirits. However, they are allowed to undertake the distilling of spirits for the nobility, government officials, etc.

The Jews must watch one another and pay attention carefully when they find any of their people on the wrong road and immediately report such a person to the proper authorities.'

Among Ashkenazi Jews the one exception to the pattern of oppression was the Court Jew. Many rulers in central Europe found themselves in need of money to pay for their armies and to finance their ever more extravagant lifestyles. To raise the necessary money, a rich Jew was often attached to the court as finance minister (*Hofjude*). Such individuals were allowed to live at court and were permitted to employ a limited number of fellow Jews from the ghetto. At the time, most of these states had no educated middle class and the land-owning aristocracy, who despised trade and commerce, had little alternative but to rely on Jews for financial expertise.

The other exceptions were the Sephardi Jews of Livorno (Italy), Amsterdam, South-West France, London and a few other places. They, being more assimilated to the prevailing culture, lived in relative dignity and freedom, in striking contrast to the lot of their unfortunate Ashkenazi brethren.

JEWISH EMANCIPATION

It was in pre-revolution France at the end of the 18th century that the new ideas generated by the Enlightenment were first applied to Jews. For the first time French thinkers questioned whether the Jews were to be included in the grand scheme of toleration? Were Jews capable of discovering reason and following its light? Could they be regenerated into useful citizens; and were they wanted in society?

After the French Revolution of 1789 the armies of Napoleon swept over Europe, literally knocking down the walls of the ghettos and liberating Jews everywhere. Napoleon, however exacted a stiff price for emancipation. The Jews were no longer to be a separate community governing its own internal affairs. Jews would become ordinary citizens, subject to all the laws of the state without exception, their only difference being that they professed the Jewish religion. In France itself the rabbis became state functionaries under state supervision and their salaries were paid by the state.

However the path to emancipation was not an easy one, even in France, but a very slow and painful process driven by the great upheavals of political revolution and the restructuring of states.

This was because of the deeply held conviction that Jews were inferior because of their relationship to commerce and money. The Enlightenment simply converted the Christian conception of the Jews' religious inferiority into the secular doctrine of moral inferiority. Jews were thought to be incapable of subscribing to natural religion or complying with natural law because of their ritualistic religion, national character or economic situation. Enlightenment thinkers almost all shared this image of Jewish inferiority.

It took a long time for the final barriers to Jewish emancipation to collapse. Relevant dates are as follows:

France 1790	Holland 1796	Belgium 1830
Italy 1848-1870	Prussia 1850	Denmark 1851
Sweden 1865	Austria-Hungary 1867	Great Britain 1870
Germany 1871	Switzerland 1874	Portugal 1910
Russia 1917		

JEWISH ENLIGHTENMENT –THE HASKALAH

Ashkenazi Jews responded to the general stimulus of the Enlightenment by a movement of their own, the Haskalah, intended to enable them to leave the close confines of the ghetto, shed their educational and cultural inferiority and take their place in society. The Haskalah, maintained that there were good reasons for the Jews to regenerate themselves in order to qualify for emancipation: the old Jewish life had decayed beyond repair. European Sephardim, with their quite different lifestyles, were not in need of regeneration and took no part in the Haskalah.

Even the great Rabbi Judah Loew of Prague had felt that Jewish education, with its narrow concentration on the Talmud, stood in need of reform and suggested also including the Bible and Mishnah. Other rabbis later echoed his complaints and suggestions. Many of the more sensitive members of the rabbinical and intellectual elite thought it a disgrace that Jews were less well educated than their Christian, neighbours and thus less well prepared to defend their faith.

This sense of dissatisfaction was encouraged by the model of Sephardi education in places such as Amsterdam, Livorno and Bordeaux, where secular subjects, including mathematics, geography and languages, were studied regularly alongside Jewish ones which included the Bible and the Hebrew language.

Moses Mendelssohn, who demonstrated by his achievements that a Jew could be a paragon of the

Enlightenment in all respects, became the outstanding symbol of the Haskalah. Although he was but one representative of the revival of Jewish culture in the eighteenth century, his life was a beacon for the Jews of Europe in their struggle for emancipation.

In the course of the eighteenth century, some 470 Jewish students were admitted to the various German universities, especially in the medical faculty. Most of them, taught by private tutors, came from wealthy urban families (Court Jews) from Berlin and elsewhere. There were also some poor students who were self-taught.

Mendelssohn did not emerge straight from ghetto Judaism to European culture and society in the way that is often imagined. He was simply the leading representative of the eighteenth century renaissance of Jewish culture.

Born in 1729 in Dessau (now Germany), a community founded in the 1680s by a Court Jew, Mendelssohn received the standard Talmudic education of his time. Yet even before his bar mitzvah, he had begun to lay the foundation of his later interests – aesthetics, literature and metaphysics through a study of the Bible, Hebrew grammar and the medieval Jewish philosopher Maimonides. In Berlin he continued to study Talmud, but also joined a circle of young Jews who, whilst educating themselves in Jewish and general culture, helped him to learn classical and modern languages and to continue his philosophical studies.

Mendelssohn was not exceptional in studying philosophy and believing in Enlightenment ideals. What singled him out was that he became one of the most important philosophers and noted personalities of the German Enlightenment while remaining a practising Jew.

His numerous works included the 'Treatise on Evidence in Metaphysical Sciences', which won him first prize in the Prussian Royal Academy of Science competition of 1763. Mendelssohn consequently became a Berlin landmark – a German and Jewish Socrates, whose wit, charm and intelligence became well known in Europe.

While Mendelssohn gained a European reputation with his German works, he also wrote in Hebrew and joined in the attempt to revive the Hebrew language. His best known work for a Jewish audience was his translation of Five Books of Moses into German, printed in Hebrew letters and with a Hebrew commentary that drew on the medieval rationalist tradition. Mendelssohn called his translation a 'first step toward culture'. He did not aim to persuade Jews to abandon Judaism, but rather to foster a renaissance of Jewish culture based on the Hebrew language and Bible. And in their revival of the Hebrew language and culture, their readiness to acquire secular education and skills, and their redefinition of Judaism (embodied in Mendelssohn's *Jerusalem*), the new Jewish intelligentsia willingly accepted the necessity of internal regeneration as the price for their eventual emancipation.

It is of interest to compare the Ashkenazim of Europe, struggling to emerge from their ghettos into the light of European civilisation, with their more fortunate Sephardi brethren; and to note that Haham Nieto of the Spanish and Portuguese Synagogue of London, a truly rounded and versatile man of the Renaissance in his secular and religious learning, died one year before the birth of Moses Mendelssohn.

Amsterdam

The movement of small groups of Portuguese New Christians, first to Antwerp and then on to the trading centres of Northern Germany, was described in an earlier lesson. Driven by fear of the Inquisition, many simply sought new and more tranquil lives for themselves and their children. Others yearned to return openly to the faith of their fathers, even if by then they could remember few of its practices.

It was in December 1601 that a group of ten adults and four boys from Portugal landed at the port of Emden in Germany. There they were befriended by Uriel Ha-Levy, an Ashkenazi rabbi, who sent them on to Amsterdam. Uriel and his family followed the refugees and rented a house in Joncker Street. The Marranos were circumcised by Uriel's son – among the nine hundred and thirty one circumcisions he performed during his lifetime – and taught the fundamentals of Judaism.

The tiny community had to behave with care, for its legal position was highly ambiguous. Though the arrival of the Jews seems to have been cautiously welcomed by the civic authorities, who hoped they would bring benefit to the city, the admission of openly professing Jews was strongly opposed by the Elders of the Dutch Reformed Church. Protestant Holland had just gained its independence from Catholic Spain and guaranteed freedom of conscience in its territory; and so protection of the lives and property of the Jews was assured. But they were not recognised as full citizens and could not work in any trade organised into a Christian guild.

The crisis came in 1603, during the course of the second Kal Nidre service ever to be held in Amsterdam. The house in Joncker Street was raided and Rabbi Uriel arrested. The record of his interrogations before the magistrates contains details of his claim to have served as Rabbi of Emden for about thirty years before coming to Amsterdam 'with the knowledge and consent of the Burgomasters'. Uriel briefed the magistrates on many details of Jewish observance and admitted that he had conducted Jewish religious services in his house as well as serving as shochet (ritual slaughterer) on a weekly basis.

More Marranos arrived; and by 1614 the community numbered over two hundred, divided into three separate congregations. Samuel Palache, who as a Moroccan ambassador to the Netherlands was able to live openly as a practising Jew, did much to help the newcomers settle in the city. That same year, land for a cemetery was bought at Ouderkerk and the community's first proper synagogue was opened with the knowledge and probably with the permission of the Burgomasters.

The Protestant Church did not easily give up its opposition to what it regarded as the scandal of open Jewish worship. Only four years before, complaints from its Elders had resulted in the temporary closure of the largest of the three Jewish houses of prayer. In 1620, Jewish acquisition of land adjacent to the synagogue for the building of classrooms prompted an anguished appeal by the Elders to the

Burgomasters of Amsterdam, complaining that the Jews were once more openly exercising their rites contrary to the ban issued by their worships the Burgomasters – but again to no avail, for the Burgomasters failed to respond and continued to extend their protection to the Jews.

By 1630 the community had grown to one thousand strong. The community's final seal of approval came in 1642 when no lesser person than Prince Frederick Henry of Orange visited the synagogue with his son, his son's new bride and her mother – Queen Henrietta Maria of England (wife of King Charles I) – and listened to an address of welcome delivered by Rabbi Menasseh ben Israel. That was the first of many marks of favour by members of the House of Orange and of a responding loyalty by the Portuguese Jews which has lasted to this day.

The splendid Portuguese Synagogue, which still stands proudly in Amsterdam, was opened in 1675. Its architecture was copied in the Marrano diaspora in places as far apart as London and Curaçao. Its laws and network of charitable institutions were also widely imitated, as was its system of 'imposta' whereby its members paid a special income tax or 'finta' to support the community.

The Portuguese Jews of Amsterdam were governed by the 'Mahamad', a standing committee of seven wardens. The Mahamad had sweeping powers over the lives of the members. Its decisions were binding on all; and no verbal or written opposition was tolerated. No Sephardi Jew could, for example, take another Jew to court without the Mahamad's permission; nor could he print a book without prior approval.

How many of the Amsterdam customs are used in this Congregation today?

Bevis Marks architecture. Synagogue music and minhag. Mahamad rule –
though no longer so sweeping. finta (income tax) ? as a fee for membership.
Many of our rules and charitable institutions.

The educational system established by the Portuguese Jews was the envy of the entire Jewish world as illustrated by the following extract from the report of an Ashkenazi who visited the city in the 1670's:

Since my arrival at the Amsterdam Community I have on several occasions visited the schools of the Sephardi Community (may their Rock preserve them) and there I saw many young children small as grasshoppers yet in my eyes as big as giants because of their great erudition in Bible, grammar, verse and poetry composition as well as in their clear spoken Hebrew. Happy are the eyes that beheld all this ...

Amsterdam with its rabbis, scholars, physicians, poets and philosophers, was the intellectual centre of the Marrano diaspora. Rabbi Menasseh ben Israel established the city's first Hebrew printing press in 1637, and was soon followed by others eager to serve the community's thinkers and men of letters.

Amsterdam became the principal staging post in the West for New Christian fleeing from the Iberian Peninsula. They underwent the rite of circumcision and studied the fundamentals of Judaism in the city before passing on to other destinations.

Where else in Western Europe were Jews able to worship openly and freely at that time?
Only in Livorno [Italy], Venice and for short periods in one or two other Italian city-states

The material conditions of Amsterdam's Sephardi community fluctuated in sympathy with that of its host city. The first century of settlement, during which the Portuguese Jewish population rose to about three thousand (in 1743), was one of tremendous expansion. Dutch merchants travelled the world – from Europe to Africa, India, the East Indies, the West Indies, Brazil and South America – bringing great prosperity to their native land.

The Sephardim, with their close network of secret family connections among the New Christians of Portugal and Spain, Italy, France and the New World, participated to the full in the opportunities provided. A few became very wealthy indeed by trading in colonial commodities such as tobacco and diamonds. Others were increasingly drawn to the financial sphere, where they were able to provide what amounted to an international system of credit because of their widespread and trustworthy connections. Sephardim also became prominent on the stock exchange, owning some one-quarter of the East India Company's shares by the end of the seventeenth century. Others concentrated on home industries such as printing.

The decline of the Dutch share of world trade during the eighteenth century, and a series of economic disasters had their effect on Amsterdam's Jews. Most were reduced to poverty as were the majority of their fellow citizens. A trend towards assimilation among the upper class became established. Ironically, many descendants of former Marranos were converted to Christianity.

The size of the community, which had remained static during much of the eighteenth and nineteenth centuries, almost doubled during the first decades of the twentieth century. But it had declined again to fewer than four thousand by 1941.

Together with the city's very much larger Ashkenazi Jewish population, the Sephardim of Amsterdam were rounded up and deported to the Nazi extermination camps following the German invasion of Holland in 1941. Fewer than five hundred survived the war.

MATERIAL FOR LESSON 27

MAP

The Jewish Traders of Amsterdam

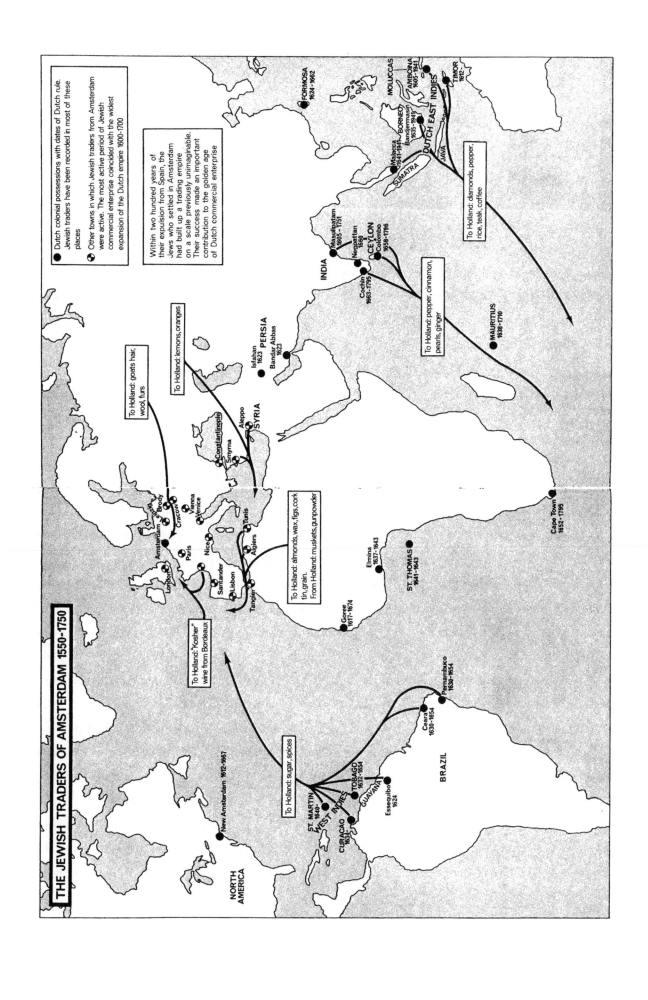

THE JEWISH TRADERS OF AMSTERDAM 1550-1750

● Dutch colonial possessions with dates of Dutch rule. Jewish traders have been recorded in most of these places

🌐 Other towns in which Jewish traders from Amsterdam were active. The most active period of Jewish commercial enterprise coincided with the widest expansion of the Dutch empire 1600-1700

Within two hundred years of their expulsion from Spain, the Jews who settled in Amsterdam had built up a trading empire on a scale previously unimaginable. Their success made an important contribution to the golden age of Dutch commercial enterprise

To Holland: diamonds, pepper, rice, teak, coffee

To Holland: pepper, cinnamon, pearls, ginger

To Holland: lemons, oranges

To Holland: goats hair, wool, furs

To Holland: almonds, wax, figs, cork tin, grain.
From Holland: muskets, gunpowder

To Holland: "Kosher" wine from Bordeaux

To Holland: sugar, spices

NORTH AMERICA

New Amsterdam 1612-1667

London
Amsterdam & Brody
Paris
Cracow
Vienna
Venice
Nice
Santander
Lisbon
Tangier
Algiers
Tunis
Constantinople
Smyrna
Aleppo
SYRIA
Isfahan 1623
Bandar Abbas 1623
PERSIA
INDIA
Masulipatam 1605-1751
Neapattan 1660
CEYLON
Colombo 1638-1796
Cochin 1663-1795
Goree 1617-1674
Elmina 1637-1643
ST. THOMAS 1641-1643
Cape Town 1652-1795
MAURITIUS 1638-1710

ST. MARTIN 1640-
WEST INDIES
CURACAO 1632-
TOBAGO 1632-1654
GUAYANA
Essequibo 1624
Ceara 1630-1654
Pernambuco 1630-1654
BRAZIL

FORMOSA 1624-1662
MOLUCCAS
AMBOINA 1605-1841
TIMOR 1612-
BORNEO
Bandermasin 1635-1841
Malacca 1641-1841
SUMATRA
JAVA
DUTCH EAST INDIES

England: Part One

Jews first arrived in England shortly after the Norman Conquest of 1066. They settled in many major cities, including London, York, Winchester, Lincoln, Canterbury and Oxford. They also lived in smaller towns; and a few families were even to be found in villages. Jealously prevented by guild and other Christian restrictions from following most occupations, the leaders of the community earned their living by money-lending – the pejorative term used to describe financial operations in which Jews were involved. In fact, the Jews provided England with its first banking system. Christians were not allowed to lend money for interest; and without interest there could be no banks. The Jews, therefore, proved invaluable to the king, the church, the nobility and ordinary townsmen and villagers.

> *Why are banks and other similar financial institutions so necessary to run a country?*
> *Could we manage without them?*

The major bankers had numerous family dependents and employed many other Jews in a variety of supporting roles, such as clerks, agents and servants.

Lower down the social scale, Jews worked as pawnbrokers, dealing also with the repair and sale of unredeemed pledges. English Jews certainly practised medicine openly as doctors; and there is evidence in Rabbinic Responsa to suggest that a few petty traders, selling goods from stalls in local markets, were also active. Apart from those occupations, it seems that the only others in which Jews were involved concerned the supply of essential services to their own communities – such as the provision of kasher food and wine.

Coming from Northern France, the community was wholly Ashkenazi in tradition. It contained several learned rabbis, who contributed to the Tosafot (Supplements to the Talmud and Rashi's Commentary on it). However, London cannot have been isolated from the Sephardi world, for Abraham ibn Ezra – the famous Spanish scholar, poet, Bible commentator, astronomer and physician – visited the city in 1158 and remained there for almost three years. Ibn Ezra, who wrote two of his works in London, described England as a 'land of darkness and gloom'; and it is supposed that he arrived during a fog.

All Jews were expelled from England in 1290 by order of King Edward I, after which none returned openly for the next four hundred and sixty five years. Several tiny communities of Marranos did come into being from the reign of Queen Elizabeth I onwards; but on discovery by the authorities, they were promptly broken up and their members deported.

England had been preparing for profound religious and social change ever since John Wycliffe first translated the Bible from Latin into English in the 1380s. The Catholic Church – and England was a Roman Catholic country then – had never encouraged lay men and women to read the Bible; and possession of an English translation of the Bible was a CRIMINAL offence in England until King Henry VIII quarrelled with the Pope in 1535, and set up his own Church of England. Henry then had the Bible translated into English and prominently displayed in every church in the land for all the read.

It would be hard to exaggerate the startling effect of the Bible's impact on the Protestants of the sixteenth and seventeenth centuries, or the revolutionary result of its message. The Bible replaced the Pope as the ultimate spiritual authority; and the Old Testament, embodying the Jewish foundation of Christianity, was favoured to counter the claims of Rome and its Church. Hebrew replaced Greek as the prime object of study. The Bible was read everywhere and its contents eagerly discussed as the people of England identified with ancient Israel and those who had struggled against tyranny. The course of ancient Jewish history became common day-to-day knowledge. Children were given the Hebrew names of Old Testament heroes in preference to those of Christian saints. The Lord's Day (Sunday) became a copy of the Jewish Sabbath. And above all, the biblical prophesies of redemption were believed in their every detail.

The Puritan revolution led directly to the Civil War of 1642-49, at the end of which King Charles I was tried and executed for high treason and the English Commonwealth was established. It was during that period of conflict with the Pope and with Roman Catholic powers in Europe – principally Spain – that public perception of the Jews softened and the ground was prepared for the eventual tolerance on English soil of Jewish refugees from Catholic Spain.

MATERIAL FOR LESSON 28: PART ONE

MAPS

The Jews of England

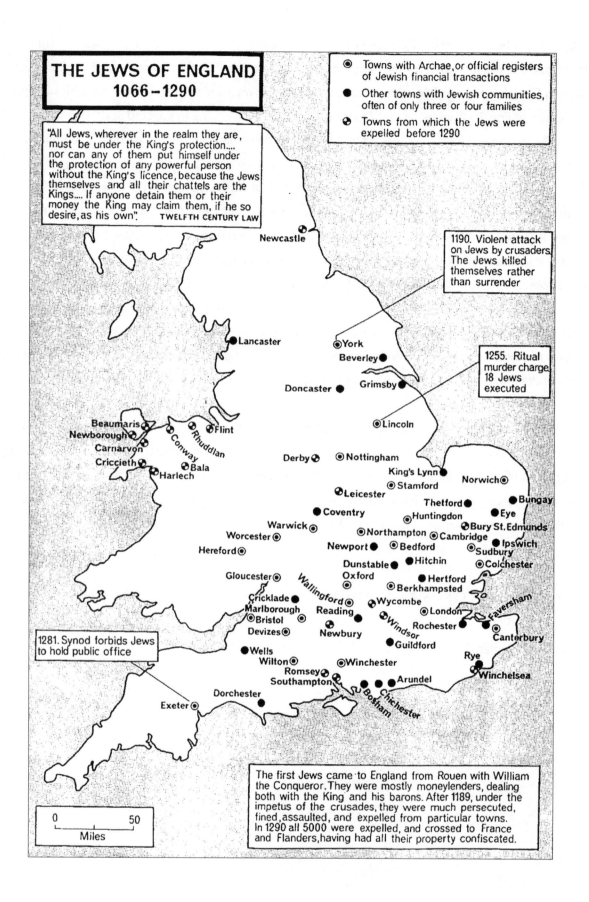

THE JEWS OF ENGLAND 1066–1290

◉ Towns with Archae, or official registers of Jewish financial transactions

● Other towns with Jewish communities, often of only three or four families

◔ Towns from which the Jews were expelled before 1290

"All Jews, wherever in the realm they are, must be under the King's protection.... nor can any of them put himself under the protection of any powerful person without the King's licence, because the Jews themselves and all their chattels are the Kings.... If anyone detain them or their money the King may claim them, if he so desire, as his own". TWELFTH CENTURY LAW

Newcastle ◔

1190. Violent attack on Jews by crusaders. The Jews killed themselves rather than surrender

Lancaster ●

York ◉
Beverley ●

1255. Ritual murder charge 18 Jews executed

Doncaster ● Grimsby ●

Lincoln ◉

Beaumaris ◔
Newborough ◔ ◔ Flint
Carnarvon ◔ ◔ Rhuddlan
Criccieth ◔ Conway
Bala ●
Harlech ●

Derby ◔ Nottingham ◉

King's Lynn ◉
Stamford ◉ Norwich ◉
Leicester ◔
Thetford ● Bungay ●
Coventry ● Eye ●
Huntingdon ◉ Bury St.Edmunds ◔
Warwick ◉ Northampton ◉ Cambridge ◉ Ipswich ●
Worcester ◉ Newport ● Bedford ◉ Sudbury ●
Hereford ◉ Dunstable ● Hitchin ● Colchester ◉
Gloucester ◉ Oxford ◉ Hertford ●
Wallingford ◉ Berkhampsted ◉
Cricklade ● Wycombe ◔ Faversham
Marlborough ● Reading ● London ◉
Bristol ◉ Windsor ◔ Rochester ●
Devizes ◉ Newbury ● Guildford ● Canterbury ◉
Wells ● Rye ◔
Wilton ◉ Winchester ◉
Romsey ◔ Arundel ● Winchelsea ◔
Southampton ◔
Dorchester ● Bosham Chichester
Exeter ◉

1281. Synod forbids Jews to hold public office

0   50
Miles

The first Jews came to England from Rouen with William the Conqueror. They were mostly moneylenders, dealing both with the King and his barons. After 1189, under the impetus of the crusades, they were much persecuted, fined, assaulted, and expelled from particular towns. In 1290 all 5000 were expelled, and crossed to France and Flanders, having had all their property confiscated.

England: Part Two

Jews and English Puritans held several important beliefs in common. They both venerated the Hebrew Bible, the Old Testament, accepting the literal truth of every detail of its prophesies. The Jews were urgently expecting their Messiah to lead them back to Jerusalem and inaugurate a New Age on earth; and the millennarian Puritans were awaiting with equal urgency the Second Coming of their Messiah, Christ, to establish his Kingdom of Saints on earth. Both groups accepted the prophesy that the Jews will be scattered to the ends of the earth, and the lost Ten Tribes will rejoin their brethren, before the return of the Jews to Zion heralds the advent of the Redeemer. The location of the Ten Tribes, the dispersion of the Jews to every known part of the world and their eventual return to Jerusalem, were thus of crucial interest to Puritan Christians as well as to Jews.

In 1644 Antonio de Montezimos, a Jewish traveller of Marrano stock, returned to Amsterdam from the New World. His story caused a sensation among the Jews of Amsterdam; and news of it soon spread to the Protestants, even coming to the ears of Oliver Cromwell in England. Antonio de Montezimos claimed to have stumbled across the lost tribe of Reuben in Colombia in South America, after a hazardous journey through jungles, across rivers and over mountain ranges. Though 'scorched by the sun', the tribesmen were bearded, spoke Hebrew, practised circumcision, and greeted him by reciting the ancient Jewish affirmation of faith, the 'Shema'.

Among those taken in by the plausible traveller was the celebrated Amsterdam rabbi, Menasseh ben Israel, a man respected by Jew and gentile alike for the breadth of his learning. Montezimos's discovery of Jews in America greatly excited Menasseh. It seemed to him that Jews were then living in every country of the world, save only for England. England suddenly become the key to the Redemption. Once the Jews were re-admitted to that country, from which they had been expelled in 1290, they would certainly be scattered to every part of the earth, thus fulfilling the prophesy and enabling the Messiah to come.

To devout Puritans the course was clear. Once Jews could be exposed to their own form of Christianity – so superior to the rank idolatry of the Roman Catholic version – their reservations would disappear, they would acknowledge Jesus as the Messiah and the Second Coming would take place. Though the ultimate motives were different, just for once Christian and Jewish ambitions converged.

Menasseh set to work with enthusiasm and high hope. He entered into correspondence with several prominent Englishmen, trying to persuade them to favour the prompt re-admission of the Jews to England.

Oliver Cromwell, who was the Chairman of the Council of State governing England, made no secret of his visionary hopes regarding the Second Coming of Jesus and the prophesies relating to the return of the Jews to their Promised Land. He also had in mind the advantages his country would derive in the way of foreign intelligence and trade from the presence in its midst of a grateful community of cultivated Jews, with links to Spain and Portugal as well as with brethren all over the world.

By this time, a small Marrano community had again established itself in London. Indeed two of them had already rendered valuable service as 'intelligencers'. In 1654 Cromwell recommended to the Council of State a petition from a gentleman of rank then living in London as an outward Spanish Catholic, but in reality a secret Jew, that the Jews be admitted to be dwellers here with the same equallness and conveniences which your inland subjects do enjoy – but the petition was rejected. The supplicant however was naturalised by Cromwell and enabled to hold private Jewish prayer meetings at his house in Bishopsgate in the City of London.

Why were Marranos so useful as 'intelligencers' – or spies?
see map: The Jewish Traders of Amsterdam

Cromwell urged Menasseh to come to England and plead his case in person. The rabbi arrived in London in 1655. He was accommodated in Whitehall, and entertained by Cromwell. He promptly petitioned the Lord Protector to admit the Jews to England on generous terms. The proposal caused a public outcry; and it soon became clear that centuries of prejudice could not easily be dispelled by newly acquired religious beliefs.

A special conference of judges, clergy and merchants was convened by the Council of State to decide the issue. The judges at once ruled that there was no legal impediment to the re-admission of the Jews; but the conference could not agree reasonable terms on which Jews might be permitted to reside in England. Cromwell intervened in person, speaking passionately in favour of Jewish settlement, and overcame many of the objections. In the end though, probably satisfied with the legal decision, he abruptly dismissed the conference without conclusion.

In March 1656 war broke out with Spain; and goods belonging to one of the Marranos, Antonio Rodrigues Robles, were seized as enemy property. Robles petitioned the Council of State for their restoration on the grounds that he was not a Spaniard, but a member of the Hebrew nation from Portugal, who had sought refuge in England. The Council restored Robles's property, thereby tacitly acknowledging that a Jew could live and trade in England.

In the same month, six heads of the most prominent of the twenty or so families of secret Jews then living in London as Catholics – regularly attending mass at the Spanish Embassy – cast off their disguise and openly joined Menasseh in a more modest attempt to regularise their position. In a 'Humble Petition of the Hebrews at present residing in the City of London' to the Lord Protector, they thanked him for 'the manifold favours and protection' he had afforded them by enabling them to meet safely for prayer in the private of their own homes. They asked for a written assurance that this freedom would continue, and for permission to open a cemetery in which their dead could be buried with Jewish rites.

That 'address' is in the Congregation's records. A copy hangs on the wall of the Print Room. See it for yourself.

Cromwell referred this Address to the Council of State, which apparently decided that no written assurance should be given. Instead, it seems that Cromwell met the petitioners personally and gave a verbal guarantee of security under which they might open a synagogue for public prayer, acquire land for a burial place, trade as brokers on the Exchange, and enlarge their community by bringing other Sephardi merchants of good standing to London.

Why was Menasseh ben Israel deeply disappointed by that compromise?

In 1657 the Jews opened their first synagogue in a converted house in Creechurch Lane in the City of London, to be replaced forty four years later by the elegant building in Bevis Marks which is still in use. They also bought a plot of land in Stepney for burials. Their precarious privileges survived the death of Cromwell and the overthrow of the Protectorate. They were confirmed by King Charles II in 1664, and by him again ten years later. Jewish resettlement in England had started, even if at first very cautiously and very slowly.

MATERIAL FOR LESSON 28: ENGLAND PART TWO

MAP

The Jewish Traders of Amsterdam

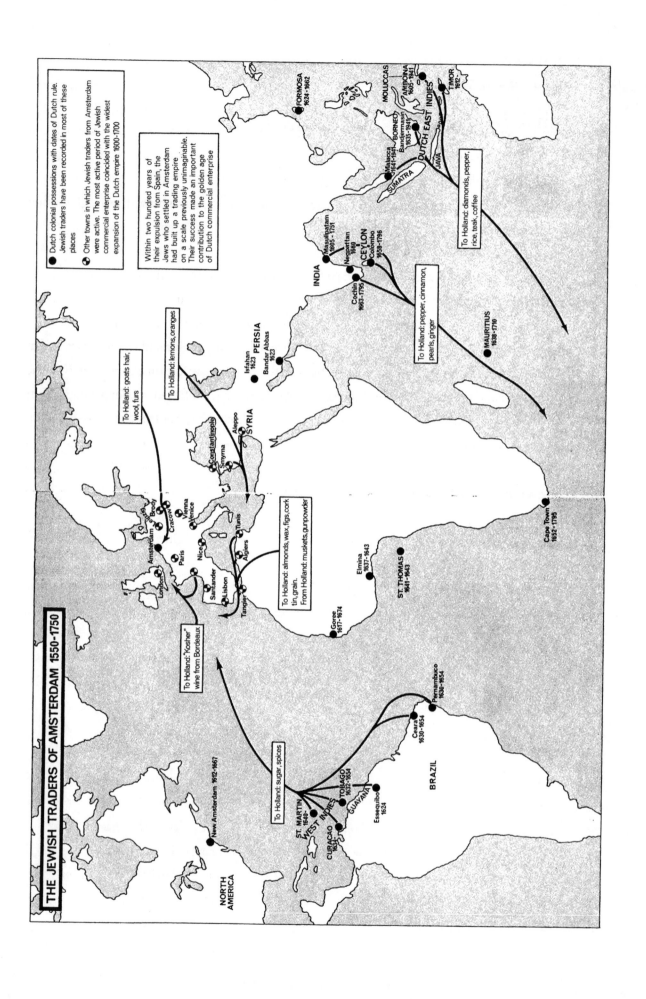

THE JEWISH TRADERS OF AMSTERDAM 1550-1750

● Dutch colonial possessions with dates of Dutch rule.
Jewish traders have been recorded in most of these
places

⊙ Other towns in which Jewish traders from Amsterdam
were active. The most active period of Jewish
commercial enterprise coincided with the widest
expansion of the Dutch empire 1600-1700

Within two hundred years of
their expulsion from Spain, the
Jews who settled in Amsterdam
had built up a trading empire
on a scale previously unimaginable.
Their success made an important
contribution to the golden age
of Dutch commercial enterprise

To Holland: diamonds, pepper,
rice, teak, coffee

To Holland: pepper, cinnamon,
pearls, ginger

To Holland: goats hair,
wool, furs

To Holland: lemons, oranges

To Holland: almonds, wax, figs, cork
tin, grain.
From Holland: muskets, gunpowder

To Holland: "Kosher"
wine from Bordeaux

To Holland: sugar, spices

FORMOSA
1624-1662

MOLUCCAS
AMBOINA 1605-1941
BORNEO Bandjermasin
1635-1941 1635-1941
Malacca 1641-1941
SUMATRA
JAVA
TIMOR 1612-
DUTCH EAST INDIES

Masulipatam 1605-1751
Negapattam 1660
CEYLON
Cochin Colombo 1658-1796
1663-1795
INDIA

MAURITIUS 1638-1710

Isfahan 1623 PERSIA
Bandar Abbas 1623

Aleppo
SYRIA
Constantinople
Smyrna

To Brody
Cracow
Vienna
Venice
Amsterdam
London
Paris
Nice Tunis
Algiers
Santander
Lisbon
Tangier

Goree
1617-1674

Elmina
1637-1643

ST. THOMAS
1641-1643

Cape Town
1652-1795

New Amsterdam 1612-1667

NORTH
AMERICA

ST. MARTIN
1640-
WEST INDIES
CURACAO
TOBAGO 1632-1654
GUAYANA
Essequibo 1624

Ceara
1630-1654
Pernambuco
1630-1654

BRAZIL

Spanish & Portuguese Jews of London

The founders of the Spanish and Portuguese Jews' Congregation of London, who had so boldly cast off their protective cloak of Christianity and openly declared themselves to be Jews – some having themselves circumcised at the age of seventy – had great courage. They and their immediate descendants were people of vision for, during the course of their first hundred years, they set up the structures necessary to maintain the integrity of the community in a still hostile environment and to assist its members to live in England as practising Jews.

The Congregation framed a series of laws to govern the conduct of its members and levied what amounted to an income tax on them. It then set about the building of institutions, some of which survive to this day. First to be established was the Burial Society. Next came the Dower Society to provide dowries to fatherless brides. This was followed by a Boy's School, a Girls' School and a Learned Society. A special charity assisted poor boys to obtain apprenticeships or otherwise start work. A Board of Guardians cared for the destitute. A hospital with a special ward for maternity cases was endowed; and a ward for the aged was added later.

Nor were suffering Jews overseas neglected. Money was raised to redeem Jewish captives from the slave markets of the Mediterranean ports and to assist the needy in the holy cities of Jerusalem, Tiberias, Safed and Hebron.

The former Marranos and their descendants also made a small but pleasing contribution to the life of their adopted country in other ways than business – mainly in medicine, letters and politics. A famous boxer, Daniel Mendoza, is also mentioned with pride in communal publications.

Benjamin Disraeli, the baptised son of a member of the Congregation, founded the Conservative Party and became Prime Minister of England. His father Isaac d'Israeli (1766-1848), a minor poet and literary critic, was chosen to be a Warden of the Congregation in 1813. But he declined to accept office and also refused to pay the fine of £40 which, according to the rules, was imposed in such cases. When the Synagogue attempted to enforce payment, d'Israeli resigned and had his children baptised as Christians. Jews were not allowed to become Members of Parliament until 1858; so had it not been for the quarrel, it is unlikely that Benjamin Disraeli would ever have become Prime Minister. Despite his conversion, he always took great pride in his origins and remained a well-wisher of the Jews. The Congregation still possesses the Register of Births in which Benjamin's name and the details of his circumcision are entered.

Moses Montefiore (1784-1885), whose family came from Leghorn (Livorno) in Italy, was without doubt the most famous son of the Congregation. Retiring from the stock exchange at the age of thirty-seven, he devoted the rest of his long life to helping poor and oppressed Jews at home and abroad. He was knighted by Queen Victoria in 1837 and created a baronet in 1846 – an unique honour for a practising Jew at that time. His charitable endeavours in England were on a large scale. But even more important, he established himself as the outstanding Jewish leader of his generation by his journeys to Palestine, Morocco, Rome, Turkey and Russia. Those journeys, some undertaken in old age and in very hazardous conditions, caused him to became a hero to countless Jews all over the world. He visited the Holy Land seven times, where he endowed hospitals and alms houses as well as devising schemes to encourage agriculture.

The journey that most captured the popular imagination was the one Sir Moses made in connection with the Damascus Affair. Jews were being savagely persecuted in Damascus in 1840 after the revival there of the mediaeval libel that Jews had used the blood of a Christian for the making of their Passover wine. Sir Moses, accompanied by the French-Jewish leader Adolphe CrÈmieux and with the support of Lord Palmerston, obtained a firman from the Sultan of Turkey. This cancelled the charges against the Jews of Damascus and guaranteed protection to all the Sultan's Jewish subjects.

A copy of this firman is mounted on the wall of the Montefiore Hall.
See it for yourself. See also the portraits of Sir Moses and his wife.

At first members of the Congregation described themselves as The Portuguese 'nation'. They spoke Portuguese amongst themselves: Hebrew and Spanish were the languages of prayer. The records of the Congregation continued to be kept in Portuguese or Spanish until well into the 19th century and it was only in 1819 that it was decided to write them in English and to use English for announcements in the Synagogue. The first sermon in English was preached in 1831.

Is Portuguese still used in our synagogue? Where?
in the announcements for the awarding of the "mizvot"

Were the Jews justified in describing themselves as a separate "nation" in England?
How many of their institutions survive today?

Synagogue and cemetery organisation, Board of Guardians (Welfare Board),
School (Sha'are Tikvah Classes and the Naima Jewish Preparatory School),
Hospital (Edinburgh House Old Peoples Home), many differ¬ent charities)

An intermittent stream of Marranos refugees continued to reach London until the Inquisitions of Spain and Portugal were abolished in the early years of the nineteenth century. Most of them were helped and absorbed by the London community; but others were sent on their way with small grants of money to settle in the British colonies of America and West Indies. Towards the end of the eighteenth century, the

Congregation was also enlarged by a wave of immigration from Italy, North Africa and Gibraltar.

From the start, the leaders of London's Jews were wealthy, educated and cultivated people who could associate with the best English society on more or less equal terms. They established themselves as shippers, brokers, financiers, bullion and gem merchants, army victuallers and commodity traders. Some even assisted in the starting of several of the City's financial institutions, including the Bank of England. But contrary to popular belief, the Sephardim were not all rich and educated. There were many humble craftsmen and artisans among them, as well as unskilled, unlettered poor.

The historic Spanish and Portuguese Jews' Congregation of London now has a membership of about seventeen hundred. Fewer than ten per cent of them still bear the Portuguese or Spanish names of the original Marrano settlers or of those who followed later, the large majority consisting of much more recent immigrants and their descendants.

How many of you have Spanish or Portuguese names?

Where do the rest of your families come from?
Are those communities newer or more ancient than that of London?

Which is the very oldest Jewish community of all?
Iraq

When did the Jews first come to Iraq?

How many ancient Jewish communities are represented in London?
Iraq, Iran, Egypt, Syria, Lebanon, Persia, Salonika, Istanbul, Tunisia, Morocco,
Italy, Amsterdam and many more.

The Congregation maintains three synagogues. The one in Bevis Marks, opened in 1701, has scarcely altered in appearance with the passing of time; but being far from the residential districts of London, it now attracts only small attendances. A recent project to expand its use to serve also as a religious and part-time educational centre for all Jews working in the City of London has made an encouraging start. The second synagogue, opened in Maida Vale in 1896, is the present focus of communal activity. The Congregation's third synagogue, in the suburb of Wembley, opened in 1977. It was originally intended to serve refugees from Egypt; but it soon attracted younger married members of the parent congregation who settled in the locality, as well as other Sephardim for the Middle East.

History of the Torah: Note for Teachers

NOTE FOR TEACHERS

This is a 'heavy' topic but also a very important one. It is suggested that it should be taken towards the end of the two-year history course.

Much will depend on the teacher to make the content interesting by means of anecdotes, quizzes and similar exercises.

THE HISTORICAL BACKGROUND

Most of this will already have been covered in the History section of the Junior Curriculum; but as very long periods of time are involved, some revision may be useful – for teacher too!

586 BCE	Jerusalem razed to the ground by King Nebuchadnezzar and most Jews deported to Babylon.
528-428 BCE	Some of the exiles return to rebuild Jerusalem and the Temple. Others stay behind in Babylon where they are well treated and prosper.
63 BCE	Roman armies conquer Judea, which was then incorporated into the Roman Empire. The community of exiles in Babylon continues to flourish under Persian rule.
70 BCE	The Temple was destroyed by the Romans as the result of a Jewish revolt against Roman rule. An academy (a yeshiva) was started in Yavneh.
132 CE	Another Jewish revolt against Roman rule, led by Bar Kochba and Rabbi Akiva, was savagely suppressed by the Romans.
200 CE	Rabbi Judah the Prince, for the first time, summarised and then wrote down the accumulated mass of oral law. This was called the Mishnah.
220	The death of Rabbi Judah. The Holy Land declines as a centre of organised Jewish learning. Many leading scholars begin to leave in order to settle in

Babylon, where the Jewish community had continued to thrive under its own princes and its own laws.

220-500	The Gemara was compiled in Babylon, thus completing the Babylonian Talmud.
650-750	The Arabs conquer most of the civilised world in the name of Islam. The vast majority of the Jewish people now live in the Muslim empire.
762-942	Baghdad was established as the centre of the great Muslim empire. The Jewish world was also ruled from Baghdad by the Geonim – the heads of the two great academies of learning – through the method of Responsa. The Talmud was accepted everywhere as an authority second only to the Torah itself, and Jewish practice – much as we know it today – crystallised and became standardised.
942-1492	North Africa and then Spain replace Baghdad as the centre of the Jewish world. The work of codifying Talmudic law started in earnest.
1040	Rashi was born in Northern France. His commentary on the Talmud and the supplements of his successors, the Tosafists, were included alongside the text of the Talmud.
1492	All Jews expelled from Spain
1565	First printed edition of the Shulhan Arukh.
1565	Responsa continues to be employed to develop to the present Jewish law. It is now the only method in use.

The History of the Torah: The Lesson

A) TORAH

1. What does the word 'Torah' mean?

It is usually translated into English as 'the Law', but a better meaning is 'the Teaching'.

2. What is the Torah?

The word is used in two different ways. In its narrow sense, the Torah means simply the Five Books of Moses:

Bereshit (Genesis)

Shemot (Exodus)

Vayikra (Leviticus)

Bemidbar (Numbers)

and

Debarim (Deuteronomy).

These are the sacred scrolls kept in the ark of the synagogue and read out regularly to the people on the Sabbath, on festivals and fasts.

When else is the Torah read regularly, and why?

On Mondays and Thursdays, the original market days when all the farmers would come to town.

In its wider sense the word 'Torah' is also used to include the Oral Law, by tradition simultaneously given to Moshe at Sinai, and its study and interpretation over thousands of years to this day.

Why do we need the Oral Law as well as the Written Law?

The Five Books of Moses, do not contain sufficient detail for use as a complete code of practical law, morality and religious practice. The Oral Law was therefore provided to interpret and amplify the information contained in the Written Law.

B) JEWISH LAW

What do we mean by Jewish law?

Though in the narrow legal sense, Jewish law embraces all the civil and criminal
law required to run society – for that was its original intention – it is far wider in
its scope than, say, English law.

Jewish Law makes no distinction between religious, civil, criminal and moral law, regarding them
all as part of the same system that regulates all aspects of life lived in obedience to God's commandments.

Jewish law fully covers the relations between man and man, and between man and God.

What topics are included in Jewish law?

C) EARLY ORAL LAW

The Oral Law was originally transmitted by word of mouth from teacher to pupil by endless repetition,
from generation to generation. It was never written down to avoid risk of confusion in the popular
mind with the Written Law – the Five Books of Moses.

What is the danger of such confusion?

A part of the Jewish people returned to Jerusalem from exile in Babylon in the years before 428 BCE,
under the leadership of Ezra and Nehemia; and it was then that the practice of public readings of the
Torah was established.

The leaders of the newly established state of Judah were faced with the problem of adapting and
expanding the ancient laws of the Torah for use in their own day. It was then that the rapid growth of
the oral tradition became vitally important.

Can you image running a country without detailed laws? What might happen?

How was the oral law developed?

The early scholars developed the oral law from the detailed study and explanation of texts found
in the written law – the Five Books of Moses. This method was called MIDRASH.

Later teachers then accepted the interpretations of the earlier sages as authoritative. They added contributions of their own to further expand the laws. This method was known as MISHNAH. (Note: not
'the' Mishnah).

Naturally, different rabbis interpreted the same laws in slightly different ways; and different schools of law arose.

The best known are those of Hillel and Shammai in the first century BCE. Hillel's interpretations tended to be more lenient, while Shammai's were sterner and far more closely bound to the literal meaning of the Biblical texts.

Can you think of a 'lenient' and a 'strict' answer to a particular question?
Teacher to help!

Hillel, one of the greatest of our sages, was gentle and patient. He was once asked by a pagan to summarise all the teachings of Judaism whilst standing on one foot.

How would you have answered?

Instead of sending away the impudent man, Hillel answered:

Do not do to your neighbour what is hateful to yourself. This is the essence of the Torah and the rest is commentary. Now go and learn.

As can be imagined, the Oral Law grew rapidly, both in size and in complexity – and remember, none of it was written down in those days. Think what problems that caused!

D) HOW THE TORAH SURVIVED DISASTER

1 THE TEMPLE

The Temple had stood in Jerusalem with only one interruption of seventy years (Babylonian exile) since the days of King Solomon, a thousand years before. It was the centre of Jewish national existence and the focus of Jewish faith.

The destruction of the Temple by the Romans in 70 CE was a catastrophe – a disaster so keenly felt that to this day, some two thousand years later, we still fast on each anniversary.

What is the fast called? What other fast commemorates the destruction of Jerusalem?

2 YAVNE

Yet Judaism itself survived that terrible event. At the height of the siege of Jerusalem a leading rabbi, Yohanan ben Zakkai, pretended to have died of the plague. His followers carried him out of the city in a sealed coffin, through the ring of Roman soldiers, for burial beyond the walls. Once within reach of the Roman camp, ben Zakkai emerged from his coffin and demanded to see the Roman general. He then persuaded the general to give him the small town of Yavneh, remote from the fighting, so that he could set up a religious school there.

Why do you think the Roman general agreed to help the rabbi in the middle of a brutal war?

It was in Yavneh that the study of Torah and the development of the oral tradition reached new heights which enabled Judaism to survive the series of terrible destructions that then overcame the Jewish people.

In Yavneh the first serious attempt was made to sort out the accumulated mass of oral law. This must have been very difficult indeed as none of it was written down.

What sort of problems and conflicts could arise if the laws of this country were oral and not written down?

3 THE MISHNAH

Catastrophe followed catastrophe for the Jewish people in its conflict with Rome. Eventually, round about the year 200 CE. Yehuda ha-Nasi (or Rabbi Judah the Prince, as he is known in English) decided that he would have to prepare an authoritative compilation of the oral law if Judaism was to have any chance of surviving the even harder times still to come.

He summarised the accumulated oral tradition of the ages in a monumental Hebrew book called THE MISHNAH. Rabbi Judah was the intellectual giant of his age; and the Mishnah was immediately accepted as defining Jewish law, custom and practice.

What did a 'book' look like in those days?

On what was it written? and with what?

4 THE TALMUD

Jewish life in the Holy Land became even more difficult after the death of Yehudah ha-Nasi, just as he had predicted. Many scholars left to join the flourishing Jewish community that had remained in exile in Babylon; and Babylon rapidly became the new centre of Jewish life and learning.

Even the Mishnah was not sufficiently detailed to deal with the complexity of life in Babylon; and so, for the next three hundred years, generations of scholars commented on and expanded its text. Their work, the GEMARA, (written in Aramaic, the everyday language of the time) was completed in about 500 CE.

The combined Mishnah and Gemara called the TALMUD (or the Babylonian Talmud), became and has remained the most authoritative source of Jewish law next to the Torah itself.

At the same time, another Gemara was written by the rabbis who, despite severe persecution, had remained in the Holy Land. Their work, the Jerusalem Talmud, is shorter and not equal in authority to the Babylonian Talmud.

5 BAGHDAD AND THE GEONIM

Babylon, and then nearby Baghdad, remained the centre of the Jewish world for many hundreds of years – for Baghdad became the centre of the Muslim world in which the vast majority of the Jewish people then lived.

> *Look at the map of the Muslim empire. What was happening in Europe and in England,*
> *when Baghdad was the most civilised, the richest and the most beautiful city in the world?*

> *Did you know that more people lived in Baghdad at that time than in the whole of England?*

6 THE JEWISH WORLD

Scholars at its great colleges of learning in Babylon continued to polish, explain and even add to the text of the Talmud.

More than that, the heads of the academies – the GEONIM – saw to it that the Talmud became the accepted authority on Jewish law everywhere. Copies were sent to distant communities.

> *How were books copied in those days?*
> *When was printing invented?*

The Geonim were consulted for rulings on all kinds of religious and legal matters by rabbis from distant countries. Scholars flocked to Baghdad from far and wide to study with the masters; and they later returned to their own countries with their newly acquired knowledge.

> *Look again at the map of the Jewish world ruled by the Geonim.*

> *On what kind of matters were the Geonim asked to judge? Could a dispute between two Jews*
> *in Morocco over the purchase of a plot of land be sent to Baghdad for adjudication? –*
> Yes, not unusual

It was due largely to the Geonim that Jewish religious practices and law became, and have remained so uniform all over the world, despite the large distance and the difficulty of travel between the different communities.

What differences can you think of between the modern Ashkenazi and Sephardi traditions?
Are they important?

E) RASHI AND THE TOSAFISTS

When did the Ashkenazi tradition really start developing?

It was just before the year 1000 that Rabbenu Gershom of Maintz, and some of his contemporaries laid the foundations for what developed into the Ahskenazi branch of Judaism?

Rashi was born in Northern France in 1040 at a time when Jews were suffering bitter persecution at the hands of the Christian Crusaders.

What was Rashi's full name?

Rashi produced a detailed Hebrew commentary on the Talmud, which is the most frequently consulted of such works. The generations of scholars who followed him wrote supplements (called TOSAFOT) to the text.

Rashi's commentary and the Tosafot are so highly regarded that they are printed alongside the text in standard editions of the Talmud.

F) THE CODES

Is the Talmud hard to read?
Despite all the commentaries, the Talmud remains a very difficult work to read, for it contains shorthand accounts of the discussions, including the disagreements, of the sages on the whole scope of human knowledge of the time at which it was written. It is not arranged in logical order and requires years of intensive study to master.

What is a code?
A Code is a précis of a much longer and more complex book, arranged in a special way for easy reference.

Of what work is the Highway Code a précis?

When were the codes written?

At roughly at the same time as William the Conqueror was invading Britain, rabbis in North Africa, Spain and Egypt (including of course Maimonides, the 'Rambam'), were beginning in earnest to produce summaries of the material contained in the Talmud – Codes, as they are called. Their intention was to provide shorter works of reference that could be consulted for decisions far more easily than by going to the Talmud itself.

Much later, in the sixteenth century, Rabbi Joseph Caro produced a condensed version of his own Code, which he called the Shulhan Arukh (The Prepared Table). This is regarded as a standard source of reference and is still used extensively to this day.

Extracts from some of the Codes are also printed alongside the text of standard editions of the Talmud.

As can be seen from the photograph of one of its pages, even the printed layout of Talmud is complicated.

Can you think of another example of a book printed in this way? What is our nearest modern equivalent?

Footnotes in modern books.

G) RESPONSA

Since the days of the Geonim in ninth-century Baghdad, Jewish law has also been developed by means of RESPONSA and that method continues today.

What are Responsa?

Responsa are the written answers given by famous rabbis to written questions on Jewish law put to them by less learned rabbis. If the rabbi delivering the judgment is sufficiently learned to command respect, and most other rabbis also accept his ruling, it becomes part of the accepted teaching – part of the oral tradition.

Can you think of modern situations requiring answers that are not covered in the Torah or the Talmud?

What about what happened when the use of electricity was discovered in the last century. Was the switching on of a light permitted or not permitted on Shabbat?

MATERIAL FOR LESSON 30

MAP *of the Jews living under the sway of Islam*

A page from a standard edition of the Talmud

Chart showing the development of the Torah

Further Note on the Torah in more depth

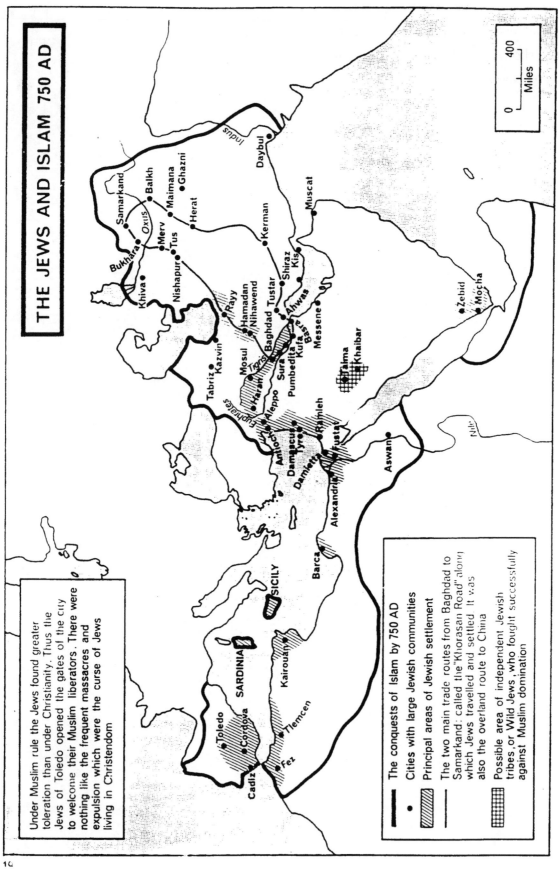

THE JEWS AND ISLAM 750 AD

Under Muslim rule the Jews found greater toleration than under Christianity. Thus the Jews of Toledo opened the gates of the city to welcome their Muslim liberators. There were nothing like the frequent massacres and expulsion which were the curse of Jews living in Christendom

Samarkand
Balkh
Ghazni
Daybul
Maimana
Herat
Bukhára
Oxus
Merv
Tus
Kerman
Muscat
Khiva
Nishapur
Ràyy
Hamadan
Nihawend
Shiraz
Kis
Mosul
Baghdad Tustar
Ahwaz
Tabriz
Kazvin
Tigris
Sura
Basra
Messene
Żebid
Mocha
Harun
Pumbedita
Kufa
Aleppo
Ramleh
Telma
Khaibar
Euphrates
Antioch
Damascus
Tyre
Fustat
Damietta
Aswan
Alexandria
Barca
SICILY
SARDINIA
Kairouan
Tlemcen
Toledo
Cordova
Fez
Cadiz
Nile
Indus

0   400
Miles

The conquests of Islam by 750 AD

● Cities with large Jewish communities

Principal areas of Jewish settlement

The two main trade routes from Baghdad to Samarkand: called the "Khorasan Road" along which Jews travelled and settled. It was also the overland route to China

Possible area of independent Jewish tribes, or Wild Jews, who fought successfully against Muslim domination

10

A PAGE FROM A STANDARD EDITION OF THE TALMUD

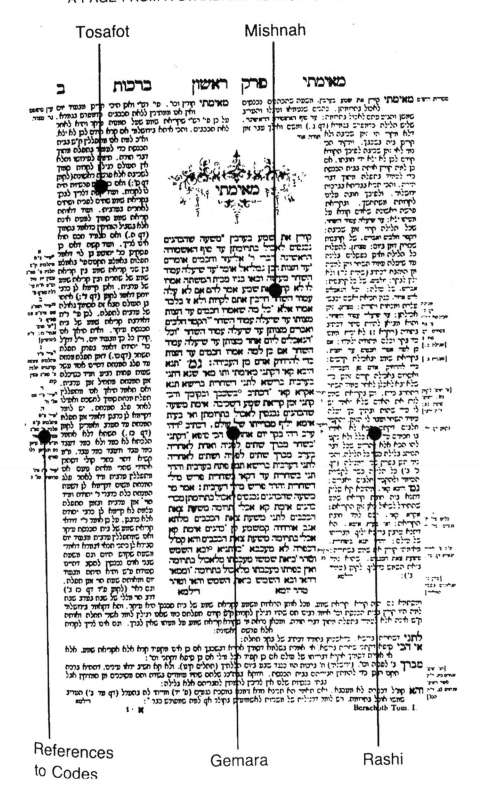

Tosafot

Mishnah

References to Codes

Gemara

Rashi

ב   ברכות   פרק ראשון   מאימתי

Berachoth Tom. I.

1 · א

LESSON 30   HISTORY OF THE TORAH: THE LESSON

409

DEVELOPMENT OF THE TORAH

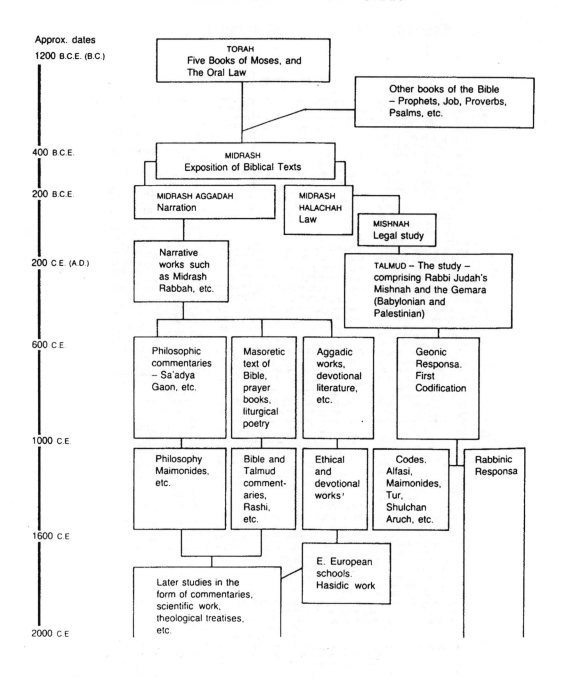

Approx. dates

1200 B.C.E. (B.C.)

400 B.C.E.

200 B.C.E.

200 C.E. (A.D.)

600 C.E.

1000 C.E.

1600 C.E.

2000 C.E.

TORAH
Five Books of Moses, and The Oral Law

Other books of the Bible – Prophets, Job, Proverbs, Psalms, etc.

MIDRASH
Exposition of Biblical Texts

MIDRASH AGGADAH
Narration

MIDRASH HALACHAH
Law

MISHNAH
Legal study

Narrative works such as Midrash Rabbah, etc.

TALMUD – The study – comprising Rabbi Judah's Mishnah and the Gemara (Babylonian and Palestinian)

Philosophic commentaries – Sa'adya Gaon, etc.

Masoretic text of Bible, prayer books, liturgical poetry

Aggadic works, devotional literature, etc.

Geonic Responsa. First Codification

Philosophy Maimonides, etc.

Bible and Talmud commentaries, Rashi, etc.

Ethical and devotional works'

Codes. Alfasi, Maimonides, Tur, Shulchan Aruch, etc.

Rabbinic Responsa

E. European schools. Hasidic work

Later studies in the form of commentaries, scientific work, theological treatises, etc.

NOTE FOR TEACHERS

THE TORAH IN MORE DEPTH

INTRODUCTION

The Hebrew word *Torah*, meaning Teaching, is often inadequately translated into English as Law. It is used in two senses. In its narrow meaning the Torah is the Five Books of Moses (Genesis, Exodus, Leviticus, Numbers and Deuteronomy), divine in origin and unchallengeable in authority. These are the sacred scrolls that are read aloud and treated with such reverence in the synagogue. In its broader sense the term Torah is also taken to include the Oral Law, which encompasses the entire range of Jewish religious practice and belief, law, morality and mysticism. The Written Law, together with the beginning of the Oral Law, was transmitted to Moses at Sinai.

As shown by the following quotation from the Talmud, the Rabbis do not seem to have been troubled by the apparent contradiction between the belief that the Oral Law was revealed on Mount Sinai and its continuous development over thousands of years.

> ... when Moses ascended on high to receive the Torah, he found the Holy One, blessed be He, adding tittles (crown-like symbols) to the actual letters of the text. Moses said "Lord of the Universe, what is the purpose of this ... ". He replied "After many generations a man called Akiva will arise, who will elaborate many, many laws on each tittle". "Lord of the Universe, permit me to see him", said Moses. He replied "Turn around". Moses was transported into the Academy of Rabbi Akiva, over a thousand years later, where he sat at the back of the class. He became more and more perplexed for he could not follow the arguments; but when a pupil asked on a certain subject, "From what source do you derive it" and was given the answer "It is a law given to Moses at Sinai", Moses was comforted.[1]

NB The subject matter of *Ages of Man* is Torah in its widest sense. This note is devoted to an outline of the historical development of Torah as a system of law and ethical rules. Mysticism, beliefs, practices and customs are described later.)

In about 1200 B.C.E., roughly when the Greeks were engaged in the Trojan war, Moses led the Hebrew tribes out of Egypt to the boundaries of the Promised Land. On the way there, in the desert of Sinai, the Written Torah (Five Books of Moses) and the beginings of the Oral Torah were revealed to Moses for onward transmission to the people.

It is clear from even a casual inspection of the Five Books of Moses that a great deal of amplification is needed before they can be used as a manual of law and morality. The Oral Law was provided in answer to that need: its purpose is partly to interpret and partly to supplement the Written Law. A convenient way of looking at many of the paragraphs of the written text is to regard them as the headings for laws whose details will be added later.

An interesting example of the beginning of this process can be seen in one of the narrative sections of the Book of Numbers. Zelophehad died in the wilderness. He left no sons and so, according to custom, his entire estate would have been awarded to his brothers. Zelophehad's daughters appealed to Moses against the ruling that they, as females, could not inherit their father's property. Moses, after communing with God, declared that the girls must share the estate between them – thus establishing in law the basic principle of female inheritance, later to be developed by the Rabbis.

The later books of the Bible, though considered less sacred than the Five Books of Moses and ranked in descending order of sanctity, record further progress. The Hebrew prophets, with their passionate concern for righteousness, emphasised as never before the unity of morality and religion. They strove to realise a vision in which first the Jews and then the whole of mankind will come to acknowledge the rule of a just and merciful God. The wisdom, practical ethics and poetry of the Psalms, Job, Proverbs, Ecclesiastes and the Song of Songs added further dimensions to the growing tradition and supplied many of the factors necessary for a balanced structure of morality and law.

At the time when the ancient Athenians were engaged in their life and death struggle with the Persians at Marathon and when the Roman Republic was being founded, two former high officers of the Persian court were busily at work reconstructing Jewish life in Jerusalem. Ezra and Nehemiah, who had returned with many of their countrymen from exile in Babylon, set about their self-appointed task with vigour. The Five Books of Moses were rescued from oblivion. The practice of regularly reading the Torah aloud to the assembled people was established in 444 B.C.E.. During such recitations, professional interpreters stood alongside the reader to translate difficult passages into Aramaic – the spoken language of the people – and also to interpret and extend the ancient laws for contemporary use.

The Oral Tradition continued to grow during the period of Ezra's successors, when the 'Scribes' or 'Men of the Great Assembly' introduced a great deal of innovative legislation. Ancient laws were interpreted flexibly for contemporary use and an elaborate series of new rules devised 'to make a fence around the Torah' to protect people against the risk of accidental transgression.

The method used by the Scribes to expand and transmit the Oral Law was firmly based on detailed study of texts from the Five Books of Moses. This is known as *Midrash* (Exposition) and is divided into two main branches. A *Midrash Halachah* is a lesson with legal implications; and a *Midrash Aggadah* is a lesson from which spiritual or moral lessons can be learned. Halachah ('The way in which they shall walk') has come to mean Jewish law. Aggadah is narrative, such as parables, homilies, sermons and the like – but all tied to particular texts.

One example of an Aggadic Midrash is a commentary on the biblical verse that describes what happened when Noah sent a dove out of the ark to determine whether or not the great flood had subsided – 'the dove came back to him in the evening and in her mouth was an olive leaf, freshly plucked.'[2] The Midrash pictures the dove as saying to the Almighty "Lord of the Universe, may my food be dove as saying to the Almighty "Lord of the Universe, may my food be bitter as the olive but given to me from your hand rather than it be as sweet as honey but given by the hand of man'.[3]

An example of a Halachic Midrash concerns the commandment forbidding work on the Sabbath. As no definition of work is given in the text, the Rabbis directed their attention to Exodus 35 where a short passage concerning the prohibition of Sabbath labour is followed immediately by detailed instructions governing the building of the Tabernacle in the wilderness. The Oral Law deduced the following lesson from that apparently inconsequential sequence of passages. 'Whatever tasks were required for the building of the Tabernacle comprise work that is forbidden on the Sabbath.' From that conclusion, the Rabbis went on to derive thirty-nine principal labours and many subsidiary ones that are not allowed on the Sabbath – including sowing, ploughing, reaping, baking, kindling fire and building. The process by which each of the prohibitions was established makes a fascinating study, typical of the legislative methods of the Oral Law.

The striking feature of all Oral Law before about 400 C.E. is that it was oral. It was never written down so as to avoid risk of confusion with the Written Law or any possible rivalry with it in the popular mind. Midrash therefore could only be transmitted from teacher to student by word of mouth and by means of constant repetition.

Alexander the Great conquered the Persian Empire in the year 333 B.C.E. and the Scribes continued their work in tranquil conditions for the next sixty years before the country was again plunged into a long period of conflict.

EARLY MISHNAH

The following centuries were a formative period for the development of Judaism. It was a time of bitter strife when Jews fought for their independence, first against the Seleucid Greeks and then against the might of the Roman Empire – whilst at the same time struggling to preserve their own religious identity from ever-encroaching waves of alien culture.

The main spiritual conflict within Jewry itself concerned the rivalry between the priestly aristocratic party of the Sadducees and that of the more democratic Pharisees (who were most unfairly maligned by early Christian writers). The Sadducees, whose faith was based mainly on the Temple cult, denied the growing authority of the Oral Law and interpreted the words of the Written Law in as literal a manner as possible. The Pharisees triumphed eventually. Their stress on a creative and flexible Oral Torah, together with their belief in the immortality of the soul and the coming of the messianic age, were ultimately accepted.

There were two rival schools within the ranks of the Pharisees. One was named after the saintly Hillel (who lived during the first century B.C.E.) and the other after the somewhat sterner Shammai. Hillel's interpretations of law tended to be more lenient and not as closely bound to the literal meaning of the biblical texts as those of Shammai, whose judgments were usually more rigorous. Members of the two opposing schools were not enemies, despite their differences, and often met to argue about and then decide contentious matters.

Another method of developing Halachah (Law) came to prominence at this time and eventually displaced Midrash Halachah as the leading system, though both continued side by side. This is known as *Mishnah* from the Hebrew for 'to repeat', referring no doubt to the way in which Oral Law had to be learned in the absence of written texts. The teachers of Mishnah were called the *Tannaim*, which is derived from an Aramaic word of similar meaning. In early Midrash, as we have explained, all comment is pinned firmly to the words of a biblical text. The Mishnaic system of legislation, though derived ultimately from the Written Law, proceeded independently of the texts and relied for its acceptance on the personal authority of succeeding generations of Tannaim.

The Oral Torah continued to grow in size and complexity through the times that preceded and then followed the great disaster of 70 C.E. when Roman legions broke into Jerusalem, burned the Temple to the ground, destroyed the city and massacred or enslaved its surviving inhabitants.

A NEW BEGINNING

Rabbi Yochanan Ben Zakkai, one of those leading Pharisees who had opposed the suicidal revolt against Roman rule, is given the credit for enabling Judaism and its Torah to survive the destruction of the Temple which for so long had been at the heart of its religious life. The Talmud relates that in the middle of the siege of Jerusalem, Ben Zakkai had his disciples declare that he had died of the plague. With much show of grief, they carried him in a coffin for burial outside the city walls. Once beyond the ring of determined defenders, Ben Zakkai emerged from his shrouds and requested an audience with the Roman general Vespasian, who was shortly to become Emperor. The rabbi asked the general for permission to start (or possibly take over) a religious school in the small town of Yabneh. We can only guess at what Vespasian must have thought of Ben Zakkai and why he granted his petition – a bizarre request during a brutal and as yet unresolved war. The fact is that Rabbi Yochanan ben Zakkai did start his famous academy at Yabneh. There the study of Torah was raised to a level that facilitated the accomplishments of succeeding generations. Judaism became a universal faith; no longer tied to the Temple and the Holy Land; and though Jerusalem could never be forgotten, for most practical purposes the Torah became a substitute for its sanctuary.

An academic *Sanhedrin* (Supreme Religious Court) was set up in Yabneh and its authority spread far outside the Holy Land. Its head or *Nasi*, who was of royal descent, often represented his people before the Roman governor. Jewish life was rebuilt painfully but surely.

Learning flourished once again. The Hebrew text of existing versions the Bible was closely scrutinised and purged of scribal errors. A serious attempt was made to come to grips with the accumulated mass of Oral Law; and many conflicting opinions were either reconciled or settled by majority vote. Rabbi Akiva, Rabbi Meir and others laboured to arrange the incoherent bulk of Mishnah into some kind of system – which cannot have been easy as this was still in oral form. What was then accomplished made Mishnah easier to teach and also to use to resolve new problems. From Yabneh also came a stream of Midrash of the highest quality, composed by rabbis such as Akiva, Judah ben Ilai and Shimon bar Yochai.

All this activity ended abruptly in the year 132 C.E. when the Roman Emperor Hadrian tried to erect a temple to the pagan god Jupiter on Temple Mount in Jerusalem. The Jews rose up in furious rebellion and the rest of Hadrian's reign was marked by savage repression, enslavement and massacre. Many fled the country. The academy and Sanhedrin at Yabneh were closed. Rabbi Akiva, an instigator and leader of the revolt, was put to death by the Romans with their usual cruelty when he refused to comply with their prohibition against teaching Torah.

RABBI JUDAH THE PRINCE – THE MISHNAH

After the death of Emperor Hadrian in 138 C.E., the surviving remnant of the Jewish population of the Holy Land began to pick up the shattered pieces of its former existence and restore its institutions. Galilee became the new centre of piety and seat of the Sanhedrin. Its second Nasi (President, or Patriarch), Yehuda ha-Nasi, or Rabbi Judah the Prince, was said to have been a personal friend of the Roman Emperor Marcus Aurelius. Such is his reputation in Jewish circles that he is simply known as 'Rabbi' (Teacher).

Rabbi Judah realised that the complex structure of the Oral Law depended for its survival almost entirely on the existence of a strong central religious authority such as the Sanhedrin. Though his long patriarchate was peaceful, he realised that this would not last for ever and that renewed bouts of determined persecution would endanger the survival of the Torah. He therefore took the decisive step of producing his own compilation of the Halachah (Law) against such a time when there might no longer be a central religious authority. This summary, The Mishnah, comprised the accumulated work of his own and previous generations of sages.

Scholars disagree as to whether Rabbi Judah chose to ignore the centuries-old prohibition against writing down the Oral Law and used his own privately written version of the text – or whether all his work was in oral form. It was certainly transmitted by word of mouth during the early years of the Babylonian academies, when certain scholars capable of reciting the entire text by heart were used very much as human tape-recorders. The Mishnah was not openly committed to writing until towards the end of the Talmudic period.

Rabbi Judah's monumental book, known as The Mishnah, is in six parts.

Zeraim (Seeds) deals mainly with religious laws relating to agriculture in the Holy Land, and also contains a section on prayer.

Moed (Seasons) is concerned with laws for the Sabbath and festivals, and with rules for fixing the calendar.

Nahsim (Women) deals with marriage, divorce, and related topics.

Nezikin (Damages) covers civil and criminal law and also includes a treatise on morals, called PIRKE AVOT (Ethics of the Fathers).

Kodashim (Holy Matters) covers the detailed regulations for maintaining all aspects of the Temple cult and also includes laws governing the slaughter of animals for food.

Tohorot (Purities) covers the laws of ritual impurity including those concerned with menstruation.

Though The Mishnah contains Rabbi Judah's own selection of earlier rulings with which agreed, its publication did not close the door to further discussion because Rabbi Judah also included many divergent opinions that he thought were also of value.

The Mishnah, written in Hebrew by the intellectual giant of his day in a noble attempt to systemise Jewish law, almost immediately came to be regarded as second only to the Five Books of Moses in authority. But The Mishnah was not sufficiently comprehensive to deal adequately with so vast a range of topics; and so Rabbi Judah's work was continued by others for many hundreds of years after his death.

THE TALMUD

The decline of the Holy Land as the prime seat of Jewish learning started after the death of Rabbi Judah. One of Rabbi Judah's pupils, Abba Arika (175–247 C.E.) – known as Rav (Aramaic for Teacher) – founded an academy at Sura, near Babylon. Samuel, another of Rav's pupils founded an academy at Nehardea: one of his most famous rulings is that Jews must obey the righteous laws of their countries of residence – 'The law of the land is the law'. A third college was started a few years later at nearby Pumbeditha. Babylonia then began to take over as the religious and cultural centre of the Jewish people.

No sooner was Rabbi Judah's Mishnah finished than the task began of extending its scope. The teachers of the Babylonian and Palestinian schools, called *Amoraim* (Speakers), subjected every detail of The Mishnah to meticulous examination and comment. Their deliberations also extended beyond Rabbi Judah's text to include teachings omitted by him in his selection – called *Baraitha* (Outside). These include the *Tosefta* (Supplement) and Midrash such as *Mehilta*, *Sifra* and *Sifrei*.

The discussions, agreements and disagreements of the Amoraim are known as *Gemara* (Aramaic for Study or Completion). These were collated and written down in Aramaic in the two centres of activity, Babylon and Tiberias (Galilee). The task was finished in about 500 C.E..

The *Talmud* (Study) consists of Rabbi Judah's The Mishnah together with the Gemara. There are in fact two different Talmuds. The first to be completed was the Palestinian Talmud, mostly compiled in Tiberias. Its Gemara was collected and recorded in the face of the harsh Roman occupation of the Holy Land, made worse by the added spur of persecution which followed the conversion of Emperor Constantine to Christianity. The Babylonian Talmud, composed in academies of Babylon, was finished about a century later. Much longer than its Palestinian counterpart, it is considered superior in many respects. Its Gemara was written in a tolerant environment where scholarship could thrive undisturbed and where the leaders of the Jewish community (the Exilarchs) were honoured by the Persian kings. The Babylonian Talmud therefore is referred to as 'The Talmud' and is regarded as the classical statement of Jewish law, practice and custom: traditional Judaism is based on its authority.

The Talmud is a vast work containing an almost universal span of human knowledge – law, religion, morals, medicine, astronomy, history and so on. It includes a bewildering welter of conflicting opinions that the reader is left to sort out for himself. Its contents are not arranged in logical sequence; and the same subject may be referred to in a dozen different places, often unexpectedly. Also the deliberations of the Amoraim are recorded with extreme brevity, which on occasion amounts to a kind of shorthand. Consequently the Talmud is very difficult to read without the help of skilled teachers and its mastery is a lifelong task. To an observant Jew, the study of Talmud is a religious duty for which there is no substitute. Yeshivot (schools of Talmudic study) are packed with men, both young and old, who think this an ideal way of spending a few years of their lives.

Scholastic activity did not cease, even in the Holy Land, after what is referred to as the closing of the Talmud. In Babylon, the Saboraim (Reflecters) polished and explained the Gemara and made some additions to the text. In both centres, Midrash continued to be produced in the form of Aggadah (narration) that included major works like Midrash Rabba, Genesis Rabba, Tanhuma Midrashim and Pesikta Midrashim.

LATER MIDRASH

In the first difficult centuries of the war of survival, first against the duality of Gnostic doctrines which maintained that there are two gods – a good god and an evil creator god – and then against Christianity, the Rabbis began to interpret biblical passages more loosely in a determined attempt to engage the hearts and minds of their followers. Those rabbis who produced Midrash in the Land of Israel then did not scruple to use their creative imaginations to the full in order to teach particular lessons of vital contemporary significance – even if that involved extending or even departing from the plain meaning of the biblical texts. Such midrashim, often contradictory in their conclusions, can be considered as subjective rather than objective interpretations. The rabbis involved assumed the right to explain the word of God for the benefit of their own and subsequent generations – a survival kit for Judaism, then under ferocious attack.

For example, at a time when Christians were teaching that the Torah had been superseded and its observance was an impediment to salvation, the Rabbis did not hesitate to reinterpret Biblical characters like Enoch and Noah, who had lived before the Torah was given, in order to teach particular lessons.

Descriptions in the Bible of its leading figures include their faults, sometimes serious ones, as well as their virtues. This conveys an unmistakeable stamp·.of authenticity: otherwise why give discreditable details when writing of the heroes of the Jewish people? But this frankness must have made some Rabbis uncomfortable when defending their religion against its detractors. Again, departing from the actual words of the Bible, some midrashim go to considerable lengths to whitewash such behaviour. For example, Esau's character is blackened in order to explain and justify Jacob's complex behaviour.

Elaborate extra-textual explanations are offered to explain away King David's relationship with Bathsheba and his sending her husband off to the frontline of the war – despite David's own acknowledgement of his sin and his acceptance of God's punishment.

Midrash, however subjective some of its explanations may be, is of great value, both for what it teaches and also for the picture it gives of the Rabbis of the time – so to speak – in their shirtsleeves, grappling fiercely with the great challenges that then faced Judaism. But it should not be forgotten that the Torah (The Five Books of Moses) always remains the ultimate authority. The subjective interpretations of some midrashim must be understood in light of the purpose for which they were written. Occasionally, they should also be viewed with caution – especially when their arguments contradict the plain meanings (*pshat*) of the biblical texts to which they relate.

THE GEONIM

The Almighty is so venerated by observant Jews that letters, manuscripts and books containing God's name may not be destroyed after use like other waste paper. They are either buried in a cemetery or else deposited in a store attached to a synagogue.

Hearing of the accidental discovery of a *Genizah* (Hidden Place) in the ninth century Ben Ezra Synagogue of Old Cairo, Solomon Shechter recovered a hoard of ancient manuscript material and brought it to Cambridge. Though that occurred in the closing years of the nineteenth century, work is still continuing to identify, classify, study and publish the 140,000 fragments of ancient letters and books. The Geniza material mainly covers Jewish life in the Mediterranean area between the ninth and the twelfth centuries: it also casts light on a period that was largely unknown before its discovery – that dominated by the Geonim of Babylon.

Arabs armies erupted from Arabia with tremendous vigour in the eighth century and, in the name of Islam, conquered a vast swathe of territory stretching from Spain in the west to India in the east. Their new capital Baghdad became the hub of a mighty empire and the centre of an impressive civilisation. Most Jews then lived in that part of the world conquered by the Arabs and so they too looked towards Baghdad for leadership.

After a decline following the Arab conquest, the condition of the Jewish population of what was once Babylonia was eventually restored to something approaching its former condition. Its leader, the Exilarch or Prince of the Captivity, was once again accorded semi-regal honours, this time by the Caliph in Baghdad. As noted by a medieval traveller,

> Horsemen, Jewish and non-Jewish, escort him every Thursday when he goes to visit the great Caliph. Heralds go before, proclaiming "Make way for our Lord, the Son of David, as is his due". He is mounted on a horse and dressed in robes of embroidered silk … the Caliph rises and places him on a throne … and all the Mohammedan princes rise up before him.[4]

The heads of the colleges of Sura and Pumbeditha became the spiritual leaders of world Jewry. They were known as the Geonim, the plural of Gaon (Excellency) the title with which each was addressed. In religious matters the authority of the Geonim was accepted throughout the Muslim empire and beyond.

Talmud continued to be taught in the academies of Sura and Pumbeditha, to which scholars from many countries flocked to study. Copies of the Talmud were despatched from Baghdad to other Jewish communities throughout the world. The first legal codes to aid understanding and observance were composed by the Geonim and then circulated. The scope of the Law was extended by means of Responsa, which were reasoned judgments on law and practice prepared by the Geonim in answer to queries sent to them by Jews from all over the world.

The text of the Hebrew Bible was again subjected to close scrutiny and scribal errors eliminated. This task was made far more difficult by the fact that the Hebrew alphabet consists only of consonants; and the

Bible was written using consonents alone, with vowel sounds and punctuation supplied from memory. The pronunciation of sacred texts thus depended entirely on oral transmission – which was unreliable and prone to error. Babylonian scholars made the first attempts to standardise reading and pronunciation beyond further dispute by adding written vowel sounds and punctuation marks to the Hebrew letters. Their efforts were finally eclipsed in the tenth century by Ben Asher of Tiberias (Galilee), whose Masoretic text (named for the Masoretes – Handers Down) became the accepted version of the Hebrew Bible.

Another important achievement of the Geonic period was the standardisation of many prayers and forms of worship. The first complete prayer book was prepared for use in Spain by Amram Gaon in 860. Another was produced some years later by Sa'adya Gaon for the Jews of Egypt.

The seventh century also saw the start of that great flow of devotional poetry that has so enriched the synagogue liturgy.

Sa'adya ben Yosef (882–942), better known as Sa'adya Gaon, was the greatest of the Geonim. In his book Emunot Vedot (Beliefs and Opinions) he attempted to reconcile reason with religion for the benefit of his own generation. Sa'adya's role was crucial in combating and ultimately defeating the Karaite movement which at that time seriously threatened the survival of Talmudic Judaism. The Karaites rejected the Oral Law and insisted on a strictly literal interpretation of Biblical texts.

The Babylonian schools began their slow decline after Sa'adya's death in 942, giving way gradually to new centres of learning in North Africa, Muslim Spain, and Christian Europe. Hai Gaon, the last of the Geonim, died in the year 1038.

RASHI AND THE TOSAFISTS

Rabbi Shelomo Itzhaki is affectionately known as Rashi from the first letters of his name. He was born in France in the year 1040, at a time when the Jews of Europe were suffering grievous persecution at the hands of the Crusaders. Rashi studied with many of the leading rabbis of his day, including pupils of the illustrious Rabbi Gershon of Mainz, before founding his own school in Troyes, northern France. Rashi was responsible for much work of lasting value including Bible commentary. He produced a detailed and up-to-date Hebrew commentary on almost the whole of the Talmud, using French words written in Hebrew characters when there was no Hebrew equivalent. Rashi's commentary, composed with impressive insight and lucidity, and imbued with deep religious feeling, has become a standard work of reference and is the most frequently consulted of such works. It is honoured by being printed in the margin of all standard editions of the Talmud.

Rashi's grandson Rabbi Jacob ben Meir, called Rabbenu Tam -'Our teacher the unblemished' – after the Patriarch Jacob who is described in the Bible as 'unblemished', was prominent in the generation of teachers that followed Rashi. He, with his pupils and other contemporaries, took particular pleasure in analysing the Talmud and Rashi's commentary in fine detail and then raising ingenious and subtle objections to many of Rashi's explanations before proposing original solutions of their own. These so-called *Tosafot* (Supplements) also appear alongside the text in printed editions of the Talmud.

Other Tosafists, whose work was published elsewhere, came from many different countries. It may interest English readers to know that learned rabbis living in England, before the expulsion of Jews from that country in the thirteenth century, were also active in this field – including Rabbi Jacob of Orleans (martyred in London in 1189), Rabbi Yomtob of Joigny (martyred in York in 1190), and Rabbi Elijah ben Menahem of London, who seems to have been allowed to die of natural causes in 1284.

Although the next part of this chapter is devoted largely to a description of the stages in which the law was developed from the tenth to the twentieth centuries, it must not be forgotten that a steady output of work classified as Midrash was also appearing at the same time – much of it as elevating in its common humanity as the Italian Tanna debe Eliyahu which declared

I call upon heaven and earth to witness that whether a person be a Jew or non-Jew, bondman or bondwoman, according to the deeds he performs will the Holy Spirit rest on him.

Following the time of Sa'adya Gaon, Jewish minds were increasingly drawn to the application of philosophical methods to the study of religious law. In contrast, as described below, development of the semi-secret mystical core of Judaism (the Kabbalah) was also proceeding with significant effect.

THE CODES

After the Tosafists, the development of the Oral Law continued without pause along two main paths – that of the Legal Codes, and that of Rabbinic Responsa. Though these activities proceeded in tandem, each will be described separately for greater clarity.

The bulk of Jewish law and its interpretation had by then become so voluminous as to demand the preparation of succinct summaries of its contents in order to make it intelligible to non-scholars. Most of the rabbis who contributed to this process of codification were Sephardim, or Ashkenazim who had come to live in Spain, North Africa or the Middle East. This is often explained by contrasting the restricted lifestyles of Ashkenazim, compelled to live in the narrow ghettos of northern Europe, with the Sephardim who were usually able to participate fully in the general life of their countries of residence. The Sephardim, it was said, were generally too busy with their secular careers to be able to devote the years of study necessary to master the Talmud itself. In any event, Ashkenazi rabbis do still display a distinct preference for the exclusive study of Talmud which, after the Bible, is the primary source of Jewish religious knowledge.

Rabbi Isaac of Fez, called *Alfasi*, was one of the first outside Babylon to produce a code of law. Alfasi was born in 1013 and lived in North Africa at roughly the same time as the Norman Conquest of England. His code drastically simplified the contents of the Talmud by omitting much of the recorded argument and all the opinions with which Alfasi himself did not agree.

Rabbi Moses ben Maimon, known to Jews as the *Rambam* after the first letters of his name and as Maimonides to the outside world, was the outstanding codifier of his time and one of the most brilliant men of the age. Born in 1135, Maimonides fled from fanatical Almohade rule in Spain and finally settled in Cairo where he became a physician to the Sultan as well as head of the Jewish community. His monumental code is one thousand chapters long. Written with deep religious feeling and with an unusual clarity for the time, it contains an authoritative summary of developed Jewish law. The book was called the *Mishneh Torah* (Second Torah) because, according to its author, it was sufficiently comprehensive to determine the law on any subject without the need to consult further authorities.

The Rambam's approach to religion was guided essentially by the principles of reason. He was an admirer of Aristotle and an accomplished philosopher in his own right. Maimonides possessed the rare facility and the courage to differentiate between the fundamentals of the faith and those aspects that can be varied – in his own words 'as a physician will amputate the hand or the foot of a patient in order to save his life'. His concept of religion was universal and he taught that the righteous of all nations are sanctified in the sight of God.

'From Moses to Moses, there has not arisen one to equal Moses.' This popular saying implies that Maimonides in his lifetime was regarded as a second Moses. That did not however prevent severe criticism of the Mishneh Torah – much of it justified. In order to present his rulings with maximum clarity, Rambam did not name the sources on which he relied and omitted all the Talmudic argument from his text. Even more important, he neglected the views of distinguished Ashkenazi scholars. Attempts were made by others to remedy some of these defects; and their comments may be found printed alongside Maimonides's own text in later editions of the Mishneh Torah.

Another influential code was written by Rabbi Jacob ben Asher. This is called the *Tur* (Rows – after the four rows of gems on the ceremonial breastplate of the High Priest). Jacob was the son of the famous Rabbi Asher ben Yehiel (1250–1327), known as the Rosh after the first letters of his name (and also known as Asheri). The Rosh, who had fled from persecution in Germany, became Rabbi of Toledo in Spain where he produced a valuable legal commentary. His ideas are included in the Tur – even though Rabbi Jacob's code is an original work in its own right.

The names of other codes of law produced then and subsequently will be of lesser interest to the general reader; so the only one mentioned here is the *Shulhan Aruch* (The Prepared Table), printed first in Venice in 1565. Its author, Joseph Caro, was forced to quit Spain when its Jews were expelled in 1492 – the year in which Columbus first set sail for America. Caro settled in Safed in Galilee, from where his fame spread throughout the Jewish world. The Shulhan Aruch is based on the results of a meticulous twenty year long study of the Tur and the works of Alfasi, Maimonides and Asheri. Where those disagreed on any point, Caro generally adopted the majority opinion. However that proved to be the Shulhan Aruch's main failing – for the views and customs of the Ashkenazim were once again ignored. Poland had by this time become an important centre of Jewish life; and Rabbi Moses Isserles of Cracow wrote a *Mappah* (Tablecloth) for The Prepared Table in which he set out the differing Ashkenazi customs and opinions. From that time on, the Mappah was always printed alongside the text of the Shulhan Aruch. This modified version soon became and still remains definitive.

The formal position in Jewish law is that the further each generation gets from the revelation on Sinai, the less authoritative is its interpretation of the Oral Tradition. Hence teachers of Torah are listed in descending order of seniority.

The *Tannaim* – up to the 'closing' of the Mishnah in the third century C.E.

The *Amoraim* – up to the 'closing' of the Talmud in the sixth century.

The *Rishonim* (The First Ones) – up to the 'closing' of the Shulhan Aruch in the sixteenth century.

The *Aharonim* (The Later Ones) – after the Shulhan Aruch.

In practice though, the principle that 'the law follows the latest ruling' usually prevails. A later master who has studied all the earlier rulings is usually deferred to by virtue of his accumulated knowledge.

The Written Law, The Five Books of Moses, always remains the ultimate authority.

RESPONSA

Law was also developed through the general acceptance of pronouncements of individual rabbis of great distinction. An early example was Hillel's devising of a legal instrument known as a Prozbul in the first century B.C.E.. His prozbul circumvented the biblical law requiring all debts to be cancelled each seventh year (The Year of Release), as this was having an adverse effect on commercial activity.

As described earlier in this chapter, the Geonim of Babylon made much use of Responsa to regulate Jewish life between 600 and 1000 C.E. Their work was continued by the rabbis of the medieval period and is still employed today.

Responsa are the written replies to legal queries addressed to outstanding rabbis by less learned colleagues. They deal with individual points not specifically mentioned in the Talmud or the Codes. In general, each responsum refers to a particular case brought to the attention of the rabbi concerned and consists of a description and analysis of the sources consulted, a survey of similar problems and relevant rulings and a final statement determining the law – in other words, what we would now describe as a reasoned judgment.

Responsa literature has had a far-reaching effect on Jewish thought and practice. A few examples are given here. Rabbi Gershon of Mainz, born in 960 C.E. and known as 'The Light of the Exile', departed from Talmudic law by prohibiting polygamy: in similar manner he also ruled that no woman could be divorced without her consent. Some years later Rashi decreed that forced converts to Christianity must be welcomed back to the Jewish faith and should not suffer reproach or disability because of their lapse. Rabbenu Tam forbade Jews to 'wash their dirty linen in public' by submitting civil disputes between themselves to non-Jewish courts for resolution rather than taking them to a Beth Din (rabbinical court). In more recent times, rabbis who survived the German concentration camps had to rule on painful topics such as whether or not the crime of murder had been committed when a child died as the result of its mouth being held closed to silence its cries – so as to prevent the Germans from discovering the family's hiding place.

DEVELOPMENT OF THE TORAH

Since the acceptance of the Shulhan Aruch as definitive, responsa became the main medium for deciding points of law not specifically covered by the Talmud or that code. For those who govern their lives by the teachings of the Torah, it still fulfils that function, by dealing with contemporary questions requiring decision – such as the permissibility of certain human organ transplants, the use of modern drugs to prolong life articicially, 'in vitro' fertilisation, surrogate motherhood, homosexuality, stem cell research, cloning and many other topics.

Of course, individual responsa may differ in their conclusions. When this happens the majority view prevails and becomes law. One example is the furore that followed the discovery of electricity and its widespread use for lighting and heating. Is switching on a light equivalent to the biblical concept of 'kindling' forbidden on the Sabbath, or is it permissible? Initially there was much disagreement until a consensus was achieved forbidding the operation of a light switch as a form of 'kindling' – which is the present law. (Lights may however be turned on by the use of a pre-set time switch.)

As well as responsa, other important contributions to Torah emerged from the thriving centres of Jewish piety and learning in eastern Europe from the seventeenth century onwards. These included incomparable contributions to Aggadic literature in the form of the fables, legends and parables composed by the followers of Israel ben Eliezer (1700–60) – better known as the Ba'al Shem Tov (Master of the Holy Name).

Jesus and the Rise of Christianity

NOTES FOR TEACHERS

A) GENERAL

Living as they do within a Christian culture, it is necessary for our children to have some historical knowledge of Jesus and the rise of Christianity from its Jewish and non-Jewish roots.

B) WARNING

The picture of the historical Jesus outlined in this lesson derives from many modern studies – both Jewish and non-Jewish. It is, of course, nothing like the picture of Jesus given by the Christian Church.

The piecing together of the portrait is one requiring critical reading of texts as well as knowledge of Aramaic, Greek and Hebrew. It is not simple – even though the main conclusions are presented here in a very simple manner.

Children should be warned to beware of proclaiming their knowledge to Christian friends. It may well give offence and they will be at a disadvantage in not having the argument necessary to defend this point of view.

C) ACCOMPANYING MATERIAL

Photocopies of extracts from *Quest for the Messiah* are enclosed to give teachers the necessary background knowledge.

Jesus the Jew and the Rise of Christianity

1) THE REDEEMER

Even since Nebuchadnezzar destroyed Jerusalem and carried the Jewish people off to Babylon in exile, they longed for the fulfilment of God's promise to send them Redeemer.

> *Where does God's promise to send the Messiah appear?*
>
> This Redeemer – the Messiah – was to be a descendent of King David. He would be a king who would bring victory to the Jews over their enemies and lead the exiles back to Jerusalem in triumph. From Jerusalem the Messiah would, with divine help, rule over the whole world in justice and peace.

> *What does the word Mashiah (Messiah) mean?*

> *Who else was anointed with oil on being appointed to office?*
>
> The High Priest

The important point here is that, in Jewish expectation, the Messiah, though indeed very special, is a mortal man – and not God, as in Christianity.

> *Has the Messiah come yet? Which of our daily prayers include prayers for the coming of the Messiah?*

2) HISTORICAL BACKGROUND

The Romans conquered Judea in the year 63 BCE and their rule grew more and more oppressive with the years.

As never before, Jews longed for the Messiah to come and liberate them from the Romans. They eagerly awaited him; and there were several false starts – with different people claiming to be the promised Redeemer, attracting followers and starting armed revolts against the Romans. They were all defeated.

3) THE JEWISH RELIGION

Jews lived all over the Roman Empire; and those outside Judea lived in peace under Roman rule. Something like one in ten of the inhabitants of the Roman Empire was Jewish.

The Jewish religion was respected by the Romans. In fact, it was the only religion – other than the Roman religion – that was allowed by the state.

What was the religion of the Romans?

Jews were the only people excused from having to worship the Emperor and the Roman gods. They were also excused military service to allow them to keep Shabbat and Kashrut.

Many people were interested in Judaism at that time – for the religion of the pagan gods was gradually losing its attraction.

A large number of pagans also partly followed the Jewish faith by loosely attaching themselves to synagogues. But they did not go the whole way in accepting all the commandments of the Torah. Known as 'God-Fearers', they were sympathetic to Judaism but not fully committed. They sat in a special section in the synagogues.

What would pagans have found most difficult in Judaism?
Circumcision and Kashrut

4) HOW DO WE KNOW ABOUT JESUS?

There are no surviving contemporary accounts of Jesus's life and death. All we have are four books called gospels, each written in Greek in countries far away from Judea, between about 40 and 60 years after his death. As might be expected, they are muddled and contradict each other in important respects.

From three of the gospels – those written by Matthew, Mark and Luke – we can derive a picture of Jesus as a fairly conventional Jew of his time. From the other – that written by John – we get a picture far closer to that given by the Christian Church.

Modern scholars have been able to reconstruct a fairly convincing historical picture of Jesus from a critical reading of the first three gospels:

1) His name was Yehoshua (Joshua) – Yeshu for short – Jesus in Greek.

2) He had four brothers and more than one sister.

3) He and his followers were countrymen from Galilee. The sophisticated Jews of Jerusalem sneered at their provincial accents.

4) He was not a carpenter but earned his living as a faith healer and popular preacher. In those days people depended on prayer as well as on doctors for curing disease. He was very successful and people thought this was because he

was close to God.

5) Jesus thought that the coming of the Messiah, to be followed by the end of the world, was approaching fast. He and his followers urged people to repent before it was too late. This was his urgent message to all Jews who would listen.

6) Jesus preached only to Jews and had very little patience with pagans. In fact he forbad his followers to waste their time with non-Jews.

7) He thought that the rabbis of his day paid too much attention to the details of Jewish observance and not enough to its inner meaning. He may have been a little careless about minor breaches of Shabbath laws and suchlike.

8) On the other hand, he was a fully observant Jew who declared that the Torah – the Law of Moses – would never be changed and would stand for ever.

9) As related by the first three gospels, Jesus never claimed to be the Messiah. Indeed very few of his ideas would not have been fully accepted by the most orthodox Jews of his time.

5) WHAT HAPPENED TO HIM?

Passover was always a very difficult time in Jerusalem. The city was then crowded with thousands of pilgrims, who had come to sacrifice in the Temple.

As the Jewish nation was in a state of incipient revolt against Rome, the Romans garrison was on full alert at Passover; and every effort was made by the Jewish leadership as well as by the Romans to keep the city quiet and prevent trouble.

Why do you think the Jewish leaders wanted to avoid trouble then?

Jesus and his Galilean followers came to Jerusalem and caused a disturbance in the Temple. He was arrested as an agitator, probably by the Jewish Temple police, and then surrendered to the Romans who promptly executed him by crucifixion – the Roman method. His followers fled in dismay.

6) WHO CRUCIFIED JESUS?

According to the gospels, the Jews of Jerusalem insisted that the Romans should crucify Jesus. This is unlikely – and the gospels accounts are full of contradictions and absurdities. Jesus was executed as a troublemaker by the Romans.

The Jews had power to arrest and execute anyone who broke Jewish law; and they would not willingly have handed one of their own over to the Roman oppressors for crucifixion – a method of execution hated by them. Also, it was certainly no crime in Jewish law to claim to be the Messiah – and it is not even likely that Jesus himself ever made that claim.

The men who wrote the gospels, between forty and sixty years after his death, were trying to 'sell' their new (and persecuted) religion to the Roman world. The Jews of Judea had by then become highly unpopular rebels against Rome. It was natural therefore for the gospel writers to try to distance themselves as far as possible from the Jewish rebels and to portray the Romans in the best light possible.

7) WHAT HAPPENED NEXT?

Those of Jesus's followers who remained in Jerusalem were, like he had been, good Jews. They continued to pray at the Temple every day and to obey the Torah. They seem to have been generally respected; for the only difference between them and other Jews was that they believed Jesus to have been the promised Messiah and that he would soon return to the earth in glory to start the Messianic Age.

Then, some years later, a group of Jews from the Diaspora who also believed that Jesus was the Messiah, caused trouble in Jerusalem. Their leader, Stephen, was killed by a furious Jewish mob who accused him of blasphemy; and his followers – but not the Palestinian believers – were driven out of Jerusalem. The original Jerusalem followers of Jesus were left in peace.

8) SAUL OF TARSUS

Saul, a member of the Temple police, claimed to have had a vision of Jesus on his way from Jerusalem to Damascus in order to preach against Jesus's followers in that city. He then changed his name to Paul and very gradually broke away from Judaism to found a new religion which we now call Christianity.

Paul taught that the Torah had been superseded by the coming of Jesus. He spent the rest of his life touring the Jewish communities of the Roman world to spread his message. Most Jews resisted Paul and treated him badly.

Paul's ideas were quite new and were most certainly not those of Jesus himself. Paul, and not Jesus, was the true founder of Christianity.

Paul's ideas:

1) The Torah is no longer valid since the coming of Jesus, the Messiah, who would shortly return to earth in glory to rule over the whole of man kind, not just the Jews.

2) Man is burdened with sin from the moment of birth. This can only be lifted by belief in Jesus as the Messiah (the 'Christ' – from the Greek

Kristos) and by no other means. To be 'saved', one only has to believe.

3) Pagans can become Christians without first having to
become Jews. No more need for circumcision, kashrut, etc.

What does Judaism teach about the forgiveness of sin?
To be truly sorry, to resolve never to do it again and to do one's best to repair
the injury. It is by actions and not by belief that sin is forgiven. God is ready to
forgive repentant sinners.

Paul's new religion became popular with non-Jews, and especially with the God-Fearers attached to many of the synagogues. There were many disagreements with the Jewish followers of Jesus who had remained in Jerusalem as good Torah-abiding Jews; but Paul's party gradually gained the upper hand.

The crisis came after the siege of Jerusalem and the destruction of the Temple by the Romans in the year 70 – for the followers of Jesus refused to join their brethren in the general mourning for the Temple. The Bar Kochba revolt in the year 132 was the last straw – for the Jewish believers in Jesus stood aside from the war and merely looked on. They were accused of disloyalty by the other Jews and were driven from the synagogues. Christianity was on its own – a new religion.

9) PERSECUTION

Christianity spread rapidly within the Roman Empire, especially amongst the poor, amongst women and slaves – the lower classes.

Only Judaism was considered a legitimate religion by the Romans; and so Christians were savagely persecuted.

Jews too persecuted the Christians whenever they could, for they considered the new religion as a threat.

Why did most Jews reject Jesus as Messiah?
He was unsuccessful – the world did not change and he did not return in glory
to start the Messianic Age.

10) TRIUMPH

Constantine, the son of a Roman army general, was born in Britain and was stationed there whilst the Roman army, commanded by his father, waged war on the barbarian Scots. When his father died in the year 306, Constantine was acclaimed Emperor by the Roman legions in Britain.

He then marched across Europe at the head of his army to in a bid to make good his claim and seize the throne.

Though never before interested in Christianity, which was being savagely persecuted by the Romans at that time, Constantine made much use of the Church as an ally in his struggle to become Emperor; and he greatly rewarded the Church as soon as he had achieved that aim.

Roman persecution of Christians was stopped completely; and the process was started by which Christianity eventually became the state religion of the Roman Empire.

Equally significant, at a great Church council convened by Constantine, a basic principle of Christian belief was fixed for the first time – and those who disagreed were driven out. In turn they were persecuted as heretics.

That principle concerns the nature of Jesus, Constantine's Council declared, as an article of faith, that Jesus is of the same substance as God. In other words, the humble Jewish preacher who had travelled through the villages of Galilee three hundred years before, urging his fellow Jews to repent, had become God.

11) A DISASTER FOR THE JEWS

That was an unmitigated disaster for the Jews.

Before then, Judaism was a 'licit' faith, tolerated by the pagan Roman emperors; and loyal Jewish subjects enjoyed valuable privileges as Roman citizens.

All that changed when Christianity became the state religion of the Roman Empire, for the Church lost no time in exacting its revenge on the Jews. Their status as Roman citizens was steadily eroded.

> *Did it serve the Jews right for not having accepted Paul's teachings?*

Far worse, since Jesus had been recognised as God, and the Jews had killed Jesus (according to the gospels), the whole Jewish people was – in Christian eyes – guilty of the foul crime of having killed God.

This is the basis of Christian anti-Semitism, which grew worse and worse though the ages until it culminated in the holocaust.

responsible for some of the writings of the Dead Sea Scrolls believed in three messianic figures – the Priest of Righteousness, the King from the House of David, and the Prophet of the Last Days. There was also a recurring tradition that the Prophet Elijah would return to earth at the End of Days. However, it was the warrior king from the House of David who retained the dominant position in popular imagination. Particularly in Roman times, it was this Davidic king who was referred to as the Messiah. His actual personality aroused little interest though, for he was not regarded as the initiator of the final drama – but rather as an instrument of divine purpose, or simply a feature of the new age.

★ ★ ★

Some further knowledge of history is necessary for proper understanding of the events that occurred during the early period of Roman domination of the Holy Land, and which were so important for the later development of Judaism and Christianity. The Jewish state, established at such cost as the result of the Maccabean revolt, expanded to take in Galilee in the north as well as Idumea (Edom) in the south. Its borders approximated to those of modern Israel today, with the addition of most of the present Kingdom of Jordan. In the upsurge of national religious enthusiasm that accompanied the overthrow of Greek domination, many of the pagan inhabitants of the land were incorporated into the nation by mass conversion to Judaism. Judea, as it was called, managed to preserve its independence for the next eighty years.

In 63 B.C., each of two rival claimants to the throne made the disastrous mistake of appealing for help to a Roman army recently arrived in neighbouring Syria. Pompey did not need to be asked twice. He promptly invaded the country and entered Jerusalem at the head of his troops. Temple Mount was besieged for three months before it was finally conquered and thousands of its defenders killed. The Temple was sacked; and Pompey committed the ultimate sacrilege of entering its sanctuary, the Holy of Holies.

Judea was firmly incorporated into the Roman world. It was stripped of most of its territory; and what was left became part of the new Roman province of Syria. The truncated country was allowed a measure of local autonomy under its former king, who

4

The word 'messiah' has not appeared previously in this book, mainly because it only came to have its present meaning after the end of the period covered by the Hebrew Bible. The ceremony of conferring office on the kings and high priests of Judah and Israel was known as anointing. It consisted of pouring special oil over their heads as the visible sign of election and consecration to God's service. Those so favoured were referred to as the Lord's anointed. King David, for example, is described in the Hebrew Bible as (HA-MELECH) HA-MASHIAH – THE ANOINTED (KING) – from which the English word 'messiah' (meaning 'anointed') was ultimately derived.

The word 'Messiah' acquired new and special significance in the Roman era, when it came to be used as the title of the warrior king, descended from King David, who will be raised up by God to restore the fortunes of Israel and inaugurate the final utopian age of human history. Though Christians later attributed divine qualities to the Messiah, it is important to appreciate that this was not a Jewish concept. For Jews, the Messiah would be human and mortal.

Jews were fascinated by the prospect of the Messianic Age to come. They devoted a great deal of energy to speculations about its character and the terrible events that were expected to precede it. Some accounts of the last days make no mention at all of the Messiah himself: others contain a variety of messianic figures. The Old Testament Book of Zechariah had two messiahs – the Priest of Righteousness (descended from Aaron the High Priest) and the Royal Messiah (descended from King David). The Jewish sect lost his royal title. Life was hard and taxation heavy under the Romans. Having enjoyed their freedom for the past eighty years, the Jews did not take kindly to foreign rule. They proved turbulent subjects; and revolted against their new masters again and again – but to no avail. Conditions only improved after Julius Caesar's victory over Pompey in 48 B.C. The Jews helped Caesar in his further struggles; and in return were treated as friends and allies. Caesar reversed previous Roman policy by restoring the port of Jaffa and other territories, by permitting the rebuilding of the walls of Jerusalem and by fixing taxes to a reasonable limit. Bad times returned with the murder of Julius Caesar in 44 B.C., after which Cassius took control in person and introduced a sterner regime. The Jews deeply mourned the death of Julius Caesar; and it was reported that groups of them were to be seen lamenting over his tomb in Rome long after he had been forgotten by the Romans.

The new order was not accepted by the people of Judea. They rebelled once again; and even regained their liberty for a short period in alliance with the Parthians, Rome's enemies in the East. Herod, the Roman governor of Galilee, resisted the Jewish independence movement and fled to Rome where he was well received by its joint rulers, Anthony and Octavian. Herod was declared King of Judea by the Romans. After the Parthians had been beaten, a Roman army helped Herod's own forces to secure his kingdom. Jerusalem fell to the Romans in 37 B.C.; and the new reign began with the execution of large numbers of Herod's opponents and the confiscation of their property to buy off the rapacious Roman soldiers, intent on looting the captured city and Temple.

· Herod was a shrewd and capable monarch with great personal charm. He was liked and trusted by the Roman leaders; and he repaid that trust with unswerving loyalty. He first assisted his patron Mark Anthony in his war with Octavian. Undismayed by Anthony's downfall, he lost no time in ingratiating himself with the triumphant Octavian (later called Augustus), by boasting of his past devotion to Mark Anthony and promising the same loyalty to his successor. Herod was duly confirmed as King of Judea. Under Herod, Judea's borders expanded to include all the land lost as the result of the Roman conquest of 63 B.C. To the world at large, and to the many Jews who lived outside Judea, Herod was a brilliant and successful king who well deserved his unofficial title of King Herod the Great.

It was different inside Judea, for Herod ruled his vassal kingdom more as an oriental despot than as a Jewish king bound by Jewish

law. He came from an Idumean family converted to Judaism in the time of the Maccabees. The Jews hated him as a foreign usurper, indifferent to their faith and customs. The cosmopolitan Greek character of his court, his generous treatment of his pagan subjects and his lavish gifts to foreign cities caused great offence to religious Jews. The country was heavily taxed for the benefit of Rome, and to pay for Herod's foreign gifts, for the maintenance of his court and for the magnificent buildings he erected all over the country. He rebuilt the Temple on such a scale as to make it one of the wonders of the ancient world – but even that did little to endear him to the people, for he placed a golden Roman eagle over its Great Gate in flagrant violation of the second of the Ten Commandments forbidding graven images.

Herod maintained his grip on the country with cruel efficiency. His private behaviour was a standing reproach to the upright of the nation; and this grew worse towards the end of his reign when he was even accused of planning to prevent his Jewish subjects from rejoicing at his death. Representative leading citizens from every town and village in the country were imprisoned in Jerusalem. Their guards had orders to kill every one of them at the announcement of the king's death – thus compelling all Judea to weep for him. That plan was frustrated; but any rejoicing that did take place was premature. His surviving sons proved incapable of maintaining their inheritance; and after ten years of strife and bloodshed, Rome was forced to intervene once again in Judean affairs.

Herod's former kingdom was fragmented by the Romans, who imposed a new order on the eastern edge of their empire. Galilee and Transjordan were detached and given to one of Herod's sons to rule on Rome's behalf. Judea lost most of its coastal plain, as well as Idumea (Edom) in the south, and Samaria which divided it from Galilee in the north. The remaining territory, centred on Jerusalem, became the Roman province of Judea, governed directly by a Roman governor and permanently garrisoned with Roman troops. The status of Jerusalem was downgraded in favour of Caesarea, the new capital. The bad old days had returned with a vengeance. The scene was set for the events described in the books of the New Testament.

The Roman occupation of Judea was oppressive, with Roman insensitivity to Jewish national and religious aspirations fully matched by Jewish refusal to accept a situation in which they were ruled by pagan foreigners instead of by the God of Israel through

LESSON 32   JESUS THE JEW AND THE RISE OF CHRISTIANITY

his anointed kings and high priests. The Jews were allowed some self-government, especially in religious affairs; but the succession to the High Priesthood was closely controlled by the Roman governor, who kept the sacred robes of office in his custody. Though the Roman army respected Jewish religious feeling to the extent of not bringing its standards into the Holy City (as they bore 'images' of the Emperor, forbidden by the second of the Ten Commandments), the presence of a permanent garrison in Jerusalem overlooking the Temple was an affront. A heavy burden of taxation was imposed to meet the demands of Rome and the costs of the occupation, as well as to satisfy the personal greed of the governors. The collection of taxes was sub-contracted to Jewish tax collectors, the so-called 'publicans' of the New Testament, who earned the hatred of the people by also lining their own pockets in the process.

Judea seethed with discontent. The three great religious festivals of the year, when hundreds of thousands of Jews from inside the country and abroad flocked to sacrifice at the Temple, were times of special tension during which the governor himself took up residence in Jerusalem and the garrison was placed on full alert. Any rebellious act or even suspicion of disobedience was ruthlessly punished; and thousands met their death by crucifixion, an atrocious form of punishment abominated by the Jews. Two thousand religious Jews were crucified by the Romans on one occasion alone.

Pontius Pilate was one of the most unpleasant of the Roman governors. A reliable contemporary source describes him as a man of limited ability, inflexible, corrupt, vicious and cruel. His first significant act on arriving in the province in 26 A.D. was to have standards containing the effigy of the Emperor secretly carried into Jerusalem at night, no doubt as a demonstration of scorn for the religious beliefs of the subject population. The images were later removed after a large number of Jews declared that they would rather forfeit their lives than tolerate such desecration of the Holy City. Pilate is reputed to have been responsible for the murder of many innocent people and for much other savagery. He was eventually recalled to Rome in disgrace after a particularly senseless massacre of Samaritans. One report has it that once there, he was ordered to take his own life.

Galilee, divided from Judea by the territory of non-Jewish Samaria, was spared the indignity of a direct Roman presence. Together with Transjordan it was ruled on behalf of Rome by Herod

32

Antipas, a son of King Herod the Great. However the illusion of independence cannot have been very convincing, for Galilee was reputed to be the most troublesome of the Jewish districts. Its fertile countryside, far from the corrupting sophistication of city life, nourished a proud and independent people who did not take kindly to foreign taxes or to foreign rule of any kind, even by proxy. Rebellion was endemic; and in the Roman world, the very word Galilean conveyed overtones of revolt.

★　★　★

The growing Jewish conflict with Rome resulted in an intensification of the prophesies of redemption, and in the production of many writings dealing with the dawning Messianic Age. In adversity, Jews always yearned for the End of Days which would bring about the predicted final triumph over their enemies. There was no shortage of men prepared to raise the standard of revolt. Judah the Galilean, founder of the Zealot movement which caused Rome much trouble, taught that is was shameful for Jews to pay taxes to the Romans and acknowledge them as masters, when God alone should rule over Israel. His passion for liberty led directly to several unsuccessful attempts to cast off the Roman yoke and inaugurate God's kingdom on earth. Theudas, another self-proclaimed messiah, persuaded a multitude of people to follow him to the River Jordan where, like Moses at the Red Sea, the waters would part for him to cross over. Most of his followers were massacred by the Romans; and Theudas himself was beheaded. Another hopeful messiah from Egypt led several thousand followers to the Mount of Olives, from where he intended to liberate Jerusalem in fulfilment of a prophesy. The Romans dealt with that rising in their usual manner. The Egyptian messiah escaped the resulting slaughter; and the Romans later arrested the Christian apostle Paul in mistake for him.

A prophet called Yochanaan – John (the Baptist) – arose in Galilee. He caused a sensation by declaring that the Kingdom of God was at hand, and calling on the Jews to repent whilst there was still time. Herod Antipas, the cautious ruler of Galilee, was alarmed by the potentially revolutionary effect of such eloquence on the masses. Presumably discounting the possibility that John was truly the prophet Elijah returned to earth, Herod first imprisoned him and then silenced him for ever. Amongst those baptised by John with the waters of repentance was a thirty-year old faith healer and popular preacher from Nazareth called Yeshu, short for Yehoshua (Joshua). Accompanied by a crowd of his Galilean followers, Yeshu (Jesus in Greek) later visited Jerusalem and caused a disturbance in the Temple at a time when the city was packed with pilgrims for the Passover festival, and when both the Jewish Temple authorities and the Roman garrison must have been at their most anxious to avoid trouble. Jesus was promptly arrested and crucified by the Romans. His followers dispersed at once and went into hiding.

For the Romans the execution of Jesus was a very minor episode that merited a single paragraph in the first-century writings of the Roman (Jewish) historian Josephus, and only a sentence in Tacitus's second-century history of the period. It is a long step from the above bald account to the Christian concept of Jesus as the Son of God, made man, crucified for the sins of the world, ascended to heaven and now sitting in glory at the right hand of the Father. Many Christians think it wrong even to attempt to bridge that gap with a critical assessment of the historical Jesus. For them it is the resurrected Jesus seen through the eyes of faith that counts, rather than actual details of his earthly life; and they are content to accept at face value the muddled picture presented in the Gospels. The apostle Paul, whose New Testament letters were written twenty years or more after the crucifixion, held a similar opinion. Paul never met Jesus, and displayed little interest in his contemporary. he declared that:

Even if we did know Jesus Christ in the flesh, that is not how we know him any longer.

However for those without such faith the topic remains one of abiding interest. And even for those with faith, a more accurate picture of Jesus's life and times need not detract from their own special view of his true nature. Some modern scholars have tried to fit the Gospel accounts into what now is known of the period. They have attempted to correct misunderstandings caused by a lack of awareness of the nuances of original Aramaic terms translated into the Greek of the Gospels by men removed in culture, place and time from the events they described. Such critical appraisal is valuable, and much of it convincing.

Nearly all of what we now know of Jesus's life comes from the four New Testament Gospels. These are the survivors of a larger number of similar gospels, each written for a particular Christian community in the pagan world outside Palestine. The society in which Jesus lived and preached, together with its written records, perished in the year 70 A.D. when the Romans destroyed Jerusalem and its Temple after four years of ferocious warfare. Scholarly opinion is far from unanimous in dating the Gospels; but it is generally accepted that Mark's gospel was written in Rome around 70 A.D., some forty years after the crucifixion; and that those of Matthew, Luke and John followed after Mark in that order during the next twenty or thirty years. The first three gospels all include much common material; and it is believed that Mark's gospel and another gospel now lost were the primary sources for those of Matthew and Luke. John's gospel stands apart from the other three. It is the least historical and differs in several details – such as in the reported duration of Jesus's ministry. It also differs in its style of presentation, which is heavily influenced by Church doctrine.

Errors in Palestinian geography, and in Jewish law, custom, language and chronology indicate that the Gospels were compiled by men remote from Jesus's world. On the other hand, the frank reporting of incidents in which Jesus expressed attitudes and ideas contrary to those of the later Christian Church – including his evident indifference to gentiles – seems authentic. At least part of the gospel material was translated into Greek from Aramaic, the everyday language of Galilean Jews of Jesus's time. A reasonable explanation of the problem of origins may be that the authors relied on older Aramaic documents for their historical data; and these may even have included accounts written by one or more of Jesus's own disciples.

Though frankly propagandist in intent, the Gospels are not dishonest. They do not purport to be accurate biographies in the modern sense; but contain special selections of incidents and teachings corresponding to the image of Jesus already formed by the Church of the period in which they were written. They are also closely geared to the particular needs of vulnerable groups of early Christians. Thus for the gentile Christians of Rome, pains were taken to portray their fellow Romans in the best possible light; and also to distance the founder of their faith as far as possible from the highly unpopular Jews of Judea, whose bitter insurrection had only just been crushed at high cost in Roman lives. It will never

LESSON 32   JESUS THE JEW AND THE RISE OF CHRISTIANITY

be known whether or not the figure portrayed in the Gospels – and particularly in those of Mark, Matthew and Luke – is the authentic Jesus who was crucified by the Romans in 30 A.D.; but it is the closest that we will ever get to him.

Jesus was a countryman from an obscure village in Galilee called Nazareth; and he spent most of his time in the countryside. He spoke Aramaic in his everyday life, reserving Hebrew for his prayers. Galileans were considered ignorant bumpkins by the more educated and worldly Judeans, who constantly poked fun at their crude behaviour and accents. Jesus was popular in his home province where he attracted large crowds, but seems to have had less success outside Galilee.

Matthew and Luke, eager to demonstrate that Jesus was the expected Messiah, first named Joseph as his father and then carefully traced his descent from King David. On the other hand, they also say that he was born of a virgin. That idea was alien to the Jewish traditions and expectations of the time, though not to those of the gentile Greek-Roman world from which it sprang. Mark and John made no such claim for Jesus's birth; nor did the later Jewish-Christian sect, the Ebionites. The historian Geza Vermes has pointed out that the word for 'virgin' in the popular languages of the period did not necessarily denote a woman who has never had sexual relations with a man, though that was definitely the way it was later interpreted by the Church – and there may possibly be a clue there.

In any event, the Gospels relate that Jesus was a member of a large family. He had four brothers and more than one sister. His family's reported exclamation of incredulity on first hearing of his mission – 'He is out of his mind' – sounds genuine in the context. Jesus was a wandering prophet, a holy man in true Jewish tradition; and as stressed in the Gospels, his power of healing derived directly from his closeness to God. He earned his living in the Galilean countryside by healing the sick, casting out evil spirits and preaching to the people – a profession by no means unusual, for we know of similar miracle workers such as the famous Rabbi Hanina ben Dosa, also from Galilee. People of the time regarded physical and mental illness as God's punishment for sin. Healing by faith and prayer was thought more proper than relying only on doctors of medicine.

Jesus preached his urgent message of repentance to all Jews prepared to listen. His teaching was restricted to Jews alone; and he expressly forbad his disciples to go among the gentiles. There

is little trace in the first three gospels of the universal Church later created by Paul; for Jesus himself seems to have had little time for pagan outsiders. A gentile woman's request for help was at first rebuffed with the retort 'It is not fair to take the children's bread and throw it to the dogs', before her humbleness caused Jesus to relent – and in first-century Palestine, dogs were not the pampered pets they have since become. He carried his message to the outcasts of Jewish society such as collaborators with the occupying Roman power and prostitutes, declaring that such people had the greatest need for him. He also seems to have had more personal contact with women than would an orthodox Jewish rabbi of his time, brushing ritual restrictions aside with unconcealed impatience.

★ ★ ★

The Jewish religion was in an exciting stage of development in the first century A.D. The aristocratic Sadducees, with their rigid interpretation of the written laws contained in the Bible and their emphasis on the Temple cult, were steadily losing ground to the more democratic Pharisees. Unfairly maligned in the Gospels, the Pharisees were the party of progress, willing to interpret the older traditions flexibly in the light of the conditions of the time and more in accordance with their underlying intentions. Unlike the Sadducees, they believed in the resurrection of the dead. The saintly Hillel was the leader of a school of Pharisees which pre-dated Jesus. When challenged to summarise the teachings of Judaism while standing on one foot, he responded:

'Whatever is hateful to you, do not do to your neighbour. That is the essence of the Law. Now go and learn.'

His reply was, of course, a paraphrase of a sentence in the Old Testament Book of Leviticus:

'You shall love your neighbour as yourself: I am the Lord'.

Jews were taught that man was created in the image of God; and that he is required to imitate God in 'holiness' by doing justice, loving mercy and carrying out the ritual requirements of the faith.

LESSON 32 JESUS THE JEW AND THE RISE OF CHRISTIANITY

Their sages had erected an elaborate protective framework of regulations on the basic laws of the Bible to preserve the people from risk of transgressing – a 'fence' around the Law, as it was called. Consequently the many details of everyday life were closely regulated, including which activities were forbidden on the Sabbath, what food to eat and what not to eat, when to wash the hands, when to leave the fields fallow, when to pay wages, how to conduct business affairs, etc. Scrupulous observance of all aspects of their holy Law was not thought to be a burden by the Jews of the time, any more than it is today, but as a way of life accepted with love and gratitude. Standards of observance were naturally higher in the Judean centres of learning than in rural Galilee.

First-century Judaism also produced several variant sects, such as the Essenes who withdrew to the desert to await the End of Days. The early followers of Jesus formed another such group, called the Nazarenes.

When asked to summarise his beliefs, Jesus first quoted the great confession of Jewish faith, the 'Shema', which was proclaimed regularly in the Temple and which is still recited by observant Jews every day of their lives:

Hear O Israel, the Lord is our God, the Lord is one. And you shall love the Lord your God with all your heart and with all your soul and with all your might...

Jesus continued very much as Hillel might have done with the passage from the Old Testament Book of Leviticus:

You shall love your neighbour as yourself...

Jesus preached that the Kingdom of God – the expected Messianic Age – was at hand. He called on his fellow Jews to repent, and follow him in renouncing the material things of this world. His main teachings were well within the scope of what was acceptable to the Pharisaic wing of Judaism; and the first three gospels contain very little that can be described as strikingly original or revolutionary. Though Jesus was not a Pharisee, he differed from them only in that he did not believe that the path to salvation lay in meticulous observance of the complex network of commandments – but rather in renunciation and absolute faith. Like other Jewish

religious reformers before and since, Jesus stressed the inner spiritual meaning of the commandments, and warned against the danger of obeying the letter of the Law but ignoring its spirit. His opponents criticised him for minor infringements of Sabbath laws, and for behaviour such as sitting down to meals before first washing his hands (a ritual requirement) and for allowing himself to be touched by impure women; but Jesus poured scorn on such quibbles. All the same, he never called for the alteration of the Law; and even declared his belief that it would stand for ever.

The really unusual aspect of Jesus's religious approach was his uncompromising other-worldliness. Judaism was a faith which concentrated more on practical measures for righting the wrongs of this world than on the life of the spirit. Jesus's teachings may not have been particularly original; but nowhere else in Jewish teaching is the extreme idealism implied in the giving up of all material possessions, loving one's enemies and turning the other cheek when wronged, presented together so plainly and with such force. Jesus possessed the unerring ability to summarise the noblest ideals of human behaviour in a coherent message, intelligible to all. He pressed that lesson home against a background in which the establishment of the Kingdom of God on earth was to be expected within a period of months rather than years. His striking success in healing the sick and exorcising the evil spirits deemed responsible for mental illness convinced admirers that Jesus was very close to God. It invested his teaching with special authority.

The Gospels do not depict Jesus as a scholar, but as a Galilean countryman who lived far from the hothouse atmosphere of the religious academies of Jerusalem. His way, in the tradition of the Hebrew prophets, was the way of inspiration rather than learning. Jesus employed the medium of rabbinic parables to convey his message – a standard teaching method, familiar to Jews though not necessarily to pagan gentiles.

The interpretation of the basic concepts of Judaism contained in the Bible (the Law of Moses) was developed by Jewish sages to cover every aspect of human behaviour. The process of continuous refinement to meet the needs of each age was partly carried out by means of learned discussions or disputes. Differing opinions were argued out by the leading rabbis, and eventual agreement reached by consensus or majority vote; and this continues among religious Jews to this day. Jesus must also have employed the same process for testing ideas. On occasion he evidently enjoyed getting the better of more learned opponents in such argument. Many of his 'disputes' with the Pharisees mentioned in the Gospels probably relate to discussions of this kind.

* * *

Whatever Jesus himself may have thought, to the Jews of Roman Palestine the expected Kingdom of God was seen first and foremost in material terms. Its main characteristic would be victory over the hated Roman occupiers – a victory so complete as to ensure permanent dominance of the Jewish people over their neighbours. The Messiah, a mortal descendant of King David, would lead the people in battle to their final triumph. He would then rule over a spiritual and moral utopia in which all the nations of the world would acknowledge the one true God of Israel. There were many variations of this basic belief; but these never included any suggestion that the Messiah would have divine qualities, or that he would perish miserably before achieving his purpose.

Nowhere in the first three gospels – those written by Mark, Matthew and Luke – did Jesus actually claim to be the Messiah. He was curiously reticent when acclaimed Messiah by his followers – neither accepting nor denying, but just ordering them not to tell anyone of their belief. Even titles, such as 'Son of God' used to describe Jesus in the Gospels need not necessarily relate to messianic pretensions, as they may have been understood in quite another sense by the Jews of the period. In fact, but for John's gospel, it would be reasonable to suppose from the evidence of the other three that Jesus never saw himself as the royal Messiah, descendant of King David. Indeed his rôle may be better be understood in terms similar to those used to describe the Prophet of the Last Days mentioned in the Dead Sea Scrolls – or even as a prophetic herald of the Messianic Age. John's gospel, on the other hand, fully supports the Christian view of Jesus as the Messiah.

* * *

Not all the gospel accounts of Jesus's last days, in which he came

to Jerusalem at the head of a crowd of enthusiastic Galilean followers, stand up well to critical scrutiny. Jesus entered the city in triumph when it was thronged with pilgrims for the Passover festival, and created a disturbance in the Temple. The story of his chasing the money-changers from one of the outer courts of the Temple sounds splendidly idealistic until one realises that the Temple complex was a major cult centre, not a synagogue or a church. The huge influx of pilgrims from all over the world needed a spacious market place close to the Sanctuary to change their money and buy the proper animals for sacrifice.

The rest of the story in which Jesus was arrested by the Temple police, tried in secret by the Jewish supreme court on the first evening of the Passover and then handed over to the Romans for crucifixion seems as improbable as do the details given to embellish it. Incredibly, for the Jews were a very legally minded people, the court proceedings as reported were entirely contrary to established law and procedure. Jesus would not have committed an offence in religious law, even if he had claimed to be the Messiah. As to being the Son of God, all prophets regarded themselves as sons of God in the Jewish sense – which implied closeness to God and no more. Also a Jewish court, which itself had the power to impose the death penalty for religious offences (as it did later in the case of Stephen), was hardly likely to have handed a fellow countryman over to the hated Romans for execution in a manner so repugnant to the sensibilities of the people.

Only one day after Jesus had entered the city in triumph to the acclamation of his followers, a crowd is supposed to have assembled to howl for his blood in front of the Roman governor, who himself was public enemy number one. And all this is said to have happened on the first morning of the Passover festival, when most would have been at the Temple or in the synagogues. Of course the High Priest could always have hired a mob for the occasion, if he had been crazy enough to have wanted to draw attention to the sorry event. There is no record anywhere other than in the gospel story of Barabbas of the supposed Roman custom of pardoning a condemned man specially for Passover. To cap it all, the image of the brutal and inflexible Pontius Pilate repeatedly pleading with a chanting mob of despised colonials for the life of one of their holy men is frankly ridiculous.

It is of course possible that Jesus was surrendered to the Romans (at their insistence?) by the Jewish leaders, on the principle of having

LESSON 32   JESUS THE JEW AND THE RISE OF CHRISTIANITY

to sacrifice one person to save the entire people – for the consequences of any kind of popular insurrection in Jerusalem at Passover would have been disastrous. This is hinted at in John's gospel, where the account given of Jesus's hurried night-time interrogation by the High Priest and a colleague makes a lot more sense than the alternative trial scene described in the three other gospels. Another possibility is that Jesus was simply arrested and executed by the Romans as a potentially dangerous agitator – as suggested by the biting irony of the inscription on his cross:

Jesus of Nazareth, King of the Jews'

Many other theories have been advanced by scholars, some plausible and others more fanciful.

Jesus was in great agony of spirit just before his arrest; and Luke's gospel has it that:

'His sweat fell to the ground like great drops of blood'.

According to Mark and Matthew, though not repeated by Luke or John, Jesus's last utterance on the cross was the bleak cry of total despair:

My God, my God, why have you forsaken me.'

Jesus's disciples scattered in panic at his death. They fled for their lives. Their dream was over.

5

TO MOVE MOUNTAINS

In terms of traditional expectation, Jesus's career ended in despair and utter failure. Yet for some of his followers that very failure was transformed into sublime triumph. The Messiah had perished miserably before leading his people to victory. But on the third day he had risen from the dead and told his disciples that he would shortly return in glory to start the Messianic Age. For most Jews – and only Jews followed Jesus then – the concept of a crucified Messiah was too much of a contradiction ever to be accepted. In Paul's words, the Cross of Christ was:

'a stumbling block. . . . an obstacle that they cannot get over'.

In any event, conditions on earth, and particularly in Roman Palestine, continued to deteriorate. Many saw little purpose in a Kingdom of God confined only to the spirit, and which did nothing to help them in their very real troubles.

Few Palestinian Jewish records survived the two terrible wars with Rome which came to an end in 135 A.D. Also the early Christian records of the time were destroyed during the Emperor Diocletian's persecution of Christians in the fourth century. Some information on the first years after the crucifixion can be gleaned from the New Testament, from the writings of the Roman-Jewish historian Josephus, from later historians and from remaining fragments of ancient manuscripts. A most important source is the New Testament letters of St. Paul, some of which may have been written as early as twenty years after Jesus's death in 30 A.D. Another is the New

Testament book 'Acts of the Apostles', written by Luke at the end of the first century.

Belief in Jesus as the Jewish Messiah remained strong among his original Galilean followers who remained in Jerusalem after the crucifixion. According to 'Acts of the Apostles', Peter taught that God had promised King David that one of his direct descendants would sit on the throne; and he urged all Israel to accept it as certain that the promised Messiah was none other than the crucified Jesus. The impatience with which Jesus was expected to return to earth to establish the Kingdom of God is illustrated by the reported question put to the risen Jesus by the apostles:

'Lord is this the time when you are to establish again the sovereignty of Israel'

and Jesus's reply:

'It is not for you to know dates or times'.

Jerusalem continued for a time to be the centre of the new Jewish sect. Though Peter is the main figure described in 'Acts of the Apostles', it is probable that Jesus's brother James (James the Just) was the first leader of the Nazarenes. The disciples continued to live very much as they had in Jesus's lifetime, proclaiming his message, healing the sick, visiting the Temple together every day, and scrupulously observing the commandments of the Jewish faith. They sold their goods and possessions in order to live in communes, sharing all things according to need. Unlike the Essenes, who also practised a form of primitive communism in their desert retreat, the Nazarenes sent a stream of missionaries to spread their gospel to centres of Jewish life outside Palestine.

The new belief attracted many, particularly among the Greek-speaking Jews of the Roman empire. It also spread to large groups of gentiles who existed on the fringe of Judaism, loosely attached to synagogues but not fully converted to the faith. Before long there were believers in most of the Jewish communities of the Greek-Roman world. Jesus the Messiah became known as Jesus the Christ, Krystos being the Greek for Messiah (Anointed); and this was later shortened to Jesus Christ, or just Christ. Believers were called Christians.

Though the Apostles followed Jesus in remaining fully within

the Jewish fold, the Greek-speaking Jews were more radical in their approach to the Law of Moses and the Temple cult; and they soon incurred the wrath of the Temple authorities. One of their leaders, Stephen, was tried by the Jewish supreme court in 36 A.D.; and, without reference to the Roman governor, was promptly executed for blasphemy. Christians were then attacked; and the Greeks – but not the Apostles – were driven from Jerusalem. This marked the beginning of the rift between Greek-speaking Jews and their Palestinian brethren.

★ ★ ★

Saul of Tarsus, better known as St. Paul, was one of the greatest religious innovators of all time. But for his intervention, the Nazarenes would probably have remained just another obscure Jewish sect, doomed to eventual extinction like the others. Because of him, they became the precursors of one of the principal religious communities of mankind.

Saul, who possessed the rare privilege (for a non-Roman Jew) of Roman citizenship, was born in the cultured and prosperous self-governing Greek city of Tarsus in what now is modern Turkey. According to Jerome, his family originated in Galilee. Saul was a tent-maker by trade, and supported himself in that way for long periods of his career. He always managed to combine genuine admiration for the Roman Empire with pride in his Jewish descent – in stark contrast to the attitude of the Palestinian Jews who suffered under the Roman yoke. It is to his credit that he barely wavered in either loyalty despite the many trials to which he was subjected. Saul's native tongue was Greek, but his religion and background were impeccably Jewish. He was a Pharisee; and was said by Luke to have studied in Jerusalem under the celebrated sage Rabbi Gamaliel the Elder – though there is no hint of this in his writings.

Saul himself claimed to have been a zealous persecutor of the followers of Jesus. It was on a mission to deal with the troublesome Nazarenes of Damascus, shortly after Stephen's death, that he was literally stopped short in his tracks by a vision of the risen Christ. Fourteen years later, he wrote that he was:

'. . . caught up as far as the third heaven . . . whether in the body or out of it I do not know, God knows . . . was caught up into paradise, and heard words so secret that human lips may not repeat them.'

That vision was so overwhelming that it left Saul blinded, changed his entire life and made an indelible impression on world history. Saul recovered his sight after three days and was baptised in Damascus. He promptly assumed a new role in life as Apostle to the gentiles, using his Roman name Paulus (Paul) in preference to his Hebrew one. Some half dozen of the New Testament letters attributed to him are unreservedly accepted as genuine by scholars. They are unique in that they are the only surviving first-hand Christian documents of the period, free from the muddle that makes the much later written Gospels so difficult to evaluate historically. The letters set out Paul's religious message clearly. They also afford fascinating glimpses of the conflicts that beset the early Christians, and from which the outlines of the new religion were to emerge.

Paul had very little to say about the historical Jesus, the Galilean teacher who came to so abject an end on his cross. Except when unavoidable, he kept well away from those leaders of the Jerusalem Church who had known Jesus in person and were intent in following in his steps. For Paul it was his vision of the risen Christ that mattered, and he had nothing to learn from other men. He proudly asserted:

'. . . the good news I bring is not a human message that I was given by men. It is something that I learnt only through a revelation of Jesus Christ.'

Paul had good reason to avoid James, Peter and the other leading members of the Nazarene sect in Jerusalem. As one of their former persecutors he may not at first have been completely trusted; and far more important, his version of Christ's message differed from theirs in several important respects. Of course both parties had much in common and did meet from time to time to reconcile their conflicts. They both recognised Jesus of Nazareth as the promised Messiah. But for Paul the concept of the Jewish Messiah was enlarged into that of a universal figure. Though Paul's expectation of the Kingdom of God was more spiritual and less nationalistic than that held in Jerusalem, both parties expected Christ to return to earth in glory during their own lifetimes. Also some of Paul's more idealistic teachings must have evoked poignant memories:

'And I will show you the best way of all . . . I may have faith strong enough to move mountains; but if I have no love I am nothing. I may dole out all I possess, or even give my body to be burnt; but if I have no love I am none the better. Love is patient; love is kind and envies no one. Love is never boastful, nor conceited, nor rude; never selfish, not quick to take offence . . . There is nothing that love cannot face; there is no limit to its faith, its hope and its endurance.'

The central theme of Paul's 'good news' was that the risen Christ was the full and final revelation of God's purpose in the world, superseding that of the Law of Moses by which Jews had hitherto regulated their lives; also that Jesus's death had cancelled God's covenant with Israel. Paul wrote:

'The Law was to be our guardian until Christ came and we could be justified by faith. Now that time has come and we are no longer under that guardian . . .'

The disciples who were living the lives of observant Jews, as Jesus had before them, must have been horrified by this sudden abrogation of their most sacred traditions. But worse was to follow, for Paul had also developed a new and extreme theory of original sin, far from that held by Judaism. Jews were not unduly burdened by a sense of sin for they believed that God would forgive sins when offered true repentence, evidence of reparation and appropriate sacrifice. According to Paul, unredeemed man is a helpless slave of sin, unable to free himself from its shackles even by means of the Law. Jesus had died on his Cross as a sacrifice to redeem all men from the power of sin. By means of that sacrifice, the whole of mankind may be saved – all men and not just Jews for:

'. . . there are no more distinctions between Jew and Greek, slave or free, male or female . . . merely by belonging to Christ you are the posterity of Abraham, the heirs he was promised.'

As a direct consequence of this new theology, Paul declared that gentile converts were not bound by the Law of Moses; and that they should not undergo the rite of circumcision. In other words, they need not first become Jews in order to qualify for salvation through Christ. Understandably those revolutionary ideas were opposed by James and Peter, the Palestinian-born Jewish leaders of the Jerusalem Church, who could not conceive of an independent existence outside the Jewish fold. Though Luke in his 'Acts of the Apostles' glosses over the difficulties and depicts all the Apostles in eventual agreement, it seems from Paul's letters that the conflict was resolved only by the destruction of Jerusalem and its Church by the Romans in 70 A.D.

Apart from the two main factions – one headed by Paul and the other by James – a bewildering variety of fringe movements also sprang up in the early years of the Church. Each group of these so-called Gnostic Christians relied on its own particular and secret revelation of Jesus in preference to the generally accepted one. Paul himself complained of a group in Corinth whose members believed that they had risen from the dead with Jesus, were already perfect and could do no wrong. Another sect mentioned elsewhere in the New Testament denied the reality of Jesus's earthly life, and asserted that his nature was purely divine. Yet another sect totally denied Jesus's divinity... and so on. In the end Paul's views triumphed over those of his opponents. All the books now included in the New Testament were written from Paul's standpoint, which became the basis of Christianity as we know it.

Paul tried to carry his message to all parts of the Roman world. He was impelled by a sense of extreme urgency, for he expected Christ's Second Coming to follow closely on the completion of his own mission. Time was short. In his own words:

'...the time we live in will not last long. While it lasts, married men should be as if they had no wives; mourners should be as if they had nothing to grieve them, the joyful as if they did not rejoice; buyers must not count on keeping what they buy... For the whole frame of this world is passing away.'

Despite considerable hardship as most Jews violently rejected him, Paul persisted in his missionary activity. This met with increasing success among the Greek-speaking gentiles. Though Paul can justly be described as the true founder of Christianity, he never turned his back on his own nation, maintaining with pride that God had saved the world through the agency of the Jews. He believed that God would never reject his chosen people, and that:

'...partial blindness has come upon Israel only until the gentiles have been admitted in full strength; when that has happened, the whole of Israel will be saved'.

The time of the Apostles did not last long. A newly-appointed High Priest, taking advantage of the temporary absence from the country of a Roman governor in the year 62, had James put to death in Jerusalem. He also executed a large number of Pharisees who had protested against the injustice – for James was popular, a man of great piety who worshipped regularly in the Temple. The High Priest was deposed after only three months in office, following complaints to the governor by what the historian Josephus described as 'the most moderate of the citizens, strict in their observance of the Law'. Within a few years of James's death, Peter and Paul both perished in Rome during the Emperor Nero's massacre of Christians following a fire that destroyed much of the city. Goaded beyond endurance, the Jews of Palestine rose in revolt against the Romans in the year 66. The war lasted for four years and cost Rome dear. But in the end Jerusalem was totally destroyed, its inhabitants killed or enslaved, and the Temple burnt to the ground.

★ ★ ★

The Temple had stood in Jerusalem with only one interruption of seventy years since the days of King Solomon, a thousand years before. For Jews it was the centre of their national existence, the focus of their faith. The Temple was the holiest place on earth. God's presence hovered in its sanctuary – a bare room considered so sacred that entry was restricted to the High Priest, and then only once a year on the Day of Atonement. The destruction of the Temple was a catastrophe – a disaster so keenly felt that, almost two thousand years later, observant Jews still fast and drape their synagogues in black on each anniversary. The sacrificial cult ended with the loss of the Temple; and the conservative Sadducean party and priesthood, against whose corruption Jesus had protested, disappeared for ever.

Yet for Judaism itself, seeds of renewal in a more vital form were also present at that terrible event. At the height of the siege of Jerusalem a leading Pharisee, Rabbi Yohanaan ben Zakkai, had his disciples declare that he had died of the plague. With great show of grief, they carried him in a sealed coffin for burial outside the city walls. Once beyond the ring of determined defenders, Ben Zakkai emerged from his shrouds and demanded to see the Roman commander, General Vespasian, who actually became Emperor shortly afterwards. The rabbi asked the general for permission to start a religious college in Yavneh, a small town in the north of the country. What Vespasian thought of Ben Zakkai, and just why he granted his petition – so bizarre a request during a brutal and as yet unresolved war – will never be known. But Rabbi Yohanaan ben Zakkai did found his famous academy at Yavneh. From that new beginning Judaism developed into a progressive and universal religion, no longer dependent on the Temple and the Holy Land for its continuation.

For the mass of the people, steeped in the expectation that God would intervene in human affairs when the forces of evil had finally achieved world domination, the End of Days seemed close. The burning of the Temple was seen as one of the last events preceding the Messianic Age; and one rabbinic parable stated that the Messiah was born on the day the Temple was destroyed – which really meant that redemption was implicit in the very act of destruction.

Economic distress and harsh political repression inflamed this messianic tension. Matters came to a head some sixty years later when rumours spread that the Emperor Hadrian intended to rebuild the Temple. The eventual disappointment of that hope was aggravated by the realisation that what Hadrian actually planned was the rebuilding of Jerusalem as an exclusively Roman city. Though the Emperor was probably unaware of the implications for his Jewish subjects of his decree forbidding the mutilation of the human body – for it seems that what he really intended was to forbid the pagan practice of castration – the law was interpreted in Judea as a ban on circumcision. That was the last straw for the Jews of Judea. Insurrection broke out all over the country.

Simon bar Kosevah led the rebellion which started in the year 132 and was actively supported by Jews in other parts of the Empire outside Palestine. The uprising was also encouraged by the great sage Rabbi Akivah. Simon at first succeeded in liberating most of Judea; but he was defeated three years later after a period of almost unprecedented bloodshed. The struggle was in vain, for Jerusalem was rebuilt after the war as a Roman City to which Jews were denied access on pain of death. A temple

to the pagan god Jupiter was erected on Temple Mount. And in a series of enactments recalling the severity of Antiochus Epiphanes, many of the rites and practices of Judaism were banned. Rabbi Akivah himself was executed by the Romans with even more than their customary cruelty when he defied their order forbidding the teaching of Judaism.

Though not himself of Davidic descent or in any way noted for his piety, Simon bar Kosevah was given the messianic title of Bar Kokhba (Son of the Star). He was actually proclaimed Messiah by Rabbi Akivah, one of a minority of the spiritual leaders of the nation who backed the suicidal war against Rome. Other rabbis vehemently denied that Bar Kokhba was the Messiah; and one rabbinic source even has it that he was eventually put to death because he could not substantiate his messianic claim. That seems unlikely, despite the despair caused by this disastrous failure; but as there are very few surviving contemporary Jewish references to Bar Kokhba, the truth may never be known. However there can be no doubt that the fanatical heroism displayed by the Jewish rebels against the overwhelming power of Imperial Rome was directly inspired by messianic hope.

Indeed, a new messianic figure appeared in literature after the defeat – that of the tragic Messiah Son of Joseph, destined to fall in battle at the head of his people in the last wars with the power of evil, in order to pave the way for the triumphant Messiah Son of David. There is no suggestion here that people continued to believe in Bar Kokhba after his defeat. The separation of the Messiah into two distinct persons was probably due more to a logical division of the Messiah's two roles – that of political saviour from that of spiritual redeemer. The creation of the legend of a simple warrior Messiah, such as Bar Kokhba might have been, freed the royal Messiah Son of David from the having to engage in warfare. It enabled him to be a spiritual redeemer, a Prince of Peace. Belief in the Messiah Son of Joseph became fairly common; but this was not shared by all the people or by all their religious leaders.

The war of 132-135 was the Jews' last attempt to inaugurate the Messianic Age directly by force of arms. From then on, messianic activity took other forms. The following gloomy passage from the Talmud aptly conveys the mood of the years that followed the revolt:

'In the footsteps of the Messiah presumption will increase and respect disappear. . . There will be none to offer reproach and the Empire will turn to heresy. The meeting place of scholars will become a brothel. . . Galilee will be laid waste and the people of the frontiers will wander from city to city with none to take pity on them. . . . The wisdom of the scribes will become odious, and those who shun sin will be despised: truth will nowhere be found. . . . The face of the generation is like the face of a dog. . . On whom then shall we rely? On our Father in heaven.'

★   ★   ★

Jesus's brother James (James the Just) was succeeded as head of the Jerusalem Church by his first cousin Simon. Simon was followed in turn by thirteen other 'bishops', including other members of Jesus's family. Most of the Jewish Christians survived the siege of Jerusalem; for they stood aside from the war, leaving in time to settle on the far side of the river Jordan. But their attitude to events increasingly set them apart from their fellow Jews. Not only had the Nazarenes not participated in the war, but they also held aloof from the deep mourning that followed the destruction of the Temple – believing either that it was a necessary fulfilment of Jesus's mission, or that it was just punishment for the Jews' rejection of Jesus. The period in which Peter, James and the others had lived the lives of pious Jews, differing from the majority only in their belief that the Messiah had already arrived, soon became only a memory. The majority turned on the Nazarenes bitterly with accusations of disloyalty. Eventually, all believers in Jesus were ejected from the synagogues.

The ill-treatment meted out to them by their fellow Jews during the Bar Kokhba revolt, coupled with Hadrian's stringent restrictions on all Jews after the war, proved too much even for the long-suffering Nazarenes. They took the decisive step of electing a gentile as head of the Judean Church; and then followed his lead in renouncing the Law of Moses. The break with Judaism was complete.

Some few, known as Ebionites, tried desperately to follow the Nazarene tradition of keeping a foot in both camps. They continued to observe the Jewish Law; but had their own Jewish language gospel in which Jesus was recognised as Messiah but not as God. The Ebionites, spurned by the Jews and condemned as heretics by the Church, eventually disappeared.

The far more successful Greek-speaking branch of the Church, founded by Paul, had long suffered persecution for its missionary activity at the hands of Jews outside Palestine. For Paul's successors, the destruction of Jerusalem and the consequent diminution in the authority of its Church was a decisive turning point. They increasingly veered away from the Jews towards the pagan gentiles among whom they were doing so well; and they re-interpreted the Christian message in terms more compatible with Greek understanding and culture.

The Jews, with their strange invisible God, were the only people of the Roman Empire who had been exempted from worshipping the Emperor. Gentile Christians, and Jewish Christians who had ceased to be Jews, were therefore required to confirm fully to the religious policy of the Empire. They were hounded by the Roman state when they refused to comply. To the Romans, Christianity was a mysterious and illicit religion which threatened to unsettle the lower classes of society. According to the first century historian Tacitus:

'There dwelt in Christians a hatred of mankind'

By the year 70, Palestinian Jews too had become highly unpopular subjects of Rome, partly on account of the ferocity with which they had just fought their four-year long war, and partly because of the unreasonable stubbornness with which they 'resisted repeated Roman attempts to impose cultural and religious uniformity on the Empire. There was little improvement after the end of the war, when Jews outside Palestine joined in several further rebellions against Rome. Palestine itself continued to seethe with discontent; and the Roman forces were so badly mauled in the second Jewish revolt of 132-135 that the Emperor Hadrian was obliged to omit the customary opening phrase 'I and my army are well' when reporting his victory to the Senate.

★   ★   ★

In those circumstances, Christian missionaries to the gentiles must have had a bad time. Already rejected violently by the very Jews from whose midst their Saviour and his Apostles had sprung, they were also persecuted by their fellow Romans for refusing to join in the cult of the Emperor. Their mission was particularly difficult in Rome itself; for its purpose was to convert the Romans to belief in a provincial Redeemer from the unpopular Jewish race who had been executed by the Roman governor for subversion.

The first New Testament gospel is believed to have been written in Rome by Mark in the year 70; and the other three were compiled in different parts of the Empire during the following thirty years. Understandably in that context, the Gospels go to great lengths to distance Jesus as far as possible from the Judaism of his day. Quite forgetting the elevated language of his 'Sermon on the Mount' and the idealistic tenor of much of his more inspired teaching, Matthew, for example, portrays Jesus as crudely abusing the Pharisees with whom he must have had so much in common:

'. . . hypocrites. You are like tombs covered with whitewash . . . inside they are full of dead men's bones and all kinds of filth . . . you are the sons of the men who killed the prophets . . . you snakes, you viper's brood, how can you escape being condemned to hell'

The Romans, of course, are shown in the best possible light. Although it could not be disguised that crucifixion was an exclusively Roman punishment abhorred by Jews, it was argued that Jesus was only crucified by the Romans at the insistence of the Jews; and that the good natured but weak Roman governor – the brutal Pontius Pilate – pleaded unsuccessfully for Jesus's life before a crowd of his own colonial subjects.

Matthew's report that the Jewish mob howled –

'His blood be on us and on our children'

may well have made his task easier with his flock. But it also was the foundation of the anti-semitism, created and nurtured by the Church, which caused untold misery throughout the ages and culminated in the murder of six million Jews during the Second World War.

★

★

★

Muhammad and the Rise of Islam

A) ARABIA

Arabia is a vast area, bigger than France and Spain combined. Most of it consists of dry semi-desert land, suitable only for nomadic grazing. Only in the south (Yemen) were there ancient civilised kingdoms and much cultivated land.

The Beduin Arabs were nomads, moving from place to place with their flocks of sheep and goats. They were organised into clans and tribes; and their only loyalty was to their tribe. Part of their way of life consisted of raiding other tribes for booty and sport – they did not want to kill each other. They were pagans.

Scattered throughout Arabia were fertile oases, in which date palms and other crops were grown and traded with the Beduin.

The inhabitants of Mecca were international traders who had become very rich . They travelled down to the south of Arabia to meet ships arriving from India, bought their precious cargoes – incense and spices – and then took them up to Syria, Egypt and Iraq, where they exchanged them for manufactured goods – textiles – which they then brought back to Mecca for trade with the Beduins.

Mecca was the home of the main pagan shrine, the Ka'aba, to which Arabs travelled once a year to pray – as they still do to this day, but now pray to Allah the one God and no longer to idols. The annual pilgrimage was a time of truce between all the warring clans of Beduin and was the ideal time for the great trade fairs during which the Meccans sold their goods.

The religion of the Arabs was very primitive. They had no sacred books, as did the Jews and the Christians, and worshipped idols, set up around the Ka'aba in Mecca. They did have a High God, al-Llah, who may have been the same as the God of the Jews and Christians – but that is not certain. It seems that the Arabs were not very satisfied with their religion and felt inferior to Jews and Christians, particularly because they had no scriptures of their own.

Though hardly mentioned in Jewish history, Jews also lived in Arabia. The kingdom of Himyar (Yemen) in the south contained many Jews, including the royal family for a period.

The story is told that a king of Himyar took his army up to conquer the north of Arabia. On his return, he fell seriously ill outside the oasis of Medina. Two rabbis came out from the town and cured the king. He was so impressed that he and his generals converted to Judaism. The rabbis accompanied the king back to Himyar, where they converted the royal family and many of the people.

Many of the oases in central and northern Arabia were inhabited by Jews, some exclusively so; and Jews were particularly good cultivators and growers of date palms.

Where did the Arabian Jews come from?

No one really knows. Perhaps they fled there from Roman persecution in the Holy Land. Some may have come from Iraq. Others may have been converts.

B) THE WORLD BEFORE MUHAMMAD

In the east was the Persian Empire in which most of the Jewish people lived. On the whole they had fared well under the Persians, despite occasional difficulties.

In the west was the Eastern Roman Empire, centred on Constantinople. This was Christian and becoming increasingly intolerant to Jews.

Western Europe, originally the Western Roman Empire, had been overrun by barbarian tribes. As the tribes converted to Christianity, they had gradually turned against the Jews and persecuted them badly.

C) MUHAMMAD

Muhammad was born in the year 570. He started on his mission to the world in 613 and died in 632.

Muhammad was an orphan from one of the poorest and least influential clans of Mecca. He had a good reputation for honesty and reliability and successfully headed a trading expedition to Syria on behalf of a rich widow from Mecca. He married the widow on his return to Mecca; and his financial future was thus secured.

Muhammad was a spiritual man who was looking for more than the pagan religion could provide. He had met both Christian and Jews during his trading trips up to the north and had been impressed by them. He used to spend days at a time alone in a cave outside the town, where he meditated and prayed.

Which Hebrew prophet used to retire to a cave for solitary meditation and prayer to God?

One day, in his cave, Muhammad had an overwhelming vision. It was of the angel Gabriel, who came to him and compelled him to recite. What he then recited was the first verse (sura) of the Qur'an. At first Muhammad found it hard to accept what had happened but eventually he started on his mission as the self-styled Messenger of God to the Arabs.

According to Muhammad, the angel Gabriel appeared to him regularly – usually at night – and gave him God's messages. Muhammad, who could neither read nor write, recited those same words in the morning. They were then written down by his family and disciples; and eventually collected together to form the Qur'an – God's message to the Arabs in the Arabic language.

Muhammad's new religion was based on what he had learned from the Jews and Christians, adapted to his own people's needs. In the very early days of his mission, he summed up its main points as follows:

1. There is no god but Allah, the one and only God.

2. Do not steal.

3. Do not fornicate.

4. Do not bury alive your unwanted female babies.

5. Do not slander your neighbours.

6. Do not disobey the Messenger of God in what is right.

Of what do these rules remind you?

There was much resistance to Muhammad's new ideas in Mecca, most particularly because the idea of only one God, and the abolition of idols, was bad for business. The prosperity of Mecca depended on the annual pilgrimage to worship the idols around the Ka'ba.

In the end, Muhammad and his followers fled from Mecca to Medina, about 250 miles away. Medina was a fertile oasis which contained two pagan Arab tribes and three Jewish tribes, each living in its own fortified village.

The Arab tribes welcomed Muhammad as their leader and adopted his new religion of Islam. They did not care about the idols in Mecca and were thrilled to have their own prophet who was bringing God's revelations to the Arabs in their own language.

Muhammad did his best to make friends with the Jewish tribes and hoped that they would come to accept him as the Messiah. He modelled his new religion on what he had learned from the Jews, such as:

1. Facing towards Jerusalem in prayer.

2. Regarding himself as the successor of Moses.

3. Including much of the Bible in the Qur'an.

4. Adopting Kippur as a celebration of his own victories. He had completely misunderstood its purpose.

5. Adopted Friday evening prayer in imitation of Shabbat.

6. Adopted 3 daily prayers.

7. Jewish-type washing and forms of prayer.

8. Rejected the Christian idea of the divinity of Jesus – though he did accept Jesus as a prophet.

But Muhammad had no opportunity to learn Torah and his idea of what it contained was often garbled and wrong. The Jews of Medina did their best to exposed his ignorance and make him look ridiculous. They often asked him trick questions such as:

Which were the 9 plagues of Egypt? and

Why did Pharaoh ask his vizier Haman to build the tower of Babel?

Muhammad therefore turned against the Jews and altered his religion to demonstrate his rejection of them:

> 1. Muslims turn towards Mecca in prayer and not towards Jerusalem.
> 2 Ramadan (a month of daily fasts) was instituted instead of Kippur.
> 3.Five daily prayers instead of the Jewish three.

Eventually, he turned against the Jewish tribes. Some were expelled by force from the oasis. The others were massacred.

Muhammad and his followers then went on to conquer the whole of Arabia for Islam. Jews and Christians were allowed to remain providing they submitted to the rule of Islam and paid a special tax to demonstrate that submission. Pagans who did not convert to Islam were put to death or enslaved.

D) THE CONQUESTS OF ISLAM

In the 100 years after Mohammad's death, his followers – in the name of Islam – conquered the largest empire the world had yet known. It stretched from Spain in the west into Pakistan and India in the east. Look at the map.

> *How close to England did the Muslim warriors reach?*
> As far as Poitiers in northern France, about 250 miles from Dover, before they
> turned back.

Pagans were given the choice of Islam or death. Christians and Jews, as people who had already received a revelation from God, were not molested if they accepted certain rules.

E) ISLAM AND JUDAISM

In their developed forms, Islam and Judaism have much in common. Some of the main similarities are listed below:

> 1. Belief in the one God. Islam accepts Jesus as a prophet but sharply rejects any
> suggestion of his divinity.
> 2. Belief in Abraham as the first Muslim; also of all the Jewish prophets.
> 3. Islam, like Judaism, is a religion of revelation. The Qur'an is the revealed,
> unchangeable word of God.
> 4. Muslim forms of worship and prayer are based on the Synagogue and not on

the Church. Similarly the function of rabbis and alim (Sunni) are similar – quite different from that of Christian priests.

5. Islam, like Judaism, is a religion of holy law, given by God and interpreted by scholars.

6. Much Jewish teaching – halacha, aggadah and Torah – is incorporated in the holy writings of Islam.

However, it is important to note that any Jewish influence on Islam is rejected with vehemence. Muslims believe that Jews and Christians were both given God's revelation – but that those revelations were distorted and falsified over the years. To Muhammad alone was granted God's final and true revelation. Any similarities are only survivals of God's original revelations; the very idea that God could be influenced by anyone or anything is blasphemous and inconceivable.

F) THE DHIMMA

This is explained as a treaty whereby Jews and Christians were protected by Islamic law. They were guaranteed their lives and property, guaranteed freedom of worship and allowed to live as separate communities under their own laws. In return, they had to observe certain conditions:

1. Each dhimmi (protected person) had to pay the special poll tax as a sign of submission.

2. They had to show respect for Islam and deference to Muslims at all times. They could not defend themselves against attack by Muslims.

3. They could not convert to a faith other than Islam. (They could not help being born into their original religion but to convert was an act of choice)

4. They could not hold any public office in the Muslim state or own Muslim slaves.

5. They could not build new synagogues and churches, but could repair existing ones. No synagogue, church or dhimmi dwelling house could be higher than Muslim ones in the neighbourhood.

6. Dhimmis had to dress in distinctive ways, so as to remain separate from Muslims. They could not bear arms or ride horses.

The Dhimma was the basis of Islam's relationship with the unbelievers in its midst. The poll tax was always enforced. But apart from that, the application of the other rules varied widely. In good times, for example, Jews rose almost to the highest positions in Muslim states, rode horses and wore costly clothes. In other, harder, times they were severely restricted.

On the whole, though, the lot of the Jews under Islam was far happier than that of their brethren under Christian rule. Though second-class citizens, they were still citizens with certain rights guaranteed by holy Islamic law. They were never expelled from their countries, as they were in Christian Europe, and only very rarely were they compelled to give up their religion.

In what year were all Jews expelled from England?
In 1290

Of course during the 1400 years that Jews lived under Muslim rule, there were disasters, persecutions and massacres. But those were violent times when all sections of the population also suffered very similar tribulations. Jews, being defenceless, probably suffered more. But on the whole the restrictions of second-class citizenship must have seemed a reasonable price to pay for the freedom to live fully Jewish lives without restriction within their own communities.

MATERIAL FOR LESSONS 33

MAP

The Conquests of Islam

BACKGROUND NOTE FOR TEACHERS

Note on Muhammad

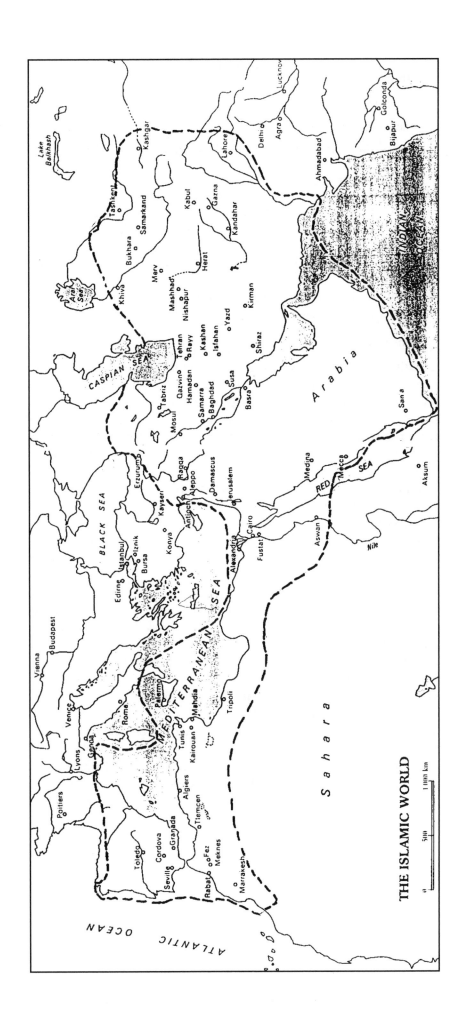

THE ISLAMIC WORLD

MUḤAMMAD, MESSENGER OF GOD

All we know about the life of Muḥammad and the early years of Islam comes from Muslim sources. First and foremost is the Qur'ān, comprising verses claimed to have been revealed by God to Muḥammad. These were dictated by him to his disciples, who wrote them down on palm leaves, stones and whatever else was to hand, and collected together into a single volume twenty years or so after the Prophet's death in 632. The final version of the Qur'ān was fixed from seven different readings in the year 933.

The other main sources, based on material repeated by word of mouth for many years before finally being committed to writing, are the Histories and the Books of Traditions (Ḥadīths). The principal Histories were produced one hundred and twenty years after Muḥammad's death; and the six standard Books of Traditions over a hundred years later. Of course they suffer from contradictions caused by lapses of memory and the differing viewpoints of their writers; but taken as a whole, they present a coherent and convincing account of those early years.

Muḥammad was born in Mecca in the year 570, at a time when guardianship of the Ka'aba and successful international trade had greatly enriched its ruling clans. We are told that the Meccans were swollen with pride and their society was an unhappy one, differing from that of other Arabs because of its rivalries, greed, and great disparity between rich and poor.

Muḥammad came from one of the poorer and less influential of the ruling families of Mecca. Orphaned at an early age, he had a reputation for honesty and reliability. Muḥammad had already accompanied his uncle on trading missions to Syria, where he had come into contact with Christian monks and with Jews, when he was asked to lead a similar expedition himself on behalf of the wealthy widow Khadījah. This was successful; and he accepted Khadījah's proposal of marriage on his return to Mecca. The marriage was a happy one. Khadījah bore him six children; and Muḥammad took no other wife or concubine until after her death.

Thus freed from financial anxiety for the first time, Muḥammad was able to devote himself increasingly to spiritual concerns. He distributed much of his money to the poor, making his own family live frugally, and was conspicuously kind to slaves. He used to retire alone to an isolated mountain cave for days at a time in order to meditate and pray.

Muslims proudly claim that Muhammad was unable to read or write, which enhances the miraculous nature of God's revelations to him. The Prophet's inability to read was not that unusual for a successful merchant of that time, or even of today, in some parts of the Middle East. But as one of mankind's most outstanding and charismatic religious leaders, Muhammad was very, very far removed from the "ignorant camel driver" or the "dangerous madman" portrayed in some Christian and Jewish writings.

Muhammad received his first revelation in the year 610, when he was forty years old. An angel appeared to him in his cave and commanded "Iqra" – recite! When Muhammad demurred, the angel "overwhelmed me in his embrace until I reached the limits of my endurance". Then the angel proclaimed:

Recite in the name of your Lord, the Creator,
who created man from clots of blood.
Recite: your Lord is the most bountiful one,
who by the pen has taught mankind things they
did not know.

At first Muhammad recoiled in horror from the memory of what had happened and doubted his own sanity. It was only three years later, when other revelations began to follow in quick succession, that he recovered his self-confidence and commenced his mission to the Arabs as the "Messenger of God".

The revelations, transmitted by the angel Gabriel to Muhammad when in a state of trance, were taken down in writing by his followers as he repeated them later. They were collected together after the Messenger's death to form the sūras (verses) of the Qur'ān.

The message of the Qur'ān is similar in essence to much Jewish and Christian teaching – there is no god but Allah, the all-powerful Creator, and Muhammad is his Messenger: there will be a Day of Judgement: there is an afterlife in which the good will be rewarded and the wicked will burn in hell: life is to be lived according to divine law, with prayer and fasting, the giving of alms and the supporting of widows and orphans. When he secretly persuaded a number of pilgrims from Medina to accept his authority, Muhammad's terms simply required them to accept the one God and to refrain from stealing, from fornicating, from burying alive newly born female babies and from slandering their neighbours. In addition they had to promise total obedience to the Messenger of God in "what is right".

Though Muḥammad had some success with the young and the poor, he was ridiculed by the leaders of Meccan society. The fact that he could not work miracles was held against him. The required total allegiance to the new community of Islam cut right across traditional tribal loyalties; and Muḥammad's teaching that their idol-worshipping ancestors were in gross error outraged the Arabs, who venerated their forefathers. Above all, the concept of only one God, and the resulting rejection of idols, seemed almost to have been designed to ruin the basis of Meccan prosperity: it would, quite simply, have been bad for business.

Some converts to Islam had been made amongst pilgrims who visited Mecca on the haj. A group from Medina, a desert oasis some two hundred and fifty miles away, secretly invited Muḥammad and his followers to join them there as their judge. So, in the year 622, Muḥammad and seventy of his followers fled from Mecca to Medina.

Medina was occupied by three Jewish tribes and two pagan tribes who had once forced their way into the oasis: each tribe lived in its own fortified village. Muḥammad was soon accepted as leader by the pagans and reached a modus vivendi with the Jews.

Unlike the Meccans, the pagans of Medina – who had long lived alongside Jews – were not shocked by the rejection of their gods under the new order. It did not affect their livelihood; and they were thrilled by the presence in their midst of the Prophet for the Arabs, with his revelations in their own tongue. There was a rapid tide of conversions to Islam.

It is clear that Muḥammad knew the Torah only from hearsay and cannot have read it for himself. The Jews of Medina probably assumed that the newly arisen Prophet was much confused by his imperfect knowledge of scripture and rabbinic legend – while to the Muslims, the Messenger's knowledge derived from divine revelation and it was the Jews who had confused and distorted their own version of the divine message.

As a fellow monotheist, Muḥammad looked to the Jews as his natural allies; and he no doubt hoped they would come to accept him as their long-awaited Messiah. He promptly adopted the Aramaic name "Medinta" used by the Jews ("al-Madinat" in Arabic) in place of Yathrib, the old name of the oasis. His followers were directed to face towards

Jerusalem in prayer and to recite three daily prayer services and special Friday evening prayers as did the Jews. Ablutions and forms of worship followed the Jewish pattern. It seems that the Muslims may have misunderstood the solemn Jewish fast of Kippur to be a celebration of victory over Pharaoh, for they too adopted the same day to celebrate their own successes. Above all, the Qur'ān itself is full of elements that had previously appeared in Jewish sources.

Though respecting Christians and accepting Jesus as a major prophet, Muḥammad vehemently rejected the notion that Jesus was the Son of God as well as all idea of a Trinity. In fact he compared himself to Moses many times and clearly regarded himself as his successor. According to the Qur'ān:

Before this book there was Moses's book ... and this book confirms it in the Arabic language.

And again, in response to taunts arising from the Jewish origin of one of his wives, Muḥammad proudly declared:

Aaron was my father and Moses my uncle.

Sadly for them and for future generations of their people, the Jews of Medina not only refused to accept Muḥammad but also subjected him to increasing criticism and mockery. Realising how little he knew about events described in their own Bible, they lost no opportunity of exposing what they took to be his ignorance. In repeated attempts to make him look ridiculous, they harassed him with trick questions such as "Name the nine plagues of Egypt". The Jews were also accused of conspiring with Muḥammad's enemies among the pagan Arabs, and among those who had recently converted to Islam, in order to undermine the new faith.

The Messenger was a proud man who could not tolerate public ridicule; and so, only eighteen months after his arrival in Medina, his attitude changed radically. Arab poets who had satirised him were assassinated together with certain Jews who had opposed him in one way or another.

Muḥammad demonstrated his displeasure with the Jews as a whole, and his growing self-confidence and independence of them, by adopting measures designed to steer his followers firmly against Jewish practices. Muslims were ordered to turn towards Mecca in prayer and no longer towards Jerusalem – now with five daily prayer services instead of the Jewish three. All traces of the Sabbath were eliminated when Friday was declared a day of public prayer on which work was allowed. Ramadan was instituted in place of Kippur. In a complete change of emphasis, Muhammad began to lay far greater stress on Abraham, whom he claimed as the first Muslim, than on Moses. He also took over Christian arguments against Jewish interpretations of scripture and repeated the Christian calumny that the Jews had killed their prophets.

Non-Muslim scholars disagree as to whether Muhammad was influenced more by Jewish or by Christian ideas. Although Moses is mentioned over one hundred times and Jesus only twice in the Meccan period of the Qur'ān, Muhammad's often repeated dread of the Day of Judgement and hellfire is certainly more akin to Christian monasticism than to rabbinic Judaism. A suggestion has been made that he may have been swayed by the doctrines of a deviant Jewish sect – there were many around at the time – which might explain the sharp hostility to him displayed by the Jews of Medina. To Muslim scholars, it is of course inconceivable that the Prophet was influenced by any source other than the divine: his revelations came from God alone.

The three Jewish tribes of Medina, by then considered a threat to the Muslim community in its struggle against its enemies in Mecca, were accused of treachery. Curiously enough, the Jewish tribes made no attempt to defend one another against the common foe when pretexts were found to attack and besiege each of their villages in turn. They were eliminated one by one.

The first tribe was expelled from the oasis in 624, leaving much of its property behind to be shared out amongst the Muslims. The following year saw the expulsion of the second tribe which, being originally in a less vulnerable position, marched out of Medina with their heads held high and carrying their possessions with them. The remaining tribe did not fare so well. In a rare bout of savagery after their surrender, they were offered the choice of Islam or the sword. Even some Arabs admired their courage as the seven hundred men who had refused to convert were lined up alongside a trench and beheaded: their women and children were enslaved.

Muhammad's actions were prompted by the politics of the situation and not by hatred of Jews as such. Individual Jews, not perceived as a threat to Islam, continued to live freely in both Medina and Mecca.

The Muslims spent the years between 623 and the Messenger's death in 632 in a series of raids and minor wars, first against the Mecca and the

Jewish tribes, and then against other tribes and oases.

Muḥammad did not always have to fight to get his way, for news of his great achievement in forcing the submission of Mecca soon became known throughout Arabia. In 631 he declared war against all idol-worshippers; and his reputation was by then sufficient for that declaration to be taken seriously. A stream of deputations flocked to Medina from all over the peninsula, there to be both awed and charmed by the charismatic new leader. Without exception they bowed to his authority and returned home bearing gifts and the faith of Islam. It is claimed that the leader of the Jewish tribes of Afghanistan, who proudly claimed and still claim descent from King Saul, visited the Prophet at this time and accepted Islam for himself and his people.

The Messenger offered generous terms to Jews and Christians to persuade them to submit quietly to the new order. Typical, and forming a precedent for the later conquests of Islam, were those contained in his long letter to the Christians of Najrān and the Jewish princes of Ḥimyar:

If a Jew or Christian becomes a Muslim he is a believer with the same rights and obligations as other Muslims. Those however who hold fast to their own religion, whether Jews or Christians, will not be obliged to change it. They must pay the poll tax, one dinar for every adult ... He who pays this tax to God and his Apostle has his security guaranteed ... but he who withholds the tax is an enemy ...

Muḥammad died of natural causes in the year 632, leaving Arabia united under Islam.

The Holocaust

An excellent pack specially prepared for schools is available from the London Jewish Cultural Centre, Ivy Pavlova House, 94 North End Road, London NW11 7SX. Tel. 020 8457 5000.

LESSON 34

The Foundations of Modern Israel

INTRODUCTION

If you are under 50 years old, you will not remember a world without Israel, a country ruled by Jews speaking Hebrew, the language of the Jewish people.

You may take it for granted that this beautiful country always looked as it does today – with its tree-covered hills, its houses, its modern highways and means of transport, its shopping centres with plentiful goods, all its everyday facilities and its happy people. If so, you would be mistaken. The land was once desolate and barren, covered in rocks and malarial swamps: then it sustained only a small population of Arabs, eking out a frugal existence from the arid countryside.

You may find it difficult to imagine how life was for the Jews of the Diaspora before the State of Israel existed, when they were persecuted, assaulted and massacred – not just by the Nazis, but throughout the centuries since the loss of their own land. The study of our history gives us some insight into what our ancestors suffered in the years when there was no State of Israel to which they could flee when persecuted. So the founding of Israel in 1948 came as a blessing for which Jews throughout the world gave thanks to God for his great goodness. It is important for us always to remember today how very fortunate we are in this respect.

In this lesson we will learn something of the struggle throughout the centuries to maintain a Jewish presence in the Holy Land and how that led eventually to the establishment of the Jewish state. We will learn how, even before the state was declared, Jews cleared the rocks, drained the swamps, and planted the land to bring it to life. We will learn how, when the goal of an independent Jewish state was at last attained, Jews fought bravely for its existence at a cost of thousands of lives. We will learn also how Jews from all over the world were welcomed to the new State of Israel and how they transformed the country from a neglected wasteland into the vibrant modern state it has become.

THE CENTURIES OF EXILE

The Temple was destroyed by the Romans in the year 70; and the Romans suppressed the last Jewish revolt against their rule with exceptional severity some 65 years later. Jerusalem was then rebuilt as a Roman city and Jews were forbidden to live there on pain of death.

However Jews continued to live in the Holy Land despite steadily increasing hardship. Jewish scholarship continued, mainly at Tiberias where the Jerusalem Talmud was completed towards the end of the 4th century. The adoption of Christianity, a religion bitterly hostile to Jews, by the Roman Empire brought about a further worsening of conditions for the Jews who had remained in the country.

It is estimated that only about 10% of the population was Jewish at the time of the Persian invasion in the year 614. The Jews allied themselves with the invaders against their Byzantine Christian rulers. As a reward they were given Jerusalem to rule on behalf of the Persians. However they suffered badly for this when the Byzantines reconquered the country from the Persians several years later.

There cannot have been very many Jews left in Palestine to witness its conquest by the Muslim Arabs in the 7th century; but those there helped the Arabs take the country. The Jews benefited greatly from the change of rule. By the year 1000, the Muslim authorities in Egypt were actually sending regular subsidies to maintain the Jewish academy of Tiberias. However, Jews suffered with the rest of the population as Arab rule weakened and the region plunged into anarchy and constant warfare.

The incorporation of Palestine into the Ottoman Empire in the early years of the 16th century established conditions more favourable to Jewish settlement. Many Jewish refugees from Spain and Portugal made their way there after the expulsion of 1492. The Jewish population of Jerusalem was doubled and transformed by this new immigration; and S'fat (Safed) in Galilee became a centre of religious leadership, with its influence spreading over the entire Jewish world.

The Turkish Sultan granted a lease of Tiberias and its surrounding countryside to one of his Jewish courtiers, Joseph Nasi, Duke of Naxos. Nasi, a former Marrano who had formally returned to Judaism on reaching Turkish shores, worked hard to establish Tiberias as a haven for Jews throughout the world. Pioneers came to Tiberias, built houses, planted crops and orchards and developed some industry: for the new colony was intended to be self-supporting. For a time the ruined countryside around Tiberias blossomed; but unfortunately the colony proved impossible to sustain in the long term for it seemed that the Jewish people was not yet ready to make the supreme effort necessary to return and build up the land..

As the Ottoman Empire declined, so too did Palestine and its Jewish community sink slowly into poverty and obscurity. The ambition to end one's days in the Holy Land was often fulfilled by pious Jews, who journeyed to Jerusalem in their old age for that purpose, but the community remained small, poor and dependent on charity from abroad for its survival.

It was only in the 19th century that philanthropists such as Sir Moses Montefiore (from the Spanish and Portuguese Congregation of London), Baron Maurice de Hirsch, Baron Edmond de Rothschild and others took the first practical steps to improve the lot of Palestine's Jewish inhabitants by enabling them to sustain themselves on the land by their own efforts. These were perhaps the beginnings of the modern Zionist movement.

THE FIRST ALIYAH

Severe persecution of Jews in Russia towards the end of the 19th century, coupled with the realisation that Jews could expect little from a Europe steeped in hatred, led directly to the birth of political Zionism. It was not long before young Russian Jews, desperate to escape from the worsening terror, began to organise themselves into groups of chalutzim ('pioneers') in order to set out for the land of Zion. In the period between 1882 and 1903 some 25,000 Jews entered Palestine.

The first pioneers experienced terrible hardships from hunger and malaria as they tried to create settlements on barren land bought from Arab landowners: but they persisted.

One by one, settlements, villages and farm communities were set up – Rishon Letzion, Petah Tikvah, Gederah, Rosh Pinah, Yesod Hama'aleh, Mishmar Hayarden, Haderah and Metullah. An agricultural college was established at Mikveh Yisrael.

POLITICAL ZIONISM

The Zionist movement, which aimed at a physical return of the mass of the Jewish people to the historic land of Israel, was at first resisted by many of the well-established Jews of western Europe, who saw in it a threat to their continued well-being in the countries of their adoption. However the tragic events which overtook the Jewish population of Europe during the twentieth century served to sweep aside most doubts and precipitated the chain of events that led in 1948 to the establishment of the independent Jewish State.

Political Zionism was carefully planned and orchestrated. Two dominant personalities influenced Zionism more than any other individuals. They were Theodore Herzl and Chaim Weizmann.

THEODORE HERZL

Herzl was born in Budapest, Hungary, in 1860. He was an assimilated Jew, with very little Jewish knowledge or education, who became a well-known writer and journalist. In 1894, as Paris correspondent of an important newspaper, he attended the trial of Captain Alfred Dreyfus. Dreyfus was a Jewish officer in the French Army, who was accused of treason only because he was a Jew. It was one of his fellow officers who had sold military secrets to the Germans; but even when the real culprit was uncovered, the authorities still could not bring themselves to declare Dreyfus innocent. He was sentenced to a long term on the penal settlement in Central America known as Devil's Island. Dreyfus was freed eventually but only after considerable protest which split French society, riddled as it was with anti-Semitism.

Herzl was deeply affected by the trial and the events that followed. He realised that the only way to eliminate such outrageous treatment of Jews was for them to be able to live freely in a land of their own. He set forth his views in a booklet entitled The Jewish State, writing that no matter how patriotic Jews were to their host country, they would always be persecuted. The only solution was for them to be granted somewhere where they could manage their own affairs and rule themselves. He suggested Palestine or a part of Argentina. That was a revolutionary concept.

Undaunted by criticism, Herzl proceeded to put his plan into action. He called a meeting of representatives of the Jewish people, the first such gathering for 1,800 years. Herzl succeeded in convening the First Zionist Congress in Basle, Switzerland, in 1897. He wrote in his diary:

At Basle I founded the Jewish State. If I were to say this today, I would be met with universal laughter: in five years, perhaps, and certainly in fifty, everyone will see it.

We now know that the Jewish state envisaged by Herzl was born exactly 51 years later!

Heartened by the success of the Congress, and bolstered by the enthusiastic support of its participants, Herzl set to work with vigour. He travelled the world, meeting prominent leaders and personalities in an effort to convince them of the practicality and the urgency of his plan. He met the British Colonial Secretary, the German Emperor, the King of Italy, the Sultan of Turkey, Lord Rothschild (the head of the Anglo-Jewish community), Lord Lansdowne (the British Foreign Secretary), as well as the editors of influential newspapers who, he hoped, would promote Zionism as a worthy cause.

Moved by the plight of eastern European Jewry, and especially by Herzl's persuasive pleading and obvious sincerity, Britain offered him the area around Al Arish in the northern part of the Sinai Peninsula. But that was barren land that would need extensive irrigation to make it suitable for settlement; and so the offer was declined.

This was followed by the offer of the central African territory of Uganda, then a British colony, which was potentially fertile. Though the offer of Uganda coincided with a series of particularly vicious pogroms in Kishinev and other Russian towns, and Herzl was in favour of accepting, the Sixth Zionist Congress of 1903 totally rejected, it. The opposition came mainly from the Russian delegates themselves who, despite the suffering of their people, ridiculed the Uganda scheme as 'Zionism without Zion'.

Herzl died in the following year at the early age of 44. In his will, he asked for his remains to be eventually re-interred in the Jewish state. In 1949, one year after the state became a reality, Herzl was reburied on Har Herzl (Mount Herzl) in Jerusalem.

THE SECOND ALIYAH

Between 1905 and the outbreak of the First World War in 1914, no fewer than 30,000 Jews went on Aliyah. If that does not sound like very many, remember that the land in those days was virtually bare and that it was difficult to absorb people.

Unlike other nations who gained their independence last century, the Jews were in a unique position. Their state had to be built from scratch. They had to remove the rocks from the soil by hand and plant trees before they could farm the eroded land: that was a backbreaking task but one which they tackled with enthusiasm and devotion. They loved the land, the country of their forefathers, only waiting to be reclaimed and again brought to life.

They set up schools, clinics, hospitals, factories and bus services – all the everyday infrastructure we take for granted in a civilised country. In addition, they had to defend themselves against armed Arab marauders, who became more dangerous as time passed. Anyone seeing a picture of Palestine in those days would not recognise it today. Those people were true chalutzim – pioneers. They reclaimed the land, drained its malarial swamps and turned them into fertile tracts of countryside. This took a heavy toll for many died in the harsh conditions: but that did not daunt others from following in their steps.

In 1909, the first houses were built on the sand dunes adjacent to the port of Jaffa. That modest settlement, named Tel Aviv (Hill of Spring), rapidly grew into the large sprawling city it is today. Soon workshops sprang up all over Palestine, followed by larger factories. Transport facilities were developed and the seaports expanded.

THE FIRST WORLD WAR OF 1914-1918

When war broke out in 1914, Palestine was one of the possessions of the Ottoman Empire (Turkey), which sided with Germany against Britain, France and the USA. This was a hard time for the Jews in Palestine for the Turks treated them as Allied sympathisers and spies. Disease spread, immigration from Europe slackened because of the war, and the population declined.

CHAIM WEIZMANN

In Europe, a new Jewish leader assumed centre stage in the struggle for Palestine. Chaim Weizmann was born in Russia, where he had seen the wretched condition of the Jews there at first hand. Unlike Herzl, he came from a strongly traditional Jewish background.

Weizmann settled in England in 1903, after accepting a lectureship in Chemistry at Manchester University. He became active in Zionist affairs and rapidly assumed a position of leadership. He was an eloquent speaker and a persuasive advocate, thoroughly committed to the Zionist cause.

That was a period of intense activity on the political front as Weizmann went around meeting people in positions of power, trying hard to convince them of the justice of his cause. He concentrated on British statesmen, many of whom held him in high regard. He met David Lloyd George (Prime Minister), Arthur Balfour (Foreign Secretary), Winston Churchill, Lord Robert Cecil and others. He also cultivated a close relationship with C. P. Scott, the editor of the influential Manchester Guardian newspaper. Weizmann, in his old age, was later to become the first President of the State of Israel.

THE BALFOUR DECLARATION

Weizmann's frantic activity led to the issuing of the famous Balfour Declaration by the British government. This declaration of British intentions was due largely to two separate causes.

Firstly, Britain's wartime leaders were indebted to Weizmann for his discovery of a new way of making acetone, then very difficult to obtain. Acetone was an essential ingredient for explosives used by the navy; and Weizmann's discovery was a valuable contribution to the war effort, long remembered by grateful members of the War Cabinet.

The second factor which helped bring about the favourable situation was that a British army, commanded by General Allenby, was then making its way up from Egypt towards Jerusalem and was on the point of gaining control of Palestine from the Turks. It was thought that a grateful Jewish population would be helpful to British interests in the region.

The Cabinet issued its statement that the British Government viewed with favour the establishment of a Jewish National Home in Palestine. This document, known as the Balfour Declaration, was signed, on behalf of the government by Arthur James Balfour, the Foreign Secretary.

THE CALM BEFORE THE STORM

Weizmann was jubilant and persuaded the Zionist movement to undertake a vigorous policy of immigration, building, planting and expanding.

Gradually the Yishuv (the Jewish community of Palestine) grew in numbers. One of the wonders of the time was the revival of the ancient Hebrew language, which was adapted with skill and ingenuity to become a spoken language able to serve the needs of a modern society.

Britain was granted the mandate (a form of temporary trusteeship) over Palestine by the League of Nations (the predecessor of the United Nations). In 1920 Herbert Samuel, a Jew, was appointed as the first High Commissioner for Palestine. The future looked rosy, but storm clouds were gathering.

THE ARAB RESPONSE

Trouble began when Arab leaders began encouraging mobs to attack the Jews. Riots erupted in Hebron, Jerusalem and Haifa. Hundreds of peaceful Jewish citizens were cruelly slaughtered. Roaming bands of Arabs from neighbouring countries terrorised settlements, burning and pillaging, ambushing vehicles and uprooting trees. Their guiding words were 'kill and destroy'.

To protect themselves, the Jewish settlers founded their own self-defence organisation which they called Haganah (defence), but the British regarded it as an illegal body and did its best to suppress it.

Worse still, the turmoil made the British government decide to limit Jewish immigration. This was a severe set back to the Zionist movement, to the Yishuv, and especially to the Jews of Europe – for Hitler came to power in 1933.

In 1939, on the eve of the Second World War, the British decreed that only 75,000 Jews would be admitted to Palestine during the next five years and that thereafter immigration would be severely limited. Furthermore, Jews were only permitted to buy land in restricted areas of the country. This statement was contained in a White Paper – which for Jews was black indeed. Harsh as this seemed at the time, worse was to follow.

TOTAL WAR AGAINST THE JEWS

The Second World War began in 1939. Since 1933, Hitler and his Nazi party had been persecuting German Jews, robbing and humiliating them, and throwing them into concentration camps. Their only crime was to have been born Jewish. Most non-Jewish Germans joined in the persecution willingly, or pretended not to notice what was going on – an unpleasant fact that many Germans would now rather ignore.

Thousands of Jews fled from countries occupied by the Germans or sent their children away to escape the terror. Yet most countries of the world slammed their doors in the faces of the Jewish refugees. The unfortunate Jews had nowhere to go; and even Palestine was closed to them by order of the British Government. The Yishuv protested, first with meetings, demonstrations and marches; but later with attacks on the British forces.

Despite their anger at the British Government for halting immigration, the Jews of Palestine sided with the British during the war and put all their efforts into supporting it. They enlisted in the British army and eventually, after much hesitation, were allowed to have their own fighting unit, called the Jewish Brigade – with the Magen David as its emblem. Meanwhile, the Arabs sided with Germany.

THE HOLOCAUST

The full extent of the Nazi horror became known in 1945, after the end of the Second World War. German crimes against the Jews had been fearful and without precedent.

Men, women and children had been sent to special extermination camps, dedicated to the destruction of the entire Jewish nation. There they were murdered and their bodies burned. The efficiency and enthusiasm with which the Germans worked was amazing; and the number they killed is staggering. In total, about six million Jews perished during the war. This figure can hardly be disputed for it was compiled from the Nazis' own records, captured by the Allied armies.

FRUSTRATION

Jewish leaders in Palestine and around the world fondly imagined that, in view of the suffering of the Jewish people and the fact of Jewish support for the Allies during the war, the gates of Palestine would be thrown open to admit those few Jews who had survived.

To their dismay, Britain stood by the White Paper of 1939. The Yishuv, which had expected to be able to welcome fellow Jews to the country, was forced to resort to other tactics to bring Jewish survivors into the country.

ILLEGAL IMMIGRATION

Even while the War was still in progress, the Jews of Palestine had succeeded in evacuating a limited number of refugees from Hitler's Europe and smuggling them into the country.

Tragically, not all of them reached their goal and many perished on the way. In 1940 for example, 1,900 people crammed into an old ship called the Patria sank with the loss of 257 lives. Again, in 1941, a ship named the Struma went down with nearly 800 refugees on board. All were on their way to Palestine and were classed by the British as 'illegal immigrants'.

After the war, when it became obvious that Britain would not relent by allowing the survivors of the Holocaust into Palestine, illegal immigration was stepped up. What had started as a trickle now became a flood. Old boats were bought and converted for use as conveyors of human cargo, whilst the groups of 'DPs' (DP means 'displaced person', the term used by the Allies for the survivors left in Europe with no home.) were secretly led to the ports in Italy, Bulgaria, and Greece and smuggled aboard under cover of darkness.

The entire operation had to be carried out in secret because the British dispatched agents to seek out the immigrant vessels and inform the local authorities of the 'illegal' activities. But not every government co-operated; many were in sympathy with the Palestinian Jews, and secretly helped them.

The Royal Navy patrolled along the entire coast of Palestine. When an immigrant boat was discovered, it was intercepted, boarded and then taken to the Palestinian port of Haifa, where the Jewish refugees were taken off and sent to internment camps in Cyprus. Often, considerable force had to be used against them to overcome their resistance.

The best-known case is that of the ship Exodus which carried 4,500 survivors. Those aboard were not allowed to disembark and the ship was sent back to Germany, of all places. This incident was followed with astonishment around the world and was very embarrassing indeed for Britain.

JEWISH RESISTANCE

The Jews of Palestine responded in another way to Britain's closed-door policy. They set up underground resistance movements to destroy British military installations and attack British soldiers.

The Haganah played only a small part in this campaign. Far more prominent were the operations of the Irgun Zvai Le'umi (National Military Organisation) which was commanded by Menachem Begin who later became a Prime Minister of Israel.

The British reinforced their troops stationed in Palestine; but this did not stop the attacks from continuing. The British travelled only in heavily guarded convoys; they put a high price on Begin's head; they hanged members of the Irgun whom they captured; and the Irgun retaliated by hanging two British soldiers – yet the attacks increased. The morale of the British troops plummeted. This, together with worldwide criticism over the Exodus affair, forced the British government to give up and pass the problem to the United Nations. Britain announced its intention to leave Palestine by 15 May 1948.

INDEPENDENCE AT LAST

The United Nations promptly set up a special Committee to investigate on the spot, report back and make recommendations. Weizmann, now an elderly man of 73, created a very favourable impression when he answered the searching questions fired at him by the committee members. The Arabs boycotted the hearings.

The Committee recommended that Palestine be partitioned into Jewish and Arab states and that Jerusalem be internationalised. There was intense diplomatic activity before the vote on that proposal in the General Assembly of the United Nations. Chaim Weizmann and other Jewish leaders lobbied and canvassed frantically to ensure a favourable outcome: pressure was exerted at every level. There was a majority for partition when the vote was taken on 29 November 1947.

In Tel Aviv, Jews danced in the streets – at long last they would have their own state and they could admit to it whoever they liked. But the Arabs did not rejoice. They cleaned their rifles and sharpened their knives.

It was not long before Jewish laughter turned to tears as the Arabs attacked. They attacked the Jews with guns and bombs. The Jews defended themselves as best they could, but were hampered by the British, who tended to side with the Arabs. The British disarmed the Jews, but not the Arabs, and many lives were lost. As the date for the departure of the British, approached, Arab attacks increased in number and intensity.

On Friday 14 May 1948, the Union Jack was lowered for the last time and the last British soldier sailed from Haifa. On that same day, 5 Iyyar 5748, the State of Israel was proclaimed, after a break of 1,878 years.

THE DECLARATION OF INDEPENDENCE

This momentous event took place in Tel Aviv because Jerusalem, the capital, was in a state of siege. All the leaders of the Yishuv, headed by David Ben Gurion (the first Prime Minister of Israel) assembled in the Tel Aviv Museum, from which the ceremony was broadcast. A rabbi pronounced the blessing 'Sheheheyanu' with great emotion, and the entire Jewish population of the world responded with a resounding 'Amen'.

THE WAR OF INDEPENDENCE

On that same day the armies of the surrounding countries Egypt, Syria, Lebanon and Transjordan (now called Jordan) invaded Palestine. They were joined by Iraq, an Arab state that did not even have a common border with Palestine. In addition to those well-supplied and organised armies, the Jews were attacked by armed bands of Arab irregulars.

In the War of Independence, the Jews, who at first did not have many guns, tanks and aircraft, sustained heavy losses: 6,000 men were killed and 30,000 were wounded out of a Jewish population of only 600,000,

At first, the Arab forces advanced steadily; but gradually, as the Jews acquired more armaments and their morale rose, the tide began to turn. With God's help, they steadily pushed back the invaders and saved their main cities and settlements – although some settlements in the south were overrun. This seemed a miraculous achievement, for the Jews were fighting against well-armed professional soldiers.

Only in Jerusalem did the Israelis suffer severe set-backs. The soldiers of Transjordan (now Jordan), commanded by British officers, captured the Old City of Jerusalem. Even West Jerusalem was under siege. Food, water and fuel, as well as arms and reinforcements had to be transported there in convoys which were ambushed and attacked by the Arab irregulars with the loss of many lives. The remains of some of the burnt-out lorries can still be seen lying by the side of the road leading up to Jerusalem, specially preserved to serve as reminders of the courage of those drivers. Meanwhile, the country was governed from Tel Aviv.

Eventually Israel was able to take the initiative and win some brilliant victories. Many Arab civilians fled to neighbouring lands. In one campaign, thousands of Egyptian soldiers were surrounded in southern Israel before being released under United Nations supervision.

On 3rd April 1949 an armistice was signed on the Greek island of Rhodes. The warring nations, with the exception of Iraq, agreed to stop fighting . The war was over. Now Israel could at last get down to the business of running its affairs and developing its economy.

Israel was at peace but its capital, Jerusalem, was divided. Only the modern section of the city remained in Israel. The Old City, which contained the Western Wall of the Second Temple, was firmly in Jordanian hands and no Jew was allowed to visit it. During the long Jordanian occupation of the Old City of Jerusalem, its Jewish Quarter with its synagogues was systematically vandalised and the ancient Jewish cemetery on the Mount of Olives was desecrated. It was not until the Six Day War of 1967 that Jerusalem was reunited by Israel; and the Jewish soldiers who finally fought their way to the Western Wall swore an oath that Israel would never again lose possession of this holy site.

THE INGATHERING OF THE EXILES

The first act of the new State of Israel was to abolish all restrictions on Jewish immigration, thus permitting the start of the long-awaited ingathering of the exiles. The subsequent 'Law of the Return' confirmed the right of all Jews to settle in their ancestral homeland, regardless of economic circumstances, cultural background or skin colour.

The first to benefit were the wretched survivors of the European holocaust during which an estimated six million Jews were murdered. Next to follow were the ancient Jewish communities of the Near East, driven from their homes by the rising tide of Arab nationalism and militant Islam.

During the first twenty years or so of its existence the new State welcomed and resettled over 600,000 Jews from Europe, a similar number from Arab lands, and others from North and South America, South Africa, and elsewhere. The flow of Jews to the Holy Land continues, and now includes many people from the former Soviet Empire.

Who paid the bill for this enormous undertaking? Who paid for transporting, housing and feeding all these destitute people? Who provided the additional schools, clinics and other services for them and their families? Israel was a new country without the industry or resources to cover the staggering cost. Without hesitation, Jews (as individuals and as communities) in the developed countries, in a display of unprecedented generosity, provided the funds necessary. Also, after much hesitation and soul searching, a reparations payment of $820 million was accepted from the German government as part compensation for the suffering Germany had inflicted on the Jewish people.

Some of Israel's efforts to rescue whole communities were truly spectacular. Operation Magic Carpet brought Jews from medieval conditions in Yemen to twentieth-century Israel. The later Operation Moses saved a primitive tribe of black Ethiopian Jews (the Falashas) from the persecution of their Christian neighbours and the even more urgent ravages of famine.

PEACE

The ending of the War of Independence did not bring peace to Israel and Israelis have had to endure continuing terrorist attacks and fight several further wars with their Arab neighbours since that time. Even now, the problems of the Palestinians have still to be resolved and the hostility of some of the Arab states continues unabated. A great deal has already been achieved but perhaps several generations will have to pass before Israel will truly be at peace.

But during the half century or more since the establishment of the Jewish state, Israel has developed in ways few people could have foreseen at the time. The dream of 2,000 years has at last become concrete reality. Israel is not perfect – what human institution is perfect? – but it is a country of which we can all be proud.

A few small groups of religious Jews still maintain that the establishment of a secular state in Israel is an impious act, a revolt against God's will. They refuse to recognise modern Israel and its laws, believing that Israel can only be re-established by God in the messianic age. But the overwhelming mass of the Jewish people interpret the rebirth of Israel in terms of an abiding miracle, a miracle in which many have helped in one way or another, a miracle which all have been privileged to witness.

MATERIAL FOR LESSON 34

MAP

The boundary of Israel in 1948

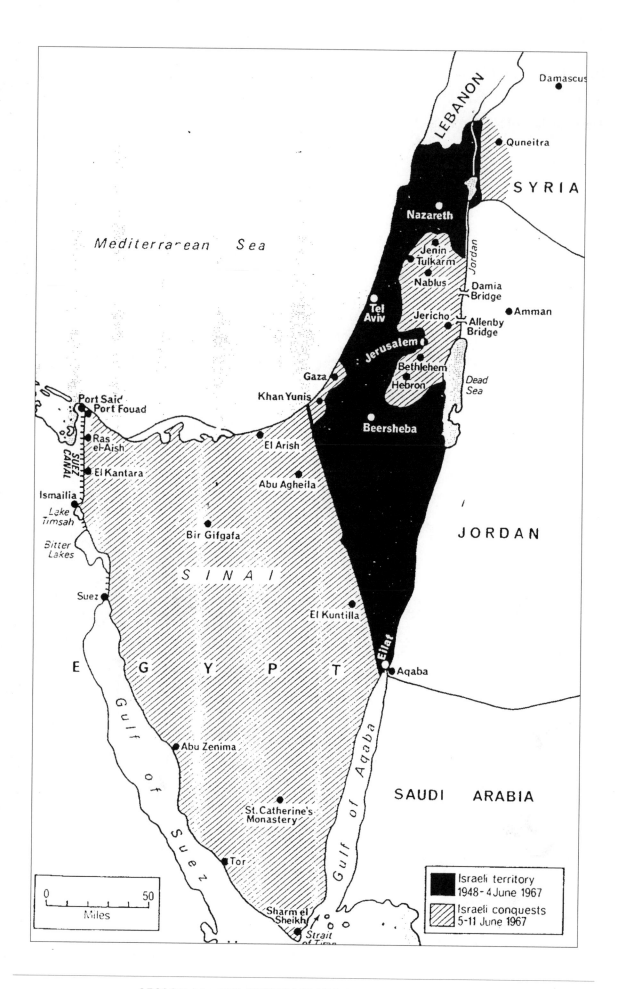

Israeli territory
1948 – 4 June 1967

Israeli conquests
5–11 June 1967

LESSON 34   THE FOUNDATIONS OF MODERN ISRAEL